DECOLONIZING EPISTEMOLOGIES

TRANSDISCIPLINARY THEOLOGICAL COLLOQUIA

Theology has hovered for two millennia between scriptural metaphor and philosophical thinking; it takes flesh in its symbolic, communal, and ethical practices. With the gift of this history and in the spirit of its unrealized potential, the Transdisciplinary Theological Colloquia intensify movement between and beyond the fields of religion. A multivocal discourse of theology takes place in the interstices, at once self-deconstructive in its pluralism and constructive in its affirmations.

Hosted annually by Drew University's Theological School, the colloquia provide a matrix for such conversations, while Fordham University Press serves as the midwife for their publication. Committed to the slow transformation of religio-cultural symbolism, the colloquia continue Drew's long history of engaging historical, biblical, and philosophical hermeneutics, practices of social justice, and experiments in theopoetics.

STEERING COMMITTEE

Catherine Keller, *Director*

Virginia Burrus

Stephen D. Moore

DECOLONIZING EPISTEMOLOGIES

Latina/o Theology and Philosophy

EDITED BY

ADA MARÍA ISASI-DÍAZ

AND EDUARDO MENDIETA

FORDHAM UNIVERSITY PRESS ❖ NEW YORK ❖ 2012

Library of Congress Cataloging-in-Publication Data

Decolonizing epistemologies : Latina/o theology and philosophy / edited by Ada María Isasi-Díaz and Eduardo Mendieta.—1st ed.
p.   cm.— (Transdisciplinary theological colloquia)
Proceedings of a colloquium, the 8th in a series of colloquia, held in 2008 at the Theological School of Drew University.
Includes bibliographical references (p.   ) and index.
ISBN 978-0-8232-4135-4 (cloth : alk. paper)—ISBN 978-0-8232-4136-1 (pbk. : alk. paper)
1. Hispanic American theology—Congresses.
2. Social epistemology—United States—Congresses. I. Isasi-Díaz, Ada María.
II. Mendieta, Eduardo.
BT83.575.D43   2012
230.089′68073—dc23

2011028549

Printed in the United States of America

14 13 12   5 4 3 2 1

First edition

*To grassroots Latinas and Latinos in our communities
whose voices are not heard, no matter how loud you speak.
For not listening to you, we ask pardon.
Do not give up on us, your sisters and brothers in the academy.
Keep speaking your truth.*

CONTENTS

Acknowledgments   xi

Introduction: Freeing Subjugated Knowledge |
Ada María Isasi-Díaz
and Eduardo Mendieta   1

KNOWING REALITY

Decolonizing Western Epistemology / Building Decolonial
Epistemologies | Walter Mignolo   19

Mujerista Discourse: A Platform for Latinas' Subjugated
Knowledge | Ada María Isasi-Díaz   44

Methodological Notes toward a Decolonial Feminism |
María Lugones   68

An(other) Invitation to Epistemological Humility: Notes toward
a Self-Critical Approach to Counter-Knowledges | Otto Maduro   87

LATINA/O LOCUS HISTORICUS

Anti-Latino Racism | Linda Martín Alcoff   107

The Act of Remembering: The Reconstruction of U.S. Latina/o
Identities by U.S. Latina/o Muslims | Hjamil A. Martínez-Vázquez   127

If It Is Not Catholic, Is It Popular Catholicism? Evil Eye,
Espiritismo, and Santería: Latina/o Religion within Latina/o
Theology | Michelle A. González   151

"Racism is not intellectual": Interracial Friendship, Multicultural
Literature, and Decolonizing Epistemologies | *Paula M. L. Moya*   169

MAPPING LATINA/O FUTURES

Epistemology, Ethics, and the Time/Space of Decolonization:
Perspectives from the Caribbean and the Latina/o Americas |
Nelson Maldonado-Torres   193

Thinking Bodies: The Spirit of a Latina Incarnational
Imagination | *Mayra Rivera Rivera*   207

Decolonizing Religion: Pragmatism and Latina/o Religious
Experience | *Christopher Tirres*   226

The Ethics of (Not) Knowing: Take Care of Ethics and
Knowledge Will Come of Its Own Accord | *Eduardo Mendieta*   247

Notes   265

List of Contributors   311

Index   313

ACKNOWLEDGMENTS

The Transdisciplinary Colloquium that provided the opportunity for the conversations that resulted in the articles gathered in this book was the eighth one that has been held at the Theological School of Drew University. We are most grateful to Catherine Keller, the main conspirator of these colloquia, for so graciously turning over the 2008 colloquium to us, thus providing the opportunity and space for Latina/o theologians and philosophers to come together. The seriousness with which she has always taken Latina/o scholarship is but one of the many indications of her unflinching commitment to the struggles for liberation. For her sisterly help and encouragement during this whole project, we are most grateful.

As can well be imagined, no academic event that brings together scholars from all over the United States is possible without many helping hands and hearts. Matilde Moros, a PhD candidate at Drew University, was the administrative assistant to Professor Isasi-Díaz for this event. Our deepest gratitude to her and to the other Drew PhD candidates who contributed their time and expertise to this project: Geoffrey Pollack, who designed the web page for the colloquium and whose art work graces the cover of the book; Sam Laurent, Christopher Haynes, and Lydia York, who facilitated details too numerous to mention; and the many other students and staff at Drew University who helped us make this gathering possible.

We are particularly grateful to the contributors to this book for their willingness to come together and engage one another, and for their patient and diligent work revising their essays, taking into consideration our initial comments after the Transdisciplinary Colloquium and those of the anonymous scholars who participated in the peer review of the manuscript. Eduardo wants to express his particular gratitude to Ada, for inviting him to collaborate on what was her brainchild. It is his honor to publish with Ada, a pioneer Latina mujerista theologian, and with some of the most inspirational Latina/o scholars today. Ada María, on her part, is most grateful for Eduardo's willingness to work with her in the many tasks that birthing a book requires. Without Eduardo's energy, breadth of knowledge, and positive attitude, this project could not have been brought to completion. Both Ada and Eduardo express their gratitude to Teresa Jesionowski for her outstanding copy editing and to Lori Gallegos de Castillo for her help with the index.

We are also grateful to Helen Tartar, who continues to oversee the publication of the proceedings from the Drew Colloquium, and to all those at Fordham University Press who helped make this book a reality.

DECOLONIZING EPISTEMOLOGIES

Introduction: Freeing Subjugated Knowledge

ADA MARÍA ISASI-DÍAZ
AND EDUARDO MENDIETA

Sitting in crowded bleachers amid a sea of Asian faces, our little group stood out like a sore thumb. Two of us were Latinas, one quite pale from a northern Spain ancestry, the other one with a dark *café con leche* skin that speaks of her African roots. The third in our group was tall and thin with that light copper skin hue that, together with her sari, indicated her Southern Asian roots. The circus in Shanghai was simply fascinating; we were spectators, but we also were part of the spectacle. Our different phenotypes drew the attention of all those around us, and as we watched and enjoyed the feats of the acrobats, we were watched intensely. It was toward the end of our two-week tour of China, and by then we were somewhat accustomed to the stares and murmuring of the people in the streets when they noticed us.

As the lights went on, signaling intermission, we immediately saw them. Across from us, on the other side of the round, sunken stage, there were two men, obviously non-Asians, moving quickly down from the bleachers and walking in our direction. They jostled their way through the crowd, and in no time they were standing before us, greeting us with ample smiles, as if we were long-lost relatives. They were Cuban men who had been sent to work in China and had been in Shanghai for almost a year. "We could not believe it when we saw you," they said in Spanish, as we effusively shook hands. When we replied also in Spanish, they burst out laughing! "What luck we have had to find people who look like us among the millions who live in this city," the older one of them said. Our visit was short, for in no time the lights dimmed, and, being part of a group with a tight schedule, we could not make plans to see them later.

During the music that served as the introduction to the second part of the show, we translated for our friend from Pakistan what the men had said and to explain to her who they were. That night the three of us sat on our beds and talked about what had happened. Myriam helped us with her questions to debrief what it had meant for the two of us Latinas to meet the Cuban men. We reflected on the joy of being recognized, on how it provided us with an affirming sense of self. We spoke about how, for a few minutes, the fact that we were different became of paramount importance, providing us with an opportunity to make contact with others. For once we had experienced being different as good and positive, leading to recognition and appreciation.

That we, as Latinas/os living in the United States, are different is most of the time ignored or considered by others to be at best a burden, at worst a threat. Our religions, languages, and cultural practices are perceived to be too different from what is considered the fundamental culture of this nation, commonly referred to as the American Way of Life. We are treated as a problem, although we have been part of the territory occupied by the United States since before the arrival of the European settlers. Today anti-immigration feelings have been fanned to such extremes that about twenty of the states are ready to pass laws that allow for open discrimination against Latinas/os and other immigrant groups. Immigrants today in the United States are seen as a threat. That the majority of us Latinas/os came to live in this country obliged by circumstances in which most of the time the U.S. government has had a hand, or were crossed by the border after the United States took one-third of northern Mexico or appropriated Puerto Rico, means nothing to the dominant group. The fact that in the twenty-first century the movement of peoples across national borders is an intrinsic element of globalization, which is promoted and sustained by the economic system of the United States and other first world countries, is ignored or considered irrelevant in the United States. That the violence in Mexico that spills into the United States is the result of the use of drugs in the United States and that the vast majority of weapons used by the drug cartel come from this side of the border are never taken into consideration; the media never refer to these facts. No one ever mentions the responsibility the U.S.

economic system bears for the present economic difficulties being experienced around the world, difficulties that fuel immigration with or without the required documents.

The racism that has characterized U.S. society has expanded into what Linda Martín Alcoff calls in her essay in this book "ethnoracism." Institutionalized discrimination was effectively battled in the 1960s, but today in the United States it again raises its head, this time finding a broader target: immigrants at large. The racialization of Latinas/os is at the base of our being marginalized, of being considered incapable of having anything to contribute to society. Our only possibility of survival seems to be to Americanize ourselves, to diminish ourselves, and in the process deprive the United States of the richness that our diversity can contribute to this nation. The dominant society seems to be incapable of decentralizing itself and welcoming the voices of others—a society that itself is formed of immigrants who violently took this land from First Nation peoples, Puerto Ricans, Mexicans, native Hawaiians, and native Alaskans.

Faced with this reality, Latina and Latino scholars, as a corrective to the inability of the dominant group to open spaces for and to listen to minoritized and racialized voices, have insisted on privileging epistemologically and hermeneutically experiences and understandings of Latinas/os. Such insistence, though praised, has met with widespread resistance from the dominant group. Latina/o thinkers, philosophers, and theologians have articulated a critical self-reflexivity that begins with an avowed and explicit identification of the locus of our knowledge and whose understandings we privilege, thus making evident where knowledge is being produced. Latina/o thinkers, aware of the ways in which the dominant society is ignorant of our experiences and ways of understanding, have a rich insight into how such self-ignorance affects us and affects the larger society. The dominant group, in contrast, being blind to its own privilege, has created an epistemic hegemony: an epistemic hegemony that makes it possible for those in the dominant group to ignore or disavow their epistemic privilege. Little or no effort has been made to facilitate and encourage the elaboration of knowledge that does not use the dominant episteme, that is, the dominant system of understanding and the ideas that emerge from the experience of the dominant group. The center continues to hold; it continues to exclude Latina/o epistemology and hermeneutics and, therefore, it continues to oppress.

In the fall of 2008, the Drew University Transdisciplinary Theological Colloquium focused on opening a space for marginalized and derogated voices to take center stage, for suppressed knowledge to see the light of day. The colloquium set out to challenge the dominant episteme, not by engaging it—to do so only reinforces it—but by creating a scholarly space that invited Latina/o scholars to elaborate the central elements for a different episteme focused on contributing to the flourishing not only of Latina/o life but of all life. The colloquium focused on and pursued Latina/o knowledge by fostering speaking a different language from the one spoken by the dominant systems of knowledge. The invitation to the colloquium challenged Latina/o scholars to unleash the knowledge that we have—subjugated knowledge—that we whisper at the edges of the academy and society. The colloquium was thought and lived as a safe space of knowing differently and one in which Latinas/os could be agents/subjects in a different way than is authorized by the dominant academic world.

The colloquium aimed to go beyond what is considered possible within the reigning understandings and perceptions of knowledge; it facilitated the elaboration of knowledge in terms of the needs of oppressed Latinas/os, the majority of whom are poor. The colloquium, conceived as a revolutionary praxis, rooted its rationale and criteria in the need to unequivocally promote the flourishing of all life—*el buen vivir,* as Indigenous People of Latin America call it—rather than rooting them in the rules that govern present-day political, social, economic, and religious discourse. A search for our own Latina/o building blocks that make it possible to free subjugated knowledges in order to construct a life-giving episteme—that is what this colloquium set out to be.

The organizers of the colloquium deliberately orchestrated a dialogue among Latina/o philosophers and theologians, for many of us are convinced that these two areas of knowledge and expertise, philosophy and theology, need to be in dialogue with each other. Latina/o philosophy must take into consideration the importance of religion for our communities, importance that is easily observable in the multiple manifestations of popular religion, in the role that churches play in Latina/o barrios (as they have in the past for other immigrant groups), and in the fact that the only sustained growth in U.S. churches comes from Latinas/os. Just as philosophy must consider theology, so too Latina/o theology must continue the centuries-old tradition of taking into consideration the discourses of our Latina/o philosophers in the elaboration of a decolonizing and liberating theology. The intellectual spirit of the gathering was guided by the conviction that if we affirm and respond to the religious understandings and practices of Latinas/os, and to how religion is an integral element of our reality, we need to work from an epistemic locus that puts religious practices and understandings at the center. To do this we need a sustained dialogue with the philosophical insights about epistemology, hermeneutics, and praxis that are elaborated by Latina/o philosophers, and, likewise, we need an appreciation of the vibrant contemporary theological enterprise of Latina/o theologians. The orchestrating of this dialogue was guided by the belief that the respective disciplines of Latina/o theology and philosophy are two of the most original areas of the Latina/o discourse that is produced at present. It is from within theology, philosophy, cultural studies, and literature that Latina/o scholars have produced distinct ways of thinking that emerge from Latina/o experiences.

The colloquium organizers brought into dialogue at least three different generations of Latina/o scholars, who, up till then, had not been together in the same space of critical and productive dialogue. Among those who participated in the colloquium were well-established scholars, recognized nationally and internationally, whose books are textbooks in different disciplines and, therefore, whose influence has reached beyond the Latina/o world. A second group of scholars included tenured professors who are recognized as "Latina/o" scholars. A third group included younger colleagues who are at an earlier stage of their academic and professional careers. Attentiveness to the locus of epistemic production requires also attentiveness to the issue of different generations as knowledge producers.

The essays in this book are at the intersection of two axes: liberation epistemology and decolonizing epistemology. Liberation epistemology, born from the struggles of oppressed peoples all over the world, emerged originally in Latin America, the roots of Latinas/os living in the United States. The centrality of *comunidades de base*—base communities—in this movement and the insistence on the richness of popular religion that is fed by Amerindian, African, and European beliefs clearly indicate that the experiences and understandings of grassroots people are the source and locus of liberating Latina/o subjugated knowledge. The decolonizing axis, a more recently developed one, emerged as a response/reaction to the way that over the last half a century most theories have synergistically conspired to exclude the non-West, the non-Male, the non-White, and the non-European, which means the privileging of European, Anglo-Saxon, Protestant, becoming-White-in-the-United-States experience. The decolonizing axis points to how a group of Latina/o scholars has challenged the way Latinas/os have been written off the epistemic geopolitical maps produced by the West—Europe and now the United States. Latinas/os are not postcolonial subjects the way that Indians or South Africans are postcolonial subjects. Nor are we imperial subjects, in the way one can say that the Spaniards, the French, and the British are imperial subjects. Latina/o political and cultural identities have been forged in the cauldron of struggles to resist postimperialism (after Spain, Portugal, England, France) and neoimperialism (U.S.). Latinas/os are not national subjects of one given nation, for we occupy at the same time different national imaginaries and have plural allegiances; nor are we postnationals, for most of us are U.S. citizens, and our Latina/o identities are forged in and are part of the United States. All of these forces, political vectors, spaces of belonging, sites of dispossession, claimed interstices, erased memories, and hushed stories have been theorized under a group of terms that aim to reorient the way we approach knowledge production. At the center of this new epistemic matrix is an understanding of our "coloniality/neocoloniality," which we live in the streets of New York, Miami, Chicago, and San Francisco and in the agricultural fields of Florida, Michigan, Ohio, and California. We are the children of a West, a Europe, and a United States, whose lies about themselves refuse and negate our histories. To survive and flourish we have to decolonize ourselves. Our confrontation with the "coloniality of power," to use Anibal Quijano's generative expression, requires a relentless and ceaseless struggle to value our past as our peoples experienced it and not as the West has written it. Our past is part of our present, as it continues to frame what becomes actuality from a horizon of possibilities. Our decolonizing enterprise to free subjugated knowledges is a creative process that works at uncovering how to determine, from our own Latina/o perspectives, horizons of possibility and knowability. Both axes—liberation and decolonizAtion—focus their knowing gaze on the ignored histories of Latinas/os;

they also embody archaeologies and genealogies that deliberately explore "sites of exception, fracture, dehumanization, and liminality" (Nelson Maldonado-Torres).

SUMMARY AND RELATIONSHIP OF THE ESSAYS

This book presents the fruits of the 2008 Drew University Transdisciplinary Theological Colloquium. The thesis of each essay was discussed at the colloquium or is the fruit of our discussions. Presentations at the colloquium were kept brief, and the time was judiciously used for discussion, making sure that all those present contributed to the different topics. After the essays were first submitted, the editors of the volume sent detailed comments and notes to each author, notes and comments that aimed to continue the discussion initiated over the three days of our colloquium. The essays in this book, therefore, are products of a collective process of knowledge production, even if each one rests on the shoulders of a named author. Each essay attempts to make a contribution to the liberation/decolonization of Latina/o knowledge. Each author approaches this task from her or his own discipline and the way they are situated in Latina/o communities.

The first part of the book, "Knowing Reality," includes essays that provide insights into what decolonizing epistemology is all about and how this task intersects with that of liberation. The essays in this part elucidate what we believe about knowledge; the procession of essays takes the reader slowly but progressively into the Latina/o world.

The essay by Walter Mignolo is an excellent starting point for understanding the thinking behind this book, which is part of the project of decolonizing epistemology by freeing subjugated knowledge. Mignolo starts by defining the decolonial option: decolonizing "naturalized principles on which knowledge is built, in disciplinary formations as well as in ideological discourses." He differentiates it from anticolonial struggles, which were anti-imperialist, and the anticapitalist struggles framed within Western civilization. Decoloniality, is different from these struggles, for it "opens up the domain of the epistemic and the hermeneutical, explanation and understanding, political and ethical processes delegitimizing the colonial matrix of power and building a world that is nonimperial and noncapitalist." The goal of decoloniality is to build epistemologies "that legitimate 'living in harmony and reciprocity,' rather than 'living in competition and meritocracy.'" Mignolo presents geopolitical epistemology and biographic political epistemology as the two pillars of decolonial thinking. The latter is political epistemology that refuses to be managed and instead works "toward communal futures" and toward building states that are at the service of the people and not vice versa; the former refers to the geohistorical configurations that respond to local needs, habits, and memories that emerge from the Third World. After highlighting the work of Partha Chatterjee, an Indian historian and political theorist, and Linda Tuhiwai Smith, a Maori national who is an anthropologist, as scholars who make decolonial moves by claiming the right to produce knowledge and advance their own people, Mignolo returns to his task of clarifying decoloniality by explaining what it has in common with de-Westernization.

The main thesis of Ada María Isasi-Díaz's essay is that Latina/o scholars must turn their attention to grassroots Latino communities as the source for decolonial/liberation epistemologies. After explaining how she brings together liberation and decoloniality, and who are included under the expression "the oppressed and impoverished" that she uses throughout the essay, she turns to describing lo cotidiano, the everyday, a key concept of mujerista thinking. She understands lo cotidiano, in an expansive though specific way, as an ethical space—time and place—in which one moves with a certain autonomy, takes decisions and put them into play, decisions that might seem unimportant but that woven together constitute the ethical and moral horizon of the person. Isasi-Díaz clarifies that the cotidiano she refers to is that of grassroots Latinas and not that of the dominant group, which often shows lack of reflexivity and ignorance of how its everyday impinges on lo cotidiano of two thirds of the world. The author links the importance she gives to lo cotidiano to the option for the poor. She denounces the attempts that are made to moderate such an option by referring to it as a "preferential" option and explains why "preferential option" is an oxymoron. The essay ends with theological reflections on using the religious understandings and praxis of Latinas as the *locus theologicus* for mujerista theology, and on the assertion that God chooses the poor and that God does not love the rich as rich. God's love for the rich and the oppressors is a call to radical conversion, to stop exploiting and oppressing others.

María Lugones' essay gives valuable insights into how a scholar frees subjugated knowledge. She starts by reasserting the importance of understanding the inseparability of race and gender and the coalitional meaning of Women of Color: a term that reveals the self as well as reality as multiple by indicating a complex social construction that includes how Women of Color are perceived by others as inferior as well as how they reject such a construction. Lugones' valuing of coalitional understanding and praxis emphasizes how collectivities and communities are the fractured locus from which emerges a subjective/intersubjective understanding of self that leads Latinas and other Women of Color to an "infrapolitical way of moving toward each other." This becomes a social linking that commits those involved to learn from one another and to envision the power of "infrapolitically resistant collectives." Lugones then complicates the understanding of racialized gender by introducing the "coloniality of gender," emphasizing that this is not merely a classification but also refers to the process of dehumanizing people to fit them into this category. To oppose the coloniality of gender she introduces "decolonial feminism," which she thinks from the grassroots and at the grassroots, emphasizing "historicized incarnate intersubjectivity." As a theorist, she places herself in the midst of the "oppressing → ← resisting relation" that takes place at the heart of the colonial difference, as women exercise their agency in order "to unveil what is obscured." Lugones' commitment to coalitional thinking and praxis leads her to learn from indigenous Bolivian women a cosmology that understands the relationship between men and women as inseparable from the flourishing of the community, an understanding different from that of Western thought. Lugones ends her essay with a call to coalition building that has as a starting point the fractured locus that oppressing → ← resisting peoples have in common.

The last essay in this section is by Otto Maduro. In a series of "notes" Maduro undertakes the task of demystifying knowledge. Maduro's text sets out from the distinct locus of hermeneutical humility. It is for this reason that Maduro deliberately titled his chapter "notes," precisely to underscore the provisional, unfinished, and nondogmatic character of his reflections. Knowledge, Maduro argues, is always collective and communal. There is no single knower, in the same way that there is no Robinson Crusoe in economic society. The autonomous single economic producer is just as much a fiction as is the single knower. Consequently, knowledge also is always accumulated communal labor. Behind all knowledge claims there is power, but also stored communal investment. Knowledge is thus "capital," in the broadest sense of the term. It allows a collectivity to achieve goals, but it is also the site of communal struggle. Some may have been granted access to it, and some may have been denied access to it, although they participated in its production and accumulation. Inasmuch as the stability and reach of knowledge is determined by its efficacy and dependability, its evocation is always a "political move." Knowledge claims are moves within a political strategy. Thus, the struggle between knowledge and ignorance, knowledge and illusion or belief, must always be read as a struggle between claims over, against, and despite political power. There is no knowledge claim that is not involved in some sort of power struggle. For this very reason, the "form" or the "how" of knowledge claims is more important than the "what" of knowledge claims. That is, the genre or style of both claiming and presenting knowledge claims may have more impact than what is being claimed as knowledge. Still, for Maduro, since all knowledge is always collectively produced, from and within very specific conditions of privation or privilege, and since it is the accumulation of societal energies, we have to approach all knowledge claims with great hermeneutical humility.

The second part of the book, "Latina/o *locus historicus*," brings the reader to the world of Latinas and Latinos, which is not a world of our own making. Ethnorace, as Linda Martín Alcoff teaches us, is the reality the dominant group has imposed on us. Our minoritized and marginalized reality leaves us no option but to deal with the world from that imposed position. The mantles of identities not of our own elaboration are dealt with as interstices out of which we operate, trying to be as self-defining as possible, valuing what the dominant group disvalues.

Linda Martín Alcoff's essay develops three concepts relevant to understanding the conditions of Latinas/os in the United States. She first discusses anti-Latino racism, which gets lost in the exclusively focused-on black-white binary discussion of racism. There is a need to understand that "what is at stake in this analysis is not only a more adequate understanding of racism but also a recognition that if racism is not a one-size-fits-all category, then antiracist policy cannot be either." Martín Alcoff then discusses the term "ethnoracism," which she defines "as pertaining to groups of people who have both ethnic and racialized characteristics, who are a historical people with customs and conventions developed out of collective agency, but who are also identified and identifiable by bodily morphology that allows for both group affinity and group exclusion." The term is not intended to replace the use of the terms "race" and "ethnicity" entirely but "to provide more linguistic options in order to develop better descriptive tools to characterize and understand current realities." Finally, Martín Alcoff discusses identity proliferation. She contends that given the complexities of the global identities and global markets, what is needed is "increased specificity rather than only broad-brush categories." For this author, analyzing and accounting for specificities does not entail an increase in conflict but rather enhances the ability to see more clearly the need for negotiation and compromise in order to make common cause. Martín Alcoff ends by emphasizing that "identity proliferation requires us to redraw and revise some borders . . . , to include the light-skinned or more assimilated among us as near-white, . . . and to take language, national origin, and ethnicity to create borders within racial groups that are often treated as monolithic."

Hjamil Martínez-Vázquez's chapter focuses our attention on a different dimension of the Latina/o experience, but it does so following a similar methodological gesture and thrust as Michelle González's contribution, which follows his. Martínez-Vázquez's essay offers an unsuspecting and almost unknown dimension of Latina/o history. There are Muslim Latinas/os, including some who have recently converted to Islam. Martínez-Vázquez shows that such acts of conversion are acts of re-membering, or reconstructing memories, in order to construct a new identity that challenges the orthodox narrative. Against the view that Latinas/os are descendants of the Iberian Spaniards who came to the Americas in order to impose their "Hispanic" culture, Muslim Latinas/os argue for a pre-Hispanic, Iberian identity that acknowledge and celebrates the Moorish and Jewish, or Marrano, histories. Martínez-Vázquez shows how contemporary Latina/o identity is predicated on the uncritical acceptance of a Hispanic *latinidad* that excludes, erases, and denigrates a Muslim past that in fact was very rich and determining for the basic elements of Latino culture. Yet, the author's aims are not simply to reconstruct history. He also aims to articulate the power of acts of remembering as deliberate

acts of fashioning new cultural identities. In this case, the act of excavating, reweaving, and remembering the Moorish background of early
Hispanic and now Latina/o culture historicizes the cultures we have
uncritically accepted. By excavating the Muslim/Moorish background of
our Latina/o identity, we resist the tendency to produce homogenizing
identities that exclude and oppress.

Michelle González's contribution may be read as a rich exemplification
of some key ideas in Maduro's "notes." Through a synthesis of personal
ethnography, sociological and theological reflection, González takes aim
at the Christocentric, church-focused, and hyperphilosophical discourse
of recent Latina/o theology. By focusing on three forms of popular religiosity, González aims to show that if Latina/o theologians are to address
the religious needs of Latinas/os they must take seriously practices that
church hierarchy and orthodox Catholic theology deride and frown on.
Evil eye, Santería, and Espiritismo are syncretic forms of Christianity
that decenter religious practice, relocating it in ritual and communal
memory. As against the primacy of the written text, these three forms
of popular Catholicism are primarily forms of ritualistic religiosity. If
Latina/o theologians, González urges, are to give credence to the epistemic productivity of Latina/o communities, they must challenge their
orthodox Catholic assumptions, namely a focus on textual exegeses that
presupposes a hierarchical system of knowledge certification that always
devalues the experiences of subjects. Catholicism, after all, is based on
two thousand years of the appropriation and exclusion of texts by boards
of authorized subjects, who have been authorized to legitimize certain
practices and texts as canonical. González's essay brings us to the edge
of that process where religious experience in a community is both generative and liminal. Sometimes its only force of conviction is its affirmation
of belief in the midst of ritual practice that nonetheless awaits the process
of rational translation and deliberation. Religions are always born as either heresy or syncretism. Catholicism forgets its own heretical and syncretic birth, González reminds us.

In a different key but with the same focus on ethnoracism as the previous essays in the second part of the book, Paula Moya offers the reader
two possible strategies for decolonial action: interracial friendships and
multicultural literature. She grounds her argument in an exposition of
the role of emotions in cognition. She asserts that emotions have "crucial

epistemic value," for they make it possible to discern "larger social meanings and entrenched social arrangements." Based on the importance of
emotions, Moya then turns to explain how in interracial friendships there
is a sharing of experiences about race and racism that can lead to moral
growth and to the increased knowledge for the interracial friends of how
race functions in society. Her goal in this argument is to propose that
interracial friendships, because of their epistemic and emotional dimensions, can be an effective antiracist project. In the last part of her essay,
Moya explains how literature written by racial and cultural minorities.
can expand "people's epistemic and moral horizons," leading to antiracist
moral growth. She sees the reading of a multicultural novel as an intellectual and emotional engagement that "expands a reader's horizon of possibility for experiential encounters." She sees the multicultural novel as a
text that mediates "complex social relations." For Moya a novel enables
a reader to "engage dialogically at a deep emotional and epistemic level
with the difficult questions around race, culture, and inequality." For her,
then, reading multicultural novels can also be an antiracist project.

   The last part of the book, "Mapping Latina/o Futures," moves with
confidence ahead—in reality, so does the whole book—offering insights
into "ethnic studies" in the academy as a locus of struggle, a theopoetic
vision of Latinas/os' struggle, and what Latinas/os have to contribute to
what some consider an autochthonous U.S. philosophy, American pragmatism. The book ends with a call to vigilance to what Latina/o claims
could ignore, and a warning about the need to continue to reassert ethics
over epistemology.

   Nelson Maldonado-Torres's essay starts with an exposition of some of
the key concepts of decolonial thought, which he calls postcontinental
philosophy. He does so by discussing and connecting Frantz Fanon's
view of subjectivity and his Caribbean migrant imaginary with that of
Gloria Anzaldúa's borderlands, a spatial reference that informs her views
on subjectivity and knowledge. For Fanon the self is constituted by "desires for entering in relation with others." Maldonado-Torres sees this as
the possible inspiration for "a decolonial politics that opposes anything
that betrays the ethical orientation of the self." This led Fanon to resist
appeals for cultural unity and instead seek "the human in the spaces
between human beings themselves." Anzaldúa is committed to relationality and, therefore, refuses to see as a positive element of cultural

identity "whatever betrays the condition of the human as a bordered subject who is open to others in relations of hospitality and generosity." For Anzaldúa, ethnic identity is about "care for the sub-other and the determination of the tasks of responsibility." Maldonado-Torres considers Fanon and Anzaldúa to be postcontinental theorists in that they propose "innovative views of time, space, self, and knowledge that facilitate decolonization." In the second section of the essay, the author argues that ethnic studies is the place where decolonial thinking flourishes. Ethnic studies exposes the complicity of the modern research university with the first world vision of the world by denouncing "the established geography of reason" and by exploring "a larger cognitive map and a deeper knowledge of self and society." For Maldonado-Torres, ethnic studies is similar to the Renaissance and the Enlightenment in that it breaks with the dominant epistemes. Ethnic studies does so by relating knowledges with histories of struggle and resistance, and by overcoming the logic of colonization of natural resources and of the body and mind, particularly of people of color. The author sees ethnic studies as the theoretical arm of the decolonizing project, which is the systematic critique and overcoming of the modernity.

Mayra Rivera Rivera's essay, a poetic reconstruction of what the author evocatively calls Latina "body-words," sets out to lay the building blocks of a Latina incarnational theology. Knowledge is produced, indeed, but it is produced by and through bodies. The power effects of knowledge claims take corporeal form. Bodies, clarifies Rivera Rivera, are the bearers of the memory of knowledge power. They are the site where we can uncover the ways in which "subjugated knowledge" has been suppressed by both physical and rhetorical violence. These clarifications, however, are only preliminary to the central theme of Rivera Rivera's contribution, namely to point the direction toward a theology that emerges and returns to the body-words, the corporeal memory, of Latinas. Incarnational theology, it bears clarifying, is that thinking about God that has as its point of departure the fundamental fact that Jesus Christ was a mortal human who suffered the inequity of human society in his flesh. God became human flesh. Christian theology is therefore most fundamentally incarnational theology, theology about God's incarnation in mortal human carnality. This embodiment, however, took place in Mary's, the mother of God's, body. Incarnational theology thus

also starts from gendered embodiment. Rivera Rivera takes these fundamental theological tenets and rearticulates them through what she calls
"Latina body-words." And for her, these body-words issue from the fact
of mestizaje and what Isasi-Díaz calls lo cotidiano—the everydayness of
our embodiments. Beginning with these racialized bodies that have produced their own poetry, we may start to understand spirit in a new way.

Christopher Tirres's essay turns our attention to another site of the
production of Latina/o knowledges, namely the appropriation and engagement by Latina/o scholars with what is taken to be the autochthonous U.S. philosophical tradition. Latina/o scholars not only bring their
Latin American and Caribbean philosophical, theological, literary traditions to bear on their intellectual production in the United States. They
also are engaged in a creative process of rescue and appropriation of U.S.-
grown pragmatism. In his richly synoptic essay, Tirres documents the
extensive and already long-established dialogue by Latina/o with pragmatism, whether in the version articulated by Dewey, James, Rorty, or
West. In this essay, Tirres aims to show how both James and Dewey can
provide us with some tools to engage the religious experiences of Lat-
inas/os productively and approvingly. At the same time, the Latina/o
experience raises a series of challenges for pragmatism as a distinct U.S.
philosophical tradition that has yet to be engaged seriously by the mainstream. Tirres argues that Latina/o reflections on the ineradicable social
dimension of faith and religious practice can be a major corrective to the
subjectivistic and individualistic appreciation of religion that is found in
pragmatist classical thinkers, such as Dewey and James. Latina/o scholars
of religion have articulated eloquently and substantively the intrinsic and
extrinsic social dimension of faith. They have also given a privileged place
to reflection on the pastoral dimension of religion, whereby "pastoral"
signals a focus on the efficacy of communities of faith to engage not just
in their own ministering but also in reflecting on their own religious
experiences. Communities of faith are also communities of religious analysis and reflection. Tirres's advocacy for a Latina/o appropriation of
pragmatism, however, is predicated on the argument that it provides
epistemic tools that can be judiciously and productively used in the project of decolonizing religion as a by-product of the decolonization of
epistemology.

Eduardo Mendieta's essay, which closes the book, focuses on what he calls "the shadowing of knowledge by ignorance." Knowledge is not found, nor is it the product of a passive receptivity on the part of some isolated knower. Knowledge is always produced, but this production entails the production of ignorance. Knowing is also "not knowing" other things. Taking up the work of Charles Mills and Linda Martín Alcoff, Mendieta sets out to link the simultaneous production of knowledge and ignorance to Toni Morrison's provocative notion of "the crime of innocence." There is culpable ignorance for which we are accountable. Ignorance is not simply the absence of knowledge. Ignorance is not simply a privative, or negation. It is also positive. It always reflects some deliberate act of turning away, neglecting, discounting, undermining, and denying. We are never innocent in our ignorance. Knowledge, for this reason, claims Mendieta, reflects a prior ethical stance. Reading Socrates less as a historical figure and more as the embodiment of a certain ethical stance, Mendieta argues for the priority of "truthfulness" over "truth." Socrates is the epitome of the ethical subject who approaches knowledge claims with hermeneutical humility, confessing ignorance, in order to be able to arrive at truth. Knowledge claims inure us to the fragility and incompleteness of truth. Truthfulness, in contrast, ceaselessly reminds us that knowledge is a path and not a destination. Yet, all of this is elaborated by Mendieta in order to issue a challenge to the Latina/o scholars who have called for a "decolonial" and "decolonizing epistemology." Such a project risks, warns Mendieta, undermining and reversing the gains made by their critiques. For aiming to "decolonize epistemology" reinforces the primacy of epistemology over ethics. His essay points out that this book is but the starting point for further reflection and elaboration of a decolonizing/liberation episteme as the grounding of Latina/o theology and philosophy.

❧ Knowing Reality

◆ Decolonizing Western Epistemology / Building Decolonial Epistemologies

WALTER MIGNOLO

The maintenance of life is an expression of knowledge, a manifestation of adequate behavior in the domain of existence. In the form of an aphorism: "Once we have accepted that there is no possibility of making testable claims about an observer-independent reality, the fundamental change in our epistemology has been completed. All forms of observation and explanation are now expressions of the system's operation with whose production we may now deal. A re-orientation has come about, a change from Being to Doing, a transformation of the classic philosophical questions."[1]

IN GENERAL: THE LEFT AND THE DECOLONIAL

What shall we understand by decolonizing Western epistemology and by building decolonial epistemologies? In answering these questions my essay is an attempt in conceptual elucidation. The words "decolonial" and "decolonization" have been used widely since the second half of the twentieth century, during the Cold War, to describe processes of liberation mainly in Asia and Africa. "Liberation" and "decolonization" were synonymous words. From the Algerian Front de Liberation (1954–62) to the Ejército Zapatista de Liberación Nacional (1994) the word "liberation" prevails. However, these movements shall be distinguished from the Colombian Ejército de Liberación Nacional (1964), which was founded on Marxist-Leninist principles. The Algerians' Front and Zapatistas' Ejército have in common a decolonial horizon, not a Marxist-Leninist one. What are the differences? And does it really matter for the issue at hand?

Decoloniality is a double-faced concept. On one side, it points toward the analytic of coloniality, the darker side of modernity. On the other, it points toward building decolonial futures. In the first case, it is analytic and theoretical. In the second it is utopian. However, the analytic procedures are already decolonial: Coloniality is always already a decolonial concept, a concept that was not created by any other way of thinking, discipline, or ideological frame than decoloniality. The first sentence of the announcement that Roberto Esposito was to deliver a lecture on biopolitics at ICI (Institute for Cultural Inquiry)-Berlin[2] stated that in the past few decades no global-political phenomenon could be explained without the concept of biopolitics. One can say also that in the last few decades no global-political, epistemic, and aesthetic phenomenon can be explained without the concept of coloniality. And more so: The same phenomena can be explained by both biopolitics and coloniality. One will be a eurocentered explanation; the other a decolonial one. For that reason, decolonizing epistemology is the first step toward building decolonial epistemologies. In the last analysis, to build future decolonial epistemologies implies to begin by decolonizing Western epistemology. However, that will be another essay and another argument. For this essay my intention, as stated in the title, is to remind the reader that decoloniality is always a double-faced concept.[3]

The Algerian uprising and final outcome were not inspired by Marxism-Leninism but by more than a century of French colonialism. The recent upheavals in North Africa and the Gulf are not the outcome of reading Marx and Lenin, but of the simple fact that living is knowing and knowing is living. And when living is no longer possible, it requires a different epistemic path. In Algeria in the fifties and in North Africa and the Gulf in the second decade of the twenty-first century, the upheavals are decolonial responses to the persistence of coloniality. Certainly, Egypt and Tunisia were not lately colonized by the British and the French. But both countries had governments that were local regimes taking the place of colonial posts of yesterday. For this simple reason, the upheavals are both against the local dictators and against their Western supporters (the European Union and the United States of America). Not only are a few governments changing, but, more radically, a certain way of sensing and knowing is changing. Knowledge is not created by political theorists, philosophers, or ethicists, but by the global political society. The struggles were not and are not against capitalism, not directly, but against Western civilization and its imperial/colonial arrogance, which of course includes capitalism. And capitalism is not merely an economic structure; it involves the subjectivities and belief systems that go with it, without which it couldn't be sustained. Decolonization is a struggle prompted and provoked by the management of coloniality (a shorthand for the colonial matrix of power), which is more than colonialism and more than capitalism. Both are constitutive of what is generally understood by Western civilization.

Marx and Lenin had not much to say—or at least they did not say much—about the struggle against Western civilization. Marx was part of it, and Lenin belongs to a historical tradition (Russia of the last two centuries before the revolution) that wanted to see itself as part of Europe and the West. Algeria is different; its past is part of the Arab-Islamic world with a strong presence of the Berber population, whose history goes back well beyond the Christian era. In 1517 Algeria became part of the Ottoman Sultanate. With the arrival of French civilization after Napoleon, the counter-perspective was that of Indigenous, not Marxist-Leninist, cosmology. Patrice Lumumba in Congo established relations with the Soviet Union not because he had converted to communism but because he couldn't sustain the decolonial project and had to fall into the hands of one of the two competing imperial projects, capitalism or communism. The anticolonial struggles of Algeria and Congo (as well as others struggles for decolonization in Africa) are not the same as anticapitalist struggles. Anticolonial struggles are defined by racism, whereas anticapitalist struggles are defined by classism. Anticapitalist struggles emphasize the working class (proletarian and peasant) but are not specifically concerned with occidentalism. Fausto Reynaga puts it in a clear and straightforward way.

> The Manifesto of the Bolivian Indian Party (PIB) does not have to subject itself to a model, formal logical and intellectual rule of the political parties of the white-mestizo mélange of Bolivia and Indigenous America. It is not the manifesto of a social class. It is the manifesto of a race, a people, a nation; of an oppressed and silenced

culture. No comparison can be established with Marx's *Communist Manifesto* because the brilliant "Moor" did not confront the West. He confronted the proletarian class against the bourgeois, and proposed as solution the class struggle, and within "Western Civilization" the communist revolution.[4]

My intention is not to evaluate whether one option is better than the other. I am just trying to clarify the distinction and to align my argument with the decolonial option. Decolonizing epistemology means to decolonize naturalized principles on which knowledge is built, in disciplinary formations as well as in ideological discourses in the public sphere. In this case, decolonizing epistemology impinges on the possible dialogues between Marxist Left orientations and decolonial options in the field of political theory.[5] The fact that I prefer decolonial options to the Marxist, or to the options offered by "the theological Left," both Christian and Islamic, doesn't mean that I attribute universal value to the option of my preference. The question is not which one is "right"—since no one is in transcendental terms—but which one is right for you. The Christian Left, in the West, is against capitalism, and we know also that there is a sector of the church that is not critical of capitalism. Briefly, there is no safe place. You can be Black and follow Martin Luther King Jr.'s or Condoleezza Rice's paths. Similarly, what we can call the Islamic theological Left is also against capitalism. But in Indonesia, for example, the official discourse of the State argues that Islam is compatible with capitalism.

Thus, although "decolonization" during the Cold War was basically connected to armed rebellion to expel imperial forces from the colonies, it was also a struggle confronting Western civilization and imperialism, rather than directly aimed against capitalism. It was also the struggle of the Third World against the First World. Capitalism as the focus of struggle defines the European Left more than decolonial thinking and doing. For that reason, Islamic intellectuals and activists, such as Ali Shari'ati (1933–1977) in Iran and Malik Bennabi (1905–1973) in Algeria, defined their decolonial positions at the intersection of Islamism and Third Worldism. In Latin America, Third Worldism was basically aligned with (although not necessarily surrendering to) the legacies of Marx, Lenin, and Mao (as they were projects basically endorsed by leftist Creoles/Mestizos since

Indians and Afro were not part of the picture). There was no other alternative than to conceive this particular version of the Third World in Latin America within European civilization. Discourses were then framed against imperialism and capitalism (basically the United States) but not confronting Western civilization. It is in this context that Fausto Reynaga defines la Revolución India and distinguishes it from Marxism.

The concepts of "coloniality" and "decoloniality" as introduced in the early nineties and as used subsequently indicate a new dimension in understanding the differences between—on the one hand—colonialism and coloniality and—on the other hand—postcolonialism and decoloniality. The experience of decolonization during the Cold War taught all of us that decolonization cannot be advanced if the principles of knowledge and understanding that regulate Western society, its imperial expansion, and its adaptations in non-European nations (Russia, the Soviet Union, Japan) are not called into question. Anibal Quijano's turning point was to link eurocentrism with knowledge and coloniality with eurocentrism. Thus, decolonization was redefined: Without decolonizing knowledge and changing the terms of the conversation, the rules of the game would be maintained and only the content, not the terms of the conversation, would be disputed. That is the trap the Christian theology of liberation and Marxism find themselves in—they are both part of Western civilization. And what is the option that decolonial projects envision so as not to be caught in the same trap? To answer this question is to answer what decolonizing epistemology and decolonial epistemology mean. Let's start then from the beginning.

In his foundational statement, Anibal Quijano proposed that decolonizing means to disengage (de-link) from eurocentrism (once again, not as a geography but as eurologocentrism), controlled by Western languages and institutions, since the Renaissance, grounded in Greek and Latin as the ultimate linguistic ground in which epistemic categories are lodged. Thus Quijano urged:

The critique of the European paradigm of rationality/modernity is indispensable—even more, urgent. But it is doubtful if the criticism consists of a simple negation of the idea and the perspective of totality in cognition. It is necessary to extricate oneself from the links between rationality/modernity and coloniality, first of all, and definitely from all power which is not constituted by free decisions made by free people. It is the instrumentalisation of the reasons for power, of colonial power in the first place, which produced distorted paradigms of knowledge and spoiled liberating promises of modernization. The alternative then is clear: the destruction of the coloniality of world power. First of all, epistemological decolonization, as decoloniality, is needed to clear the way for new intercultural communication, for an interchange of experiences and meanings as the basis of another rationality that legitimately pretends to some universality.[6]

That is the blueprint for decolonizing knowledge and creating decolonial knowledges. The process started a long time ago, since decoloniality is part of the package modernity/coloniality/decoloniality. I have argued elsewhere that Guaman Poma de Ayala in sixteenth- and seventeenth-century Tawantinsuyu and Ottobah Cugoano in eighteenth-century Africa/Caribbean/England wrote decolonial political treatises that were not acknowledged as such because coloniality of knowledge precisely ruled out everything that was not useful for the ruling ethnoclass and was not in the tradition of Aristotle, Plato, and Machiavelli.[7] The process has been accelerating in the past ten years, and the conference that originated this volume is part of such process.

My argument here is based on the work done by the collective modernity/coloniality/decoloniality in the past ten years. I am not representing the collective. Nobody does, for that matter. I am just arguing in tune and in dialogue with the contributions made by every member of the collective. There are two shared principles I assume as the two pillars of my own work: that (a) coloniality is constitutive of modernity and therefore there is no modernity without coloniality and (b) colonization (and therefore decolonization) shall be distinguished from coloniality (and therefore decoloniality). Whereas decoloniality refers to specific historical periods and applies to different imperial/colonial formations since 1500, mainly Western imperial formations but also those of Russia, the Soviet Union, and Japan, coloniality refers to a matrix for management and control of the economy, authority, knowledge, gender, sexuality, and subjectivity. Consequently, whereas decolonization refers mainly to specific moments of political struggles to send the invaders back home, decoloniality opens up the domain of the epistemic and the hermeneutical, explanation and understanding, political and ethical processes delegitimating the colonial matrix of power and building a world that is nonimperial and noncapitalist. Building a world regulated by the principle "living in harmony" requires both decolonizing the epistemic foundation of the colonial matrix of power and building decolonial epistemologies that legitimate "living in harmony and reciprocity" rather than "living in competition and meritocracy."

Let's move closer to ongoing processes of decolonization of knowledge and building decolonial epistemologies. The following argument is in tune and in conversation with María Lugones's and Nelson Maldonado-Torres's contributions to this volume, and with the work of Emma Perez.[8] You will see decolonial thinking at work grounded in particular, although similar, genealogies of thoughts and experiences of embedded in colonial epistemic and ontological differences. In my view, this distinguishes us (in the project modernity/coloniality or at least myself) from the genealogy of thought, experiences, and issues that generated the great work of thinkers such as Max Horkheimer, Simone de Beauvoir, and Michel Foucault, to give a few examples. If all of us are concerned and working toward a just and nonimperial world order (Ecuadorian quichua "sumak kawsay," to live in plenitude, living in harmony; Mandarin's "Ho" peace, harmony, union; or Western languages' "democracy") we do it in different ways because—due to the modern/colonial world order we are all living in—we share the same goals but have different ways to march toward them: Some are imperial, religious, or secular; others, national; others, decolonial. And that is the simple "fact" that requires geopolitics and body-politics of knowing, understanding, and being, to avoid modernity/rationality, as Quijano said, in its variegated forms: the imperial Right, the modern liberating secular Left (Marxism), and the modern theology of liberation. To extricate oneself (to de-link from modernity/rationality) means to de-link from the Right, the Left, and liberation theology. It means simply that the decolonial options need to be asserted in order to "extricate oneself" not only from the imperial/dominating option but also from current Western liberating options such as Marxism and theology of liberation. Decolonizing epistemology means, in the long run, liberating thinking from sacralized texts, whether religious or secular.

IN PARTICULAR: THE DECOLONIAL OPTION

The previous section is already engaged in decolonizing epistemology and in working toward decolonial epistemologies. How come? By decolonizing Western epistemology I understand an analytic task. The analytic decolonial task consists in unveiling beliefs and assumptions, anchored in common sense, that naturalizes the world as we have been taught to see it.

The first task of decolonizing epistemology (and I will say more about "epistemology" below) consists in learning to unlearn in order to relearn and to rebuild. We will find our sources not necessarily in the canon of Western thought but in the corpus of decolonial thinkers, such as Fausto Reynaga and a hundred others.

Decolonial thinking means to dwell and think in the border (the slash "/" that divides and unites modernity/coloniality); which means in *exteriority*. *Exteriority* is not the outside, but the outside built from the inside in the process of building itself as inside. Exteriority is the dwelling place of the world population who do not belong to the house of civilization and democracy. Thus, modernity is a discourse defining its interiority by creating the difference to be marginalized and eliminated. The rhetoric of modernity has an abundant vocabulary to mark the difference, to create exteriority spatially and temporally: pagans, barbarians, primitives, women, gays, lesbians, Blacks, Indians, underdeveloped, emerging economies, communists, terrorists, yellows, etc. All of these will be incorporated into modernity or left out when necessary (see María Lugones in this volume).[9] Dwelling in exteriority means dwelling in the borders traced by the colonial difference from where border and queer thinking are already engaged in decolonizing epistemology and engaging decolonial epistemologies.[10] In fact, what is remarkable and groundbreaking in the work of Pérez and Lugones is the bringing together of decolonial and queer thinking (see below, "Coda").[11] The two enunciative pillars of the colonial matrix of power (racism and patriarchy supported by theo- and ego-epistemologies) are eroded and undermined, and from their ruins decolonial epistemologies emerge. We see in the work of Enrique Dussel, Lugones, and Pérez how modern rationality does something that is not explicit: It implements the logic of coloniality that appears as the benevolent action of the savior.

Thus, the first step would be to de-link from Western modernity's pretense to universality and to open up to what Partha Chatterjee calls unapologetically "our modernity." "Our modernity" is a claim made from India with full acknowledgment that British imperialism is and will be forever a part of the history and the memories of India and Indians. In the inverse situation, if India will be forever in the history of Britain, it will also be part of the imperial memories of England. So then, from the perspective of "our modernity," "their modernity" has a different trajectory and a history of power differential: the epistemic colonial difference that entangled both civilizations in imperial/colonial relations. So then, Aristotle and Plato are still necessary but hardly sufficient. It would be necessary to bring next to the tradition of Western modernity the tradition of colonial India: the Vedic Age, the Southern Kingdom, the arrival of the Portuguese in 1498, the Muslim invasion, and the foundation of the Mughal Sultanate that would eventually fall under British rule. Ancient Greece and Rome and Christianity will constitute just a quantitatively small dimension, although a significant power component (the Western imperial component) that can hardly rule out and replace Vedanta rationality. Certainly, today India's state and economy have opted to embrace Western political theory and capitalist economy. It may last and erase all intent and possibility of engaging with its own past and find a new dignity as Western subjects. Or it may not. In any event, the fact that India's ruling elite took one of the four BRICs (Brazil, Russia, India, China) doesn't mean that this state of affairs is totalitarian and that there is no room for advancing decolonial projects, particularly in the sphere of epistemology.

I have been arguing, following on Quijano's and Dussel's landmark epistemic insights, that decolonizing epistemology and decolonial epistemology have to be anchored in geo- and body-politics of knowledge.[12] Both are necessary to de-link from the theological and egological politics of knowledge in which Western modernity/rationality has been anchored.[13] Let me explain.

The colonial matrix of power, put in place in the sixteenth and seventeenth centuries, was framed in and by Christian theology. Christian theology was the ultimate horizon of knowledge—since and after the

Renaissance—that incorporated Greek rationality (through the monumental work of Saint Thomas Aquinas), invented the Middle Age as its own tradition, and placed Islam in its exteriority, disavowing Muslim knowledge of Greek philosophy and Muslim contributions to Western civilization. Theology was then the ultimate and the supreme court of knowledge and understanding built on the foundation of Greek philosophy and biblical wisdom. All that was called into question, in the eighteenth century, when a new ethno-class, in France, Germany, and England slowed down theology to make room for secular egology. Carl Schmitt summarizes it with the clarity that characterizes his prose.

> It should have been noticed that any elaboration of political theology [is] not grounded in a diffuse metaphysics. They [theology and secularism] bring to light the classical case of a transposition of distinct concepts which has occurred within the systematic thought of the two—historically and discursively—most developed constellations of "western rationalism": the Catholic church with its entire juridical rationality and the state of the *ius publicum Europaeum*, which was supposed to be Christian in even Thomas Hobbes's system.[14]

There you have it in a nutshell. By 1651, the year *The Leviathan* was published, secularism was not yet accomplished, merely a decade or so after Descartes turned theology into egology, which had displaced God and put Reason in his place. Catholicism was the legal authority in matters of law, as Protestantism would be the authority in matters of economy, according to Weber. Law and economy under theological rules were supplanted by secular political economy (Smith) and the secular state (Locke, Montesquieu). Thus the theo-politics of knowing and understanding moved to the second row, but never disappeared. Now, to decolonize the European paradigm of rationality/modernity could not be successful if we remain within the theo- and ego-politics of knowledge.

Political theology and political egology are the epistemic foundations for the classification of the world in regions or continents and hierarchies (Europe, Africa, Asia, and America) and in sectors of the population and religious/secular racialization (Christians, Moors, Jews, Confucians, Buddhists, people without religion; white, yellow, blacks, reds). Both political theology and political egology assumed that masculinity and heterosexuality were the norm and used them to classify and rank gender hierarchies and sexual relations. Theological politics and egological politics of knowledge are grounded on racial presuppositions and male heterosexuality. Thus to decolonize knowledge means to move away from all of that, to de-link from rules of the game managed by modern imperial languages and institutions.

To take seriously and act on the awareness that knowing responds to local needs (habits, memories) and that the politics of knowing is not in the clouds but rooted in the earth of geohistorical, body, racial, and patriarchal configurations (both of the individual and the community) means to take seriously the fact that in the "Third World" (a racist classification that puts together people and region of the planet [e.g., the Third World is inhabited by underdeveloped people]) needs and desires are not necessarily those that prompted the thoughts of modern, postmodern, and poststructuralist European thinkers. Certainly, there are eurocentered critiques of modernity that we can call demodernity, and there has been, since the sixteenth century, a critique of modernity from the receiving end of its effects, which configure the decolonial project. And therefore, whatever knowledge was generated in France or Germany to address their problems can be a hindrance and a distraction in addressing the problems in Bolivia or India. However, coloniality of knowledge has been so successful and pervasive that in the same way that political and economic leaders in the Third World, for personal convenience or conviction, thought that development and Western democracy would be good for Bolivia and India, these leaders have prevented themselves from thinking on their own; they have not been building "our own modernity." Political biography, or corpo-politics, was a similar phenomenon but enacted in relation to racialized, genderized, and sexualized bodies, bodies made inferior from theo- and egological epistemic hegemony in such a way that to be respected those bodies for belief or convenience had to become what they were not (Michael Jackson was a sad example). Thus, geopolitical epistemology and biographic political epistemology are two pillars of decolonial thinking. Notice that biographic political epistemology (or corpo-politics of knowledge) is exactly the opposite of biopolitics. Whereas biopolitics studies how the state manages the population, biographic politics of knowledge is political epistemology that refuses to be managed, that de-links and works toward communal futures and toward building states at the service of the population rather than a population at the service of the state.

TWO CASES

I

A landmark essay in which geo- and body-politics of knowledge comes clearly to the fore was written by the Indian historian and political theorist Partha Chatterjee.[15] The essay is the English version of a lecture he delivered in Bengali language and in the city of Calcutta. The English version is not just a translation but also a theoretical reflection on geopolitics of knowledge and epistemic and political de-linking.

Unapologetically and forcefully, Chatterjee structured his talk on the distinction between "our modernity" and "their modernity." Rather than a single modernity defended by postmodern intellectuals in the First World, or the most dependent take on "peripheral," "subaltern," and "marginal" modernities, and so on, Chatterjee plants a solid pillar to build the future of "our" modernity—not independent from "their modernity" (because Western expansion is a fact), but unrepentantly, unashamedly, impenitently "ours."

This is one of the strengths of Chatterjee's argument. But remember, first, that the British entered India, commercially, toward the end of the eighteenth century and, politically, during the first half of the nineteenth century when England and France, after Napoleon, extended their tentacles into Asia and Africa. So for Chatterjee, in contradistinction to South American and Caribbean intellectuals, "modernity" means Enlightenment and not Renaissance. Not surprisingly Chatterjee takes Immanuel Kant's "What Is Enlightenment?" as a pillar of modernity. Enlightenment meant—for Kant—that Man (in the sense of human being) was coming of age, abandoning his immaturity, reaching his freedom. Chatterjee points out Kant's silence (intentional or not) and Foucault's shortsightedness when reading Kant's essays: Missing in Kant's celebration of freedom and maturity and in Foucault's celebration was the fact that Kant's concept of Man and humanity was based on the European concept of Man from the Renaissance to the Enlightenment and not on the "lesser humans" who populated the world beyond the heart of Europe. So, "enlightenment" was not for everybody. Thus, if you do not embody Kant's

and Foucault's local history, memory, language, and "embodied" experience, what will you do? Buy a pair of Kant's and Foucault's shoes or cut
your own feet?[16]

One point in Chatterjee's insightful interpretation of Kant-Foucault
is relevant for the argument I am developing here. Paraphrasing Kant,
Chatterjee states that in the "universal domain of the pursuit of knowledge," which Kant locates in the "public" (not the "private") sphere,
where "freedom of thought" has its function, he (Kant) is presupposing
and claiming the right of free speech only for those who have the requi-
site qualifications for engaging in the exercise of reason and the pursuit
of knowledge, and those who can use that freedom in a responsible manner.[17] Chatterjee notices that Foucault did not raise this issue, although
he could have, given the interests of his own research. I surmise, following Chatterjee's argument, that what Foucault did not have was the colonial experience and political interest propelled by the colonial wound that
allowed Chatterjee to feel and see beyond both Kant and Foucault. Thus,
Chatterjee concludes this argument by stating that vis-à-vis both Kant
and Foucault:

> It is the specialists, a phenomenon which appears alongside the gen-
> eral social acceptance of the principle of unrestricted entry into edu-
> cation and learning . . . In other words, just as we have meant by
> enlightenment an unrestricted and universal field for the exercise of
> reason, so have we built up an intricately differentiated structure of
> authorities which specifies who has the right to say what on which
> subjects.[18]

Chatterjee acknowledges, like Pauline J. Hountondji and Kwasi Wiredu
in Africa (although independent of each other, since "influence" goes
from Europe to the United States to Africa and India, but not yet in
conversations between Africa and India), that the Third World (in Carl
Pletsch's terms) has been mainly a "consumer" of First World scholarship; and like his African colleagues, Chatterjee bases his argument "on
the way the history of our modernity has been intertwined with the
history of colonialism. For that reason, 'we' have never quite been
able to believe that there exists a universal domain of free discourse,

unfettered by differences of race or nationality." Chatterjee closes his argument:

> Somehow, from the very beginning, we had made a shrewd guess that given the close complicity between modern knowledge and modern regimes of power, we would forever remain consumers of universal modernity; never would we be taken as serious producers. It is for this reason that we have tried, for over a hundred years, to take our eyes away from this chimera of universal modernity and clear up a space where we might become the creators of our own modernity.[19]

I imagine you are getting the point. The argument is similar to arguments advanced by Guaman Poma in the early seventeenth century and Ottobah Cugoano in the late eighteenth, when both appropriated Christianity instead of submitting to it with the humility of the humiliated; it was indeed a slap in the face of European Christians when an Indian of Tawantinsuyu and an ex-enslaved African in the Caribbean, who reached London, unveiled the unhumanity of European ideals, visions, and self-fulfilling prophecies. Both paid dearly for their epistemic de-linking, their epistemic insolence. Kant thought, like Hume, that no Negro was able to reach the level of the least gifted white and that Indians were at an equal level of intelligence with Blacks.[20]

Yes, indeed, Chatterjee is aware that European nationalism in the nineteenth century and Hindu nationalism made similar claims. From the recognition of the shortcomings of the ways in which promoters of Hindu national ideals deal with "our" modernity, it doesn't follow that the solution is to fall into the arms of "their" modernity. The point is this: Thanks, Immanuel Kant, but now let us figure out how to pursue "our modernity," now that we have reached maturity by having gained India's independence in 1947 and expelling British colonists, their institutions, and their ideals of progress, development, and civilization. We have, so to speak, "our own" ways of being. In fact, I would translate Chatterjee into my own vocabulary: "We know that we have to decolonize being, and to do so we have to start by decolonizing knowledge."

II

Linda Tuhiwai Smith is an anthropologist in New Zealand. And she is a Maori national. Maori nationals live next to nationals of European descent, people who have coexisted in the same land since the British started their management of New Zealand. James Busby was named "Official British Resident" in May 1833 and was instructed to organize the Maori chiefs into a united body to deal with the increasing instability provoked by the greediness manifested by the French, the Americans, and the British themselves. As is well known, Maoris did not care about "private property," but Europeans did. The "New World" increased their appetite to transform land into private property since the sixteenth century.

Anthropology (that is, the Western discipline thus named) was assigned to study the non-European world in the human sciences distribution of labor; and it took charge of the Third World that reorganized during the Cold War. Now, it is not a secret that quantitatively the majority of anthropologists, men and women, were white and Euro-Americans. However, anthropology as a discipline also found its niche in the Third World. What then would a Third World anthropologist do when he or she was part of the "object of study" of a First World anthropologist? Well, one answer to the question is that a Third World anthropologist would do the same job and ask similar questions as a First World anthropologist and the difference would be that he or she is "studying" people living in his or her own country. There will be variations depending on whether in a given country the nationals are "natives" or "of European descent." It was more commonly accepted that anthropologists in the Third World would be of European descent—for example, in South America, South Africa, or Australia. The end result is that, in general, anthropological research in ex-colonial regions would be dependent on and secondary to anthropology as taught and practiced in the First World—nothing new or remarkable here.

The remarkable novelty comes when a Maori becomes an anthropologist, and she practices anthropology as a Maori rather than studying the Maori as an anthropologist. This is one way to understand and engage in shifting the geography of reason and the geopolitics of knowledge. Let me explain, starting with a quotation from Linda T. Smith's *Decolonizing*

Methodologies: Research and Indigenous Peoples (1999). One section of the first chapter is titled "On Being Human."

> One of the supposed characteristics of primitive peoples was that we could not use our minds or intellects. We could not invent things, we could not create institutions or history, we could not imagine, we could not produce anything of value, we did not know how to use land and other resources from the natural world, we did not practice the "arts" of civilization. By lacking such values we disqualified ourselves, not just from civilization but also from humanity itself. In other words, we were not "fully human"; some of us were not even considered partially human. *Ideas about what counted as human in association with the power to define people as human or not human were already encoded in imperial and colonial discourses prior to the period of imperialism covered here.*[21]

Well, you get the idea of the interrelations between the politics of identity and epistemology. You could certainly be a Maori, Black Caribbean, or Aymara and an anthropologist and by being an anthropologist suppress the fact that you are Maori or Black Caribbean or Aymara. Or you can chose the decolonial option: Engage in knowledge-making to advance the Maori (or Black Caribbean or Aymara) cause rather that to advance the discipline. Why would someone be interested in advancing the discipline if not for either alienation or self-interest?

If you engage in the decolonial option and put anthropology "at your service," as Smith does, then you engage *identity in* politics, unveiling and enacting geopolitics and body-politics of knowledge. You can also say that there are non-Maori anthropologists of Euro-American descent who really are for and concerned with the mistreatment of Maori and that they really are working to remedy the situation. In that case, the anthropologists could follow two different paths. One would be in line with Father Bartolomé de Las Casas and with Marxism (Marxism being a European invention responding to European problems). When Marxism encounters "people of color," men or women, the situation becomes parallel to anthropology: Being Maori (or Aymara, or Afro-Caribbean like Aimé Césaire and Frantz Fanon) is not necessarily a smooth relation, because Marxism privileged class relations over racial hierarchies and patriarchal and heterosexual normativity. The other path would be to "submit" to the guidance of Maori or Aymara anthropologists and engage, with them, the decolonial option. Politics of identity is different from identity politics—the former is open to whoever wants to join whereas the second tends to be closed by the definition of a given identity.

I am not saying that a Maori anthropologist has epistemic privileges over a New Zealand anthropologist of Anglo descent (or a British or U.S. anthropologist). I am saying that a New Zealand anthropologist of Anglo descent *has no right* to guide the "locals" in what is good or bad for the Maori population. Granted, there are many locals in developing countries who, because of imperial and capitalist cosmology, were led to believe (or pretended they believed) that what is good for developed countries is good for underdeveloped countries, because the former know "how to get there" and could lead the way for underdeveloped countries to reach the same level. And there is also a good chance that an expert from England or the United States may "know" what is good for him or her and his or her people, even when he or she thinks that they are stating what is good for "them," the underdeveloped countries and people.

Returning to the quotation by Smith, it would also be possible to object that "we" denounces an essentialist conception of being Maori or that "we" indeed is not a tenable posture at the time when postmodernist theories really ended with the idea of a coherent and homogenous subject, be it individual or collective. Indeed, such a posture could be defended. But . . . remember Chatterjee. It would be fine and comfortable for modern subjects (that is, embodying the languages, memories, and cosmology of Western modernity, "their" modernity). It would not be convenient for a Maori, Aymara, or Ghanaian philosopher or an Indian from Calcutta, who are modern / colonial subjects and would rather have "our modernity" than listen to vanguard postmodern critics or Western experts on developing underdeveloped countries. Thus, geopolitics of knowledge comes to the fore. There are many "our modernities" around the globe—Ghanaian, Indian from Calcutta, Maori from New Zealand, Afro Caribbean, North African, Islamic in their extended diversity—while there is one "their" modernity within the "heterogeneity" of France, England, Germany, and the United States.

If you are getting the idea of what shifting the geography of reason and enacting geopolitics of knowledge means, you will also understand what the decolonial option (in general) means, or what decolonial options (in each particular and local history) mean. The decolonial option means, in the first place, to engage in *epistemic disobedience*, as is clear from the two examples I offered. Epistemic disobedience is necessary to take on *civil disobedience* (Gandhi, Martin Luther King Jr.) to its point of nonreturn. Civil disobedience within modern Western epistemology (and remember: Greek and Latin, and six vernacular European modern and imperial languages) could lead only to reforms, not to transformations. For this simple reason, the task of decolonial thinking and the enactment of the decolonial option in the twenty-first century starts from epistemic de-linking: from acts of epistemic disobedience.

THINKING DECOLONIALLY

A basic, vexing question since decolonizing epistemology and building decolonial epistemologies began has been formulated in different languages around the world (at different times and places, that is, in different local histories) in the past five hundred years. The question is: How does one respond to the uninvited interference of Western ideas and ideals in the non-Western world? "Modernity" (whether by that name or under the name of "Christianity" in the sixteenth and seventeenth centuries) was always a problem for non-Western people. And it was always a solution for Westerners. Granted, you could find plenty of cases in the non-Western world defending and promoting modernity or Christianity and vice versa: Westerners criticized Christianity (Nietzsche, for example) and modernity (Foucault, perhaps), but the point is that chanting the glories of modernity is not a non-Western project, and decolonial critiques of modernity are not a Western project. Western critiques of modernity inside Western cosmology did not originate as anticolonial or decolonial critiques but as postmodern. In any event, the non-Western world had to deal with modernity either by jumping on the bandwagon, rejecting it, or figuring out what to do.

Fazlur Rahman has written one of the clearest and most compelling books on the issues at hand: *Islam and Modernity: Transformation of an Intellectual Tradition* (1982).[22] He summarizes the dilemma as follows:

Two basic approaches to modern knowledge have been adopted by modern Muslim theorists: (1) that the acquisition of modern knowledge be limited to the practical technological sphere, since at the level of pure thought Muslims do not need Western intellectual products—indeed, these should be avoided, since they might create doubt and disruption in the Muslim mind, for which the traditional Islamic system of belief already provides satisfactory answers to ultimate questions of world view; and (2) that Muslims without fear can and ought to acquire not only Western technology but also its intellectualism, since no type of knowledge can be harmful, and that in any case science and pure thought were assiduously cultivated by Muslims in the early medieval centuries, whence they were taken over by Europeans themselves. To be sure, there are various nuances of these views and also "middle-term" positions.[23]

That is the dilemma not only in the Islamic world, beyond the classic responses: One consisted in adopting either a pro-Western orientation to solve non-Western problems (e.g., Ataturk in Turkey), and the other was a radical rejection of Western modernity and its local representatives (e.g., the Muslim Brotherhood). Lately, two new orientations emerged that are relevant for the topic at hand: One is de-Westernization and the other, closer to what I see in South America, the Caribbean, and the United States (particularly among Latina/o and Native American scholars and intellectuals), is understood as decoloniality.

De-Westernization and decoloniality share the common goal of de-Westernizing and decolonizing epistemology. Where de-Westernization and decoloniality break apart is in that de-Westernization doesn't question the "nature" of the world economy, capitalism, but it questions the control of authority and the control of knowledge (or the complicity between principles of knowledge and Western political theory). In that process, the racist foundations of Western knowledge are called into question. A powerful argument has been advanced in this respect by the strongest advocate of de-Westernization, Kishore Mahbubani, in his book *Can Asians Think?* (1999). The argument begins by making explicit the meaning of the question in the title. I can ask that question and get away with it, Mahbubani explains, "because I am Asian." If, instead, he ponders, he would ask the question "Can Europeans Think?" most likely it would be taken as an insult or as incredible arrogance, since the logic of the question is connatural to the European idea of thinking and how the idea of thinking was used to disqualify or suspect thinking beyond Greco-Latin conceptual genealogies of thought and practice. And, he adds, "if I were to ask 'Can Africans Think?' I would be taken as an ally to the European Kantian tradition where Africans were closer to the animal kingdom than to the human race."[24] The question is potent in that it questions epistemology and racism, that is, epistemic racism. It could be a decolonial argument. However, since de-Westernization remains faithful to development and the capitalist economy, the challenge is to Western control of authority and Western control of knowledge. De-Westernization is contributing to the polycentric world order of the twenty-first century in which the West (the European Union and the United States) is becoming one player (a powerful one, no doubt) among many forces in contention. What de-Westernization is doing, in other words, is taking to its limit the second trajectory outlined by Rahman: appropriating and making their own, without fear and without imitating and wanting to become Western, what Western civilization has contributed to world history. Beyond de-Westernization in China there is a revaluation of Confucianism, not as a religion, but as a philosophy of living, thinking, and doing. And in the case of Islam, de-Westernization is based on arguments showing the compatibility of Islam and capitalism.[25]

Decolonizing epistemology and decolonial epistemology have a different pedigree than de-Westernization, although both share the confrontation with Westernization or occidentalism. For that reason, it is common to find references to Japan among progressive and radical Islamic thinkers. Why, they ask, was Japan able to take a route of its own since 1895 whereas the Islamic world kept falling into desuetude? Such claims could go either way, de-Westernization or decoloniality. Claiming "our modernity," instead, as Chatterjee does without invoking the example of Japan, not only means that there is no one modernity, or a model of it, that is European, and then peripheral, subaltern, or alternative modernities, but that "modernity" belongs to everyone and to no one. To claim "our modernity" in this way is already a decolonial claim, whereas Japan's modernity is conceived and enacted as de-Westernization. Although de-Westernization takes issue with two major spheres of the colonial matrix of power (control of authority and control of knowledge/subjectivity, focusing on racism and human rights), decolonial thinking confronts the entire colonial matrix. Nonetheless, the starting point of decolonial thinking is to de-link from Eurocentrism (or occidentalism).

What do de-Westernization and decolonization have in common? A paragraph by Malik Bennabi helps us understand the point where both projects meet rather than where each project follows the path of its own local history.

> It is abundantly clear that the problem facing us does not concern the nature of Western culture. It actually concerns the particular character of our relationship to it. In this respect, the Muslim who stood as a student at the school of Western culture was one of two types: genuine student or the "tourist" student. Neither of them goes to the real roots of a civilization. Rather, they go either to its distilled products or to its garbage. That is to say, they go to where it loses its life, its warmth as well as its reality embodied by the ploughman, the craftsman, the artist and the scientist, that is, those multitudes of men and women who daily perform, in the cities and the countryside alike, the great work of civilization.[26]

Malik Bennabi wrote these words in Algiers in 1970. "We" refer to "we the Muslims." However, the situation depicted is common to all local histories of the non-Western world that had to confront the West. The problem is "the particular character of our relationship with it," and "we" are all those who are in the same trap and dwell in diverse local histories. Here we find the colonial difference that María Lugones elaborates in her essay. The observation is useful to distinguish Western culture and civilization from Eurocentrism. Western culture is one among many other cultures or civilizations in the world, past and present. For, in the present, Western civilization is not the only one. Such thinking is Eurocentric thinking, whose latest version was neoliberalism. Western civilization coexists today with Chinese, Japanese, Indian, African, Islamic, and Indigenous civilizations in the Americas, Australasia, and Africa. We can debate how we characterize and define civilizations, but that is another matter. The point I am trying to make is that Western civilization is not universal; it is one among several today. But because of the Eurocentric (and imperial) bent of Western civilization and its

"success" in slaughtering people and expropriating lands and natural resources in the name of civilization, all other civilizations have to deal
with it, have to define the particular "character of our relationship with
it," to define "our modernity," with reference to it. There is the starting
point of decolonial thinking, of decolonizing epistemology and creating
decolonial epistemologies. This is also where the decolonial option
emerges next to existing liberating projects such as the Marxist Left, the
theologies of liberation (Christian, Jewish, and Muslim), and countless
social movements that are in the process of forming a new social actor
(next to the state, the market, and the civil society)—this new political
actor is the global political society. There is no one-to-one correlation
between the political society and decolonial projects, but there are some
projects that are clearly decolonial, that is, projects that could be understood as responses to the making, transformations, and persistence of
coloniality. Among them we can count Sovereignty of Food and La Via
Campesina, on the one hand, and, on the other hand, the politicization
of African religions in the Americas (Candomblé, Voudou, Santería, Ras-
tafarian). In the academy, decolonial thinking, decolonial philosophical
thinking as Nelson Maldonado-Torres has articulated, and decolonial
queer thinking, as Emma Pérez argues, are radical epistemic transformations (e.g., decolonizing epistemologies) that are becoming integral parts
of the political society at large.

CODA

"Decolonizing Western epistemology" is in principle a scholarly and disciplinary proposition. However, I understand it as affecting both the *episteme* and the *doxa*. By this I mean that the task of all of us who are
engaged in decolonial thinking, decolonizing Western epistemology, and
generating decolonial epistemologies want to have a transformative impact on public opinion, through our teaching and interventions in the
public domain through whatever means (blogs, independent media,
inter-net-working, radio when it applies, video-making, etc.).

Zero-point epistemology was historically founded in Christian theology and sixteenth-century Western cartography (e.g., mappemonde); and
it was logically founded in the separation between the knower and the
known, the knowing subject and the known object. Max Horkheimer
described it as "traditional theory," pervasively infecting secular sciences

in the nineteenth century, which he confronted with "critical theory." One of the key distinctive and transformative features of critical theory is to fuse the knower with the known, the knowing subject with the known object. In other words, there is no object or phenomenon to be known independently of the knowing subject. It is the knowing subject that constructs the known in the process of knowing. Horkheimer was defending this thesis in 1937. By that time Einstein and Heisenberg had already been arguing in the same direction in the field of physics. Lately, Horkheimer's "critical theory" has been accepted in the reorientation of the social sciences and continues to be argued in the physical sciences.

Although "critical theory" was a welcome corrective to zero-point epistemology, it still remained caught in its web. Or better yet, critical theory calls into question the knowing subject but not the epistemic presupposition in which he or she is grounded—that of the *modern* subject. But it so happens that since the sixteenth century, coexisting with the European modern subject was the *colonial subject*. And the colonial subject was exterior to zero-point epistemology: He was the object being described, the *anthropos*, he who is beyond Western rationality, she who was different from *humanitas*. And when critical theory came into the picture, things did not change for the colonial subject: If the knower was fused with the known, the known remained exterior to critical theoretical minds. In the best of all possible situations, there is a "recognition," and as result of the recognition, he or she can learn the basics of Western epistemology: That is, recognition means epistemic instead of religious conversion.

Until the *colonial subject* would be able (through five hundred years of struggle in the Americas, three hundred in Asia, and, depending on from when you count, five hundred or three hundred years in Africa, and three hundred years in Central Asia and the Caucasus [counting from Peter the Great]) to understand, analyze, and figure out, not how to stop what cannot be stopped, but how to move away, to be in and out, to de-link, from the colonial matrix that will remain in place, flexible as it is to adapt to changing circumstances. In order to de-link and move forward, decolonial epistemologies are needed. And they are already in the making. And they have been for five hundred years although little known, and when known celebrated as "resistance," as "opposition," not in the affirmation of something else in relation to what was being negated.

Thus, decolonial thinking is what colonial subjects do when they do not want to assimilate and are not happy with remaining colonial subjects. That is the difference between critical theory and decolonial thinking.[27] Decolonial thinking means engaging in knowledge making and transformation at the edge, in and of, the disciplines. There are already countless examples, testimonies, and statements, and perhaps a collection of essays should be made out of this dispersed creativity. I end by quoting in this regard Gloria Anzaldúa, reflecting on the process of writing. Let's read this paragraph both as it is and then sometimes replacing "writing and speaking" by "knowing and understanding" and other times adding it. And keep in mind that Anzaldúa is not part of the group of Tel Quel, who, in the seventies, were expressing similar concepts of "writing" (and you have Jacques Derrida elaborating on "writing" and "philosophy"). Remember the coexisting views of the critical modern subject (of critical theory) and the critical colonial subject. The critical colonial subject is decolonial, in writing, thinking, doing, knowing, and understanding. That is where decolonial epistemologies found their "morada" (their dwelling).

> One thing I urge you to do when you are reading and writing is to figure out, literally, where your feet stand, what position you are taking. Are you speaking from a white, male, middle-class perspective? Are you speaking from a working-class, colored, ethnic location? For whom are you speaking? What is the context, where do you locate your experience? In the Bronx, in Southern California? Why are you doing this research? What are your motivations? What are the stakes, what is at stake—to use a popular theoretical expression. In other words, what's in it for you? What are the terms of the debate and who set up the terms? . . . These may be some of the stakes for people of color. As a white person you may have similar stakes or you may be doing it because you are tired of living in a racist country, you are tired of your ignorance and you want to learn about other peoples, other cultures. You may want to make a better world in which we all can live and in relative peace. Or you may do it out of guilt.[28]

We have here in a nutshell the cross-fertilization of decolonial thinking and queer theory. Decolonial thinking in its specific formulation, that is, as responses to the logic of coloniality and the rhetoric of modernity, has its foundation in the concept of race/racism whereas queer theory finds its motivation contesting the heteronormativity founded in patriarchy. If we take racism and patriarchy to be the two pillars upon which imperial enunciations are supported, the intersection of decolonial and queer thinking can productively join forces in decolonizing and queering epistemology, and work together toward the future in building decolonial and queer epistemologies.

❧ Mujerista Discourse: A Platform for Latinas' Subjugated Knowledge

ADA MARÍA ISASI-DÍAZ

One of the main goals of mujerista discourse has been to provide a platform for the voices of Latinas living in the United States. Mujerista discourse, particularly focused on Christian ethics and theology, has as its goal the liberation/flourishing of Latinas. It uses as its source the understandings and practices of Latinas, in particular the religious understandings and practices of grassroots Latinas who struggle against oppression in their everyday lives. Mujerista discourse, originally a liberationist one, highlights the voices of Latinas, which as a group are ignored by U.S. society.[1] Often considered intellectually inferior, Latinas' understandings are indeed one of the many subjugated knowledges that are ignored to the detriment not only of our own community but also of the whole of society.[2]

Mujerista thought is a "thinking-with" grassroots Latinas rather than a "thinking-about" them.[3] Mujerista discourse is a "we" discourse that embraces commitment to being community while not ignoring specificity and particularity. Elaborated by academic Latinas, mujerista discourse takes very seriously what Paulo Freire noted long ago: At the heart of all liberation thinking there has to be a commitment to the people, what he calls a "communion with the people."[4] This communion, or solidarity, with the people has to find expression in an ongoing dialogue that profoundly respects the people's ability to reason and to participate reflectively in their own struggles against oppression.[5]

In order to remain true to the struggle for liberation, one needs to continuously find ways of creating knowledge from the underside of history. This is why mujerista thought attempts to be beyond the controlling rationality of dominant discourses. To do this, we use the experience of Latinas as the source for knowledge: This is a nonnegotiable understanding in the struggle for our liberation. Our work is not to elaborate and explain our understandings against the background of "regular" knowledge, using the dominant discourse to validate our insights. As a decolonial discourse, mujerista thought seeks adequacy and validation from its usefulness in Latinas' struggles. This does not mean, however, that we can claim to be free of "dominant thinking" or that we can always evade its categories, or that we always find it necessary to do so. As a matter of fact, the goal of mujerista discourse, the liberation/flourishing of Latinas, obliges us to use in our methods, in our categories, and in our strategies whatever we find valuable to achieve our goal.

This makes clear that though mujerista theology and ethics have used the language of liberation discourse, they certainly understand liberation not as a project possible within Western civilization but rather one that has as its goal radical structural changes. Our attempt has always been to enable and further Latinas' thinking, that is, to shed light on the epistemological richness that emerges from our lived experiences and to value what we know and how we know it as our contribution to building a different world. Undoubtedly, we find many similarities between mujerista discourse and decolonial thinking—postcolonial philosophy—which we began to explore at the beginning of the twenty-first century. Though we agree with Walter Mignolo that liberation theology, one of the "parenting" discourses of mujerista thinking, was conceived within the Western episteme, mujerista thinking, as one of the instances of Latina/o thought, has taken liberation thought beyond its initial articulations.[6] Perhaps because of our condition as an ethnoracial, minoritized, and marginalized group within the United States, mujerista theology, though indebted to Latin American liberation theology, also drinks from many of the same fountains as does decolonial thinking. It is not a matter of merely "changing dresses" but rather a welcoming of decolonial thinking as an addition to liberation thought and as a way of creating "coalitions" among scholars and schools of thought that are committed to local communities and that seek to contribute to the articulation of shared meanings.

That said, I turn to the themes of this essay that indeed fall within the paradigms of both decoloniality and liberation. This essay is about two elements at the heart of our communion with grassroots Latinas: an ongoing option for the oppressed, which, as mujeristas, is an option for Latinas, and a commitment to value lo cotidiano—the everyday of Latinas. Without these two commitments, one cannot contribute to unveiling subjugated knowledges. In this essay I first explain what I mean by the oppressed, of which Latinas are but one group. I then clarify the meaning of lo cotidiano in an attempt to discover and highlight its richness. In the third section of the essay, I analyze the option for the oppressed and why it has to be at the heart of all liberative and decolonial discourses. I conclude the essay with some important theological considerations.

THE OPPRESSED

Injustice, which from the perspective of those suffering is called oppression, has different causes that need to be made explicit in order to struggle for justice in a more effective way than we have done since the 1960s. Different causes lead to different modes of oppression, which are interrelated but do not operate in the same way. There are five different modes of oppression: exploitation, marginalization, ethnoracism, powerlessness, and structural violence.[7] None of these different forms of oppression is more unjust or causes more destruction than the others. All of them are interconnected, creating institutions, organizations, laws, and customs that reinforce one another and create structural oppression. The dominant group, the group that has power, considers oppressed people as having no value or significance. Those who are oppressed—Latinas and Latinos, the impoverished, lesbians, gays, transsexuals, and transgender people, among many others—are not taken into consideration in determining what is normative for society.

Often when referring to the oppressed, I specify "the impoverished" because I am a middle-class Latina and though I have suffered economic exploitation, i.e., my salary in comparable situations has not been the same as that of my male colleagues,[8] being middle class can easily lead me to ignore poverty. Consciously mentioning the impoverished is a way of reminding myself that I have to struggle for societal changes even if such changes will "cost me" some of the economic advantages and privileges I have being a middle-class Latina.

When I refer to the oppressed and the impoverished, I am referring to those who are conscious of their oppression and who struggle for their liberation, taking into consideration their communities. In this category I include those who know that liberation is about a radical change of structures and not about participation in oppressive structures. The oppressed and the impoverished are those who are conscious of being historical agents, though they would most probably not talk about it using this phrase. They are those who can and do explain to themselves what happens to them and in doing so take responsibility for their experience of being oppressed, for who they are as oppressed people and how they face the situation in which they find themselves.[9] I do not include, however, the impoverished whose struggle to survive makes it impossible for them to reflect on their circumstances. In no way does this mean that I devalue them or ignore them. A commitment to the impoverished and the oppressed is precisely a commitment to create spaces that will allow them the opportunity to become more conscious of the reasons for the injustices they suffer. Though one cannot "conscienticize" anyone else, we can facilitate opportunities for the oppressed and impoverished to reflect on their own reality.[10]

Not part of this category are those who consider themselves oppressed but whose situations are due to personal circumstances and not to structural ones. One needs to keep in mind, at least in the United States, that it has become somewhat fashionable to claim to be oppressed in order to benefit from government programs such as scholarships for minority children and youth. Therefore, in conclusion, the oppressed and impoverished are conscious of their oppression, and they know that their reality is not due solely or mainly to personal shortcomings; they neither seek an individualistic way out of their situation nor attempt to simply "move ahead" within oppressive structures.[11]

LO COTIDIANO

I start this section with a quotation from Martin Buber's work, for it situates me and my interest in lo cotidiano, and indicates the reason for my commitment to value it.

I possess nothing but the everyday out of which I am never taken. . . . I know no full but each mortal hour's fullness of claim and responsibility. Though far from been equal to it, yet I know that in the claim I am claimed and may respond in responsibility, and know who speaks and demands a response.[12]

My interest in lo cotidiano is intrinsically linked to the principal axis of my ethical-theological work: an option for the impoverished and the oppressed. Therefore, lo cotidiano that interests me and to which I refer is that of the impoverished and the oppressed, particularly that of my community of accountability, Latinas living in the United States. I struggle to describe lo cotidiano in order to be able to make it concrete, for if not, I will not be able to affect it, that is, to change it.

The description of lo cotidiano that follows, which I propose not as a definition but as a heuristic device that has as its goal a better—deeper—understanding of both the oppression of Latinas and our liberative praxis, has hermeneutical and epistemological implications.

> Lo cotidiano refers to the immediate space—time and place—of daily life, the first horizon of our experiences, in which our experiences take place. It is where we first meet and relate to the material world—by which I mean not just physical reality but also the way in which we relate to that reality (culture) and how we understand and evaluate our relationships with reality (our memories of what we have lived, which we refer to as "history").
>
> The materiality of lo cotidiano brings into focus the fact that it always refers to embodied experiences; the embodied quality of lo cotidiano is consciously important to the oppressed and the impoverished.
>
> Lo cotidiano has to do with the practices and beliefs that we have inherited, and with those habitual judgments that are part of our "facing life," of how we face and what we do with our reality.[13]
>
> Lo cotidiano does not refer to the a-critical reproduction or repetition of all that we have learned or to which we have become accustomed. Instead it refers to what is reproduced or repeated in a conscious manner, that which is part of the struggle for life and for liberation. Lo cotidiano, therefore, refers to the problematized daily reality—that is, to the limitations imposed by the material-historical

reality one faces every day, and to the personal situations in which we find ourselves as we try to deal with such problematized reality. Lo cotidiano, then, refers to the space—time and place—which we face daily, but it also refers to how we face it and to our way of dealing with it. Realizing that lo cotidiano has hermeneutical value, that is, that it is not only what is but also the interpretative framework we use to understand what is, lo cotidiano is a powerful point of reference from where to begin to imagine a different world, a different societal structure, a different way of relating to the divine (or to what we consider transcendental/radical immanence), as well as a different way of relating to ourselves: to who we are and what we do. Lo cotidiano, therefore, has an extremely important role in our attempt to create an alternative symbolic order.

It is precisely because lo cotidiano refers to a problematized reality, that one can find in it subversive and creative elements that enable questioning oppression and resisting it.

Lo cotidiano is what makes specific—concrete—the reality of each person and, therefore, it is *in view of* it and *in* it that one lives the multiple relationships that constitute each one as a specific person, as me and not someone else.

Lo cotidiano has to do with our emotional and physical strengths and weaknesses, with the work we do, with the frustrations and hopes we have. Lo cotidiano refers to our family relationships and to our friendships; to the way we relate to our neighbors and to our different communities; to our experience of power and powerlessness—that is, how we relate to those who have power over us and to those over whom we have power; and to the role religious beliefs or other beliefs have in our lives.[14]

The specificity of lo cotidiano makes focusing on the particular possible while it helps to question abstract universals that often ignore or falsify lo cotidiano.[15]

Lo cotidiano does not relate only to what is specific, but it also enters into contact with and is part of social systems. Lo cotidiano impacts structures and its mechanisms and is, in turn, affected by them. It is in lo cotidiano that the oppressed live, socially marginalized, economically exploited, and struggling against sexism and ethnoracism.[16]

Lo cotidiano is closely related to what is referred to as "common sense," which is why it is considered "natural." Natural here refers to the sense given to "of course," and not to the philosophical naturalism that limits reality to what the human mind can conceptualize. I use "natural" to insist on how lo cotidiano is enmeshed with the concrete and specific.[17]

Because lo cotidiano refers to what is specific about each of us, it is the main locus for considering diversity in a positive way. Now in the second decade of the twenty-first century we are certain that homogeneity turns people into masses easy to control and to manipulate. It is the diversity made present by and in lo cotidiano and the particularity and specificity of lo cotidiano that makes it possible to highlight differences and generate shared meanings as the basis for creating liberating societal structures. It is out of this diversity present in lo cotidiano of many different communities that subjugated knowledge emerges, helping the oppressed survive in the present-day suffocating globalization that ignores them.

Lo cotidiano refers to the simple reality of our world, which is not a simplistic reality. By simple reality I mean the one that we have to urgently tend to, that is dispersed throughout each day, and that we run into whether we want to or not. Without forgetting to deal with the reasons behind the reality, the urgency of surviving for the oppressed makes it necessary at times to leave for later the "whys," a later that often does not arrive because we do not conquer the urgency. Of course, that some have no time, energy, and/or resources to deal with the reasons for oppression does not mean that they are not conscious of them. In short, then, lo cotidiano is the reality strung along the hours in a day; it has to do with the food we eat *today*, with the subway or bus fare we have to pay *today*, with how to pay *today* for the medicine for a sick child or an elderly parent. Claiming that lo cotidiano has to do with the simple reality of our lives refers to the obviousness and the immediacy of lo cotidiano, to the many crises that grassroots people face with a wisdom and creativity made obvious by the fact that somehow they survive today and are ready to face tomorrow.

It is in lo cotidiano that we have and exercise power, appropriating information that we filter and shape according to our needs, our hopes, and oue goals. This is why the powers that be might kill us but cannot conquer us, as Hemingway said.

Lo cotidiano is an ethical space—time and place—for in it we can move with a certain autonomy, take decisions and put them into play—decisions that might seem unimportant but which woven together constitute our ethical and moral horizon.[18]

There are, of course, different cotidianos. Lo cotidiano that I refer to is that of the base/grassroots/Latino communities, mainly to lo cotidiano of Latinas. It refers to how Latinas understand and use the elements of our culture in common, ordinary, everyday realities, to how we appropriate traditions, language, symbols, and art. This cotidiano is very different from that of the dominant group. An example might be useful here.

When using a public bus in New York City, many times I see two Latinas approach the bus but only one gets in. The other one waits outside until the first one uses the fare card and then quickly turns around and gives it to the woman who has stayed on the sidewalk. That they have to pay a $2.25 fare to ride the bus powerfully impacts their lives. They have to coordinate their efforts to face this reality of their cotidiano. They have to give it much thought: coordinate schedules, decide who pays for the card, how they are going to keep track of its use, and so forth. On the other hand, for those of us who do not have to worry about how we are going to pay for local transportation, lo cotidiano is less demanding, and we hardly pay attention to it. Often we stand on the sidewalk and signal a taxi, or those who are upper middle class or rich simply wait inside until the doorman of the building gets them one. When one gets in a taxi, how much it is going to cost is something one does not know until the end, but having more than a minimal amount of money means one does not worry. The taxis in the area where I live, an area of middle-class and working-class people, are different. Here you negotiate with the driver how much the taxi ride is going to cost before you get in.

This example reveals the aspect of lo cotidiano that Certeau called the tactics of lo cotidiano: the "what" and the "how" at the level of the particular situation. Grassroots people, of course, would like to have a general strategy to deal with their transportation expenses, an established way of paying for them, but they simply do not have the resources to do this. Their cotidiano is full of struggles to make ends meet. It is an *a pie cotidiano*—an on-foot cotidiano—in the sense that they have to deal with it with little resources other than their wit and popular wisdom. Their cotidiano deals with a reality that for the dominant group is a matter of routine. The dominant group does not have to decide whether to take the bus and pay $2.25 or walk fifteen blocks in order to have that money to buy food or soap to do the laundry. Those of us with resources often go through the day without having to think much about how to feed and dress ourselves, how to pay for transportation to get where we are going, or to pay for doing the laundry. It is at this level of facing the particularity and specificity of everyday life that grassroots people—Latinas—embrace lo cotidiano and in doing so, lo cotidiano becomes the space—time and place—where they exercise their moral agency and determine who they are, who they become, and how they live their lives.

Why is it that lo cotidiano of the grassroots is not valued, is not taken into consideration when one analyzes reality and elaborates strategies for dealing with it? In philosophy there is both a valuing of lo cotidiano but also a disvaluing of it because it is seen often as a "place for inauthentic living."[19] When lo cotidiano enters the academic discourse it is often dislodged from the actual living of the vast majority of people. It becomes abstract; and this is not the abstraction needed to talk about any and all themes and issues. Instead it is an abstraction that loses its footing in the historical reality of peoples. This is because most of us in the academy often have no contact with lo cotidiano of the people, and ours is too different from theirs, so it does not help us to be mindful of what constitutes the reality of most people. Again, an example here might prove useful in establishing the poignancy and urgency of the grassroots people's cotidiano and its difference from that of those of us in the academy.

I was at a bus stop last Sunday on my way to church, when I noticed a woman crossing the street. She seemed to be in her mid-fifties and had a little boy with her who was about six years old. The little boy was dressed in a pair of shorts and a T-shirt, a white one clean and pressed. He happily skipped across the street and came to sit on the bench next to me. He looked healthy and rested, for he did not have a sleepy face even though it was early. The woman, in contrast, was wearing a faded dress that was not ironed. She was very thin and looked distraught. She was munching on a donut and was drinking coffee from a paper cup that indicated she had bought her breakfast at a convenience store. The little boy sat next to me, and the woman sat next to him. After a few minutes the little boy, who in order not to bother me was crowded against the woman, said to her, "Mom, you stink." He repeated it a couple of times in a soft voice. Previously the woman had talked rather sharply to him telling him he needed to behave. Now she mumbled softly to him, "Yes, I know."

Their bus came before mine, and I was left to ponder on what I had just seen and heard. First of all I was surprised that the woman was the mother of the boy—he called her Mom—for she looked too old to have such a young child. I realized that most probably she was not in her mid-fifties but in her forties. She indeed looked older, her body wasted beyond her actual age. Then I thought about how smartly dressed the little boy was in contrast to how disheveled she looked. Most probably she had poured all her attention on the little boy and had little time, energy, or money left to get herself clean, to wash and iron her dress. She could have saved money by making coffee in her house instead of buying it at a convenience store. Well, that is, if she had a house and had paid for the gas or the electricity to run the stove, and owned a coffeemaker, and had the money to buy a can of coffee plus the filters needed to brew it, which all together would cost over $5. She might not have had $5; she might only have had $2.00 to buy one cup of coffee and a donut.

I thought long and hard about all the decisions she had made by 9 AM that Sunday morning. She had to think about breakfast. She had fed the little boy, for if not, I thought, he would have been asking her for some of her donut, and she had fed him at home or his face might have smudges of powdered sugar or the glaze that covers the donuts. Her breakfast came second, given the fact that she was quickly eating before boarding the bus. She, perhaps, had to start thinking about breakfast the night before. Perhaps she had to decide not to buy a can of coffee. She needed the money for the bus fare.

In contrast, I had made no decisions about breakfast: I have all I need to make coffee at home and I have oatmeal to cook, or bread to toast. I did not have to choose between having money for the bus fare and eating a good breakfast. I have a fare-card that automatically gets recharged by debiting my bank card. I knew that if the bus did not come in time for me to make it to the church before the service started, I could and would take a taxi. I had been preoccupied with other things than the routine of surviving since I had gotten out of bed. The decisions I had taken on that Sunday morning were so trivial that I do not remember a single one of them. It was different for this woman. This woman probably had made half a dozen decisions that impacted her values, her commitments, her responsibilities, and her obligations. How important the child was for her was obvious by the contrast between his appearance and hers. And the fact that he felt he could tell her that she was smelly meant that, though she had spoken roughly to him at first, he was not afraid of her. Her soft reply to the child, I thought, was one of embarrassment, embarrassment that I too might have noticed her condition. However, even if she paid no attention to me, how embarrassing for your own child to tell you that you stink!

From the perspective of liberation, socio-political-economic liberation, I also had many questions. I wondered if she is alone or has a family or community that helps her in her daily struggle to make ends meet. I doubt she is paid a just wage that would make it possible for her to care for herself and her child. Maybe she does not even have a job, a reality today in the United States for almost 10 percent of the population. The terrible economic situation of the world today is a consequence of a neoliberal economics that does not take seriously the lives of the majority of people around the globe, people like this woman and this little boy. Neoliberal economics considers this woman and this child surplus people, and they are not taken into consideration by present-day systems. She is, if anything, blamed for her situation, for the myth that in the United States anyone who is willing to work hard can "make it" continues to influence the way in which many in this country look upon this woman. Her cotidiano is not factored into the "reality" of this society, of this nation; it is never taken into consideration by the economic mechanisms at work on Wall Street. How she understands her life and how she deals with it every day are given no attention or importance by those of us whose work is to explain, in order to influence, the world in which we live, be it from a political, economic, social, philosophical, or religious perspective. Much less is the academic discourse willing to engage this woman and the millions like her in order to understand lo cotidiano of the majority of the human race. Why?

I think there are three reasons why the reality of this woman is not considered in our discourse about lo cotidiano. First, we are not in touch with our own cotidiano, maybe because we consider it trite, but I think it is because it would make us question it. Yet, one of the first considerations we need to pay attention to when dealing with lo cotidiano is that "we exist in the everyday in a permanent presence that makes all attempts to escape it useless."[20] Our cotidiano is related to that of the woman and the little boy who sat next to me at the bus stop, for the privileges and economic resources that make it possible for me not to worry about getting coffee in the morning have to do with her not having enough money for a decent breakfast and for washing her clothes. Until we understand the connection between what some of us have and what this woman does not have, we will not be able to understand her cotidiano, much less will we be able to factor it into our considerations. We do not look at her cotidiano, for we do not want our way of life to be challenged.[21]

If we claim to be about unveiling and enabling subjugated knowledges, definitely a liberation and decolonial move, then we have to enter into the world where that knowledge is produced, for there is no knowledge without "encountering" the reality we claim to know. As a Latina living in the United States, I indeed have experienced oppression. I also have some understanding of other forms of oppression—poverty and homophobia, for example—of which I have no personal experience. However, without the constant commitment to "encounter" the reality of impoverished Latinas, as a middle-class woman, I cannot claim to value Latinas' subjugated knowledges.[22]

Second, lo cotidiano is seen as trite. We consider the decisions that deal with structural issues, the ones that we believe impact society at large, and tend to not think about lo de todos los días—what happens in the dailiness of our lives and of the whole human race. We fail to value lo cotidiano of grassroots Latinas because we see it as belonging to the private sphere, not having political consequences. Yet it is the struggle about lo cotidiano that often sparks the great movements for justice, showing the political implication of everyday reality. Consider the fact that the spark for the Civil Rights movement in the United States was one trite, tiny event: Rosa Parks's refusal to move to the back of the bus, where the "people of color" where supposed to be.[23] Or think about the impact of Mexican American farmworker Cesar Chavez's fast in bringing powerful companies and rich landowners to the table ready to make concessions.[24] Or, to make it really contemporary, think what set in motion the tumultuous struggles of people in Africa and the Arabian Peninsula to rid themselves of dictators and exploiters, even as this essay is being written. It was Mohamed Bouazizi, a street vendor in the town of Sidi Bouzid, Tunisia, who on December 17 fought to defend himself from abusive power. A policewoman had confiscated his scale. Without it he could not make a living to sustain his family. When he protested, she slapped him, spat on him, and tossed aside his cart and the produce he was selling. He went to the governor's office to complain, but the governor refused to see him. Humiliated and weighed down by his situation, less than an hour after the altercation with the policewoman, he poured gasoline over himself and set himself on fire. Protests against what had been done to Bouazizi started within hours of his self-immolation and continued to grow, moving into affluent areas and eventually into the capital. Bouazizi died on January 4 and on January 14, 2011, President Ben Ali, after twenty-three years of authoritarian rule, fled Tunisia with his family.[25]

Third, I think that the lack of attention to lo cotidiano of grassroots people is because they are not valued as intellectuals; they are not thought of as having and producing knowledge. In my experience the contrary is true. I have found grassroots Latinas admirably capable of explaining what they do and the reason for doing it. Their lives are not unreflected. On the contrary; the urgency of their situation makes them think and choose constantly. Their lives are indeed a constant action-reflection-action that keeps them alive and searching for ways to flourish. They might not be able to explain their lives in terminology that we in the academy find acceptable, or even understand. But they deal with their lives intelligently, that is, in ways that illumine the structures that they face and in which they have to find ways of fitting in in order to survive.

The lack of value given to Latinas' cotidiano goes hand in hand with the lack of appreciation for the epistemology of all oppressed people. Ignorance about the value of subjugated knowledges contributes to the oppression of the vast majority of the people in the world. The recognition and valuing of their subjugated knowledge are intrinsic to their liberation, which indeed is part and partial of the flourishing of all life.[26]

THE OPTION FOR THE OPPRESSED AND THE IMPOVERISHED

For a while, for a couple of decades, at least among those calling themselves liberals in the academic and church world in which I move, it was
fashionable or politically correct to talk about an option for the oppressed
and impoverished. However, for the last ten years approximately, we
have been watering down such an option and, I propose, in doing so we
have rejected it. We do this in great measure for the same three reasons
given for not valuing lo cotidiano of the oppressed. We attempt to
assuage our consciences by talking about a "preferential" option, an understanding that allows those of us who have some privileges in the
dominant world, to keep them. A preferential option is not an option for
the oppressed. It is merely a way of straddling the fence that shows as
not true what we claim to do and invalidates much of our discourse, for
it falsifies the ethical implications of opting. I believe we soften the option
in order not to antagonize the liberals that we think are willing to struggle for justice, but who in fact are against any radical structural change.

A preferential option is an oxymoron, for to prefer is not the same as
to opt: the two are mutually exclusive. Preferences are operative before
one opts, but once an option is made, other possible preferences one
might have considered cease to exist. You can prefer more than one thing
among many others. As a matter of fact, the process of opting goes
through a process of clarifying preferences and evaluating them. But
when the moment of opting comes, one opts *for this,* and in doing so,
one opts *not for that.* The option for the oppressed, as is true of all options, cannot be qualified. It can be changed, but once this happens it is
not any longer an option for the oppressed. To claim to have a preferential option is a way of rejecting the demands of what it really means to
opt for the oppressed and impoverished.

There are three reasons given for claiming that to opt for the poor is
not correct. The first one has to do with the claim that such an option
limits one's freedom; the second reason talks about fairness and impartiality as central elements of ethics; and the third one proposes that one
cannot opt against the powerful and the rich, who constitute about one
third of the human race. The discussion about these three points follows
somewhat abstract arguments of the kind generally used in analytical
thinking, the kind that yield "knowledge that." However, as in the first

section of this essay, I also use narratives about experiences that yield "knowledge about," that is, knowledge "in which the qualia of the experience are among the salient part of the knowledge."[27] I point this out because apart from the coherent analytical explanations I give—at least I think they are coherent and, therefore, convincing—the option for the poor is a commitment to a praxis (the intertwining of reflection and doing) that requires the nourishing of knowledge that knowledge about can provide much better than knowledge that.[28]

Personal Freedom and Moral Subjectivity or Agency—Self-determination
One of the reasons given for modifying the option for the oppressed (I will refer to it simply as "the option") with the word "preferential" is that the option coerces, that it limits one's freedom and self-determination. This might be true from the liberal perspective that understands freedom in an individualistic way. However, there is a difference between an individual and a person. A person knows herself and thinks about herself as a social being. An individual, in contrast, thinks himself to be unrestrained by social ties and believes that to be fully himself he does not need to take anyone else into consideration.[29] The individual has a sense of totally unrestrained freedom. For the person, on the contrary, being herself carries a social mortgage; she knows her freedom is related to that of others.

The problem with the liberal way of thinking about freedom is that personal freedom is not without limits precisely because, even if they do not recognize it, as human beings we need others and others need us. As human beings we owe ourselves to others; we are accountable to others for who we are and what we do. As social beings, our personal freedom is restricted, and we are not free to opt without taking others into consideration. Taking others into consideration when opting does not limit one's freedom but rather helps us understand freedom in a realistic way, in a way that recognizes the sociality of human beings.[30] To recognize that we have to take others into consideration when we choose is to accept the finitude of human beings, a finitude that is ever present to the oppressed in their cotidiano.

Besides the social-relational ontology behind the claim that our personal freedom has a social mortgage and, therefore, has to take others into consideration, our freedom to be self-determining also is limited by the historical reality in which we live. The circumstances in our lives, some of our own choosing but many of them not necessarily so, also limit our freedom. Some claim that circumstances not only limit our choices but determine our choices. I believe the possible options that we have are often given to us, thus determining partially what we will choose. An example helps clarify this point.

For seven years, 1997–2004, I stayed in my birth-country, Cuba, to teach at the Seminario Evangélico de Teología in Matanzas, to work with women's groups, and to work in a Catholic parish in Santiago de Cuba. While I was there some of the options I made were different from the ones I would have made were I in New York, where I live, because the choices I had were different. I was still free to opt, but the choices I had were different; the options I would have made in New York were not possible to make when I was in Cuba. However, I did not consider myself less free to opt while I was in Cuba, but the fact is that my choices were restricted by the limited possibilities among which I had to choose. The same is true when thinking of the inverse situation. In Cuba I had choices I do not have in New York.

Not individual but personal self-determination, responsibility, and the exercise of moral subjectivity happen socially, that is, they happen in and through the communities of which we are part.

Human existence is a participatory and evaluative process, that is, a communitarian ordering by means of which a human conceives her or himself as a "self" who, precisely because of knowing that her or his own subjectivity or self-consciousness is in relation to an "other," or is a consciousness among others, conscious of others, and that, therefore, her or his subjectivity is an involved-with-others subjectivity.[31]

Human subjectivity—self-definition—therefore, which is part of the process of ethical formation, is a coming to know that to be human involves a being-with-others subjectivity. Such self-definition or affirmation of one's subjectivity is "concrete and alive, nourished by the memory of the liberation of all those who have struggled against their humanity being denied, [and is] based on a communitarian existence in resistance."[32] This resistance is not negative but refers to establishing for oneself what is right and good as we stand in solidarity with others. Resistance speaks to being human among others, particularly when one protests against oppression and struggles for liberation. The process of self-definition, or of becoming one-self/oneself is, therefore, relational-communitarian, and it happens in the process of being in solidarity with an-other. Liberal individual freedom is simply impossible.

Fairness and Impartiality

Impartiality has to do with giving the same consideration to all, without prejudice, and without being influenced by one's self-interest. Deciding what is fair takes into consideration merit and the importance of the person involved. These two moral values, fairness and impartiality, seem to be ignored or violated by the option for the oppressed and impoverished. The fact is, however, that these values, as is true of all values, cannot be considered abstractly. What we have mentioned above regarding the materiality-historicity of reality and the sociality of human beings is the basis for insisting on the need to take into consideration the situations of those involved in order to be fair.

The situation of the oppressed and impoverished is different from that of the dominant group. It is not only different. It is worse. It is extremely bad. It is precisely this difference that demands partiality. The option is not unfair because its goal is to create circumstances in which there can be fairness for the oppressed and impoverished. To be unfair because one is partial to the oppressed is the result of an undistorted and full appreciation of their situation needed for the sake of applying moral norms fairly.

Partiality, which is considered unfair and is used in arguments against the option for the oppressed, does not "violate cognitive impartiality"[33] if it is based on a reasonable gathering of relevant facts that uses a critical selectivity, aimed at presenting a picture that takes into consideration the situation at hand within the context of its societal reality and the reality of those involved. Neither is partiality in the case of the option for the oppressed intellectually dishonest; it is not "a bias that distorts experience, obstructs understanding, and undermines judgment."[34] On the contrary, partiality in favor of the oppressed urges profound honesty in examining the implications of the circumstances that are being assessed and the values used in evaluating them. Honesty requires a hermeneutics of suspicion when analyzing any situation that involves the oppressed.

The fact that the poor and impoverished constitute over two-thirds of humankind has to make one suspicious about the reason for their predicament.[35] Honesty entails a critical assessment of the persons doing the so-called impartial evaluation as well as a serious consideration of who benefits from the actions resulting from the analysis they present. Partiality in favor of the oppressed, therefore, does not undermine judgment but rather enriches it by highlighting previously ignored elements that must be taken into consideration when making decisions. The option for the oppressed does not distort but rather takes into consideration experiences that have been ignored or discounted, for example, women's experience of gender bias, Latinas/os' experience of ethnoracism, gays and lesbians' experience of heterosexism. Consequences of what is decided or chosen, that is, of how the decision or option will affect the oppressed also must play a key role in decision-making by those in charge of present structures and organizations.

Partiality in the case of the option is not only justifiable but desirable because it contributes to inclusiveness.[36] An understanding of impartiality has to include fair inclusion of the oppressed in all spheres of society and in the processes that set or influence what is normative for society.[37] The partiality of the option for the oppressed contributes to inclusiveness by insisting on the human dignity of the oppressed, remembering that lack of recognition of their dignity also diminishes that of the oppressor. It is important to note in this regard the contribution that has been made to the argument for partiality by affirmative action, a significant outcome of the U.S. Civil Rights movement in the 1960s. Affirmative action is indeed partial; it is in favor of those in society who have been systemically excluded from opportunities—economic, social, educational. It has been a way of leveling the field so that those who are members of minoritized and marginalized communities can have an opportunity to contribute to society. The inclusiveness made possible by the partiality of affirmative action contributes not only to a particular person. Its goal is the enriching of society at large, making it possible for those who have been discriminated against to participate in creating the world in which we all live. Affirmative action is not about opening doors for those who are not qualified, as those who oppose such a program often claim. It is about making possible consideration of those who have been excluded, so that their talents can be used for the good of all.

Those who benefit from affirmative action merit the jobs they are hired for, being accepted into an educational institution, and being economically successful. Partiality does not dispense with merit but rather provides opportunity for the merit of all persons regardless of their ethnicity, ethnorace, race, gender, sexual orientation, age, and so forth to be taken into consideration.

To be able to fairly concentrate on merit requires equality of opportunities and capabilities, which do not exist in our world today. Merit always has to be contextualized. And given what we have indicated about the need for partiality for the oppressed, the analysis of the context when it comes to judge merit has to pay particular attention to the oppressed. Merit as an abstract measure for judgment does not lead to fairness. Fairness is not possible if impartiality is taken to mean identical treatment for all.[38] Material and nonmaterial dissimilar needs and capabilities require a discriminate respond—a partial response.[39] Insistence on privileging the oppressed is a denunciation of "apolitical neutrality," which in reality yields not impartiality but partiality or bias in favor of the oppressors.[40]

The arguments against the option for the oppressed based on impartiality and fairness are part of the tendency to privilege the fixed, formulaic, and blandly categorical, instead of being, as is often claimed, an attempt to be theoretically rigorous.[41] Since the meaning of fairness is not static but is influenced by historical human claims, today there is an urgent need to consider those who suffer oppression, allowing them to exercise their moral agency by participating in deciding what is fair, taking into account their demands, their rights, and their human dignity. Therefore, partiality toward the oppressed emphasizes adequacy, which corrects the invalid attempts at "categorical uniformity" by "a vigorous emphasis on facing up to the particular reality of each person [the majority of whom are oppressed] . . . and on refinement of perception, acuity of communication, flexibility of perspectives, and use of a range of moral categories,"[42] such as the needs and the rights of two-thirds of humanity. Without this emphasis on the needs and rights of the oppressed the understanding of impartiality is inadequate.

In conclusion, the option not only indicates the need to reinterpret the traditional way of understanding fairness and impartiality, freedom and self-definition, but it also shows the need to highlight other values, like the value of all life, of the dignity of all human beings, the importance of needs and desires, and the importance of human beings as persons and not as individuals, and the requirements to stand for and privilege the most vulnerable.

Not an Option against the Oppressor as Person

The option for the impoverished and the oppressed is a fundamental option, one that makes clear not only what one is opting for but also what one is *not* opting for. Options always put aside other preferences because opting has consequences that cannot be ignored and that oblige until the option is rejected. No matter how much one insists that the option for the oppressed is not against the oppressor, the fact is that one cannot opt for both: to opt for one is not to opt for the other. Faced with the reality of how prevalent injustice is in our world today, one has to choose; one is forced to choose. One cannot decide not to opt, not to choose. Options must be made: One cannot escape.[43] The option for the oppressed cannot be put off; it is an urgent matter—a matter of life and death for two-thirds of humankind. Indecision and delay when it comes to the option for the oppressed and the impoverished are "as criminal as resolutely evil acts."[44] Indecision and delay bring enormous suffering and even death to the oppressed.

Is the option for the oppressed and impoverished an option *against* the oppressor? For sure, the option for the oppressed questions and negates the perspective and rationality of the oppressor. It is an option to struggle against the structures that benefit the oppressor at the expense of the oppressed. It is an option not to be on the side of the oppressor: not to think, imagine, plan, and act the way the oppressor does. The option is to struggle to bring about radical change, change that the oppressors oppose at all costs.

However, the option is *not* an option to destroy the oppressor. It is *not* wishing the oppressor evil. On the contrary; the option for the oppressed and impoverished is also an option *for* the oppressors even if they do not understand this or accept it. The option to change the present death-dealing world order benefits not only the oppressed and impoverished but also the oppressors. The economic downfall being experienced all around the world makes this obvious: The present world order—a death-dealing world order—is prejudicial to all.

THEOLOGICAL CONSIDERATIONS

Lo cotidiano and the option for the poor are of such importance for mujerista discourse that they function as intrinsic elements of a mujerista worldview, that is, mujerista assertions, values, and praxis. This is why they are part of the *locus theologicus*—the source and context—we use to do mujerista theology. In saying that they are the source of mujerista theology, we reject the traditional division of the sources of Christianity into primary sources—scripture for all Christians, to which Catholics add tradition—and secondary sources—church teaching, theology, liturgy— adding to these latter ones others such as history and context. Mujerista theology makes explicit the prima facie consideration that for some of us scripture and tradition are always mediated through those interpreting them, who are in a given context and respond to certain interests.[45] Mujerista theology insists that the context and interests that should be at play in the reading of scripture and tradition are those of the oppressed and impoverished: their reality, how they come to know such reality, and how they interpret it. The option, which carries with it a valuing of lo cotidiano of the oppressed, operates, therefore, at this very fundamental level of doing theology.

In mujerista theology, we understand God's grace—God's free and efficacious self-disclosure and self-giving—to be present mainly among the oppressed and through the oppressed.[46] Such an affirmation is not a metaphysical claim, that is, we do not claim to be talking about God's nature per se. This is what we understand and believe based on our reading of the Christian Bible, using a mujerista hermeneutical lens shaped by the struggle for justice for Latinas. One can indeed point to passages in the Bible that, though the authors of the Gospels most probably were not making metaphysical claims—in the present-day understanding of metaphysical claims—they may be read as such. For example, our belief that God is in the midst of the oppressed and impoverished is based, among other passages, on Matthew 25:31–46 where the Son of Man, a title used in the Gospels to refer to Jesus, welcomes those who have favored the impoverished and oppressed and rejects those who have not helped them. Also relevant here is the first beatitude found in Luke 6:20, "Blessed are you who are poor, for yours is the kingdom of God." We believe that Jesus made clear that God is with the oppressed and impoverished, and because we value immensely what Jesus proclaimed, we make what Jesus proclaimed a matter of belief. We find further reason to believe in God's option for the poor in the argument presented by the author of the first letter to the Corinthians 1:26–31: God chooses the unimportant and those the world judges to be fools, to shame the wise, to bring the important people to naught so that no one will be able to be presumptuous in the face of God.

We do not choose the impoverished and oppressed as a categorical good among others; one does not opt for an austere style of life in order to be coherent with the growing poverty and oppression in the world. We respond to the teachings of the Bible by believing that God makes the reality of the poor divine reality.

> If it is so, the preferential option for the poor in our times, becomes stronger, because it does not depend on empirical verifications. . . . Today the poor are more oppressed, suffering more daily dyings, and yet, the commitment to justice, the option, and hope continue to be anchored in the faithfulness and the saving workings of God.
>
> If this is so, the option for the poor is a condition for the possibility of all knowledge. Furthermore, one's personal position in view of the poor, connotes and configures the moral personality of the agent.[47]

A second theological consideration is extremely important to our argument of using the option without "preferential" as a modifier. It is important because the argument for modifying the option has emerged as an explanation of the belief in the unlimited love of God. Therefore, those who want to soften the option say that love for the oppressed and impoverished cannot limit God's love for the oppressor and the rich. The option for the poor is seen as excluding the rich and the oppressor from God's love. God's option for the oppressed and impoverished, it is claimed, leaves no room for God to love the oppressors and the rich.

Together with a few others I argue that there is no need to soften or deradicalize God's option for the oppressed in order to assert God's love of the oppressors. However, that God loves the oppressor and the rich does not mean that God loves them because they are rich and because they are oppressors. On the contrary, God's rejects the rich as rich and the oppressor as oppressor. That God loves them means precisely that God demands them to denounce unconditionally their benefits, privileges, and riches for their own sake. God's love for them comes in the guise of a demand to abjure their richness and privileges.

In God, we claim, there are no contradictions. Then God cannot love both, the oppressed and the oppressor, the impoverished and the rich. God cannot opt just a little—preferentially—for the impoverished and the oppressed. There is no possibility of "a little" when it comes to options and much less is there a possibility of "a little" when it comes to God. In opting for the oppressed and impoverished, God questions the rich and the oppressor about their richness and privileges—a questioning that cannot be ignored, to which they must respond (Luke 9:109).

> The option of the poor, which will never exclude that person of the rich—since salvation is offered to all and the ministry of the church is due to all—does exclude the way of life of the rich, . . . and its system of accumulation and privileges, which necessarily plunders and marginalizes the immense majority of the human family, whole peoples and continents.[48]

Because God's grace is extended to all, and God's grace is precisely what makes possible human acceptance of God's commands, the rich and the oppressor are constantly being given the opportunity and strength to repent and radically change their ways. Just as the oppressed and the impoverished are being given constantly the opportunity and strength not to covet what the oppressor and the rich have.

Finally, there is an important ecclesiological consideration when it comes to the option for the oppressed and the impoverished. I believe the opposition to the option is not because it is theologically questionable but because it requires a radical change of ecclesiology. The option for the oppressed and the impoverished means that the church is *not for* the oppressed and the impoverished; the church must be *from them* and must be *their* church. The option requires a radical change in church structures, structures that privilege the church's hierarchies, its ministers, and those theologians recognized by church authorities. To radically affirm the option requires from the church a willingness to consider radically changing how it understands itself and its relationship to the kin-dom of God.[49]

The church has to be a church *of* the impoverished and oppressed, not a church *for* them, which is a church where they have no say in creating its meaning. The church has to privilege the oppressed and the impoverished epistemologically, hermeneutically, and in its ongoing praxis—both how it operates within as well as its pastoral activity. This is an extreme demand, but it is a Gospel commandment. The flesh is weak, but as Christians we are called to heed the Gospel and not to change its central visions and stipulations so we can continue to sustain structures that do not privilege the oppressed and impoverished.

↬ Methodological Notes toward a Decolonial Feminism

MARÍA LUGONES

I do not seek to erase the factors of time and place that coalesce as they do only in me.
—ALFRED ARTEAGA, *Chicano Poetics*

The diasporic subject reminds us that Aztlán, the mythic homeland, shifts and moves beneath and around us. The mythic homeland is longed for, constructed, and rewritten through collective memories. Time is traversed and mythic past entwines with a future where a decolonized imaginary has possibilities. The "imagined community" of Aztlán was initially given an "essentialist identity," but if it is rethought as traveling culture, then its identity depends upon its social construction, in which memory and forgetting are as much a part of the history as the myth. Although seemingly adaptive, diaspora's transformative mobility is in actuality its most creative oppositional function.
—EMMA PEREZ, *The Decolonial Imaginary*

The colonial difference is the space where the coloniality of power is enacted.
—WALTER MIGNOLO, *Local Histories/Global Designs*

The theories of feminism developed by the coalition Women of Color in the United States in the 1980s transformed the meaning of gender. If all the "women" are "white" and all the "blacks" are "male," what does "black woman" mean? The question can be repeated for Latinas, Chicanas, Asians, and Native Americans. The coalition Women of Color was formed in part to answer this question, a question not dissimilar to Sojourner Truth's question, "Ain't I a woman?"[1] The question constitutes an existential, material, social response to the idea of a universal "woman."

The question was answered in at least two ways. The first answer revealed the inseparability of race and gender. When "woman" stands for "white woman" and "black" stands for "black man," the term "black woman" is grossly inadequate because racial formation and gender formation are inseparable processes. There is no underlying, core, irreducible meaning to "man" or "woman" apart from race. It is not just that the meaning of "man" and "woman" cannot be reduced to the reproductive; the reproductive itself cannot be thought apart from the racialization of procreation.

The additive understanding of the relation between race and gender has received many and varied forms of critique. The critique of the logic of addition moved to the logic of *intersection*. Intersectionality looked for Latina, black, Asian, and indigenous women at the intersection of race and gender. In particular, it considered the relation of race and gender in the U.S. legal system. Intersectionality points to the erasure of nonwhite women from the legal system. To say that nonwhite women are erased from the legal system is to say that they will not find redress regarding issues such as racialized sexual harassment because there are no subjects that could be abused in this manner who are recognized by the law. The legal system recognizes categories that disentangle gender from race. Thus at the intersection we find an absence. All structuring of social life in the United States mirrors the law in this erasing of black, Native American, Latina, and Asian women. At the intersection of "woman" and "black" or "Latino" or "Native American" or "Asian" one finds an absence or a distortion, such as an understanding of Native American women as the addition of white women and Native American men. To notice the inseparability of race and gender, to "see" nonwhite women, produces an important epistemological shift. One "sees" the inseparability in questions of labor, education, knowledge, legal practices, health practices, religious agency, and theology.[2] Intersectionality is also a more significant move. One looks at theoretical accounts of feminism, at feminist practices, at perceptions, and asks the intersectional question. As

such, the intersectional question reveals racism at the fundamental theoretical and epistemological levels.

The second answer to the meaning of African American, Native American, Latina, and Asian women is the coalitional meaning Women of
Color. It reveals selves and reality as multiple. Because multiplicity is also
understood in two related ways, a double meaning, this answer also
doubles. On the one hand, the racialized, gendered self is multiple in its
perceiving others perceiving her as inferior, as lacking in the fundamental
capacities of the rational modern self. Her inferiority to others' superiority is inscribed not just in how she is perceived but also in the very
complex construction of the social world. Her construction as inferior is
fictional but real because the fiction is upheld by power. The split in self-
perception is crucial for the subjectivity/intersubjectivity of the nonwhite
subject. She comes to understand herself as without authority. She understands the racial difference as establishing a cleavage, a split that cuts
through her and through her relations. But the multiplicity of reality is
complicated by her inhabitation of her self within collectivities that are
despised in the larger construction of the social world, but that reject the
construction of her as inferior. These collectivities back up meanings that
raise enduring critiques and alternative meanings. Thus she inhabits, at
least, a fractured locus.

As the fragmentation of the self is lived as double consciousness, one
comes to inhabit the multiple position that reveals the imposed quality
of the inferiority and the relation between power and that imposition.
The doubling makes vivid the injunction to see and live only in white
terms, erasing resistant subjectivities and relations within the dominant
hegemonic mainstream, marking gender as real only among real people,
white people. So hegemonically, Native American, black, and white are
not ways of marking gender. They are disconnected from gender. The
sense of split, of schizophrenia that one feels—here I am a woman/there
I am Latina—when faced within the excision of gender and race becomes
familiar. The multiplicity of Women of Color enables us to live the sense
of schizophrenia also as something we deny through our resistant presence. Women of Color's inhabitation of the multiple and fragmented
senses of self in relation is not only a denial of the denial of unity, equality, purity, authority, and coevalness[3] but also a rejection of the terms

"unity," "equality," "purity," "authority," and "coevalness." She will not be a passive being.

Multiplicity points to a way of understanding differences among women, but also to an understanding of society, intersubjectivity, and selves as fragmented by structures of power and through the use of power, including the exercise of power by some women over others. Finally, as one stands in the fragmented social world with others who provide one a sense of self that is in response to the denigration and dehumanization of racialized gendering—home places, circles of resistance, communities and collectivities with alternative understandings of reality than the ones imposed by power—one comes to understand oneself as fractured but able to both critique and to propose questions and directions hidden by the powerful unitary discourse of power. It is here, from within this fractured locus that is sustained in larger, variegated groups, collectivities, and communities that the critique of the meaning of "woman" was raised. It was raised as an issue of praxis, one marking a redirection in movement at the grassroots, a moving among the racialized gendered as inferior from within enclaves that enabled the moving. The question was taken up coalitionally. "Women of Color" is thus the coalitional identity, subject position, resistant agency, that we began inhabiting actively, in the gerund, be-ing, inhabit-ing, lov-ing. This subjectivity/intersubjectivity emphasized a multiple understanding of selves and realities and an infrapolitical way of moving toward each other.

Thus the question is answered in several complementary and radical ways that offer critique, awareness through critique, further awareness through an understanding of the consequences of the critique for the construction of the "real." Finally, and most importantly, we are enabled to follow through the looking glass to see our possibilities in deep, differential, nonreactive opposition that moves us toward each other. We are moved to see our possibilities in a multiple, differentiated social world that may be dispersed geographically, including grassroots and traditional communities, but also urban landscapes. That social linking forms us. It commits us to learning about each other and thus to encompass in our imagination the multiplicity of the powerfully oppressive constructions of the social and of the infrapolitically resistant collectives.

I have pointed out an emphasis on multiplicity, coalitional infrapolitics, intersectionality, double or multiple perception as characteristic of

Women of Color feminisms. I have also pointed out a sense of agency different from the modern sense, both in its not being univocal and unitary, and in its not being recognized institutionally or hegemonically. Thus it is a minimal but strongly infrapolitical sense of agency. Finally and importantly, from Lorde to Anzaldúa to Sandoval the coalitional sense is guided by love, a strong erotics that becomes a social erotics. This inclination to others is powerfully motivating, inspiring, and energizing as it inclines us to learn from each other in complex histories of interdependence, including betrayal, as we respond to multiple oppressions. The sense of activity and the erotic connection interweave Women of Color possibilities.

Even though understandings of the relation between colonization and racialized gender oppression have been part of the formulations of Women of Color feminisms, it has not been clear how colonization has affected the meaning of "woman." The lack of clarity has made our relation to decolonial positions difficult. I am complicating the understanding of racialized gender, going beyond intersectionality, by introducing what I call the *coloniality of gender* and moving toward a *decolonial feminism*. Going beyond the coloniality to a decolonial politics and style of living and relating asks that we become conscious inhabitants of the multiplicity of historically resistant subject positions and thus become fluent in the resources that we each bring to a coalitional decolonial solidarity.

In proposing a decolonial feminism I am not departing from Women of Color feminisms. I am providing a theoretical framework that enables us to understand both the relations of oppression and the resources that we bring to liberation. I am moving to a way of speaking that more clearly seeks coalitions among the colonized across vast histories and spaces, always honoring the local, since resistance can be seen and understood only up close. Centering of the colonial further clarifies why coalitional solidarity among Women of Color requires that we both become fluent in each other's histories and that we read each other sociohistorically in terms of the coloniality of gender.

THE COLONIALITY OF GENDER

With colonial modernity, beginning with the colonization of the Americas and the Caribbean, the modern hierarchical dichotomous distinction between men and women became known as characteristically human and a mark of civilization. Indigenous peoples of the Americas and enslaved Africans were understood as not human, as animals, as monstrously and aberrantly sexual, wild. The dichotomous gender distinction became a mark of civilization: Only the civilized are men or women. The European bourgeois man is a subject, fit for rule, for the public, a being of civilization, heterosexual, Christian, a being of mind and reason. The European bourgeois woman is not his complement, but the one who reproduces race and capital. This is tightly bound to her sexual purity, passivity, home-boundedness.

The bourgeois white Europeans are civilized; they are fully human. Being gendered in this dichotomous manner makes being a man a mark of humanity. Women are human in their relation to white, bourgeois, European men. The hierarchical dichotomy as a mark of the human becomes also a normative tool to damn the colonized. As the behavior and personalities/souls of the colonized are judged as bestial, of animals, the colonized are nongendered, promiscuous, grotesquely sexual, sinful. Though at this time the understanding of sex was not dimorphic, animals were differentiated since the conquest and colonization of the Americas as males and females, the male being the perfection, the female, the inversion, deformation of the male.[4] Hermaphrodites, sodomites, viragos were all understood as deviations from male perfection. As primitive, wild, not quite human, the colonized were also understood sexually as males and females, the female the inferior, inverted male.

But to the extent that the civilizing mission and conversion to Christianity has been always present in the ideological conception of conquest and colonization, colonized "males" are also judged from the normative understanding of "man," and colonized "females" are judged from the normative understanding of "woman."[5] The priests and the church overtly presented their mission as transforming the colonized animals into human beings through conversion. From this point of view, colonized people became males and females. Males became not-human-as-not-men, the human trait, and colonized females became not-human-as-not-women. Consequently, though sexually colonized females' lack was understood in relation to male perfection, her human lack compared her only to women. Colonized females were never understood as lacking because they were not men-like. Colonized men were not understood to be lacking as not being women-like. Notice the important distinction between sex and gender at this time, which is conflated later as sexual dimorphism becomes the companion of the dichotomous understanding of gender. What has been understood as the feminization of colonized men seems rather a gesture of humiliation, attributing sexual passivity to the threat of rape. This tension between hypersexuality and sexual passivity defines one of the domains of masculine subjection of the colonized.

The colonial civilizing mission was the euphemistic mask of brutal access to people's bodies through unimaginable exploitation, violent sexual violation, control of reproduction, and systematic terror, which included, for example, feeding living people to dogs and making pouches and hats from the vaginas of brutally killed indigenous females. The civilizing mission used the hierarchical gender dichotomy as a judgment, though the attainment of dichotomous gendering was not the point of the normative judgment. Turning the colonized into human beings was not a colonial goal. Rather, the colonizing mission included the profound transformation of the colonized into men and women—a transformation not in identity but in nature—in its repertoire of justifications for abuse. Christian confession, sin, and the Manichean division between good and evil served to imprint female sexuality as evil. There is an important separation in this respect between the treatment of *comuneros*, community members, subjects of empires, and the treatment of the indigenous nobility that needs exploration from the point of view of the coloniality of gender. Here I am highlighting the most direct and brutal conception and treatment of those whose labor and sexuality were clearly understood in terms of the coloniality of gender.

The civilizing transformation justified the colonization of memory and thus of one's sense of self, intersubjective relations, and relation to the spirit world, to land, to the very fabric of one's conception of reality, identity, social, ecological, and cosmological organization. Thus as Christianity became the most powerful instrument in the transformative mission, the normativity that tied gender and civilization became involved in the erasure of community, of ecological practices, knowledges of planting, weaving, and the cosmos, and not only in changing and controlling reproductive and sexual practices. One can begin to appreciate the tie between the colonial introduction of the instrumental modern concept of nature central to capitalism and the colonial introduction of the modern concept of gender and appreciate it as macabre and heavy in its impressive ramifications. One can also recognize the dehumanization constitutive of what Nelson Maldonado-Torres calls "the coloniality of being" in the scope of the modern colonial gender system.[6]

I use the term "coloniality" following Anibal Quijano's analysis of the capitalist world system of power in terms of coloniality of power and of modernity, two inseparable axes in the workings of this system of power.[7] Quijano's analysis provides a historical understanding of the inseparability of racialization and capitalist exploitation as constitutive of the capitalist system of power as anchored in the colonization of the Americas. In thinking of the coloniality of gender I complicate his understanding of the capitalist global system of power, but I also criticize his understanding of gender only in terms of sexual access to women. In using the term "coloniality" I mean not just classification of people in terms of the coloniality of power and gender but also the process of active reduction of people, the dehumanization that fits them for the classification, the attempt to turn the colonized into less than human beings. This is in stark contrast to the public aim of conversion, which constitutes the Christianizing mission.

DECOLONIZING GENDER

The semantic consequence of the coloniality of gender is that "colonized woman" is an empty category. No women are colonized. No colonized females are women. Thus, the colonial answer to Sojourner Truth is clearly—*No*. That gives to her defiant question a depth and complexity that is otherwise lost. Unlike colonization, the coloniality of gender is still with us; It is what lies at the intersection of gender and class and race as central constructs of the capitalist world system of power. Thinking about the coloniality of gender enables us to think of historical beings, only one-sidedly understood as oppressed. As there are no such beings as colonized women, I suggest that we focus on the beings that resist and respond critically and praxically the coloniality of gender from the colonial difference. Such beings are, as I have suggested, only partially understood as oppressed, as constructed through the coloniality of gender. The suggestion is not that we search from another side of the eurocentric construction of gender in indigenous organizations of the social world. Resistance to the coloniality of gender is historically complex.

When I think of myself as a theorist of resistance, of defiant response from an other logic, that is not because I think of resistance as the end or goal of political struggle, but rather its beginning, its possibility. I am interested in the relational subjective/intersubjective spring of liberation, as both adaptive and creatively oppositional. Resistance is the tension between subjectification (the forming/informing of the subject) and active subjectivity, that minimal sense of agency required for the oppressing → ← resisting relation to be an active one, without appeal to the maximal sense of agency of the modern subject.[8]

Resistant subjectivity often expresses itself infrapolitically. Infrapolitics marks the turn inward in a politics of resistance toward liberation. It shows the power of groups, enclaves, and communities of the oppressed constituting both resistant meaning and each other against the constitution of meaning and social organization by power. As colonized and racially gendered, we are also other than what the hegemony makes us be. That is an infrapolitical achievement. If we are exhausted, fully made through and by micro and macro mechanisms and circulations of power, "liberation" loses much of its meaning or ceases to be an intersubjective affair. The very possibility of an identity based on politics[9] and the project of decoloniality loses its peopled ground.

As I move methodologically from Women of Color feminisms to a decolonial feminism, I think feminism from and at the grassroots, and from and at the colonial difference, with a strong emphasis on ground, on a historicized incarnate intersubjectivity. The question of the relation between resistance to the coloniality of gender and decoloniality is being set up here rather than answered. But I do mean this way of understanding resistance to the coloniality of gender as key in the setting of the question and thus as crucial to a decolonial feminism. So, this work is methodological.[10]

Decolonizing gender is necessarily a task of praxis. It is to enact a critique of racialized, colonial, capitalist, heterosexualist gender oppression as a lived transformation of the social world. As such, it places the theorizer in the midst of people in a historical, subjective/intersubjective understanding of the oppressing → ← resisting relation at the intersection of complex systems of oppression. To a significant extent it has to be in accord with the subjectivities and intersubjectivities that partly construct and in part are constructed by the colonial situation. It must include "learning" peoples. I use the word "feminism" because feminism does not provide just an account of the oppression of women. It goes beyond oppression by providing materials that enable women to understand their situation without succumbing to it. Here I begin to provide a way of understanding the oppression of women who have been subalternized through the fused, inseparable processes of racialization, colonization, capitalist exploitation, and heterosexualism. My intent is to focus on the subjective-intersubjective to reveal that disaggregating oppressions disaggregates the subjective-intersubjective springs of colonized women's agency. I call the analysis of racialized capitalist gender oppression the *coloniality of gender;* I call the possibility of overcoming the coloniality of gender *decolonial feminism.*

The coloniality of gender enables me to understand the oppressive imposition as a complex interaction of economic, racializing, and gendering systems in which every person at the colonial encounter can be found, as a live, historical, fully described being. It is as such that I want to understand the resister as being oppressed, the colonizing construction of the fractured locus. But the coloniality of gender hides the resister as fully informed as a native of communities under cataclysmic attack. So the coloniality of gender is only one active ingredient in the resister's history. In focusing on the resister at the colonial difference I mean to unveil what is obscured.

The long process of coloniality begins subjectively and intersubjectively in a tense encounter that both forms and will not simply yield to capitalist modern colonial normativity. The crucial point about the encounter is that the subjective and intersubjective construction of it informs the resistance offered to the ingredients of colonial domination. The global, capitalist, colonial, modern system of power that Anibal Quijano characterizes as beginning in the sixteenth century in the Americas and enduring till today met not a world to be formed, of empty minds, evolving animals.[11] It rather encountered complex cultural, political, economic, religious beings: selves in complex relations to the cosmos, to other selves, to generation, to the earth, to living beings, to the inorganic, to production; selves whose erotic, aesthetic, and linguistic expressivity, whose knowledges, senses of space, longings, practices, institutions, and forms of government were not to be simply replaced but met, understood, and engaged in crossings and dialogues and negotiations. Instead, the process of colonization invented the colonized and attempted a full reduction of them to less than human primitives, satanically possessed, infantile, aggressively sexual, and in need of transformation. The process I want to follow is the oppressing ← → resisting process at the fractured locus of the colonial difference. That is, I want to follow subjects in intersubjective collaboration and conflict, fully informed as members of native American societies, as they take up, respond to, resist, and accommodate hostile invaders who mean to dispossess and dehumanize them. The invasive presence engages them brutally, in prepossessing, arrogant, incommunicative, and powerful ways that leave little room for adjustments that preserve their own senses of selves in community and in the world. But instead of thinking of the global, capitalist, colonial system as in every way successful in its destruction of peoples, knowledges, relations, and economies, I want to think of the process as continually resisted. And thus I want to think of the colonized neither as simply imagined and constructed by the colonizer and coloniality in accordance with the colonial imagination and the strictures of the capitalist colonial venture, but as a being who begins to inhabit a fractured locus constructed doubly, perceiving doubly, relating doubly, where the sides of the locus are in tension, in conflict, and the conflict itself, its energy and moves, actively informs the subjectivity of the colonized self in multiple relation.

A central consequence of what I called here the coloniality of gender and which elsewhere I have proposed as the modern/colonial gender system[12] is that gender is a modern colonial imposition. The modern/colonial gender system is not only hierarchical but also racially differentiated, and the racial differentiation denies humanity and thus gender to the colonized. I have clarified that gender has been thought of and treated as a civilized human trait, not extended to all. Irene Silverblatt,[13] Carolyn Dean,[14] Maria Esther Pozo,[15] Pamela Calla,[16] Sylvia Marcos,[17] Paula Gunn Allen,[18] Filipe Guaman Poma de Ayala,[19] Filomena Miranda,[20] and Oyeronke Oyewumi, among others, enable me to affirm that gender is a colonial imposition, not just as it imposes itself on life in relation that was lived in tune with cosmologies incompatible with the modern logic of dichotomies but also that such inhabitations animated the self-among-others in resistance from and at the extreme tension of the colonial difference.

The long process of subjectification of the colonized toward adoption/ internalization of the men/women dichotomy as a normative construction of the social, a mark of civilization, citizenship, membership in civil society was and is constantly renewed. It is met in the flesh over and over by oppositional responses grounded in a long history of in-the-flesh oppositional responses in a constant resistant movement. It is lived in alternative, resistant socialities at the colonial difference. It is movement toward coalition that impels us to know each other as selves that are thick, in relation, in alternative socialities, and grounded in tense, creative inhabitations of the colonial difference.

I am investigating historically and in contemporary living, concrete, lived, resistances to the coloniality of gender that issue from this tension. In particular, I want to mark the need to keep a multiple reading of the resistant self in relation. This is a consequence of the colonial imposition of gender. We see the gender dichotomy operating normatively in the construction of the social and in the processes of subjectification. But we need to bracket the gender distinction to understand resistance and the sources of resistance rather than read it into the very fabric that constitutes the self in relation resisting. Only then can we appreciate the different logic that organizes the social in the resistant response. Thus the multiple perception and inhabitation, the fracture of the locus, and the double or multiple consciousness are constituted, in part, by this logical difference. The fractured locus includes the hierarchical dichotomy that constitutes the subjectification of the colonized. But the locus is fractured by the resistant presence, the active subjectivity of the colonized against the colonial invasion of self in community from the inhabitation of that self. We see here the mirroring of the multiplicity of the Woman of Color in Women of Color feminisms.

But in the methodology of decoloniality, I recommend a move to read the social world from the cosmologies that inform it, rather than beginning with a gendered reading of cosmologies informing, constituting perception, motility, embodiment, and relation. The reading I am recommending moves in a very different direction from reading gender into the social world. The shift can enable us to understand the organization of the social world in terms that unveil the deep disruption of the gender imposition in the self in relation. Translating terms such as *koskalaka*,[21] *chachawarmi,*[22] and *obinrin*[23] into the vocabulary of gender, into the dichotomous, heterosexual, racialized, and hierarchical conception that gives meaning to the gender distinction is to exercise the coloniality of language through colonial translation.

In conversation with Filomena Miranda,[24] I asked her about the relation between the Aymara *qamaña* and *utjaña,* both often translated as "living." Her complex answer related *utjaña* to *uta,* meaning dwelling in community in the communal land. She told me that one cannot have *qamaña* without *utjaña.* In her understanding, those that do not have *utjaña* are *wachjcha* (orphans) and many become *chhixi.*[25] Though she lives much of the time in La Paz, away from her communal lands, she maintains *utjaña,* which is now calling her to share in governing. Next year she will govern with her sister. Filomena's sister will replace her father and thus she will be *chacha* twice, since her community is *chacha* as well as her *father.* Filomena herself will be *chacha* and *warmi,* as she will govern in her mother's stead in a *chacha* community. My contention is that to translate *chacha* and *warmi* as man and woman does violence to the communal relation expressed through *utjaña.* Filomena said *chachawarmi* in Spanish as complementary opposites. The new Bolivian constitution, the Morales government, and the indigenous movements of Abya Yala express a commitment to the philosophy of *suma qamaña* (often translated as "living well"). The relation between *qamaña* and *utjaña* indicates the importance of complementarity and its inseparability from communal flourishing in the constant production of cosmic balance. *Chachawarmi* is not separable in meaning and practice from *utjaña;* it is rather of a piece with it. Thus the destruction of *chachawarmi* is not compatible with *suma qamaña.*

I want to emphasize that I am not advocating not reading, or not seeing, the imposition of the dichotomy in the construction of everyday life, as if that were possible. To do so would be to hide the coloniality of gender and it would erase the very possibility of sensing and reading, the tense inhabitation of the colonial difference and the responses from it.

As I mark the colonial translation from *chachawarmi* to man/woman, I am aware of the use of man and woman in everyday life in Bolivian communities, including in interracial discourse. The success of the complex gender norming introduced with colonization that goes into the constitution of the coloniality of gender has turned this colonial translation into an everyday affair, but resistance to the coloniality of gender is also lived linguistically in the tension of the colonial wound. The political erasure, the lived tension of *languaging* between *chachawarmi* and man/woman constitutes loyalty to the coloniality of gender, as it erases the history of resistance at the colonial difference. Filomena Miranda's *utjaña* is not a living in the past, but living the tension of languaging at the colonial difference in the present with a vivid sense of the past.

THE COLONIAL DIFFERENCE

Walter Mignolo begins *Local Histories, Global Designs* by telling us: "The main topic of this book is the colonial difference in the formation and transformation of the modern/colonial world system."[26] As the phrase moves through Mignolo's writing, its meaning becomes open-ended. The colonial difference is not defined in *Local Histories*. Indeed, a definitional disposition is unfriendly to Mignolo's introduction of the concept. So as I present some of the quotes from Mignolo's text, I am not introducing them as his definition of "the colonial difference." Rather, these are quotes that, from within the complexity of his text, are guiding my thoughts on resistance to the coloniality of gender at the colonial difference.

The colonial difference is the space where coloniality of power is enacted.[27]

It is the space where the restitution of subaltern knowledge is taking place and where border thinking is emerging.[28]

It is the space where local histories inventing and implementing global designs meet local histories, the space in which global designs have to be adapted, adopted, rejected, integrated, or ignored.[29]

It is the physical as well as imaginary location where the coloniality of power is at work in the confrontation of two kinds of local histories displayed in different spaces and times across the planet. If Western cosmology is the historically unavoidable reference point, the multiple confrontations of two kinds of local histories defy dichoto-mies. Christian and Native American cosmologies, Christian and Amerindian cosmologies, Christian and Islamic cosmologies, Chris-tian and Confucian cosmologies among others only enact dichoto-mies where you look at them one at a time, not when you compare them in the geohistorical confines of the modern/colonial world system.[30]

Border thinking is a logical consequence of the colonial difference.[31]

The fractured locus of enunciation from a subaltern perspective de-fines border thinking as a response to the colonial difference.[32]

The colonial difference creates the conditions for dialogic situations in which a fractured enunciation is enacted from the subaltern per-spective as a response to the hegemonic discourse and perspective.[33]

The colonial differences around the planet are the house where bor-der epistemology dwells.[34]

Once coloniality of power is introduced into the analysis, the colonial difference becomes visible, and the epistemological fractures between the Eurocentric critique of eurocentrism as distinguished from the critique of eurocentrism, anchored in the colonial difference.[35]

The transcending of the colonial difference can only be done from the perspective of subalternity, from decolonization. And therefore, from a new epistemological terrain where border thinking works.[36]

Often in Mignolo's work the colonial difference is invoked at levels other than the subjective/intersubjective. But when he is using it to character-ize border thinking, as something that Gloria Anzaldúa[37] is enacting, the use characterizes her locus as fractured. The reading I want to perform sees the coloniality of gender and rejection, resistance, and adaptation to it always concretely from within.

COALITION

But instead of starting from my own peopled ground, I want to start *coalitionally*, following selves in relation inhabiting the tension of the colonial difference from socialities to which one is and from those to which one is not an insider, learning other resisters at the colonial difference, from the perspective of subalternity. That is not to say that in perceiving, understanding what is being resisted and from where, seeing the creations and transformation at the fracture, the wound of the colonial difference one would understand particular resistances as coalitional. Some may be, say from Quechua to Aymara and vice versa. The coalitional characterizes the spring of the reading, of seeing resistance enacted, and it also sees the coalitional possibilities in the present.[38] The reading moves against the social scientific objectifying reading, attempting rather to understand subjects, the active subjectivity emphasized as the reading looks for the fractured locus in resistance to the coloniality of gender, at a coalitional starting point.

Here I disagree with Mignolo as I move from the coloniality of power to the coloniality of gender, which includes the crucial elements of the coloniality of power. Searching for the complex active subjectivity at the colonial difference requires focusing one's attention on people's moving their hands, using and speaking signs, cooking, walking, and all that constitutes their lives as done from a different logic and meaning. This is deeply local, but the reading is attentive to global designs, since the coloniality of gender is inseparable, historically, from global designs. Learning each other is not a presentist way of perceiving. It must look at people with a history steeped in the coloniality of gender, of being, of power, of knowledge, and of language as crisscrossing historical lines of oppression and defiant responses that resist oppression. That brings us to the present in a very different way. It is a complex shift in attention and in living among our contemporaries resisting the coloniality of gender, which is inextricably connected to global designs. It is here that one is attentive to the active subjectivity of the subaltern creating nondichotomous responses from a logic that rejects dichotomies. What Mignolo calls border thinking may be more aware and politically articulate, but I think one will find border thinking in this search.

I think of the starting point as coalitional because the fractured locus at the colonial difference is present in the histories of resistance on which we need to *dwell,* learning each other. The coloniality of gender is sensed as concrete, intricately related exercises of power, some body to body, some legal, some inside a room as indigenous female-beasts-not-civilized-women are forced to weave day and night, others at the confessional. The differences in the concreteness and intricacy of power in circulation are not understood as levels of generality—embodied subjectivity and the institutional are equally concrete.

As the coloniality infiltrates every aspect of living through the circulation of power at the levels of the body, labor, law, demands for tribute, introduction of property, and land dispossession, its logic and efficacy are being met by different concrete people whose bodies, selves in relation, relations to the spirit world are not following the logic of capital. The logic they are following is not countenanced by the logic of power. The movement of these bodies and relations does not repeat itself. It does not become static and ossified. Everything and everyone continues to respond to power and responds much of the time with resistance—which is not to say in open defiance, though some of the time there is open defiance—in ways that may or may not be beneficial to capital, but which are not in its logic. From the fractured locus the movement succeeds creatively in retaining ways of thinking, behaving, and relating that are antithetical to the logic of capital. Intersubjective relations, their ground, and possibilities are continually transformed, incarnating a weave from the fractured locus that constitutes a creative, peopled re-creation. Adaptation, rejection, adoption, ignoring, and integrating are never just modes of resistance in isolation, since they are always performed by an active subject thickly constructed by inhabiting the colonial difference with a fractured locus. I am attempting to see the constantly re-created multiplicity in the fracture of the locus: both the enactment of the coloniality of gender and the resistant response from a subaltern sense of self, of the social, of the self-in-relation, of the cosmos, all grounded in a peopled memory, orality, ingrained gestures and activities. Without the tense multiplicity we only see either the coloniality of gender as accomplishment, or a freezing of memory, an ossified understanding of self in relation from a precolonial sense of the social. Part of what I see is tense movement, people moving: the tension between the dehumanization and paralysis of the coloniality of being, and the creative activity of being.

Finally, I mark here the interest in an ethics of coalition in the making in terms of Audre Lorde's sense of be-ing, and be-ing in relation that extends and interweaves its peopled ground.[39] I can think of the self in relation as responding to the coloniality of gender at the colonial difference from a fractured locus, backed by an alternative communal source of sense that makes possible elaborate responses. The direction of the possibility of strengthening the affirmation and possibility of self in relation lies not through a rethinking from the point of the oppressed of the relation with the oppressor, but through a furthering of the logic of difference and multiplicity and of coalition at the point of difference, as I think Lorde understood it. The emphasis is on maintaining multiplicity at the point of reduction, not in maintaining a hybrid (as a product, which hides the colonial difference), but in the tense workings of more than one logic, not to be synthesized but gone beyond. Among the logics at work are the many logics meeting the logic of oppression: many colonial differences, but one logic of colonial oppression. *The responses from the fragmented loci at the colonial difference can become creatively aware of interdependence, transforming the resistance into coalition.* I propose a way of thinking of the possibility of coalition that takes up the logic of decoloniality, and the logic of coalition of feminists of color: the oppositional consciousness of a social erotics[40] that makes be-ing creative,[41] that permits enactments that are thoroughly defiant of the logic of dichotomies.[42] The defiant inhabitation of the colonial difference cannot be done in dichotomous terms precisely because the logic of dichotomies places us at the fracture, but the logic of coalition at the colonial difference is constituted by a rejection of dichotomous construction of realities. The multiplicity is never reduced.

I have revisited Women of Color from the coloniality of gender proposing a decolonial feminism. I have explored the ties between them by moving back and forth between Women of Color feminisms[43] and the coloniality of gender. I was inspired methodologically and substantively by the work that Women of Color theorists have done on race/gender/coloniality. I have considered intersectionality and strengthened its application to the liberatory possibilities of the inseparability of race/gender/coloniality. I have explored the resistant and liberatory possibilities that are at the heart of Women of Color feminists. I have done so exploring

the inseparability of race/gender in both the coloniality and in the decoloniality of gender.

It is well outside the scope of this text, but certainly well within the
project to which I am committed, to argue that the coloniality of gender
is constituted by and constitutive of the coloniality of power, of knowledge, of being, of nature, and of language. They are inseparable. One
way of expressing that is that the coloniality of knowledge, for example,
is gendered and that one has not understood the coloniality of knowledge
without understanding its being gendered. But here I want to get ahead
of myself in claiming that there is no decoloniality without decoloniality
of gender. Thus, the modern colonial imposition of an oppressive, racially differentiated, hierarchical gender system permeated through and
through by the modern logic of dichotomizing, cannot be characterized
as a circulation of power that organizes the domestic sphere as opposed
to the public domain of authority and the sphere of waged labor, the
access and control of sex and reproduction, biology as contrasted to cog-
nitive/epistemic intersubjectivity, knowledge, and nature as opposed to
culture.

❧ An(other) Invitation to Epistemological Humility: Notes toward a Self-Critical Approach to Counter-Knowledges

OTTO MADURO

It is only when the dominated have the material and symbolic means of rejecting the definition of the real that is imposed on them . . . that the arbitrary principles of the prevailing classification can appear as such.
—PIERRE BOURDIEU, *Outline of a Theory of Practice*

In this essay, written as a series of short (hypo)theses, I try to construct an invitation to rethink our understandings of knowledge and truth in a perspective that I would call "epistemological humility" (as opposed to the "epistemological arrogance" of thinking that *we*—whoever *we* are—already have the definitive true knowledge of anything). This effort is explicitly and constantly inspired by the works of Pierre Bourdieu.[1] It is an effort animated by the idea that oppression, exclusion, domination, and exploitation often bring forth and stimulate, among many other consequences (most of these destructive), the production of "counter-knowledges" (knowledges and ways of knowing opposed to the dominant ones), while paradoxically often contributing to, and (only partially) benefiting from, certain new forms of "epistemological arrogance," which, somewhat as a result of producing knowledge from within a subaltern position, might often turn out to function as a "self-defeating epistemology" rather than the opposite. Connections with ethics and politics, and particularly with democracy, justice, and peace, are at the heart of this effort.

The predicament of Latinas/os in the United States—as agents of knowledge while objects of oppression, exclusion, domination, and exploitation—is what underlies and prompts this invitation. Placed, on the one hand, under the power of imperial policies toward Latin America, the greed of U.S. national elites, the racism of its "white" (dwindling) majority, and, on the other, the often contradictory urgencies of survival, solidarity, adjustment, and/or success, Latinas/os in the United States are often urged (by past experience, personal qualms, traditional wisdom, nontraditional approaches, etc.) to question, doubt, and challenge what they are concurrently pressured, expected, and/or taught by the dominant culture to accept as true. Such a predicament can at times result in the production of "counter-knowledges": alternative ideas, subversive discourses, dissident voices. However, one of the tragedies and tendencies of all knowledge produced within and under relations of oppression, exclusion, domination, and exploitation is that inadvertently, surreptitiously, at least part of the ruling patterns, relations, conceptions, and/or values permeating the larger society might be reintroduced. Thus, there is no guarantee that any counter-knowledge will forever and/or wholly avoid ending up reinforcing (rather than weakening) the prevailing ways of knowing against which it emerged (viz., hierarchical, binary, authoritarian, patriarchal, racist, elitist ways of knowing). There is, however, always chance, hope, and room for a constant self-critique—individual and collective—of our counter-knowledges, alongside the possibility that such collective self-critique helps weaken, rather than buttress, the unavoidable tendency of subaltern counter-knowledges to wind up co-opted by and/or confirming the leading ways of knowing.

It is mainly to such constant self-critique of our counter-knowledges that I want to contribute the hypotheses below, especially as they might be useful for some Latina/o activists, leaders, and thinkers within the geographic, bodily, relational, institutional, mental, and spiritual territories currently occupied by the patriarchal, "white," neoliberal, capitalist, imperial global expansion headed by the United States.

(HYPO)THESES

I

Whatever we understand by knowledge, we always and only know in community, in a culture and a language shared by a community; a shared culture and language allow us to communicate what is understood, challenged, or probed as being—or not being—knowledge. In another culture or language we could easily be at a total loss, at least at first, to claim having, achieving, or conveying anything as knowledge.

This is markedly important for Latin American immigrants, their U.S. Hispanic/Latin@ descendants, and their relatives gradually turned into *aliens*—by either xenophobia, racism, and/or the ever-moving western and southern frontiers ("we didn't cross the broder, the broder crossed us" is a piece of grassroots counter-knowledge shared by many Puerto Ricans and Mexican Americans, among others).

Part of the social paradox of knowing is that knowledge is not yet quite knowledge unless and until it is recognized as such by a group of people—both in the sense of being "understood" by them and in the sense of being "accepted" by the group. If nobody understands or (what is almost the same, but not quite) if nobody accepts what somebody "knows," for all intents and purposes that knower knows nothing (for the time being), that is, her/his/their knowledge is at least provisionally incapable of making a difference in the community where the knower/s is/are located.

"Individual" knowledge is never merely individual: It is always a knowledge claimed by an individual within a community, but not quite yet knowledge until it is understood and validated by a community (or another). Or, otherwise stated, knowledge is always in process, in an unpredictable process for that matter, and knowledge is always in struggle: the process and the struggle of trying to (re)formulate (received or "new") knowledge in such a way as to gain understanding and acceptance (recognition), indeed, but also the process and the struggle of reacting and responding to the obstacles to such knowledge's being received and acknowledged as knowledge.

Even in the extreme, hypothetical case of a hermit separated from any human contact for decades, and suffering from what could be deemed (from the outside) as dementia, whatever s/he knows, cannot be so but in response to, and with the elements of, what s/he acquired in the community of her/his years before being estranged from human contact—and it is on such a basis that her/his creativity might build. Whatever s/he knows, it will not be understood and recognized as knowledge, again, unless and until a group of people concurs with it.

Changes, conflicts, and power dynamics in any community—
unavoidable traits of any group of people, especially when time, size,
innovations, and social differentiation intervene—have consequences in
the ways in which knowledge is (differentially) understood and "used"
within human interaction. For starters, those alterations, struggles, and
forces at work tend to induce analogous changes, conflicts, and power
struggles around what people want (or desperately need) to make sense
of, to know, what we recognize (or overlook, or disqualify) as knowledge, and those whom we recognize (or dismiss) as producers or carriers
of legitimate knowledge, as authorities.

II

Whatever we understand by knowing or knowledge (or, by extension,
by true or truth), we almost invariably know amid unstable, asymmetric
power relations, interests, and dynamics. The old dictum that knowledge
is power probably contains more (and more problematic) wisdom than
what we usually would want to grant it. To know is always, at least
implicitly, a claim to know, thus an attempt to either reaffirm "what
everybody knows" (and thus gain recognition as a normal, acceptable
member of the community), or to sway others toward a more or less
novel way of understanding (and thus gain recognition as a legitimate
challenger of accepted verities). Claiming to know something, to have
knowledge, is thus always a kind of claim to power, a political move.

Knowledge might simply be, to begin with, a claim to share and accept
what all or most (or those with the weightiest say) in a community
accept and share as "true," "obvious," "mandatory," "expected," or the
like (as in "we all know that undocumented, illegal, and criminal go
together"). That is, it might be a way of claiming that the present, prevailing state of affairs is OK, is as it should be, and needs not be challenged. (Claiming) knowledge, therefore, might entail a surreptitious
threat to whoever dares to even think of challenging the prevailing
power arrangements in the community (be such community a family, a
network of specialized scientific experts, a nation, a political constituency,
a hospital, a religious congregation, etc.): a subtle summons to acquiesce
to the establishment.

Knowing, however, may involve a claim to know something that others do not know: a claim to a "new" or "hidden" knowledge, one that

does not fully mesh either with the prevailing power arrangements in the community or with the established epistemological order therein (i.e., the limits of what is socially accepted to be known and knowable). Think of the claim that "first generation immigrants have a significantly lower rate of involvement in criminal activities than U.S.-born, third generation or higher, 'white' citizens."

An utterance is then, more often than not (and regardless of the awareness of the "speaker"), simultaneously an epistemological and a political act(ion): awakening, activating, mobilizing not only knowledge/s (within a wide range of possibilities going from confirmation of the prevailing state of affairs to its questioning, interruption, and/or subversion), including in the "speaker" herself/himself as well as in her/his web of relations—but also awakening, activating, mobilizing power claims, relations, struggles, conflicts, fears, and other types of conflictual dynamics.

In fact, most utterances could be seen as being in themselves, at least to a certain degree, claims to power, to authority: appeals to assent, respect, and recognition—i.e., political moves. This is particularly the case when/if such an utterance commands (or tries to bring forth) attention—an attempt that is more likely to succeed if/when the person uttering something is capable of mobilizing significant forces (social, economic, military, political, legal, emotional, etc.) behind her/his utterances, or at least of giving the appearance and stirring the fear of having such capability.

Conversely, the "same" utterance (as seen abstractly by an "outsider"), even in the "same" community, but uttered by a different or differently located "speaker" (or by the "same" one but in a different juncture in the dynamics of the "same" community) might be entirely "inaudible," overlooked, meaningless—or worse: It might elicit rejoinders, attacks, violent silencing, or even physical suppression.

Or, to put it in yet other terms: No utterance (written, sung, spoken, iconic, gestured, or otherwise) can have only one meaning in or of itself, because meaning is not something residing in the utterance, or even in the utterer, but, rather, it is produced and can be "present" only in the relation (itself unstable and perishable) between utterance (and, if somehow present, its utterer, too) and a community of interpretation—the latter equally unstable, mobile, perishable.

Meaning is located always in an unstable relation—a relation, among others, of course, of knowledge, inexorably located amid a dynamic, larger constellation of relations, which indeed complicate the production, circulation, perception, and transformation of meaning (i.e., of knowledge): relations of identity, competition, exchange, power, domination, resistance, alliance, and so on, which include (but are by no means limited to) gender, sexual, economic, political, cultural, linguistic, military, and other types of relations, many of which (but not necessarily all, nor all necessarily reinforcing each other) involve lopsided, asymmetric, conflictual power dynamics.

Thus, the meaning of an utterance, if any, is (re)produced in relation (both specific and variable) to the history, culture, and dynamics (including power dynamics) of a specific community—be these personified in one single individual member of a community having access to that utterance, or embodied in a group.

This suggests that, in all probability, any utterance can mean anything—including what would seem from certain perspectives as absolute opposite meanings—depending on the interest/knack of the "hearer(s)" (reader/s, dancer/s, singer/s, preacher/s, professor/s, etc.) to (re)produce a particular meaning, as well as on her/his/their ability to mobilize certain forces (social, political, legal, emotional, etc.) both in favor of such meaning, and over against those different or opposite understandings of the "same" utterance (and against the bearers of those other differing senses).

What is needed to transform a certain, accepted meaning, of a "stable" discourse (text, icon, song, etc.) in a particular community into what would have been typically grasped in that same community as its exact opposite meaning is at least, probably, time (which helps forget and transform meanings), people (i.e., increased numbers of individuals and groups invested in the "new" meaning), and power (of any and/or all sorts) to both boost the "new" meaning and counter the lingering or reemerging remembrance, allegiances, and diffusion of former meanings of the "same" discourse or utterance. Is not this what happens in many of our churches with the ancient Hebrew injunction regarding hospitality to the stranger?

III

Whatever we understand by knowing or knowledge, we could submit that it is less so (held less and by fewer people as knowledge, as "real," as "true"), the less the attention, importance, and consequences (as well as its denials, refutations, rejections, and dismissals) it is capable of bringing forth—and it is more of a knowledge (held more and by more people in a community as knowledge, as "real," as "true"), the more interest, significance, and effects (no less than its denials, refutations, rejections, and dismissals) it is able to elicit. In other words, knowledge is something that (like love?) has a thinner, weaker "reality," the weaker, thinner, and more fragile the bonds among those "sharing" it are—basically dissolving if/as the interest in it (and/or the community sharing such interest) fades away, disintegrates, or dies out.

Knowledge and the interest that constitutes it as such, the importance giving it weight in a community, the recognition it awakens, and the authority it carries (or not)—all require previous and concomitant labor, an "intellectual" labor of thinking, rethinking, presenting, arguing, refuting, persuading, and so on. In addition, emotional, physical, erotic, political, economic, linguistic, esthetic, legal, cultural, police, military, and other types of labor might be necessary and/or helpful to generate, sustain, disseminate, defend, enforce, and reinforce what appears to the community as the most "important" knowledge/s, chiefly if/when other competing interests (and related knowledge/s and groups) threaten the consensus supporting the prevailing knowledge/s—and therefore the power of the groups and relations linked to it.

Whatever is shared, recognized, and accepted in a certain community as knowledge (i.e., not merely as perception or opinion, but as an important, authoritative, "true" knowledge) is such as a result of the investment of time and energy in constructing and safeguarding such knowledge as valid, legitimate, true, and important. In this sense, knowledge is accumulated labor.

Diplomas, awards, publications, reviews, interviews, citations, invitations, appointments, salaries, promotions, and so on—as Pierre Bourdieu, among others, has tirelessly endeavored to understand, analyze, and demonstrate—are often distinctions recognizing such accumulated, embodied labor (i.e., the number of hours, dollars, and connections collectively invested in being admitted, trained, promoted, and recognized as a holder of and an authority in a certain type of knowledge).

In this sense, knowledge is capital—one peculiar form of capital, which, as all forms of capital, might be used to acquire other forms of capital and might serve to enhance, reinforce, and protect different forms of capital "owned" by the "knower," those associated with her/him, as well as the institutions of which s/he is part.

In order to acquire the only form of knowledge that is worth anything in a particular community, that is, recognized knowledge or knowledge acknowledged and respected as such (as distinction, as capital, as worth, as value), a certain type of labor is required that calls for a certain degree or amount of time, energy, self-esteem, acknowledgment, training, and so on. Most people in most modern societies have not enough of these resources readily available to them so as to acquire/produce enough recognized knowledge to elicit the attention, respect, and recognition beyond, at the very best, a certain modicum of deference among a reduced group of acquaintances.

As with other forms of capital (in modern societies at least), the more widely known something is, and by a larger diversity of people, the less important it is. Otherwise stated, the more common, easily attainable, and widespread a certain type of knowledge becomes, the less valued, appreciated, esteemed, distinctive, and respected it becomes. The less often it is recognized as important, interesting knowledge, the less will it command attention, prestige, action, or obedience.

No wonder, first, that so many people, doubting their own capacity to know, for having been subject to decades of humiliation, invisibility, neglect, marginalization, abuse, and/or exploitation—without ever enjoying the respect and attention (i.e., the love) that could have awakened and nurtured in them at least the energy, self-esteem, and recognition necessary to produce recognized knowledge—end up seeking knowledge, meaning, and truth outside of themselves and their kin, among those already esteemed and recognized by most as authorities, experts, people who really know and who know what is really important. Think of a Hispanic child uttering (or not quite yet: deciding whether to utter) her dissenting knowledge of the pronunciation/use/meaning of a Spanish word in a classroom where s/he frequently finds herself/himself bullied by her/his classmates and/or scorned by the teacher, when not simply invisible, unheard, nonexistent.

No wonder, symmetrically, that, for their part, those already esteemed and recognized by most as intellectual authorities, as experts, as the people who really know, and who know what is really important, try (without knowing that they are trying) to keep their knowledge rare, either by "giving" of it only that modicum that they deem accessible to the populace (somehow letting the recipients know that this is the case and earning recognition for their charitable donations) or by denying that knowledge to the common folk, clothing their wisdom in esoteric, obscure, "specialized" jargon, thus redoubling their distinctive preeminence as experts with an impossibility of being understood save by their peers.

Unless acutely aware of such complementary epistemological tendencies between elites and the subaltern, the very groups and individuals engaged in an intellectual struggle (supposedly) in solidarity with the oppressed and against the dominant elites, might easily end up swallowed by those same dynamics of intellectual distinction, carving secondary niches of expertise (in churches, unions, NGOs, opposition parties, etc.), where authority, recognition, connections, self-esteem, and other forms of capital can be accumulated and later exchanged for yet further types of capital—probably contributing, in the end, not to dismantle, but to reinforce and further veil the role of (recognized) knowledge (theirs included) in the reproduction and cover-up of relations of domination. Ironically, this is at times the case with Bourdieu's thought and jargon—originally supposed to have emerged to expose elitist relations and oppressive hierarchies, but every so often used instead to re-create and reinforce dynamics of exclusion and self-aggrandizement.

Nobody is exempt from the temptation and possibility of slowly sliding from (honestly believing that they are) producing and using their knowledge mainly in the service of vulnerable, at-risk populations, to using the privileged position of the "intellectual" among the subaltern (and to increasingly orient their production of knowledge) to secure, enhance, and reinforce their own position of privilege—thus enabling themselves to accumulate enough capital (relations, prestige, self-esteem, etc.) to exchange for positions in other social locations, including in the service of the dominant power structures and elites. I submit that, rather than an anomaly, this is the "normal" (tragic) tendency of intellectuals, especially when we refuse to acknowledge that this is the normal tendency and to take the necessary collective measures to counter it.

IV

The easy opposition between knowledge, on the one hand, and illusion, falsehood, ignorance, and the like, on the other—an opposition that is but the inverse of the almost natural, spontaneous identification of knowledge with "truth," "reality," and "the facts"—deserves to be critically analyzed as both an outcome and an instrument of the long labor of imposition of certain forms of knowledge (certain "knowledges") over against competing claims and interests, this imposition being, more often than not, one more strategy (not necessarily conscious or deliberate, and all the more efficient if it is *not* conscious or deliberate) in the complex struggle of the dominant elites to at least preserve the power (of any and all types) thus far accumulated, to ward off threats to such accumulated power, and, if feasible, to reinforce and broaden that power.

Intellectuals, including composers, poets, theologians, storytellers, teachers, reporters, editors, novelists, philosophers, historians, economists, preachers, ministers, union leaders, and so on (i.e., people who produce and distribute one or another type of "knowledge"), all too often tend to identify my/our knowledge as "the" truth, reality, and the facts—and to cast the differing, competing knowledges as erroneous, false, wrong, or, at worst, as deliberate deceit.

The easy opposition between "truth" (i.e., the knowledge we agree with) and "error" (the knowledge that we disagree with and that therefore we refuse to recognize as knowledge) might be, especially for subaltern, dominated, marginalized groups, both necessary in the short run and self-destructive in the middle and long runs. Or, otherwise stated, the opposition might be in the end exclusively beneficial to those who have already attained enough power in a society so as to monopolize the epistemological power of defining which knowledge is knowledge, true and worthwhile, and which is not, thus doomed to ridicule, oblivion, justifiable suppression, or, at best, as relics of a surmounted past.

This might be particularly the case in junctures of increasing insecurity, fear, conflict, and/or violence—where life hangs by a thread and where the conditions of life of a growing segment of a population (including those accustomed to the highest positions of power and authority) are perceived as being on the brink of disaster. Dialogue, reflection, conciliation, serene negotiation, and compromise, as well as hopeful delegation and deferment, become for most unthinkable, intolerable—with perceptions of reality (knowledges) being polarized, frozen, oversimplified, and pitted against each other as part and parcel of the general climate of anxiety, when there is a need for a clear, prompt resolution, even at a very high, once inadmissible, cost.

Under such extreme conditions (which the contemporary processes of globalization and the ongoing worldwide economic and political crises make ever more likely and unpredictable), it is common for a tendency to emerge to promptly assemble, adopt, and/or cast a straightforward and hopeful vision of reality as the only true and admissible one (the only real knowledge) and concomitantly to see any and all other visions as both false and irreconcilable with "ours" (as not-knowledge, error, or deceit)—including among intellectuals linked to groups whose existence and/or power are perceived as being under serious threat.

It could be further hypothesized that this is the case not only on larger collective planes (nations, regions, etc.) but also at the microsocial stage (neighborhoods, families, classrooms, churches, etc.), as well as at the individual level.

Individuals experiencing radical insecurity (because of a job loss, the death of a loved one, foreclosure on their home, the onset of a fatal illness, a serious accident, a destructive addiction, a marital breakup, or violence at the hands of a close partner or relative, for instance) might be more open to a radical change of their perception of reality, including embracing forms of knowledge hitherto unacceptable to them—and to taking these up in a much more vigorous, closed, aggressive, and defensive manner than they ever embraced any other vision of reality in their past. By the same token, the way in which this embrace of new knowledge might tend to take place is by redoubling it with attempts to impose it on others, closing off any avenues for dialogue with even (formerly) loved ones, and, in the extreme, by joining in violent actions to destroy symbols or, worse, human lives, linked to those other ("false") knowledges. Think, among others, of the bombings of abortion clinics, the assassination of freedom riders in the sixties, that of Matthew Shepard, the rape and murder of the four religious women in El Salvador on 12/2/1980, and the 9/11 attacks in the United States—but think no less of the discomfort some would feel when seeing all these cases lumped together.

Neighborhoods and small groups and/or families within neighborhoods, whose lives, traditions, expectations and safety are growingly menaced by drug dealers, shootouts, police violence, unemployment, and/or city attempts to renovate their area (with the consequent, usually definitive, relocation of residents and disintegration of the community), might similarly develop or embrace ways of looking at their world that

could at times shift into closed, intolerant, even violent forms of defending and imposing one's own truth. Think of youth gangs, Pentecostal
churches, and petitions for the eviction of undocumented immigrants in
several places in contemporary New Jersey—and, again, of the possible
discomfort of some readers that these things are placed on the same
level.

However, whereas such a tendency to brandish under duress one's
own old or new knowledge as exclusive truth might translate into thriv-
ing strategies of consensus-building and self-preservation among the
elites (who actually do very often have the material and symbolic resources to spread and enforce a certain vision of the world while restraining most, if not all, other competing visions—as shown worldwide in
recent decades with the global embrace, from tabloids to graduate
schools of economics, of the neoliberal fundamentalism of the invisible
hand and free markets), tragically, this is rarely the case among the
subaltern.

What most often takes place among disadvantaged, vulnerable, marginalized groups under duress (precisely because their social location entails, among other things, the scarcity of material and symbolic resources
to spread and enforce a certain vision of the world while restraining most
other competing visions) is the multiplication of competing knowledge
claims and knowledge authorities—many indigenous, many imported,
and most a creative synthesis of both local and extraneous elements—
hardly able to sustain the onslaught from above and from the outside,
the bitter antagonisms generated by the climate and available options,
and/or the hard labor required to maintain and prolong credibility, out-
reach, cohesion, and effective mobilization. Thus, the emergence of new
knowledge under duress among the subaltern is constantly threatened
with disintegration and co-optation, and it is prone more often than not
to bring forth in the long run self-destructive developments—rather than
the purported opposite aim of furthering new knowledge(s).

Paradoxically, the affordable luxuries, in Western democracies at least,
that self-criticism and critical analysis constitute, in general, for middle-
class professionals and intellectuals—luxuries that can actually enhance,
rather than threaten, their recognition and prestige among peers and the
larger public—probably constitute among the subaltern a much more
urgent component, albeit less affordable, for the production, distribution,

exchange, and transformation of new knowledges, precisely in order to offset the (constant, inevitable) tendency to shape new knowledge(s) as closed, absolute, exclusive truths, alongside the building of a "new epistemological order" (e.g., that of Marxism, "national Catholicism," liberation theology, Zionism, Shiite Islam, national socialism, or Pentecostalism), which might easily end up—at a smaller or larger scale—birthing new, destructive dynamics and structures of oppression within, or instead of, the dominant ones.

V

As suggested by the recent tradition of popular education (since Paulo Freire), it is not only (and possibly not mainly, except rarely) through the actual content of a discourse or utterance (written, sung, spoken, iconic, gestured, or otherwise) that its most significant meaning/s are transmitted, disseminated, and/or reinforced. Equally or possibly more important in transmitting knowledge is the form of the transmission, including the actual relations between the "vessels" of knowledge (speaker, book, song, image, sensation, etc.) and the audience experiencing, perceiving the utterances expressed by/through the "vessel." The forms through which we express our knowledge (e.g., linear, "logical," academic prose) can be, in and of themselves, ways of knowing, of normalizing certain ways of knowing, of authorizing certain authorities, and—at least by omission—of delegitimating, obliterating, and/or silencing other ways of knowing, different sources of knowledge, multiple forms of expressing knowledge, and, beyond, entire cultures, regions, and traditions involving far more numerous and diverse populations (and their millennia of histories) than those represented in, privy to, and involved in the dominant ways of knowing our world.

Thus, an authoritarian form of transmission of knowledge—as in scholarly lectures, ceremonial speeches, or religious homilies, where interruptions, challenges, and questions are a priori out of order—might serve to confirm and reinforce a self-perception of oneself and one's peers as incapable of being a speaker. Such effect is frequently redoubled by a confirmation of the superiority of the speakers and their (class, gender, linguistic, ethnic, racial, and/or educational) peers, particularly when the traits of most of those occupying the positions of discursive authority are not just consistently repeated across times and places but are also constantly different from those of the segments of the population finding themselves and their peers almost invariably in the location of passive receptors, followers, believers (students, readers, hearers, audience, etc.) of authoritative discourses.

This effect of the form in which knowledge is presented and transmitted can easily offset or outweigh any and all antiauthoritarian intentions and contents in the spokesperson(s) and/or her/his/their ideas. In other words, "new" knowledges, or supposed "counter-knowledges," depending among other things on the form in which they are expressed and transmitted, could in fact transmit and induce a reinforcement of, rather than a challenge to, dominant ideas, groups, relations, and practices. Think, for instance, of authoritarian, rigid, top-down teachers teaching their students "socialist" ideas, and making clear that whoever responds to exam questions with unacceptable, contrary ideas will indeed flunk their course—or worse.

Conversely, a democratic, dialogical, horizontal, nonthreatening, welcoming, inclusive, egalitarian form of presenting and discussing "conservative" ideas could elicit discussions, reflection, research, and exchanges of opinions among participants, leading at least some of them to generate critiques and alternatives to the ideas originally presented, and/or to bring forth interpretations of such ideas, which, rather than reinforcing domineering and dominant practices and relations, might foster a novel, transformative, "progressive" take. Think, for instance, of the turn that many evangelicals, especially young ones, have recently taken in relation to hunger, poverty, homelessness, immigrants, and the environment.

The printed word as a privileged vehicle of knowledge (including as a surreptitious propaganda device to consecrate certain forms of knowledge, certain knowledges, and certain knowers, while devaluing others) presents its own kind of epistemological problems, not only insofar as it has the capacity to spread certain content widely, but also, even more significantly, as a culturally overdetermined form that, almost in and of itself (again regardless of its actual content or the intentions of its users), evokes and buttresses a certain idea of where/how worthy knowledge is expressed (in printed prose, like this one), where/how authorized knowers present worthy knowledge (in published books and journals—but not in any nor all books or journals), and what true knowledge looks like (in "stable" print form, transmissible, somewhat "always same," with a supposedly fixed meaning and appearance).

All the above are likely to be more probable if and when producers/ transmitters of knowledge and those "receiving" it are not only different but when their relations are unequal, imbalanced, lopsided power relations, or, worse, relations of oppression, exclusion, domination, and exploitation. Thus, the content of a discourse critical of asymmetrical relations (class relations, for instance, between industry shareholders and manual workers in the same industry), where the critic happens to be located in a position closer to the privileged pole of the relations, can be grasped in radically opposite ways by audiences closer to one or the other pole in such relations—for instance, as intolerably subversive by the critic's peers and as one more empty gesture of superficial sympathy by those in the weaker end of the relation.

Knowing as women, African Americans, lesbian/gay people, Hispanics, Native Americans, Asian Americans, or persons with disabilities— even when explicitly and deliberately resisting, denouncing, fighting, and subverting oppression—is knowing not just beyond and against oppression, but it is also, always, knowing under and from within oppression, and thus a knowing immensely more prone to, tempted by, and liable to being co-opted, swallowed, digested, and excreted, as it were, by the very same relations of oppression under, within, and against which such "counter-knowledge from below" emerges. And such an occurrence is all the more possible because it can develop without one's knowledge or will, all the more so if/when such counter-knowledge is produced without a consistent, deliberate, continuous effort to pinpoint and fight the very tendencies and enticements to fall back into the dominant ways of knowing while honestly thinking we are continuing to produce a genuine counter-knowledge.

VI

A claim to know, to have knowledge, to know where knowledge is, how to get it, and who has it is more and other and more perilous than just an intellectual claim. Such epistemological claims mobilize appetites, hopes, and fears. They might reactivate, reanimate, reawaken dormant memories, worries, patterns, and desires, and thus mobilize people toward or away from certain groups, thoughts, courses of action, and reflection—regardless of, and also over against, the best intentions of those (re)introducing certain knowledge claims in a particular juncture of a group's history.

VII

Globalization accelerates, multiplies, and elicits the constant criss-crossing, encounters, conflicts, clashes, and mutual influences and transformations of a multiplicity of knowledges, knowers, and ways of knowing—often unevenly able to deal openly and creatively with each other. Dialogue and syncretisms are only a few of the dynamics emerging from these encounters, sadly often overshadowed (or worse) by destructive dynamics of invisibility, denial, exclusion, persecution, (in)civil wars, and other forms of conflict generated in the encounter among diverse ways of knowing through migrations, seasonal labor, maquilas, electronic communications, and other dimensions of the contemporary processes of globalization.

VIII

The paradox of a way of knowing that aims to undermine an authoritarian, hierarchical, exploitive social system is that, in order not to mimic, legitimate, and serve as an instrument of that very system, it needs to shape itself as an open, humble, dialogical, consistently self-examining way of understanding and producing knowledge—which inevitably turns it into a more fragile, vulnerable way of understanding and producing knowledge, even more liable to be destroyed by the very social system it emerges against.

IX

All epistemological problems are simultaneously political and ethical problems. All political problems are simultaneously ethical and epistemological problems. All ethical problems are simultaneously political and epistemological problems. Actual power dynamics, our efforts toward knowledge, and our accountability toward our planet and all our fellow creatures are intricately intertwined with each other.

X

The dangerous ideal of a universal, eternal, and singular true knowledge—a delusion that is habitually part of imperial designs of forced unification, subjection, and homogenization of a variety of ways of being human—is all too often one of the most intractable hurdles to the peaceful resolution of human conflicts, to the respect and flourishing of human diversity, and to the possibility of learning from such conflicts and diversity a few new and better ways of coexisting with one another. Would it be socially thinkable to humbly and respectfully launch, at a fairly broad and durable scale, an invitation to reach partial, temporary, open agreements as to the variety of (epistemological) knowledges, (ethical) values, and (political) structures within which we can live—and within which we can revise, transform, and disagree, too, on the variety of acceptable ways of living? Would it be feasible to start among some U.S. Latina/o groupings an experiment in epistemological, ethical, and political humility that becomes someday a witness of another way of not just knowing, but of knowing justly: knowing in a way that contributes to enhancing life on earth for all?

❧ Latina/o *locus historicus*

❧ Anti-Latino Racism

LINDA MARTÍN ALCOFF

Immigrants are today the most reviled group in America.[1] While there is wide public support for instituting routine identity checks for persons who "look like" they may be immigrants, day laborers waiting on sidewalks or in parking lots for employment report routine verbal and physical harassment, from having soiled food thrown in their faces to being shot at. The Southern Poverty Law Center has recently reported 144 new groups it defines as "nativist extremists," whose main agenda is the intimidation of immigrants. These groups have been found to be stockpiling semiautomatic weapons, grenades, and ammunition, as well as assorted smaller weapons of harassment such as pepper spray, knives, and Molotov cocktails, for use against their local immigrant communities. Targeted violence against immigrants has become a routine weekly story across the country, whether instigated by high school kids or those more ideologically developed. The level of acceptable vitriol has increased in both mainstream news sources as well as the halls of Congress, such as denouncements of anyone who suggests providing education, worker protections, or health benefits—evenly privately purchased—for the 12 to 20 million undocumented persons estimated to be living in the United States, whose labor everyone of us relies on. It was this issue that elicited the unprecedented "liar" shout at the President's address to the joint meeting of Congress in September 2009. The acceptance of violence and degradations inflicted on this population is perhaps most profoundly symbolized by the popular support for Sheriff Joe Arpaio's Abu Ghraib–style prison practices in Arizona, which include public sexual humiliation.

Meanwhile, the hundreds of nameless bodies and bones uncovered every year on our southern border go unmemorialized, and largely unremarked. They die trying to achieve the chance to work in the United States under conditions in which, according to AP reports, Mexicans are killed in on-the-job accidents at a rate four times higher than U.S.-born workers.[2]

In reality, as we know, the principal target of vitriol here, whether armed or merely discursive, is not an unspecified or generic immigrant population, but Latino immigrants, especially those from Mexico and Central America. Varied nonwhite immigrant groups experience varied forms of vilified treatment, based on their representation as potential terrorists, as threats to national security, or as global intellectual competition, whereas Mexicans, Central Americans, and other Latinos receive abuse mainly as a labor supply of unskilled or semiskilled workers. Their interpellation in the public imaginary is not as generic, undifferentiated workers, but racialized workers mostly from south of the border. It is this group, I argue, that is the group principally identified as "immigrants" in the national discourse, though in some local contexts other groups may be more relevant. The actual effective meaning of the term "illegal immigrant" or "illegal alien," then, is illegal Mexican. And thus the arsenal of attacks on immigrants is largely aimed at Latinos, especially those who look like Mexicans.

Latinos occupy a particular place in the dominant imaginary for good reasons, given the location of the United States in the Americas, where Spanish is dominant throughout the hemisphere, and no border has proven to be impermeable. No other minority can realistically pose the threat of ballooning numbers that we can. Thus, public attitudes toward Latinos cannot be disentangled from the host of attitudes toward immigration.[3] Today's nativist movement, unlike some in the past, is not a paranoid projection but an accurate recognition of the imminent cultural changes soon to be wrought by losing white European American majority status by 2050, and its effects on the future of the imagined community of the U.S. nation.

In this essay I want to argue that we need a specific formulation of anti-Latino racism in order to represent this massive phenomenon, as well as to understand the specific form of white or Anglo reaction that is currently on the rise. The racist imaginary has variegated targets of attack with varied and specific representations of Latinos (and, within this group, of Mexicans and Puerto Ricans), as well as Arabs and Muslims, Asians, Africans, Jews, and others (and each of these groups needs further division and specification). Also relevant are the specific histories of U.S. international relations, and the associated historical memories they invoke. Together these specificities make a difference in the development and formation of reactive policies and informal violence. Although from one perspective all of these nonmajority groups might be thought to share some characteristics that make them subject to racism and ethnic chauvinism, given their non-European status, still, a broad brush concept of racism or xenophobia has led to inadequate analyses as well as ineffective remedial policies.

Philosophers, as we know, aim toward generalities and universals, and their work on racism is no exception. The principal competing accounts in the philosophical literature today about the nature of racism concern whether racism is a cognitive commitment (Piper) or affective disposition (Garcia), whether, in other words, it is a belief or an emotion.[4] This is on the analytic or Anglo-American side of the tradition. On the continental side, among those who work in contemporary European philosophy, racism is generally characterized as a form of negation or abjection of the Other, in which that Other is taken as something of a generic.

There is an undoubted utility in these general approaches that try to characterize the emotional attitudes and cognitive processes that make up racism. Much of this work is motivated by the important debate over how we identify *when* racism has occurred, whether racism is always a consciously held belief or perceptible emotional state, whether someone who sincerely disavows racism might yet be racist, or whether institutions as well as individuals can be racist.

But these general, even generic, accounts are not all that is necessary to understand the phenomenon. And the general accounts can mislead us to think that we can avoid specificity and stay at the level of abstract generalization. This leads some to believe that all forms of racism can be covered under the more general concept of xenophobia, and then in turn that all forms of xenophobia can be covered under the general topic of evolutionary fears of the foreign. Analyses that are this abstract have the danger of collapsing the antipathy of the U.S. public for the "snobbish"

French together with antiblack denigrations together with the love/hate relationship with immigrant populations found throughout U.S. history.

In contrast to this approach, Lewis Gordon helped inaugurate an in-depth analysis of antiblack racism using Sartrian phenomenology. In his first book, *Bad Faith and Antiblack Racism*, Gordon used general existential categories from Sartre's *Being and Nothingness,* such as the concept of the look, the facticity of the body, and the ideas of presence and absence—the very concepts that can be used to obviate distinctions—as a basis for the development of specific descriptions of the ways in which blackness is represented in antiblack cultural contexts. For example, he analyzed the way in which black bodies exist in antiblack cultures as a kind of present absence, "a body without perspective," or a body without subjec-tivity.[5] He further argued that Blackness is a paradigm case of what Sartre called *de trop,* meant to signify the superfluity of existence, but with a specific meaning in this context: The mere presence of a black body in a certain place such as university classrooms is *de trop* in the sense that it requires explanation and justification in a way that the mere presence of a white body does not. Some of the experiential aspects of antiblack racism that Gordon describes might indeed prove applicable to other groups, though others seem more specific to African Americans, such as the attribution of an a priori criminality. As Gordon puts it, criminality is so constitutive of the meaning of blackness in antiblack cultures that a black person is always guilty until proven innocent. In this effort at a thick, contextual description of the specific historical conditions and set of cultural practices and discourses facing African Americans, Gordon brought forward the specific conditions of antiblack racism as a distinct phenomenon.

My aim here is not to replicate Gordon's phenomenological account with the category of *latinidad* or perhaps Mexican identity, but rather to develop the broader contours of the specificity of anti-Latino racism. Especially in the current climate of anti-Latino-immigrant hysteria, vio-lence, and political mobilization, we need the category of "anti-Latino racism"; I'll try to unpack this, in order to name what is happening.

The argument for "anti-Latino racism" is embedded first of all within a larger argument that we need more specificity in the analyses of the ways in which groups become misrepresented as posing threats of spe-cific sorts and elicit specific and varied hostile and hysterical reactions. The variety of racist attributions cannot be boiled down to a single form that differs only in degree. Nor is there a single emotion that might serve to unify the field of reactions between disdain, fear, distrust, indifference, and disregard. Pointing out that all of these are negative is no help—consider the difference between fear and indifference, or disdain and distrust, and the different reactive behaviors these emotions might elicit. Indifference, for example, leads to neglect and *invisibilization*, while fear can lead to hypersurveillance.

What is at stake in this analysis is not only a more adequate understanding of racism but also a recognition that if racism is not a one-size-fits-all category, then antiracist policy cannot be either. We cannot address the problem of *invisibilization* by a postracial erasure, nor can we address language prejudice by traditional forms of affirmative action. As Dana Takagi explains in her analysis in *The Retreat from Race*, Asian American activists at one point argued for a greater use of standardized test scores to determine college admission as a means to thwart the influence of anti-Asian prejudice in judging extracurricular activities and self-narratives, but this form of redress proved disastrous for African Americans and Latinos, who continue to test below average even across class. The forms of racism at work here are not only different in degree but different in kind. Some groups are thought to be "too smart," others "too dumb," and these prejudgments need different kinds of redress.

Beyond a discourse of generic racism (among philosophers as well as the general public, I'd argue), there is also sometimes a generic discourse that targets immigrants, usually referred to as nativism. This is an alarming phenomenon, without a doubt. Since 2008 (the year a nonwhite was elected President, by no coincidence), the number of hate groups nationwide has increased to more than nine hundred. Antigovernment, or so-called patriot, groups have tripled in the same period so that there are now twelve hundred. The "nativist extremist" groups that harass randomly targeted immigrants in what some like to call "beaner hunting" have seen the largest change, with an 80 percent increase to a total of sixteen hundred. These groups are not all in the south or southwest: There are thirty-two hate groups in Alabama, but there are thirty-one in New York state, forty-four in New Jersey, and sixty in California. And these groups are far from harmless. The month that Obama was elected, in November 2008, gun sales reached a record high of 1.5 million.

I hope the discussion thus far has convinced readers of the need for developing a cogent and specific concept of anti-Latino racism. Yet developing this faces more than the obstacle of a preference for overly generalized accounts. In fact, there are three formidable obstacles to articulating a concept of anti-Latino racism: (1) the hegemony of colorism as the paradigm of racism, (2) the representation of Latino identity as ethnic and national rather than racial, and (3) the obvious need for a disaggregation of the category of Latino. I will explain these in turn and respond to them in the following sections.

THE HEGEMONY OF COLORISM

The most general definition of racism—as opposed to a causal account or phenomenological description—is as a negative value or set of values projected as an essential or noncontingent attribute onto a group whose members are defined through genealogical connection—i.e., as sharing some origin—and who are demarcated on the basis of some visible phenotypic features.[6] Antiblack racism is the most virulent and persistent form of current racisms, and it informs and infects other forms without a doubt. Yet we would be mistaken to assume that antiblack racism provides the model for all forms of racism. Racism's persistence, as many have noted, is due to its flexibility and vitality, its ability to change targets and morph into new and less obvious forms, especially into less ostensibly offensive forms.[7] Thus we need a correspondingly flexible analysis of the variety of forms racism can take.

Rather than taking colorism as the paradigm of racism, and then differentiating racisms on the basis of degrees of colorism, we can expand our ability to explain manifestations of racism if we understand it as working through four independent axes: colorism, physical appearance, culture, and nativism. These axes may overlap, combine, or stand alone.

The first axis of racism, color, is the most obvious and most pernicious, and it operates not only between whites and nonwhites but also, and as perniciously, within numerous ethnic and racialized communities of color who differentiate among themselves based on lightness. Yet bodily morphology, eye-shape, hair type, height, and general facial features also figure prominently in racist iconographies, as is evidenced in common racist epithets such as "slant-eyes," "pancake face," "squat-body," or "greasers." This second axis of physical appearance, then, operates more broadly to favor the range of northern European visible, physical features. Nell Painter's recent book, *The History of White People*, makes a convincing case that aesthetic hierarchies of beauty played a central rather than peripheral role in constructing racial ideologies, given the long-held association of physical attributes with moral and intellectual character.[8] Exhaustively detailed typologies of noses, ears, and head shapes, as Stuart and Elizabeth Ewen's book *Typecasting* also documents, were used to explain how one could spot criminal or sexually licentious tendencies.[9] The recent discussion in Arizona of how to tell an undocumented person by sight eerily echoes this antiquated discourse, with government leaders sharing opinions about hair type, shoe choice, and manner of walking.

The third axis of culture produces a variety of forms of cultural racism that target specific non-European cultures as less evolved, less civilized, and as a hindrance to modernity, secularism, capitalism, and rationality. Some theorists have developed the concept of "cultural racism" to note the changing developments of racist discourses after World War II, during which time overt biological claims about racial inferiority lost favor and were replaced by claims that imputed the same characteristics to specific culturally defined groups and cultural practices.[10] So although cultural racism may target visibly demarcated groups, its (purported) concern is with their cultural practices rather than their genetic inheritance. The reason to use the term "cultural racism" rather than other terms such as ethnocentrism or xenophobia is that the culture that is targeted is portrayed in the same static and fixed way that biological races were previously represented—as unsusceptible to change, improvement, or assimilation, and with bounded, impermeable borders. Thus, the presence of inferior cultures in the United States is likened to an infection, rather than a stimulus for new cultural hybridizations. It can only do harm, dragging us down, diluting our core values. To the extent a culture is portrayed as static, it operates to justify exclusionary and supremacist attitudes as securely as biological differences once did.[11]

The most pejorative terms widely used against Latinos in this country have been the terms "spic," "wetback" and "beaner," all of which denigrate cultural identity rather than any physical attribute. There is some controversy over the origin of the term "spic" but most believe it evolved from Anglos who heard people saying "no spic English" and thus is a term that denigrates a people's language. The term "wetback" denigrates how people arrived here by swimming from Mexico across the Rio Grande, and the term "beaner" denigrates a typical food group. The general racist portrayal of Latinos targets cultural identity, presenting us as premodern, primitive, less civilized or restrained, less individualistic, less reflexively rational, more dominated by our cultural traditions, including premodern religions and sexist gender practices, and more violent.

The discrimination against Latinos (among others, especially Asian Americans and now Arab and Muslim Americans) has also operated very strongly on the basis of nativism, in which the nonnative other is viewed as posing a subversive threat to the cohesion and tradition of American identity, a rupture in the body politic. European immigrants, by contrast, are no longer viewed as inassimilable cultural inferiors, nor is their difference racialized. In the past nativism was not necessarily racialized, when, for example, during World War I German immigrants were shunned, German street names were changed, and frankfurters were renamed hot dogs. But nativism today takes a racialized form, targeting groups whose racialized cultural differences are said to justify the view that they will never be assimilated and will in fact drag down the country into fractious violence. The 144 extremist militia groups are not focused on Eastern Europeans (who often occupy similar places in the labor market as semi-skilled or unskilled workers). Rather, the racialized non-European others are the ones who threaten the imaginary identity of the U.S. nation as essentially derived, or evolved, from Europe.[12]

The idea that the United States might naturally evolve into a cultural amalgamation of European and Latino elements strikes many people with horror.[13] Samuel Huntington's work usefully clarifies this response. "American values," which he defines as support for democracy and the rule of law, and having a strong work ethic, are ethnically marked, in his account, by their purported Anglo-Saxon lineage, and thus Mexicans must lose their cultural identity and language in order to adopt these values. Although Huntington was vilified by many critics for these claims, he was simply elaborating on similar arguments made by influential liberals such as Arthur Schlesinger and others.

Nativism operates to make racial discrimination appear much less offensive than colorism. Attributing problems to one's cultural identity and practices rather than physical attributes looks more rational. Yet nativism produces alarmingly similar patterns of emotional disaffection as colorism once did, so that people can turn a blind eye to what happens to the undocumented, "nonnative" peoples, such as those profiled as terrorists or those standing on the corner day-labor meat markets or those trying to cross borders. Nativism puts nonnative groups outside the pale of peer group conventions of tolerance, respect, and civil rights. It legitimates the idea that the application of human rights and humane treatment is conditioned on one's legal status and cultural identity.

Perhaps all racialized groups have experienced more than one of these axes of racism, but my argument is that we need to unpack these multiple axes and name them as forms of racism. This provides us with an expanded analysis of the varied repertoire racisms can take. Oversimplifications of racism can eclipse both the severity and the complexity of the problem, reducing the possibility of effective solutions as well as the possibility of making common cause across diverse communities.

Racism's persistence into the twenty-first century bespeaks its resilience, its flexibility of targets, and its capacity to shift from biological to cultural justifications. In this, racism is like any other language game whose practices and modes of intelligibility are grounded only in a shifting historical and cultural terrain. The very fact that racism is grounded not in natural facts but in social constructions means that it is an ever-present threat, capable of new metamorphoses and mobilizations, and resistant to a final cure.

"LATINOS ARE NOT A RACE"

The concept of anti-Latino racism may elicit confusion, given that, according to the latest U.S. census, Latinos constitute an ethnicity rather than a race. Yet the relationship we draw between ethnicity and race when such contrasts are made needs further thinking. Given that the representation of most Latinos includes both racial and ethnic elements, and given that the ethnic characteristic of Latino identity is often racialized as the purported effect of innate tendencies, this group is an obvious candidate for the term "ethnorace."[14]

The term "ethnorace" is used in David Theo Goldberg's book, *Racist Culture*, to refer to group identity categories that are viewed as interchangeably racial or ethnic, or that have moved historically from one designation to another, and then sometimes back again, or that conflate meanings that invoke both natural and social kinds.[15] Beyond this Goldberg does not develop the concept. I have found that when I used Goldberg's term in various presentations, members of the audience are often intrigued and want more elaboration, indicating that it resonates with their experience and the complexities of contemporary classification. So here I will offer a further elaboration, building from Goldberg's initial characterization.

In classic formulations of these terms in the Western literature of sociology and social theory, race and ethnicity are differentiated by their basis in genealogical and phenotypical criteria (for race) or in cultural and social criteria (for ethnicity). Thus, ethnicity and race map onto the natural and social distinction Goldberg mentions, with race viewed as natural and ethnicity viewed as social or a social product. Race connotes an unchosen, arbitrary designation of identity based or heritable physical and visible characteristics. One does not choose one's race, nor can one change it, according to this view. Ethnicity, in contrast, connotes culture, ways of being in the world, manners of dress, bodily comportment, and history. It is true that one is born into an ethnic group, and to this extent it is as arbitrary and unchosen as one's racial membership, but the ethnic group itself is defined by a set of practices or customs developed in response to historical events and geographical location that are chosen, invented, and in a process of ongoing development. Ethnicity, then, connotes subjecthood, not mere objectlike physical descriptions, and thus is potentially more consonant with notions of human dignity.

This is the way Werner Sollors, Max Weber, and other twentieth-century theorists spliced the distinction, but it is interesting to note that they too blur the boundaries. Weber notes that the *belief* in group commonalities "often delimits social circles" to create practices tending toward "monopolistic closure."[16] He then says, "We shall call 'ethnic groups' those human groups that entertain a subjective belief in their common descent because of similarities of physical type or of customs or both, or because of memories of colonization or migration."[17] Although he goes on to say that "it does not matter whether or not an objective blood relationship exists," the point is that the social closure that produces group formation, motivated by history and social conditions, then creates a reproductive community with delimited boundaries and shared physical features.

We can note three distinct commonalities between such understandings of ethnicity and today's common characterization of the socially constructed categories of race: (1) Exclusionary reproductive practices start from social and historical formations to create identity categories that are, or might be seen as, natural. In other words, a social group identified as an ethnic group will reproduce internally to create a genealogically related biological unit, or a race.[18] (2) Both ethnicities and races can be similarly characterized as having essential and stable common identities, with noncontingent features. And (3) both races and ethnic groups are treated as a political threat to democracy to the extent that they manifest in-group loyalty or deference that results in "special interest group" approaches to politics that disengage from considerations of the common good (the controversy over Sonia Sotomayor's nomination to the U.S. Supreme Court serves as a good example here).[19] These important commonalities indicate that there is not as much of either a semantic difference or a political difference between the concepts as one might initially suppose.

Weber's analysis interestingly prefigures more contemporary anti-identity accounts (e.g., those of Appiah, Gilroy, and Fraser),[20] where, for example, both ethnicity and race are often seen as founded in wrong beliefs (what Weber calls an "artificial origin"). With the belief in ethnicity, Weber claims, "the original motives or reasons for the inception of different habits of life are forgotten."[21] The purpose of this forgetting is to naturalize and perpetuate differences, according to Weber, thus circumventing possibilities of critique and change, but by producing boundaries around reproductive communities, it also creates the conditions for the actual heritability of "qualities and traits." What I find interesting is that most classical ethnicity theorists see primarily negative effects arising from the artificiality of ethnic genealogy stories, as well as from the trends toward what Weber calls "monopolistic closure," even though we might also argue that such processes of group formation in some cases enhanced survival and the ability of individuals to flourish in hostile cultural climates by creating networks of solidarity and material support. But for Weber as well as for the critics of ethnicity today, the results are by far more negative than not: because they promote in-group interaction over a wider social intercourse, because they generate "special interest" approaches to political participation, and because they prioritize identity considerations over the content of proposals (what Cornel West calls "racial reasoning"). Nathan Glazer and Daniel Patrick Moynihan's influential characterization of ethnicity in the 1960s expresses this most forthrightly: In their view, strongly felt ethnic identities are an a priori problem requiring political policies that would enhance their dissolution and irrelevance.[22]

The point that is relevant here is that, as it turns out, ethnicity no less than race is generally viewed as based in artificial origin stories and strategic forgetting with negative political effects, and thus the distinction between race and ethnicity is shallow at best. The natural/social distinction is not merely conflated by mistake by theorists such as Weber but argued to dissolve in the practice of ethnic group reproductive isolation, so that an ethnic group can turn into something like a race. And the political distinction—in which race is seen as arbitrary, without subjective control, and without dignity, whereas ethnicity is seen as the product of collective agency and praxis—is dissolved once ethnicity is viewed as formed on the basis of artificial origin stories whose motivations are consciously forgotten and thus naturalized, and whose political payoff is a decreased rationality in the public sphere. Today, given the widespread belief that the true genealogy of racial classification is social process rather than natural differentiations, these commonalities between race and ethnicity are all the more striking.

Some philosophers will view such confusions in the public domain over the distinction between ethnicity and race as just the sort of problem that philosophers can fix, by clarifying meanings and stipulating more precise usage.[23] But I argue that in regard to race and ethnicity, at least, the problem is not simply in the imprecision of ordinary speech. In fact, the slippage between race and ethnicity makes sense given a longer view of how such group category words have been used. In Greek antiquity, the word ethnic was an epithet corresponding to the origin of a group. So it began, interestingly, as a pejorative rather than a neutral description. In line with this, the first definition of "ethnic" given in the modern period was generally "heathen." Sixteenth-century definitions of the word "ethnic" in English define the term as "pertaining to nations not Christian or Jewish," thus foregrounding religious identity.[24] Also in the modern period and before, what we today call ethnic groups and races were loose terms used to refer interchangeably to "peoples" and "cultures" and "nations." In the nineteenth century, the definition of "ethnic" was given in the *Oxford English Dictionary* as "pertaining to race" and as "having common racial, cultural, religious or linguistic characteristics, esp. designating a racial or other group within a larger system."[25] This indicates that ethnicity was associated always with a minority group, never a majority. In the twentieth century, when dictionaries tried to capture common usage, the term "ethnic" was explained as connoting "foreign," "exotic," and "un-American." Today, *Webster's Unabridged* gives as its first definition of race "any of the major biological divisions of mankind, distinguished by color and texture of hair, color of skin and eyes, stature, bodily proportions, etc." thus conforming to the standard phenotypical characterization of race. But *Webster's* also gives the third definition of race as "any geographical, national, or tribal ethnic grouping," and the fourth definition as "the state of belonging to a certain ethnic stock."

Thus confusion and conflation abound. The strict differentiation of race as physical or natural and ethnicity as cultural or social does not accord with either historical etymology or common current usage, and even if we try to maintain the distinction for analytical purposes we find a slippage caused by reproductive practices of ethnic groups and a shared political analysis and critique. And given the current deconstruction of the naturalist pretensions of the concept of race, both ethnicity and race are increasingly used as social categories of identity referring to a historically created, or socially constructed, group of people.

One important conclusion we can draw from this synopsis is that it is a mistake to believe that only the concept of race can be subject to pejorative essentialism. But more than this, what I find missing from both the current dictionary definitions and the political critiques is any sense that these terms might have more than merely negative connotations or uses. In contrast, Michael Omi and Howard Winant's Foucauldian account of racial formations argues that the meaning of even the more loaded term "race" is not reducible to elite projections but is in fact the product of negotiations in which the oppressed play a role, and thus the form resistance takes has an impact on the social meanings in circulation.[26] After all, there have certainly always been positive in-group meanings divergent from the mainstream. To say that "black" has only negative connotations is to take the white Anglo dominant discourse as effectively hegemonic, a feat it has never achieved and is even less likely to achieve in the future. It is also to ignore the increasing internal diversity of white discourse itself on racial matters.

Let us return to the category of ethnorace. The point of introducing this hybridized term is not to replace the usage of race and ethnicity, since each of the latter terms continue to carry some different possibilities despite the fact that they overlap and are sometimes even equated. We can continue to use race to signify physical visible features deeper than dress and comportment, and ethnicity to signify customs and group practices developed by a people within history. We can continue to refer sometimes to "blackness" as a racial designation across national and ethnic identities, and to refer to "African Americans" as an ethnic group born of the experience of American slavery. The point of introducing the term ethnorace is to provide more linguistic options in order to develop better descriptive tools to characterize and understand current realities.

In particular, the term "ethnorace" provides a solution to the special difficulties of characterizing the ways in which Latinos are currently interpellated in north America. The conceptualization of Latinidad as a form of ethnicity, even a panethnicity, is misleading if one does not acknowledge the racialization of Latino ethnicity itself, in the sense that its purported features—being less assimilable, endemically premodern, and less rational on the whole than Europeans—are not viewed as changeable features, or features that will undergo a natural process of progressive development, which is why the prospect of a hybridization of "American" identity poses such an imagined threat. To characterize Latino identity as merely ethnic is to misunderstand the specific racisms directed at Latinos, the obstacles to acceptance, and the (often) visible nature of the identity. For reasons Weber explains, clear-cut distinctions between race and ethnicity do not always hold. Thus, there is something missing when we say that Latinos experience ethnic discrimination but not racism per se, or that only Afro-Latinos experience racism. Clearly we will often need to disaggregate the overly broad category of Latino before we can make meaningful political and economic analyses, as I argue in the next section. We are not all racialized, or racialized to the same degree or in the same way, and the racisms indigenous peoples face vary from those Afro-Latinos and mestizos face. To address these complexities as well as others, we need more terms, not fewer.

The concept of ethnorace, then, might be defined as pertaining to groups of people who have both ethnic and racialized characteristics, who are a historical people with customs and conventions developed out of collective agency, but who are also identified and identifiable by bodily morphology that allows for both group affinity and group exclusion. An ethnoracial group should not be seen as a biologically based natural kind, but as a form of identity that has evolved over time with elements of both bodily and cultural attributes.

The advantage of such a designation for Latinos is twofold. One advantage is that we can avoid having to choose between race or ethnicity to explain the meaning of Latino identity. Neither is wholly adequate to the large pan-Latino category. "Latino" incorporates too many ethnicities and races within it to operate as an analogous term to the sub-European groupings such as Italians or even Scandinavians that often serve as the paradigm for the concept of ethnicity. A second advantage is that our distinctiveness in the cultural imaginary of the United States can become more perspicuous. When we are called simply an ethnicity, it then can become difficult to explain the reason why Latinos are not viewed as equally assimilable, and why our experiences of assimilation take a different path. We need to understand the racialization of Latinos and anti-Latino racism to understand why most Latinos cannot in fact become white. The term ethnorace, then, allows us to avoid having to choose between binary concepts imagined as independent, such as our racial and our ethnic identities, at the same time that it allows for more fine-tuned analyses of the diverse political effects of increasing Latino visibility.

THE NEED TO DISAGGREGATE

In the face of imprecise, artificial, always inadequate and politically troubling categories and concepts of social identity, not a few theorists argue for retreating to class or to cosmopolitan individualism. But this would disenable an effective political analysis of how people enter the political process and what obstacles they encounter in doing so.[27] It is true that current identity categories all have some limitations, especially when we try to fit them to Latinos. The concept of a pan-Latino identity itself is subject to a vigorous debate concerning whether it is a meaningful marker of lived experience or rather too broad to capture any significant political or socioeconomic realities.[28] In the light of all these concerns, some think it would be better to stem the tide of identity categories (if not immigration) and adopt either a racial eliminativism or some pan-national or otherwise amorphous category such as "brown" under which we can all (white, black, brown, etc.) be subsumed.

The major problem with transcendence proposals and amalgamation models is that they ignore the fact that our labor markets are still strati-fied by race, ethnicity, nationality, documentation status, and gender, and that the global culture wars continue to project conflict based on intractable differences based on identity. Moreover, global capital moves to, and from, its various locations based on identities that correlate to job skills, degrees of vulnerability, levels of unionization, and flexible social practices.[29] The global labor market is tightly organized around identity and complexly differentiated. It is also capable of transition, but its capacity for transition is also correlated to shifts in identity, as light-skinned English-speaking people of color gain managerial acceptance, and as new waves of immigrant populations come to dominate certain labor sectors. Thus, to understand the complexities of global identities and global markets, we need increased specificity rather than only broad-brush categories. This is as true for whites as any group. Amalgamation proposals, along with transcendence models, are often motivated by the understandable desire to enhance the possibility of collaboration and unity. But analyzing and accounting for the specificities of our complex differences do not entail an increase in conflict but should enhance our ability to see more clearly where we need to negotiate and compromise to make more effective coalitions.

In the essay "Comparative Race, Comparative Racisms," I advance an argument for identity proliferation based on a description of real-world organizing in complex work sites where races, ethnicities, linguistic com-munities, nationalities, and ethnoraces crisscross one another in their po-litical allegiances and solidarities.[30] Union organizers and leaders use the phrase "communities of solidarity" to describe the bonds of trust, com-munication, and support they find in work sites. Solidarity is sometimes based on color, sometimes based on language, and sometimes based on nationality. Employers often try to exploit and exacerbate conflicts among workers, such as encouraging African Americans to support En-glish-only policies or drawing on the antiblack racism among Filipinas.

But communities of solidarity in workplaces also emerge organically from real and not only imagined shared experience and shared interests. In this sense, communities of solidarity are not merely based on "artificial origins" stories, or mistaken metaphysical views, but on the shared need to have bilingualism accepted as a right, to have antiblack racism seen and named as such when it affects hiring and promotion, and to have the contract committee take up the priorities immigrant workers need, such as the long vacations needed to return to home countries where their families (even partners and children) live. The task of the union or community organizer is not to convince everyone that neither race nor ethnicity is real, or that language and national differences can be set aside at the bargaining table, but to understand with precision and accuracy the nature and significance of the differences within the bargaining unit so that productive collaborations can be developed and trust across groups slowly cultivated. Only in this way can organizers thwart the exploitation of differences by bosses, identify the common enemies and common problems that can sometimes trump differences, as well as find ways to negotiate across differences for mutual benefit in mutual shows of support. The route to this expanded solidarity is neither transcendence or false commonality but accurate renditions of differences of experience and position within the labor market. In some cases this will require some groups to acknowledge their privileges, for example the fact that their light skin tone can enhance their capacity to be given a promotion. But even privileged workers cannot get their workplace rights secured without the collaborative power of a union.

The need to disaggregate our categories of identity is becoming more and more apparent. Consider, for example, important new research by the economist Sandy Darity and his collaborators that shows surprisingly negligible differences between whites and light-skinned blacks in job success, rates of unemployment, and salary differentials.[31] They found, in other words, that whether one is white or a light-skinned African American makes a statistically negligible difference. But Darity's work also shows that when those light-skinned blacks are disaggregated from the statistics on black unemployment, black poverty, and so on, the gap is even larger than previously thought. I argue that in the white imaginary, light-skinned African Americans still signify differently than whites do, raising fears of retaliation for slavery, for example. Yet the fact remains that patterns of discrimination do not operate with nearly the same intensity across the category of African American identity.

This indicates that what we have long known was true for Asian Americans and Latinos is also true for African Americans: We must disaggregate the categories to make meaningful analyses of the scope and intensity of the problems. For Latinos, skin color is relevant as well as other physical characteristics, accent, language, dress, and documentation status.[32] Tensions and political differences among Latinos spring from different opportunities for class mobility, which may solidify distinctions for the next generation. But skin color will be an inadequate predictor. For example, unlike for some Latinos, no Asian Americans can truly pass as white, and yet we need to take account of a similar collection of attributes to make useful predictions. In particular, racialized features intersect with national origin to make economic analyses that take the midpoint or mean between Laotian and Japanese wages to be completely meaningless.

An argument for identity proliferation is also at odds in some respects with the influential account of Eduardo Bonilla-Silva that racial formations in the United States are moving toward what he calls a Latin Americanization.[33] In this schema there are only three categories: white, honorary white, and collective black, into which all the various ethnoracial nationalities will be grouped. For some purposes, Bonilla-Silva's triracial map is a useful explanatory device to account for the kinds of economic data that Darity and others provide. But I argue it could be misleading if we take it as the principal way to understand racialization developments in the years to come. For example, Bonilla-Silva's account places "Middle Eastern Americans" in the honorary white category, a claim that has obvious explanatory limitations given the hysteria over Obama's innocuous middle name. And Bonilla-Silva's account is ultimately insufficient for classifying Latinos as divided into only two categories: light-skinned, which he categorizes as honorary whites, and dark-skinned, which he categorizes as collective black. This is not much of an improvement over the black-white binary. Where do mestizo-looking Mexicans and indigenous Central Americans go on this map, precisely the target populations of the new Jose Crow laws in Arizona?

Despite the limitations of Bonilla-Silva's triracial map, it, along with other versions of aggregated terms, can continue to have utility depending on what our project of inquiry is. The umbrella term "Latino" also has a persistent utility given the racialized characterization of Latin American cultural identities and the common experiences in the diaspora that can cut across national differences. Yet it is urgent today to promote more disaggregated approaches and proliferations of identity categories as routine ingredients in the public domain of discourse, so as to be able to factor in a variety of mediations and subcategories. This will allow us not only to produce more meaningful economic indicators but also political projections that can make plausible predictions. "Blackness" and "whiteness" are as much in need of analytical disaggregation as any other categories. The white vote for Obama, for example, proved meaningless in an undifferentiated lump. What was predictive was whiteness as mediated by rural or urban status, gender, age, and living in a union household.

Identity proliferation requires us to redraw and revise some borders in potentially uncomfortable ways, to include the light-skinned or more assimilated among us as near-white, as Bonilla-Silva urges, and to take language, national origin, and ethnicity to create borders within racial groups that are often treated as monolithic. This is not to say that gross categories like Latino, Asian American, black, or African American should no longer be used, but that we need to consider what the relevant degree of specificity is for a given question.[34]

We need more than simple disaggregation. We need an identity proliferation that can recognize the validity of some aggregate terms as well as considering new categories that cut across existing groups in helpfully illuminating ways.

In this essay I have addressed three issues that challenge our ability to develop the concept of anti-Latino racism: the exclusivity of colorism as a paradigm of racism, the claim that Latino identity is only about ethnicity, not race, and the argument that the pan-Latino category should be disaggregated. In response to these challenges, I have argued (1) given that there is no single yardstick for racism, but in fact four distinct axes along which racism can operate quite effectively, we need a more pluralist and flexible approach to the new formations racism can take; (2) that there has been a long-standing entwinement of ethnic and racial concepts, and both concepts are particularly necessary to comprehend the specific conditions of Latinos, a combination that the concept ethnorace provides; and (3) that we do in fact need to disaggregate in many projects of inquiry, and thus need to understand both the concept "Latino" and the concept "anti-Latino racism" as essentially umbrella terms, or cluster concepts as philosophers might call them, a fact that makes them no different, however, from other useful concepts such as "whiteness," "blackness," or "antiblack racism."

The emerging Latino population in the United States is testing existing categories and modes of conceptualizing identity, status, and political effect. The hysteria over undocumented workers needs to be unmasked, often as specifically anti-Mexican and anti-Latino racism. If one of the specific aspects of antiblack racism is its attribution of an a priori criminality to black bodies, a key aspect of anti-Latino racism is the attribution of a suspect legal status across the category. We need expanded categories of identity, as well as expanded notions of racism, to provide meaningful representations and analyses, and we need to be willing to devise new creative concepts like ethnorace to be able to avoid unproductive debates about whether Latinos are an ethnicity or a race, or whether they are closer to black or white. National and cultural cohesion and the possibility of an expanded political participation do indeed hang in the balance.

⟡ The Act of Remembering: The Reconstruction of U.S. Latina/o Identities by U.S. Latina/o Muslims

HJAMIL A. MARTÍNEZ-VÁZQUEZ

When communities begin to establish an identity as a group, one of the steps taken is that members of the community start to challenge the ideas and stereotypes that have been imposed on them by the dominant culture. In the case of U.S. Latinas/os, the confrontation takes place not only as they deconstruct the historical narratives that silence their story but also as they re-member those silenced voices and introduce them into a new narrative. The predicament of this process lies in the fact that the stories and voices that make it into the new narrative and identity may then become the norm, and thus leave out or even exclude other voices. The new identity becomes normative and somehow homogenized, and those whose stories did not make it into the new constructions are left out. The homogenized identity is supported by an imaginary, which guides the images, representations, and discourses that are acceptable.[1]

The presence of the U.S. Latina/o Muslim community in society breaks the normative aspect of U.S. Latina/o identities, and thus threatens the traditional constructs of culture and identities. Latina/o Muslims are forced to demonstrate that their religious transformation does not situate them outside of the U.S. Latina/o community. At the same time, they are also forced to prove to the Muslim community that they fit within it, even if their ethnicity is not usually recognized as part of the religious group. This in-betweenness locates U.S. Latina/o Muslims in the complex circumstance of explaining that although conversion has transformed them, making them different from stereotypical U.S. Latinas/os, it did not evaporate their *latinidad*. In other words, their new religious practices and rituals do not change their ethnicities; they do not become what traditionally and stereotypically have been considered culturally Muslim, Arab, or Middle Eastern. Since U.S. Latina/o Muslims "go back" and create, or retrieve, connections with the past, they speak of their conversion as part of their cultural tradition. The dis-covery of the historical consciousness of a Muslim Spain speaks to both a Muslim and Latino past.

In this essay, I explore the way U.S. Latina/o Muslims address this reconstruction of identity by revisiting the historical narratives and constructing a new historical consciousness. For U.S. Latina/o Muslims, the restoration of this past is not a simple process of finding stories that one can use to prove one's location within a tradition; it is a process of "putting together" pieces of a silenced past in order to re-member.[2] At the same time, this act of remembering includes a historicization of culture, in which the foundations of the normative constructions of culture are challenged. The idea of a culture based on a Christian (Catholic) past is deconstructed in order to speak of contested histories and thus contested cultural identities. These contested cultural identities have a past based on contact and exchange, both peaceful and violent, and choosing only some aspects of that contact and exchange not only limits the way historical consciousness is constructed but serves as the rationale for deciding who gets left out. For example, the Christian paradigm that dominates most U.S. Latina/o cultural-identity discourses leaves out the Muslim and Jewish voices from Spain and the voices of enslaved Africans.

U.S. Latina/o Muslims engage in a dis-covery to break these discourses, and this leads to the eventual reconstruction of their identities. Now, while these seem to be different projects, in fact they are simply different phases of an extensive project that entails that the convert, in community, be an engaged individual in the process. Thus, the product of constructing cultural identities (ever-changing, never fixed) is never delegated to those outside of the community seeking the construction. U.S. Latina/o Muslims begin this project even before conversion through being engaged in a search to find answers to their spiritual anomie. Finding in Islam a place where they fit, they convert, but this decision then places them outside of the traditional cultural understanding of their lat-inidad. In the process of searching for a cultural past (1) broken memories are found; (2) a narrative is deconstructed and a new narrative is created based on the dis-covered pasts that build a new consciousness; and (3) a new imaginary is developed based on new cultural memories that lead to new cultural identities.

The U.S. Latina/o Muslim community, like other U.S Latina/o reli-gious communities, is dependent on cultural memories through which the past is not a discourse but a lived experience that allows for the construction (or reconstruction) of identities. Because the act of remem-bering is a subversive activity, the epistemic consequence of the identity construction that follows is a direct challenge to the established narra-tives/discourses that seemed normative. Conversion to Islam leads to a subversive activity that tries to subvert the normative conception of lat-inidad, utilizing the process of remembering the Muslim past in order to confront the established imaginary. The cultural memories of a Muslim Spain allow U.S. Latina/o Muslims to locate their conversion as part of the dis-covery of a historical consciousness.

In the pages that follow, I argue that the use of cultural memory offers U.S. Latina/o Muslims, as colonial subjects, the opportunity of defining themselves and building a cultural identity grounded in their lived experi-ence. This essay is divided into seven sections. In the first two sections, I explore how cultural memory and the act of remembering serve in the process of deconstructing the narratives and discourses that have been imposed as normative. Then, in the third and fourth sections, I turn my attention to analyzing the role that religion and conversion play in the way cultural memory is used as a way of dis-covering a historical con-sciousness for U.S. Latina/o Muslims. This dis-covery allows for the real-ization that the new identities are to be built on new interpretations of the past, which is the center of the discussion in the fifth section. In the last two sections, I provide an analysis of how this process of identity reconstruction challenges the traditional normative narrative, especially the narrative that U.S. Latina/o academic discourses have constructed, and the identities put forward by those discourses.

REMEMBERING

The process of identity construction is intrinsically related to the way stories are constructed and the knowledge they create. For U.S. Latinas/os who are seeking identities independent of that imposed by normative stories fixed by stereotypes and labeling, the use of memory becomes essential. For U.S. Latina/o Muslims it becomes even more essential since the process of remembering not only confronts the normative history but also the colonial discourses embedded within the U.S. Latina/o culture. The act of remembering and building a historical consciousness becomes a subversive enterprise when we use it to escape the stereotyping process and instead use it in our self-identification process.

Memory is constantly linked to historical discourses, for the use of memory—the act of remembering—serves as the basis for constructing historical narratives. As the Puerto Rican scholar Juan Flores declares, "*Memory* has been associated, since its earliest usages, with the act of inscribing, engraving, or, in a sense that carries over into our own electronic times, 're-cording' (*grabar*)."[3] In this sense, historical discourses serve as representations/interpretations of memories. But, within the process of reconstruction of identities among U.S. Latinas/os, memory acquires a more powerful positioning within historical discourses because "it may no longer be viewed merely as the raw material of history."[4] Using memory allows colonial subjects not only to recover what is lost in the narratives of history but also to challenge the identities these narratives generate and legitimate. At the same time, the decline of the influence of these narratives of the past allows "for a proliferation of memory that talks back; not just recent memory, where it is most visible, but even distant forgotten memories that have returned to challenge history."[5] Memory becomes a subversive activity as people dis-cover their histories previously suppressed by hegemonic histories, and recover "lost or suppressed identities."[6]

Using memory as subversive activity uncovers the fragmentation within historical narratives. Normative historical discourses are portrayed as linear and continuous, but memory breaks that illusion, not in order to create a new continuous discourse but to reveal history as an ever-changing discourse. As Flores argues, since "the process of memory is open, without closure or conclusion[,] the struggle to (re)establish continuities and to tell the 'whole' story only uncovers new breaks and new exclusions."[7] The decision turns out to be between remembering and forgetting. Both are processes of selecting what to remember and what to forget, but the act of remembering works against the metanarratives used to label and marginalize people, and it helps break down their power. Traditional historical discourses silence the voices of the colonized, leaving them without a historical consciousness, but they also generate what the Puerto Rican scholar Arcadio Díaz-Quiñones has identified as "broken memories."[8] *La memoria rota* (broken memory) is the product of the mutilation of a social consciousness. As Flores argues, "A people's memory and sense of collective continuity is broken not only by the abrupt, imposed course of historical events themselves, but by the exclusionary discourses that accompany and legitimate them."[9]

U.S. Latinas/os, because of their in-betweenness, suffer from "broken memories," and the subversive act of remembering allows them to reestablish those memories. However, this subversive activity has to be rooted in the cultural experience of the people (the everyday activities of the people), and not in an esoteric or academic interpretation of the past. I am calling not for new raw material to be added to the established narratives but for a way to expose their discontinuities. Whereas those benefiting from colonial discourses may see the exposing of the discontinuities as "a threat to cultural survival and inclusion," it allows the colonial subject to "critically examine prevailing continuities and imagine and create new ones."[10] Consequently, the discontinuities exposed through the act of remembering "manifest themselves in lived experience and expression."[11]

CULTURAL MEMORY

By remembering from a particular social/cultural location, we understand the past as a lived experience. This reconceptualization of the past as a lived experience is grounded in the understanding that "history is constructed partially from the accounts of witnesses and partially from primary documents that reveal the memories of those involved in the events."[12] In essence, history should not be seen as straight recollection of facts from the past, but as "a reconstruction of culturally relative 'facts' that is always influenced by particular worldviews."[13] Cultural location adds to historical discourses not only a sense of specificity but also a meaning grounded in the experience of a particular community. Historical interpretation thus does not come from a one-dimensional impetus for understanding the past in a vacuum but from the necessity of locating oneself within the present and the future. In this way, the subversive activity of remembering is a cultural activity, which I refer to here as cultural memory.

Cultural memory can be seen as both an individual and a collective experience.[14] The use of cultural memory offers people more than the opportunity to recall the past in order to find continuity. It is a way for individuals and communities to "put together" a recollection of past events, even if they have been hidden, and build a narrative, a historical consciousness, that allows the construction of identities. The English-language words re-membering and re-collecting express with particular clarity this aspect of connection intrinsic in the concept of memory, which is essential within the process of creating identity. These terms evoke the idea of putting "members" back together (re-membering and dis-membering) and "re-collecting" things that have been dispersed.[15]

This "coming together" by "putting together" exemplifies the way communities see the past as a source of connection among their members. U.S. Latinas/os as colonial subjects in search of identities, through a process of dis-covery, re-member and re-collect, not as an individual enterprise, but as a communal and socially situated activity. But bonding memories can limit the understandings we have about the past and ourselves, and for that reason we need to go beyond simply gathering bonding memories to adding the cultural perspective. Through cultural memory, the memories of the past are not limited to organized traditions and history, but include those stories that do not get to be narrated within the official history, "the noninstrumentalizable, heretical, subversive, and disowned."[16] Cultural memory generates knowledge that is beyond traditional Western knowledge, and through the use of what the Chicana feminist Gloria Anzaldúa refers to as la facultad, the colonial subject accesses this type of memory—a vital task since traditional Western knowledge has covered, erased, and silenced history.[17]

Thus, U.S. Latinas/os will look to the past for a representation and interpretation of the "facts" and memories from their particular location, using lenses that look beyond traditional history. In this sense, "memory becomes important as a survival mechanism when it becomes part of artistic, emotionally laden ways of forming group identity and meanings."[18] This dis-covery of the past, in the light of the community's cultural memory, brings forward hybrid identities that challenge the essentialized versions of identity established by colonial discourses. Along with Jeanette Rodríguez and Ted Fortier, I understand cultural memory as "rooted in actual events and in the surrounding and resulting alignment of images, symbols, and affectivities that turn out to be even more persuasive than facts."[19] The use of cultural memory brings together the reinterpretation of the past with the lived experience of the people, allowing U.S. Latinas/os to construct hybrid identities different from those imposed by the process of stereotyping.

RELIGION AS A SOURCE OF CULTURAL MEMORY

Religion functions as one of those lived experiences that advances the act of remembering and therefore the construction of identities. For U.S. Latinas/os, religious experience "has always been an important element of their cultural fabric and ethnic identities."[20] Yet, religion is not a fixed characteristic, for those experiencing it transform it constantly, making it always hybrid. However, it is true that religious experiences through rituals and practices not only acquire meaning throughout time but may also become tradition, which may seem to be fixed. In this sense, religion needs to be understood as a sociocultural instrument, whose use depends on the social location of those experiencing it. It is a lived experience that speaks to the connection between the experience with God and the experience of a community, and thus acquires power—"but will it be a power unto life or a power of sacralized and legitimized oppression, [marginalization,] exclusion, ethnocide and even genocide?"[21] Differentiating between the roles of power is essential because religious institutions, for the most part, have been responsible for establishing fixed religious traditions that have precluded the use of religious experiences and rituals as sources for the dis-covery of cultural memory. Conversely, individuals and communities have stepped away many times from those institutionalized traditions and through the use of popular religion and local ritual have constructed identities distinct from the ones established by people in power.

By moving away from traditions imposed to isolate people, colonial subjects create rituals and experiences of faith that give meaning to the marginalization they know. For example, in the history of Latin America the colonial subjects, both indigenous communities and enslaved Africans, created religious systems to confront the domination imposed by the colonizer. These religious systems, like Afro-Latino religions, generated in most cases through syncretic activities, proved to be essential for the survival of these groups in the face of oppression and marginalization. Even in more recent history, religious experience continues to play a core role in the creation of identities in Latin America. Participation within the liberation theology movements and the Pentecostal movements has allowed Latin Americans to develop communal identities that, while not fixed, help bring people together. Religious experiences as lived experiences have become important in developing cultural identities among Latin Americans and this importance translates into the life of U.S. Latinas/os.[22]

Religious experience gives meaning to colonial subjects' history of struggle while also opening the door for the development of identities that challenge imposed identities and stereotypes. It opens the door for the dis-covery of historical consciousness. I am not implying here that religious experience serves only to challenge the system, since it is clear that religion has been used within processes of colonization and assimilation.[23] Rather, I am suggesting that, for the most part, colonial subjects, people in the middle, see religious experience as a mode of liberation, reinforcing a cultural memory and building cultural identities. This process happens in community as colonial subjects look at religious experience not only in the light of the relationship with a higher being but also of that between individuals. Sometimes religion brings a community together—it can become the fulcrum of new communal and social identities. It gives people a sense of belonging and a communal experience with a higher power, and it helps them reconstruct an identity based both on the religious past and on communal experiences. Thus, on the one hand, "Religion validates our existence by connecting us with ancestors, with spirits, with a god or gods," and mediating "the dynamic of being here in the moment while also being part of an ongoing continuum."[24] On the other hand, "Religion heightens our communal experience of life," as "it brings us together in a community that reinforces the events in our lives."[25] Moreover, in the context of people living in the middle, "Religious experience interprets the way a community defines the world, and it does so in such a way that establishes its primary values, affects, behaviors, and choices."[26]

U.S. Latinas/os experience religion in this way as they become involved in communal rituals and acquire symbols that articulate their
opposition and resistance to the discourses that fix identity. These rituals
and symbols become aspects of cultural memory. As lived experiences
they provide the opportunity to "remember," to dis-cover the history
that may have been silenced by colonial interpretations of the past. They
give meaning to the community as the community assigns meaning to
them. In the words of the Catholic theologian Virgilio Elizondo,

> These religious practices are the ultimate foundation of the people's
> innermost being and the common expression of their collective soul.
> They are supremely meaningful for the people who celebrate them,
> but often appear meaningless to the outsider. To the people whose
> very life-source they are, no explanation is necessary, but to the
> casual spectator no explanation will ever express or communicate
> their full meaning. Without them, there might be associations of
> individuals bound together by common interest (e.g., the corpora-
> tion, the state, etc.), but there will never be the experience of being
> a people, *un pueblo*.[27]

Religious experiences open up the imagination of the community to new
identities, as these experiences become cultural processes that bring together historical memories and everyday life experiences. Through them
U.S. Latinas/os are empowered to develop new religious meanings. As
Mexican American anthropologist Richard Flores suggests, "The self-
creation of Latino community with its own set of religious meanings
represents a process that constitutes social power and cultural identity
that jeopardizes the political power of the church."[28]

Latinas/os in the United States, as people in the middle, look to religion to challenge their sense of anomie and marginalization. The communal aspects of religious experiences develop cultural memories and
provide U.S. Latinas/os with an opportunity to look beyond the traditional understandings of history and knowledge. This use of religion
jeopardizes the power of the social and cultural system that silences the
voices of these communities and labels them. U.S. Latinas/os, by engaging religion as a lived experience, revisit symbols, images, and rituals that
provide an opening to the dis-covery of alternative knowledges. These

alternative knowledges, which some may characterize as counter-memo-ries, become critical in the development of cultural identities. Thus, people in the middle (displaced communities) revisit rituals and symbols as cultural artifacts, not just as simple religious experiences. This activity works as a way of connecting a collective identity (for example, a national identity) to a historical past. Religious experiences, by activating the act of remembering, become part of cultural memories that lead to the discovery of cultural identities. In this sense, cultural identities, as cultural memories, are rooted in history and in historical consciousness. This happens when colonial subjects are able to see beyond the already established labels and the static identifications. Religious experiences thus open a door not only to the experience of the divine but also to the processes of self-identification.

The conversion to Islam offers the opportunity for U.S. Latina/o Muslims to re-member history in order to try to make sense of their culture and religion as two nonexclusive aspects of their identity. In other words, because U.S. Latinas/os are mostly identified by their Catholic (or at least Christian) roots, U.S. Latina/o Muslims feel pressure to seek beyond that label and find an identity that puts together their ethnic (or national) characteristics and their religious experience. As an outsider, it seemed to me that the members of this community do not have a choice, as they are forced to reidentify themselves. I am not simply alluding to the changes that conversion brings, such as in eating habits, changing one's name, or wearing the *hijab*; I am talking about the process through which U.S. Latina/o Muslims have to reinvent themselves as people. Conversion thus implies a change in worldview, not just a transformation of practices. As Rebecca Sachs Norris acknowledges, "Conversion involves not just adopting a set of ideas but also converting to and from an embodied worldview and identity."[29] Since U.S. Latina/o Muslim converts for the most part were raised within a particular Christian worldview that has (in multiple and different ways) informed the development of most U.S. Latina/o identities, it is important for them to confront that historical consciousness and dis-cover a new cultural memory that serves as the core of their process of construction of new identities. I am not implying that the decision of converting comes as an act of subversion, but the result of the conversion and the need to reconstruct an identity make the response to conversion an act of subversion.[30]

REVERSION: GOING BACK

The historian Alberto Hernández explains that U.S. Latinas/os "have looked back upon their Iberian cultural and family heritage with an ambivalence not easily understood by persons of Anglo-European or Germanic ancestry."[31] The ambivalence developed from the connection that the Iberian heritage has with "the trappings of Spanish conquest and colonial exploitation."[32] Colonization and conquest, thus, have become the particular terms that describe the history of Spain's relationship to Latin America. In contrast, U.S. Latina/o Muslims, who do not dispute this colonial narrative, look to Spain in a different way because they look also at the history of Spain that comes before colonization and the conquest. They are interested in reconstructing the traditional and normative narratives to dis-cover the cultural memories about Islam that have been hidden. These cultural memories have been buried in order to underscore the Catholic tradition that lay behind the course of the colonization and conquest of the Americas. At the same time, "Spain and its history was marginalized by intellectuals and nationalists touting the racialized nineteenth-century discourses of Western European civilization."[33] The contact and exchange between three cultures—Muslim, Jewish, and Christian—generated a mixed society, a hybrid reality, which placed Spain outside of the paradigm European modernity created. Describing this situation, Hernández states that "when the intellectual and literary canon of European civilization was constructed by nineteenth- and early twentieth-century Euro-American intellectuals, Spain was marginalized for not being 'white' enough and still too mired in a latent 'medievalism' to have benefitted from the ideals and objectives of the Enlightenment."[34]

U.S. Latina/o Muslims reinterpret the history of Spain beyond its relation to Latin America, arguing that the period of three cultures, especially due the dominance of Islam, is not only not what reduces Spanish history but also, on the contrary, what makes it rich. The focus on the richness of this forgotten history does not simply allow for the reconstruction of historical consciousness through the dis-covery of cultural memories but also leads U.S. Latina/o Muslims to create a cultural identity that has at its core this covered part of history. Thus, after conversion, U.S. Latina/o Muslims go through a series of steps that lead to that creation of identity. They transform their personal lives, and they "go back" and re-member (put together) those silenced features of the past in order to transform normative historical consciousness and help explain how their conversion actually fits in with their latinidad. Dis-covering the cultural memories of the Islamic tradition within Spanish history and culture, U.S. Latina/o Muslims understand their conversion as a process of "going back" to the roots of what it means to be a Latina/o. For this reason, most U.S. Latina/o Muslims refer to their process of conversion as a process of reversion, a process of returning. U.S. Latino Muslim Yahya 'Abu Ayah' López explains this process.

> When we said that we "reverted" back to Islam, we therefore were, in effect, saying that we had returned, migrated back, or come home to our original condition from which we had been tragically separated in years past. After voluntarily returning to that primordial form, we then joyfully "embraced" it. We had realized, via our cognitive evaluation, its true worth and held it tightly within our arms, not wanting to let it go again.[35]

In other words, reversion represents not a stepping away from their cultural and historical memory but an actual recovering of their past and the "forgotten" (dis-membered) heritage, a Muslim Spain. This "going back" tends for the most part to romanticize Moorish culture and history. As the community leader Edmund A. Arroyo explains, "The Latino Muslim conversion can often be traced to this rediscovery of their ancestral roots."[36] This is a way of looking at the past in order to dis-cover a "new" cultural memory, hidden behind the colonial discourses. Thus, the term "reversion" becomes essential in the way conversion leads to identity. It not only explains the religious "going back" to Islam but also "going back" to the Muslim roots in the Latino cultural memory.

The concept of reversion allows us to see beyond the natural changes U.S. Latina/o Muslims go through and understand how they go beyond describing their conversion. With the concept and understanding of

"going back," they address the criticism of and challenge to their latinidad posed by other members of the U.S. Latina/o community. U.S. Lat-
ina/o Muslims typically find many similarities between Islam and Latino
culture, rather than seeing these two cultures as opposites as do many
outside this community. Establishing these connections is only the first
step in the process of building an identity founded in cultural memories
that are in need of dis-covery and a historical consciousness developed
out of these dis-coveries. When asked about how she reconciles her reversion with the challenges to her Latina identity, María, a U.S. Latina
Muslim from New York, clearly establishes that reversion has actually
reinforced her understanding of her latinidad.

> I feel it is reinforced because in my perspective I am actually going
> back to my roots. I think people who are Christian, who are Catho-
> lic, have gone away from their Latino roots because we have our
> roots in Spain. We have our roots in the Moors. Our language con-
> tains Arabic words. Our morality, our chivalry, the men, their pro-
> tection, how they are with their women and with their families, that
> comes from the Arab, from the Moors. So, I think I am reinforced.
> I think I am in an uphill battle because some people's perspectives
> are now the norm and that is what I am dealing with. But I do not
> feel displaced or like I am going against my Latino roots.[37]

Many U.S. Latina/o Muslims share this perspective and look at this history as the basis of their new identity. Some, like María, will take personal issue with the challenges and push back by challenging the
Christian privilege within history and arguing that it is in the Moorish
tradition that one can find the actual roots of latinidad.

BUILDING ON THE PAST

U.S. Latina/o Muslims focus their attention on the dis-covery of these
cultural intricacies in order to demonstrate the central role Islam plays in
their historical consciousness and in the construction of their identities.
In this regard, Juan Galván states that "Latinos today are still influenced
by Islamic Spain," and that "for example, thousands of Spanish words
are derived from Arabic."[38] Some of these words like *ojalá*, which comes
from the Arabic *insha'allah* (God willing) and words that begin with *al*

like *almohada*, which comes from *almuhádda* (pillow), are intrinsic to the Spanish language and show the connection. Raheel Rojas, a U.S. Latino Muslim writing in the *Latino Muslim Voice*, focusing on this perspective about Muslim Spain being at the core of U.S. Latina/o identity, makes a plea to U.S. Latina/o Muslims who doubt their latinidad.

> What can be more Latino that being Muslim. Spain was predominantly Muslim for 800 years. The shining light of Islam belonged to people who spoke Spanish, mashallah. Europeans came to Spain to learn sciences. Spain brought the renaissance of Christian Europe. Islam spread in Spain through the reversion of the indigenous people, not mass immigration of Moors as they have you believe.[39]

In this sense, Muslim Spain becomes the center in the process of reconstruction of identity. Kenny Yusuf Rodríguez, a Dominican Muslim, argues that most of the Latinas/os who criticize Islam do so because they may have "forgotten that Islamic and Spanish cultures were once closely knit." He goes even further to link Islam in Spain and Latin America as he stresses the Islamic influences not only in language but also in architecture.[40] In the same way, Ramón Omar Abduraheem Ocasio establishes, "We are reclaiming our history after a 500-year hiatus," because "Catholics never successfully stripped the Moors of their identity," and thus, "We are the cultural descendents of the Moors."[41] These types of argument increase the visibility of these stories from the past in order to establish the importance of Islamic culture as part of the basis for U.S. Latina/o culture. Although some scholars, like María, offer a critique of Catholicism as dominant, most U.S. Latina/o Muslims highlight Islamic culture in Spain as being not oppressive and colonizing but inclusive and tolerant. This idea of Spanish civilization is what U.S. Latina/o Muslims want to dis-cover: that Islamic culture is a culture of tolerance and that it is part of the core of Spanish identity and civilization. It has been hidden by the preponderance of the Spanish narratives that emphasize only the "occidental" aspects of its history, thus stressing the Catholic perspectives. In dis-covering the hidden stories and reconstructing the narratives, U.S. Latina/o Muslims seem to take a romantic approach to Islamic culture, but at the same time try to underscore that the Spanish

Catholic history of colonization cannot be understood without a full comprehension of the interactions between the three cultures.[42]

Their attitude resembles that of Spanish Muslims and Moriscos (Muslims or descendants who converted or were forced to convert), who after 1492 resisted the imposition by those in power (Christians) of a national myth that left Al-Andalus and Islamic tradition out of the picture, a myth "that veiled its divisive regionalism and sacralized its origin in the Crusades of the Reconquest."[43] The historian Mary Elizabeth Perry maintains that as part of the challenge to that national myth, Muslims "claimed their own myths of the past," which allowed them "to resist oppression and reclaim their position of honor and power."[44] The confrontation of these two myths created a debate regarding the legacies that served in the construction of Spanish identity, which resulted in the evolution of what Perry calls contested identities, each based on a different myth. The struggle between these contested identities forced those in power not only to expel Muslims and Jews from Spain but also to reinforce the myth of a Catholic, occidental Spain, leaving the "Other" (Muslims and Jews) outside of the myth. U.S. Latinas/os, who after conversion to Islam no longer recognize themselves in the official history, reclaim that Islamic myth and create a space of contested identities among U.S. Latinas/os.[45] In the process of reconstructing their identity, they realize that their hybrid identities are complicated even further if they can dis-cover the Islamic tradition embedded within latinidad. This process of reconstruction is comparable to the process undertaken by U.S. African American Muslims, who through their own *da'wah* search deeper into the past in order to make sense of their social condition and create new identities. This message "raised the consciousness of [U.S.] African Americans about their history, including the fact that many of them were descendants of Muslims who had been forcibly converted to Christianity."[46] They look at the history of slavery in order to find a historical consciousness that makes sense and that gives them meaning (cultural memory).

After conversion, U.S. Latina/o Muslims no longer have legitimacy among the larger U.S. Latina/o community. Because of the labeling and stereotypes created by those in power and internalized by the people, U.S. Latina/o Muslims are left outside of the normative paradigm of what constitutes a Latina/o. Although ethnically they fit the oversimplified conception of what a U.S. Latina/o is, their conversion situates them without a historical consciousness, a past, that could support their actual "membership" within this community. The absence of a historical consciousness leaves them without a cultural memory that fits the traditional narratives. At the same time, because they have felt some marginalization among the larger Muslim community, U.S. Latina/o Muslims are once again feeling that "in-betweenness." They see themselves as part of the two different communities, the Latino and the Muslim, and yet they are at the margins of both. They become the "Other." This reality triggers their search of the past and the dis-covery of a historical consciousness. The normative historical narratives did not make any sense to U.S. Latina/o Muslims because they were unable to see themselves in them.

As Guillermo Araya Goubet states, "History achieves its full meaning only when it creates an adequate awareness of the past in a community that recognizes that past as its very own."[47] Only through the remembering of the Islamic past and deconstruction of the normative narrative based on the colonial Catholic tradition, they can see a history that actually makes sense, one that is comprehensible from their social/cultural location. They "go back," dis-cover cultural memories and create new representations that connect their new lives, after conversion, and a past that is not invented or somebody else's but theirs. This uncovered past becomes a lived experience and the source of the creation of an identity that gives meaning to their conversion and legitimates their religious experiences. U.S. Latina/o Muslims argue that they should not be marginalized for what some perceive as their "going against" their own culture, because, instead, they see themselves as essentially retrieving and then transforming that culture rather than abandoning it. Certainly, it would take some time to construct a clear U.S. Latina/o Muslim identity, as Juan Galván states, but through the dis-covery and the remembering of the Islamic past, the path toward that identity or identities is created, challenging the traditional understandings of U.S. Latina/o identities.

NEW IDEAS: U.S. LATINA/O THEOLOGY/RELIGIOUS STUDIES

U.S. Latina/o theologies and other fields within U.S. Latina/o religious studies have been responsible for the construction of the discourses that examine the relationships between religious experiences and U.S. Latina/o identities. A complete assessment of these discourses lies beyond the scope of this essay, but it is important to explore and deconstruct the identities these discourses create. These identities are created through oppositional consciousness, against the normative discourses of those in power, and they demonstrate the subjecthood of U.S. Latinas/os even when they have been constructed as Other by the colonial imaginary. This process of identity construction through oppositional consciousness results in the creation of identities that appear to have a liberatory nature, a decolonial character. The problem is that in the process of constructing these identities most discourses within U.S. Latina/o religious studies have privileged some sources over others to the point of obscuring memories. The most recognizable aspect of this process is the focus on Christian religious experiences, leaving those non-Christian U.S. Latina/o religious communities outside of the imaginary it creates. Thus, these discourses, created as counter-discourses through subversive practices, acquired a new normativity as they essentialized U.S. Latina/o identities. Although these counter-discourses try to transform the normative discourses, there is always a danger of the reinscription of the same categories; the counter-discourses do not necessarily completely break the boundaries.

Even if the ideology behind these constructions is not colonial, the actual discourses it creates seem colonial in that they are responsible for covering and silencing voices that break the normative character of the imaginary. The Cuban theologian Michelle A. González argues that U.S. Latina/o scholars of religion have focused on the importance of culture "as the unifying element that links Latino/a peoples."[48] For González, this "emphasis on culture erases the diversity of the histories of Latino/a peoples and makes the experience of Spanish colonialism the thread that unites them."[49] Even when these discourses speak about difference they are closed to some differences that do not fit within the traditional historical consciousness. This is why, as Miguel De La Torre states, "To unmask how power operates within our own marginalized group, a rethinking is required—not just a rethinking of our religious concepts but, just as important, a rethinking of how we construct our very identity."[50]

U.S. Latina/o scholars, for the most part, begin their analysis of U.S. Latina/o identities with an examination of the history of the conquest of the Americas, privileging the colonization of indigenous populations and thus neglecting the presence of Muslim traditions, as well as the history of the African slave trade. González in her analysis of U.S. Latina/o theology critiques the discourse within the field for this focus, because it "has become normative," even though it does not represent the totality of the diversity, since "not all of our foremothers and forefathers were conquered."[51] She is interested in deconstructing the discourses in the light of its silences about the African elements that helped build U.S. Latina/o heritage. She argues that because of its African roots, the symbol of Our Lady of Charity not only serves as a source for the construction of Cuban identity but also underscores the significance of Africa in the construction of U.S. Latina/o identities. At the same time, she finds that one of the major problems with U.S. Latina/o theologies is that it has put at the center of its narrative Mexican American traditions to the point that, for example, the symbol of Our Lady of Guadalupe has become a normative representation of latinidad. This emphasis is nowhere more evident than in the understanding and use of the concept of mestizaje as a way to construct U.S. Latina/o identities.

Mestizaje has served to define the hybrid condition of U.S. Latinas/os, but when used as an all-encompassing concept, it hides some of the aspects that make up its hybridity. In U.S. Latina/o religious studies, mestizaje seems to have acquired an all-encompassing, essentialized meaning and thus needs to be deconstructed and open to those aspects that have been covered over. The influence of Mexican American traditions within this conception of mestizaje can be traced to the work of Mexican philosopher José Vasconcelos, and "the writings of one of the founders of [U.S.] Latino/a theology, Virgilio Elizondo."[52] Both not only offer a romantic view of the hybrid reality (as chosen people) but also limit the understanding of this concept, not fully problematizing its complexity.

In this concept Elizondo sees hope for U.S. Latinas/os who have the promise of "a new creative universal subject."[53] This promise is based on the challenge subaltern groups present to those in power because they break the normative understandings of racial purity, and Elizondo finds that the best representative of this process is Jesus, because as a Galilean, Jesus "was himself *mestizo*, laboring at a crossroads of peoples and cultures at the margins of the empire to build a new, inclusive reign of God."[54] In this sense, for Elizondo and other U.S. Latina/o religious scholars, mestizaje carries a theological meaning beyond its racial component. Manuel A. Vásquez, in his reading of Elizondo, goes further by arguing that because Elizondo understands mestizaje "through the lenses of liberationist Christianity." The concept of mestizaje, he continues, "is not the inalienable property of Ibero-American civilizations or any other ethnic or national group, but the core of humanity itself."[55] Thus, mestizaje has not only a theological meaning but also a humanistic aspect. It is not founded in racial essentialism; it actually challenges the racial constructions put forward by those in power, sustained by colonial discourses of racial purity and hierarchy that locate one race over another. Because of this function, mestizaje has become a core idea within U.S. Latina/o religious studies. The ethicist Ada María Isasi-Díaz states:

> In our theological endeavors, *mestizaje/mulatez* constitutes our *locus theologicus*—the place from which we do theology precisely because it is intrinsic to who we are. It situates us as a community in U.S. society. *Mestizaje/mulatez* is so important to us that we have suggested it as an ethical option, because it has to do with an understanding of difference that is intrinsic not only to the Latina community's identity but to everyone's sense of self.[56]

For many scholars within the field of U.S. religious studies, mestizaje is defined through an understanding of the religious experiences of U.S. Latinas/os. For example, "For Elizondo, the Christian faith plays a central role in what mestizaje is, means, and signifies."[57]

Others go beyond the traditional Christian understandings in order to include popular religious experiences, not simply institutional perspectives. Isasi-Díaz, in her scrutiny and reconceptualization of this concept from a mujerista perspective, states:

> In *mujerista* theology we have proposed an understanding of popular religion as a form of *mestizaje* in itself, as well as a key factor of *mestizaje* at large. We also recognize that both African and Amerindian religious understandings and practices are intrinsic elements of popular religion as well as of *mestizaje*. Our intention has been to broaden *mestizaje* to include African cultural, historical, and biological elements.[58]

In order to achieve this broadening of the concept, Isasi-Díaz and others "started to add *mulatez*—which refers to the mixing of the white and black races—to *mestizaje* instead of including our African heritage under this term."[59] This repositions the focus of the term away from solely the Mexican American experience, where Vasconcelos and Elizondo appear to have placed it, and includes a broader perspective, in this case the African heritage that is so prevalent in the Caribbean.

The conceptualization of mestizaje has gone through many transformations. Although it may seem that the inclusion of multiple perspectives illustrates difference, the continuous and exclusive focus on this concept as an all-encompassing term is in part responsible for the homogenization of its meaning and has prevented U.S. Latina/o scholars from looking beyond essentialized U.S. Latina/o identities. For example, the most common understandings of mestizaje, before the addition of mulatez, did not integrate the histories of those groups outside of the story of the colonization of the Americas, to the point of silencing them, as in the case of Africans, and erasing them, as in the case of Muslims. Mestizaje understood in this narrow way creates a colonial discourse, and U.S. Latina/o peoples who do not fit the discourse become Others. Even with the addition of mulatez, which Michelle González shows has not been fully integrated within U.S. Latina/o religious studies, the discourse of mestizaje is not open to difference, because it is not simply adding perspectives that will get lost in a homogenizing concept but actually having a concept (or concepts) that fully elucidate difference.

Rather than advocate for the elimination of the term, I want to show how the U.S. Latina/o Muslim perspective opens the concept of mestizaje to a larger perspective, breaking its colonial feature.[60] For example, Vásquez states that mestizaje "helps Latinos to recover and celebrate the richness of their religious and cultural resources."[61] Yet its actual use within U.S. Latina/o religious studies has fallen short of providing this opportunity. The richness that can be recovered from the present understandings of mestizaje is based on a Christian paradigm and/or a relationship to it, as in the case of Afro-Caribbean religious experiences. Those outside of this limited richness become Other, like U.S. Latina/o Muslims.

The Otherness created by the colonial discourse of mestizaje is grounded in a historical consciousness that has Christianity at its center.

Even though many times it includes a critique, the focus on the conquest of the Americas still privileges Spanish Catholicism as a central aspect of U.S. Latina/o identities. Although U.S. Latina/o Muslims in their process of reconstruction of identity do not deny the importance of this history, they do challenge its primacy. By "going back," U.S. Latina/o Muslims alter this historical consciousness and expose the silences within the narratives. Islam takes "center stage"; history is revisited; and the normative discourses are broken as memories are dis-covered. The work of Raúl Gómez-Ruiz is important in this process of dis-covery for U.S. Latina/o religious studies because it reveals the connection between Iberian and U.S. Latinas/os beyond the limited focus on Catholicism. He writes about the link between Mozarab rituals and U.S. Latina/o Catholic rituals. Because for Gómez-Ruiz, "One way that culture, identity, and therefore community develop is through rituals," he finds that the roots of the U.S. Latina/o liturgy in Spanish history should be considered part of the construction of U.S. Latina/o cultural identities.[62]

U.S. Latina/o scholars have paid no attention to Iberian history before 1492, but Gómez-Ruiz's work seems to transform that situation by opening the discourse to the understanding of this history. Alberto Hernández, talking about Gómez-Ruiz work, states:

> Thus, Gómez-Ruiz succeeds in showing us that Hispanic Christians, regardless of their contemporary Latin American stereotypes or North American racial profiling, also possess a story rooted in the early medieval cradle of European ethnic and religious culture. Hispanics, Latinos, and Latinas are not merely "recent arrivals" on the stage of Western civilization. Their story is not merely that of an insignificant "recent history," but is rather a story rooted in the dynamic multicultural tensions of the Iberian Peninsula, which long before 1492 functioned as the creative and progressive frontier of numerous Western European religious and intellectual currents.[63]

Hernández, whose own research addresses the history of medieval Spain, is clear in his analysis that the cultural identities of U.S. Latinas/os are not simply rooted in the actual events of the conquest of the Americas but also in the period before these events. Like Michelle González, Raúl Gómez-Ruiz is interested in transforming the way U.S. Latina/o cultural identities have been constructed by enhancing the discourses. He understands not only that "many [U.S.] Latinas/os have only a faint and/or dismissive sense of their connection to Iberia," but that the effects of this "heritage are often underrepresented or ignored in the works written by [U.S.] Latina/o theologians."[64] So while this dis-covery triggers "the Hispanicization of [U.S.] Latina/o identity,"[65] it also opens the discourse of identity to Islamic tradition, which is exactly what U.S. Latina/o Muslims also want, as they use cultural memory as a subversive activity.

Based on these dis-coveries, a new historical consciousness needs to be developed in order to include these memories. Thus, by dis-covering the memories of Muslim Spain and breaking the linearity of the history, the colonial discourses (e.g., mestizaje) are deconstructed. U.S. Latina/o identity can no longer be homogenized, for these dis-covered memories, even if they are contested, carry cultural meanings that then guide the construction of cultural identities.

If these silences within U.S. Latina/o religious academic discourses persist, the U.S. Latina/o identity created will be the product of coloniality.[66] With these lacunae, these discourses do not explore the fullness of the historical consciousness or recognize its shortcomings; the intent of these discourses to normativize (consciously or unconsciously) the identity of U.S. Latinas/os is exposed as a colonial enterprise. Thus, the deconstruction of these traditional discourses and the incorporation of U.S. Latina/o Muslims' cultural memories, among others, although it does not complete the discourses, does increase the diversity and difference needed to reconstruct U.S. Latina/o identities. As González argues, "We cannot afford to erase and marginalize portions of our population in favor of a more generalized description of our identity. To do so is to do violence to the communities we ignore and forget."[67] To not speak about U.S. Latina/o identities, latinidades, and continue perpetuating an imaginary that leaves people without a voice would be to reproduce the same discourses that they confront. Participants in the disciplines within the fields of U.S. Latina/o religious studies have to become involved in these discussions or else they will be reproducing the colonial character of the oppressive systems of power.

LATINIDADES

The purpose of this essay is not to fix the parameters of U.S. Latina/o identities but to expose the way U.S. Latina/o Muslims are forced to

confront the coloniality implicit in the conceptions of the present discourses. It is about dis-covering the multiplicity of voices that make up
historical consciousness, which in turn serves as a foundation for constructing cultural identities. This process entails including new voices,
silenced voices, even though "the construction of identity, whether cultural, racial, or ecclesial, is nonetheless an exclusionary process where
one group's identity is set apart from that of the other group."[68] In this
construction, one has to see cultural identities as fluid and ever-changing,
always open to dis-covered memories.

U.S. Latina/o identities are built through a process of convergence:
Different stories, different threads come together—but not to erase differences and construct a normative discourse. It is about weaving in all
the threads and looking for some of the loose threads that have gotten
excluded from the fabric. If we continue to have loose threads, the discourses will be filled with holes. The silenced voices break into the holes
and dismantle the discourses in order to reconstruct the fabric. After
conversion, U.S. Latina/o Muslims find themselves in one of those holes
as a loose thread. Through the act of remembering they have the opportunity of putting a new fabric together and restoring their thread to the
fabric. Thus, U.S. Latina/o cultural identities are "very much involved in
the cultural and religious dynamics of understanding how the now
muted voices of our Iberian forebears, and their lost cultural and religious
memories, still touch our hearts and move our minds."[69]

The thread U.S. Latina/o Muslims intend to incorporate into the fabric
is predicated on the idea of contested identities. In the same way that
medieval Spain was a contested space for multiple identities, today's situation of latinidad fits the same model. In this sense, our discourses regarding identity have to be problematized in order to make them more
comprehensive and whole: a pluralistic approach to the study of U.S.
Latina/o identities. The process of identity construction among U.S. Lat-
ina/o Muslims offers a paradigm to address this issue for communities
that have been silenced by the normativity of U.S. Latina/o identity. It
is developed in three major levels: (1) Look at the past in order to dis-
cover a historical consciousness that allows for the past to be a lived
experience; (2) use cultural memory (the act of remembering) as a source
for self-identification; (3) look beyond the normative and colonial representations and break through the holes to dismantle the imaginary that

supports its construction. This paradigm certainly does not represent an all-in-all model, but it deals with an analysis of contested spaces and contested identities without homogenizing any of them. It also allows for the convergence of different threads as one constructs U.S. Latina/o identities.

❧ If It Is Not Catholic, Is It Popular Catholicism? Evil Eye, Espiritismo, and Santería: Latina/o Religion within Latina/o Theology

MICHELLE A. GONZÁLEZ

In this essay I argue that Latina/o theology can provide only a limited understanding of Latina/o Catholicism, given its Christian focus. Latina/o popular Catholicism is much more than Christianity and is in fact influenced by non-Christian religious traditions. The three religious traditions I explore that heavily mark Latina/o popular Catholicism are the folk religion surrounding evil eye, the religio-philosophical worldview of Espiritismo, and the religion of Santería (the popular term for *Regla de Ocha*). Through highlighting their influence on Latina/o Catholicism I challenge Latina/o theology to open itself to the possibility of decentering Christianity epistemologically. After briefly explaining evil eye, Espiritismo, and Santería, I conclude with their epistemological impact on Latina/o Roman Catholic theology. The three traditions I cover bridge Latin American and U.S. Latina/o religion. It is my belief that to understand Latina/o religiosity one must understand and include the Latin American context. Latina/o theologians, I fear, often cut themselves off too sharply from Latin America in their scholarship.

In order to understand contemporary Latina/o Catholicism, we must take into consideration its historical Spanish roots. Medieval Spanish Catholicism had a distinctive flavor, marked by heavy aesthetic expression that remained relatively unscathed by the 1545–63 Council of Trent that sought to de-emphasize these devotions. This aesthetic emphasis is found in the strong presence of processions, devotionals, and performative rituals. The historian Laura de Mello e Souza argues that the absence of

Trent reforms contributed to the popular religious landscape and syncretism so predominant in Latin America. As she notes, Trent took time to root itself even in Europe. "During the seventeenth century, two different religions cohabitated in Europe—that of theologians and that of believers—despite the elites' intensified efforts to crush archaic cultural features that had for centuries survived in the hearts of these Christianized masses."[1] Regarding the religion of everyday believers, de Mello e Souza notes, "This religiosity was imbued with magic belief, more inclined to images than to what they represented, to external aspects more than to the spiritual."[2] Trent would truly be felt only in the eighteenth century. She argues, however, that this inclination for images and processions was not necessarily Iberian (Spanish and Portuguese), but in fact European. The regulation of individual rituals and devotions that Trent instituted was not in place when Catholicism sailed across the Atlantic.

However, this regulation was not an outright rejection of popular devotions. As highlighted by Anthony Stevens-Arroyo, "The council did not wish to accept the Protestant rejection of devotion to Mary and the saints, but it instituted a set of reforms that were designed to control excesses. . . . Local devotions had to be approved before they could share the benefits of indulgences, and theologically correct prayers had to be composed with ecclesiastical approbation."[3] Local public devotions were transformed into private devotionalisms. There was a movement to control the religion at the popular level that was not characteristic of Spanish and Portuguese colonial Catholicism in the Americas. Regional devotions were not exclusively the devotions of the poor. The medieval Spanish historian William Christian argues that class was not a factor in terms of local religion; both rich and poor shared these devotions, though they differed in style. "In the villages, towns, and cities of Central Spain (and, I suspect, in most other nuclear settlements of Catholic Europe) there were two levels of Catholicism—that of the Church Universal, based on the sacraments, the Roman liturgy, and the Roman calendar; and a local one based on particular sacred places, images, and relics, locally chosen patron saints, idiosyncratic ceremonies, and a unique calendar built up from the settlement's own sacred history."[4] It is important to note that this local religion did not represent a pure Catholicism but instead a Catholicism that had been mixed with folk religion. Too often the study of Latina/o Catholicism presents Catholicism as if it had been untouched

by other religious phenomena prior to its encounter with African and
Indigenous religions in the Americas. This is far from the case. The Catholicism that arrived in the Americas was one that had been thoroughly
influenced and shaped by other European and African religious worldviews. This influence would materialize in the folk religion of the
Americas.

MAL DE OJO

"Byron Manuel has evil eye." My mother-in-law said this to me omi-
nously, studying my face intently for my reaction. I shrugged and answered, "So rub an egg over him." This was my standard response to
her spiritual assessments of my son's health. It was also not what I was
truly thinking. What I was thinking was that he was eleven months old
and teething. However, I had learned that such responses were not welcome in the Guatemalan community where I had been living for the past
two years. Most afflictions, even ones that had medical explanations, also
had spiritual causes.

By now I was an old pro at evil eye. My husband was diagnosed one
day by his mother. His stomach had been bugging him, and he was
listless. I suspected parasites, something that I had become quite familiar
with since I moved to Guatemala yet that natives had certain resistances
to. My diagnosis was rejected. My mother-in-law rubbed an egg on him,
chanting Catholic prayers and making the sign of the cross over his body.
This egg was then broken in a glass of water and placed under our bed
overnight as he slept. The yolk revealed in the morning that it was indeed evil eye. Another egg was rubbed over him and he was "cured."
The next day he woke up with a fever, vomiting. I sent a sample to the
lab, purchased antibiotics, and smugly informed my mother-in-law that
he indeed had parasites. My diagnosis and my smugness were not very
welcome.

I am perhaps giving a bit too antagonistic of an impression. I get along
fabulously with my mother-in-law, and for the most part welcome her
religious beliefs (what many scholars would call superstitions or folk religion) into our lives. I avoided drunk men and dogs having sex on the
streets (a frequent site in a poor town like San Lucas) when I was pregnant and when my son was an infant, for they were sure bearers of evil
eye. I usually remembered to tie the red ribbon with a scabbard on it

around Byron Manuel's wrist when we left the house, knowing if I didn't I would be chastised by all the women in my new family. When I would come home and find my mother-in-law or my husband's aunts looking at me with a tinge of guilt, I would not reprimand them for the inevitable egg I would find under my son's crib. However, they could sense that in spite of the fact that I was Cuban American and a scholar of religion that I did not take them 100 percent seriously.

Back to my son's evil eye. This evil eye is different, I am informed. My mother-in-law does not have the power to heal it. I must take Byron Manuel to a spiritual healer, a *curandera*, for three consecutive days to cure him. My husband, upon hearing this, tells me to go. He says that it is out of respect for his mother. However, I can tell he is worried. There are tales floating around town of children that died from evil eye, whose parents did not treat the affliction. Their mothers' skepticism killed them. I can tell my husband is wondering if my skepticism will harm our son. So I go. I am a good Cuban girl who has been raised to respect her elders, and frankly the religious scholar in me wants to see what is going to happen. An old woman rubs my son with herbs making the sign of the cross repeatedly over every inch of Byron Manuel's body. He does not writhe in agony as the curse is removed. In fact, it tickles him. This satchel of herbs is thrown in the fire and crackles loudly, signaling the presence of evil eye. The same ritual is repeated each day, and by the third day, I must admit, the crackling is much weaker.

Did my son have evil eye? I don't know. He did not seem any different to me after this ritual, but everyone is relieved and much more relaxed once it is completed. The threat of evil eye has been lifted from our family. I am not sure if it is the curandera or the tube of Baby Orajel that a friend brings me from the States that cures him. I do know that this is a ritual purification that is important for the community where I was living, my second home, and that I must respect it. I also know that whether or not he had evil eye, the family believed he did, and going to the curandera healed that. Evil eye is a widespread belief in this community, and its origins date back to Spanish folk religion. Children are most susceptible to evil eye, especially infants, which is why the custom in San Lucas Tolimán is that neither a newborn nor his mother should leave their home until forty days after childbirth. What are described as "hot" forces give evil eye, which is why drunken men, menstruating and pregnant women must be avoided, for one can transmit evil eye without knowing it.[5] One can also intentionally give evil eye, and this is usually due to envy. The symptoms of evil eye include vomiting, listlessness, irritability, and waking up suddenly throughout the night.[6] Within the realm of evil eye a distinction is not made between diseases of the body and other forms of misfortune.

The anthropologist Sheila Cosminsky has noted that one of the effects of the understanding of evil eye in Guatemala is that women's social roles are limited. Indeed the burden of protecting one's child falls exclusively on the mother. Cosminsky also points out that evil is used to explain the innocent suffering of children. Since most cases of evil eye are accidental, the giver is not to blame and the receiver is an innocent victim.[7] Studies of evil eye in San Lucas open up an important discussion for scholars of religion, namely the significance of the Spanish folk Catholicism and its impact on the Latin American worldview in contrast to the common institutional approach to Spanish Catholicism. I would also argue that studies of religious beliefs such as evil eye pose a methodological challenge to scholars who are forced to rethink the manner in which they approach the study of religion.

Widespread belief in evil eye is one of the markers of the religious landscape of San Lucas. Although scholars of evil eye recognize its global, historical, and religious foundation, studies of evil eye are often relegated to folkloric and psychological studies. However, this is a deeply spiritual belief that interweaves Roman Catholicism and folk religion. My interest in evil eye is twofold. First, contrary to many Latin American studies of religion that glorify the indigenous and/or African populations and their religious worldviews, within San Lucas evil has Ladino origins. Ladino is the name used in Guatemala to describe an individual who is racially mixed, comparable to how mestizo is used in other parts of Latin America and the United States.[8] Though perhaps not as glamorous as ancient Mayan secrets, these everyday Ladino practices have come to saturate the indigenous religious worldview as well. Therefore, one finds a moment when the folk religion of the elite transforms the religion of Mayans. This is not through the imposition of institutional Catholicism, the paradigm that is most often cited. Instead, it is found in the fertilization of Mayan religion by folk Ladino Catholicism. Mayans have adapted traditional Mayan folk medicine as part of the curing of evil eye, giving this expression of evil eye its own particular Guatemalan expression. The second dimension of *mal de ojo* within the San Lucas context is its religious framework. It is not an area for folk anthropologists and psychologists to explore; rather, the heavy saturation of Roman Catholic prayers and devotions mark the diagnosis and healing of evil eye. Thus, belief in evil eye is a religious belief in San Lucas, linked to the Spanish Catholicism that has become the dominant religious ethos of the community.

ESPIRITISMO

I have been invited to a séance. This invitation is extended at the end of every month. The group that gathers consists primarily of women from my husband's family: aunts, cousins, and of course my mother-in-law. They are extremely dedicated to their spiritual organization, as they describe it, and they are fiercely Catholic. On the last Sunday of every month two mediums arrive from Guatemala City. They read from the Bible and say Roman Catholic prayers; one of the mediums gives a sermon, and then each woman goes around the room describing her personal problems and struggles. The mediums then channel a spirit and address the personal needs of some of the women, and a general prophetic message is given. If someone in the family has recently died, that spirit is channeled. The group also asks the local priest for masses several times a year, and he, knowing very well what they are about, honors their requests. Spiritual healing is a vital part of this community, and if someone in the family is ill, the mediums are contacted and the spirit of a doctor is sent to heal the individual.

I never attended the séances. Part of it was practical. My husband worked most Sundays, and with all the women in the family at the same séance there was no one to watch my son. I also felt that I would be intruding. I did not want my skepticism to be noticed and disrupt the dynamic of the group. I must admit I am uncomfortable with that type of personal disclosure in public. I also must admit that I was scared. I had many ghosts in my past, some of which I was not ready to confront in a séance. Though I did not attend a séance, I was spiritually healed on several occasions. Because I am not from Guatemala any illness I contracted was a worry for the family, since my fragile North American disposition made me prime for serious illnesses. So, if things were looking in any way serious, the mediums were contacted, and we were informed a spirit would come heal me during the night. The time was very specific, so I would have to make sure to be asleep, for one is always healed in their sleep by a spiritual doctor. My father-in-law once made the mistake of waking up when a spiritual doctor was healing his bladder infection, and the fuzzy figure of a man dressed in white with his hand inside of his hip startled him when he opened his eyes. The disapproving glare the "doctor" gave him made him quickly shut them. You have to leave a candle and a glass of water at your bedside for the doctor and cover your body in a white sheet. I remember one night lying awake, terrified I would not fall asleep before the doctor arrived. Each time I was healed I awoke the next morning feeling much better and sometimes cured. Psychological persuasion? A good night's rest? Or did the spirit of a doctor place his healing hands upon me? To this day I do not know.

Though not exactly a religion per se, Espiritismo is one of the most distinctive dimensions of Latin American religion. Espiritismo is best described as a religious metaphysics or worldview. The story of Espiritismo and its arrival in the Americas is a fascinating tale of the belief systems of a highly educated European elite transforming the religious landscape of the population as a whole. Espiritistas believe that there is a spirit world that interacts with the material world. Spirits exist in a hierarchy: The lower spirits remain attached to the material world, are ignorant, and try to do harm to human beings; the highest level of spirits are called *espíritus de luz* (spirits of light) and protect us, given their higher state of spiritual perfection. Espiritismo embraces a dualistic model of humanity where we consist of a body and spirit, though our essence is located in our spirit. After death we move on to another plane, yet our spirits still have the ability to morally and spiritually develop. Espiritistas also believe in reincarnation and the notion that actions in our past lives shape our present one. Spirits also have the ability to control us human beings, sometimes in a negative fashion. As noted by Mario A. Núñez Molina, "The influence of these ignorant spirits can also produce physical disturbances, ranging from headaches to major illness. Every person is born with a guiding spirit who protects him or her from the influence of ignorant spirits."[9] The material world in which we are living has a direct relationship with the spiritual plane. Spirits interact, communicate, and influence us. Caribbean Espiritismo has its roots in France, where the writings of a French educator became a critical alternative for Latin Americans studying in Europe and disenchanted with the Roman Catholic Church.

Espiritismo (spiritism) is one of the most widespread and least analyzed dimensions of Latin American religion. Studies that do exist often emphasize its Cuban and Puerto Rican manifestations, ignoring its prevalence in Central and South American contexts. Espiritismo was founded by Hippolyte Rivail (1804–1869), a French engineer who wrote under the pseudonym Allan Kardec.[10] A mix of Christianity, scientism, and personal mysticism, Espiritismo in its origins is best understood more as a philosophy than a religion. Throughout Latin America it initially attracted middle-class Catholics who were disenchanted with the ecclesial hierarchy and the rigidity of Catholic morality, while also open to new spiritualities. The church's association with Spanish colonial rule in the wake of colonial independence struggles furthered this alienation. Among Espiritista practices is communication with the dead. As Espiritismo spread throughout Latin America, so did its class base and expressions. Healing was emphasized, and in rural areas Espiritismo mixed with folk Catholicism. This is therefore yet another example of a European folk religious worldview that has become predominant throughout Latin American cultures. Whereas its founders saw it as a complementary system to Catholicism, it has been condemned by the church as heretical. Espiritistas today understand their beliefs and practices as parallel to and not in contradiction with Catholicism.

Though Espiritismo began in Puerto Rico and Cuba as a middle-class, intellectual movement that emphasized its philosophical and social framework, among the lower economic classes the healing dimension of Espiritismo was its greatest appeal. "They syncretized Espiritismo with popular Catholicism, *curanderismo*, herbal medicine, and other healing practices derived from Arawak and African heritages."[11] The expressions of Espiritismo in Latin America and the Caribbean take on their own characteristics as they encounter the diversity of folk religious practices in their localized contexts. The emphasis on healing is in sharp contrast to traditional Kardecan Spiritism. Kardec was wary of any reference to healing as any sort of miracle, instead emphasizing the morality of the healer. While Kardecan spiritism lays the foundation for Latin American

Espiritismo, in Latin America it remained an intellectual religiophilo-
sophical system for the urban elites, whereas the masses of rural Latin
Americans mixed Kardec's beliefs, folk Catholicism, traditional Indigenous and African healing practices, and African Diaspora religions.

SANTERÍA

I am sitting in a room full of *santeros/as* (Santería practitioners) who are
engaged in a heated debate. A panel of priestesses to the *orisha* Oshun
sits before us. They have all described their experiences of their orisha,
what she means to them, and how she is an active divine force in their
lives. This panel is part of a monthly gathering organized by the Diaspora
Cultural Center in Miami, an organization that seeks to undermine negative stereotypes about Afro-Cuban religions in Miami. The founder of
this center, Miguel "Willie" Ramos, watches the panel unfold from the
audience.

The debate is not about Oshun per se. All have agreed on her attributes, her strength, and her significance. However, the conversation
moved into her association with La Caridad del Cobre (Our Lady of
Charity), the patron saint of Cuba. And here the debate began. *La Regla
de Ocha*, popularly known as Santería, is an Afro-Cuban religion geographically associated with the West African Yoruba people that during
the slave era in Cuba came to be known as the Lucumí people. The
term "Lucumí," while very significant for understanding slave identity,
religion, and culture in Cuba, is in fact a construction that does not exist
in Africa.[12] The majority of slaves imported in the second half of the
nineteenth century were Yoruba. Santería is a mix of Yoruba religion,
Catholicism and Kardecan Espiritismo. It is the incorporation of Catholicism into this African religious tradition that sparked the heated debate
that I observed.

The supreme being of Yoruba religion is Olodumare, who is the cre-
ator and sustainer of the universe. "He is master of the skies, owner of
the universe, and the owner of character (*oluiwa*). Yet, he is manifest in
the world through *asè* (divine energy) and the collection of this energy
in the form of the *orisà*—the deities who interact with human beings."[13]
Olodumare is detached from human beings, having no places of worship
and no priesthood devoted to this being. Olodumare is never given
human attributes and is never represented in images. In order to have a

relationship with humanity, Olodumare created the orishas. Orishas can be most simply defined as superhuman beings or spirits.[14] They are beings that are worshipped, with shrines and a priesthood. Ultimately they are the expression of Olodumare in this world. They are anthropomorphic manifestations of various dimensions of the natural world and expressions of particularities of the human character.

In the colonial *cabildo* system, slaves worshipped the orishas behind the images of Catholic saints. Cabildos were mutual aid societies that existed in the Americas. For our purposes the cabildos that were associations of Africans (men and women) from the same tribe in a city, a representative body of a particular nation, are significant. They were social societies and were very active on religious feast days.[15] Cabildos played a central role in the preservation of African culture, religion, and identity. It was in cabildos that the practice of ritually hiding one's African beliefs behind Roman Catholic iconography began. Slaves, in order to continue practicing their traditional African religions, began to mask their beliefs behind Roman Catholic images, most often saints and images of Mary. This was a strategy for continuing to practice Yoruban religion while seeming to be Catholic. Every orisha in the Santería pantheon, therefore, has a Roman Catholic figure associated with him or her. The saints are not to be cosmologically confused with the orishas, though over the years they have come to be integrated with the saints.

And so the debate began. Though often reduced to merely a fertility or river goddess, Oshun is a powerful deity in the orisha pantheon and intimately linked to the destiny of humanity. She is connected to the act of divination and the creation of this world. For several in the room, the association of Oshun with La Caridad is pure iconographical, a vestige of the past, and should be removed. After all, they argued, slavery is over, and practitioners of Santería no longer have to hide their religious beliefs behind Catholic masks. For others, however, La Caridad has become a concrete expression of Oshun. Echoing the sentiments I heard that evening in Hialeah, Joseph M. Murphy proposes the thesis that La Caridad del Cobre is a manifestation of Oshun for the Cuban people. She became a way of understanding Oshun. "La Caridad del Cobre is a 'way' that Òsun is present to Cubans who come from an array of social, economic, and racial groups. A mask reveals as much as it conceals, and it is this dynamic simultaneity of inner and outer, African and Catholic, black and white, that informs my interpretation of Òsun's reflection as La Caridad del Cobre."[16] The Catholic saints hid the African gods, yet they also revealed something meaningful. La Caridad was not merely a mask of Oshun; she was simultaneously being venerated with Oshun. In other words, La Caridad had religious value for the Yoruba, she was not merely a disguise, and this religious value was intimately linked with Oshun. Through the image of La Caridad del Cobre, the island's entire population could venerate Oshun. For the Yoruba, they are empowered by their knowledge of the fullness of the Caridad/Oshun image, for they are aware that she is much more than what she seems to the broader population. La Caridad, in their eyes, becomes a manifestation of Oshun while not losing her identity as the Mother of God. The Yoruba belief in the multiplicity of the deity's identity allows for this fusion that maintains the individuality of La Caridad's and Oshun's identities.

The discussion moves from Oshun and La Caridad to the presence of Catholicism as a whole in the religion. There is much debate about the manner in which Catholicism has shaped or influenced Santería. Even though it is no longer required, Santería practitioners are often baptized. The Catholic calendar of saints is used as the liturgical calendar to celebrate particular orishas (so Oshun's feast day is La Caridad's feast day) and there is a required visit to a church immediately after initiation. One cannot deny the current presence of Catholic imagery or the historical role Catholicism has taken in the preservation of Yoruba religion. What is debatable is the theological value of Catholicism within present-day Santería. Even the myths or *patakis* of the Yoruba were transformed in Cuba. They became acculturated and acclimated to the Cuban context. So, for example, in Africa the orisha Oshun washes her clothes in a river and in Cuba she washes them in a tub.[17] One Oshun priestess proudly declares that she attends mass every Sunday, and if for some reason she can't make it physically, she always watches it on television. Santería has adopted some of the language of Catholicism. Yoruba religion in Africa is based on the family. In Cuba, this familial religion becomes transformed, and practitioners adopt the Catholic system of godparenting and gather under particular priests or priestesses. The priest or priestess who initiates you into the religion is known as your godparent.[18] The conversation that evening is never resolved, with one side of the room demanding the return to a more "authentic" African religion entirely divorced from Catholicism and the other half of the room arguing that the incorporation of Catholic elements is what makes this religion Santería, a Cuban religion grounded in but distinct from African Yoruba religion.

Fundamental to Yoruba beliefs is the presence of *ashé*. "*Ashé* is the animating force that moves both earth and cosmos. It can be found in a plant, an animal, a stone, a body of water, a hill, the heavens, the stars. But *ashé* is also present in human beings, and can be manifested through bodily actions, but is especially active in words (*afud'ashé*)."[19] Within Yoruba religion the barriers between the natural and the supernatural worlds do not exist. Ashé saturates all aspects of this material world, including plant, animal, and inanimate materials of this earth. Plants contain ashé and are used ritualistically. Initiates also receive ashé when they are possessed by their orisha. Ashé is fundamental to the manner in which santero/as view the cosmos and plays a primary role in Santería rituals, a primary one being divination. Possession by one's orisha, a religious ritual every initiate participates in, is a fundamental manner of communing with one's orisha. These possessions take place within the boundaries of ritual. Possession also allows the orishas to commune with the natural world. *Ebó*, or sacrifice, is the primary means of communicating between the supernatural and natural worlds and a means of honoring a particular orisha. "*Ebo eye* entails the offering of an animal to a deity in exchange for the orisha's protection or involvement in the affairs of the living. Worshipers consider the sacrifice of an animal as the most intimate contact between the spheres of the sacred and the profane. It is a communion, the establishment of a bond between worshiper and deity that serves as a medium of exchange."[20] Animal sacrifice is not only essential or the orisha's presence in this world, but also the community's relationship with the orishas.

DECENTERING LATINA/O CATHOLIC EPISTEMOLOGY

A common thread shared by the three religious traditions examined in this essay is their appropriation of Catholic elements into their rituals. Curing evil eye involves the chanting of Catholic prayers and making the sign of the cross. Espiritismo draws from Catholic ritual life as well. Santería also incorporates elements of Catholic symbolism, ritual, and prayers. However, the three are not accepted by the official Catholic Church. In this concluding section I examine the particularity of the three and the manner in which they exist in a tense relationship as insiders/ outsiders in relation to Catholicism. I approach this through their episte-mological implications for Latina/o theology, which remains very Chris-tian in its focus. A serious consideration of the three would expand the ways in which Latina/o theology constructs theological knowledge.

The particularity of evil eye in certain Latin American contexts is found in its assumption that individuals (and in some cases animals) are able to harm or curse others, often unknowingly, and that in some cases evil eye can be cured by an ordinary individual, and in extreme cases curanderas are needed. In this worldview the victims are most often children. Interestingly, at least in the Guatemalan setting, anyone can give evil eye, and it is often not intentional. This is a worldview where negative energy can be transmitted from one to another, and unknow-ingly one can cause ill to the innocent. This ill will manifests itself physi-cally. It is through physical maladies that evil eye is diagnosed. This does not mean that all ailments are attributed to evil eye. People go to doctors; however, when illness is deemed a result of evil eye, only faith healing is effective. The diagnosis of evil eye is through an egg that is rubbed on the body. It is through an everyday object that knowledge of the affliction is attained. Similarly, the healing of evil eye is through either an egg or satchel of herbs that is rubbed over the body or though drinking an herbal remedy. The whole diagnosis and treatment of evil eye is there-fore through everyday herbal medicine. The combination of *curanderismo* (faith healing) and Roman Catholic belief reveals a point of tension within Latina/o Catholicism. Though well aware of the church's de-nouncement and rejection of such faith healing, Latina/o Catholics con-tinue to engage in this activity. The curandero is said to have the *don* (gift) of healing. That gift is sacred. As Luis León has thoughtfully high-lighted, for many who visit a curandera/o, the contradiction with Ca-tholicism is not an issue.[21] This tolerance for contradictions reveals a religious worldview that is grounded in Catholicism but incorporates other knowledge and rituals of the sacred with ease.

Perhaps the greatest epistemological hallmark of Espiritismo is the be-lief in communication with the dead. This is not to be confused with the Catholic belief in the value of prayers for the dead (and the efficacy of indulgences). To pray for the dead is not to communicate with the dead. Communication with the dead is seen as un-Christian.[22] In Espiritismo communication with the dead is fundamental. Not only do the dead you know speak to you through mediums, but certain dead have healing powers. The dead are an active force of knowledge, advice, and participants in the community of the living. Within certain Espiritista circles the medium serves as the vessel for the dead's communication. This often appears very similar to spirit possession, in which the medium is taken over by the spirit of the dead. During this time consultations and advice can be given, healing rituals can occur, and future events can even be predicted. A community often gathers in these settings. Again, although these rituals go against official Roman Catholic teachings, many Latinas/os inhabit both the world of Catholicism and the world of the spirits without feeling conflicted.

Espiritistas and those who believe in evil eye share the fact that they often consider themselves institutional Catholics despite the fact that their rituals and beliefs go against the grain of institutional Catholicism. They do not see their rituals as problematic though the institutional church readily does. This ambiguity, while given a cursory mention in the writings of Latina/o theologians, needs a more systematic approach. It is quite easy for Latina/o theologians to describe and acknowledge beliefs and practices that are institutionally rejected by the Catholic Church, but those who are claiming a Catholic theological voice must respond with more than a respectful nod. Latina/o theologians will remain limited in their ability to describe Latina/o Catholic religious worldviews if they narrow their focus exclusively to Catholicism. Similarly, both Espiritismo and evil eye challenge Latina/o theologians' sources of theological knowledge through their everyday approach to matters of faith and the presence of the "supernatural" through spirit possession and communication. This encounter of Catholicism, the importance of ancestors, and non-Christian worldviews is also concretely revealed in the Day of the Dead.

The Mexican American celebration of the Day of the Dead is a classic example of the importance of family and ancestors for Latinas/os. The Day of the Dead is usually celebrated on November 1, though in some contexts it is celebrated on November 2 as well. The Day of the Dead has both Aztec and Roman Catholic roots. The Aztec contribution is marked by the presence of food, music, dance, and gravesite visits. Aztecs also understood the dead and their ancestors as intercessors between the living and the realm of the supernatural. From the Roman Catholic side comes the tradition of Masses for the dead; the tradition of bringing flowers and food to cemetery visits; the celebration of All Saints and All Souls days; and the belief in the Communion of Saints. Lara Medina and Gilbert R. Cadena have studied the Day of the Dead celebrations in Los Angeles, and they note that many of the rituals and objects used in the Day of the Dead celebrations have medieval Catholic roots.[23] These include Masses for the dead, flower and food offerings, skull images, and the tradition of baking bread on All Souls Day. On the Day of the Dead families often spend the evening at the graves of their deceased relatives, bringing them their favorite foods and drinks. This is a manner of honoring the dead and remaining in communion with them. The bringing of favorite food and drinks to one's deceased family members is a way to affirm their continued presence within the family. Though they have passed away, they are still alive to the families and active participants in the construction of family identity.

The Day of the Dead also reveals a worldview that emphasizes the interconnectedness of life and death. The dead are not gone and departed, they continue to be a part of the present. On the Day of the Dead we remember our ancestors. In a community such as the Mexican American community in the United States, one whose culture is constantly threatened by the dominant U.S. ethos of assimilation, celebration of this Day, and remembering who you are and where you come from is a political and subversive act. For Mexican Americans, the Day of the Dead also raises interesting questions about the relationship between popular religion and official religion. It represents an event in which the church is involved but not in charge. Catholics and non-Catholics celebrate side by side. Many of the activities surrounding the Day of the Dead involve families, with children, parents, and grandparents working together. Women play a prominent role in these activities, especially in the preparation of the *ofrenda* (altar piece) at the Roman Catholic Church. The skills of the parish altar makers are passed down from mother to daughter, woman to woman. The work they contribute to the church's celebration is a source of pride. The Day of the Dead celebration incorporates not only the traditional Mass, processions, and gravesite visits, but also poetry, art, and dance.

Although an entirely different religious tradition from Catholicism, Santería shares the ritual of spirit possession and is also heavily influenced by Espiritismo. One may ask where Santería fits into this picture, since it is a religion with elements of Catholicism, though in no way claims to be Catholic. Nonetheless, the incorporation of Catholic sacraments into Santería rituals (i.e., baptism before initiation) makes this religious tradition a concern for Catholic theologians, particularly those studying Caribbean populations. Also, there are practitioners of Santería who equally claim a Roman Catholic identity. The impact on Santería for Catholic theological epistemology is twofold. First, this poses a methodological question regarding where the line is drawn for the subject matter of Catholic theology, especially when other religious traditions are incorporating elements of its sacramental life. Second, the rituals of spirit possession and animal sacrifice, while not practiced by nonmembers of Santería, are part of the cultural framework of Caribbean Catholicism. In other words, there are Catholic Latinas/os who may not practice these rituals but see them as efficacious. There are even those who dabble in African Diaspora religions.

The hybridity of Latina/o religion is expressed in the mestizaje and mulatez that characterize the Latina/o condition. Within Ada María Isasi-Díaz's scholarship, these terms function at various levels: as descriptors of the Latina/o condition, ethical standpoints, and epistemological categories. Mestizaje and mulatez are a theological locus of her mujerista theology and function as a hermeneutical tool and paradigm that reveal the nature of Latina/o epistemology.[24] They contribute to a new understanding of plurality, diversity, and difference. For Isasi-Díaz, mestizaje and mulatez are both descriptors of the Latinas/os' cultural condition and an explicit decision by Latinas/os to embrace an identity within the dominant U.S. paradigm. However, the role of normativity must be added to this discussion in the light of Catholic theology. What does this mean for the religious worldview, or, to put it more concretely, epistemological horizon, of Caribbean Latinas/os? Can Latina/o theology authentically describe Latina/o religion broadly and Latina/o Catholicism specifically without considering these traditions? What does it mean to believe that you can communicate with the dead, become possessed, and inflict physical harm on others spiritually? As Roman Catholic theologians that take the faith of Latina/o communities as the foundation

and starting point of their theologies, Latina/o theologians are in a difficult position when the normativity that exists within their communities
is in tension with official Catholic theology. Underlying this tension is
the role of the Latina/o theologian as intellectual elite and his or her
relationship with the masses of theologians, the Latina/o community in
its diversity, that also make critical claims about their faith through their
ritual life. Indeed, unlike the heavily written tradition of ecclesial Christianity and academic theology, the popular Catholicism of Latinas/os is
transmitted primarily ritually and orally. Thus ritual, not text, becomes
revelatory of Latina/o popular Catholicism's underlying epistemology.
Similarly, belief in evil eye, Espiritismo, and Santería do not have the
written traditions that Christianity, Judaism, and Islam share.

Epistemology plays a foundational role in the manner in which theology constructs knowledge and in deciding which sources of knowledge
are authentic. The religious practices outlined in this essay inform the
ethos of Latina/o religion as a whole. They are part of, whether officially
sanctioned or not, the Latina/o Catholic imagination. Their presence
poses some serious methodological challenges to Latina/o theology.
First, Latina/o theologians must determine their stance on the incorporation of non-Catholic elements into Latina/o Catholicism. It is one thing
to acknowledge their presence, but as Roman Catholic theologians, what
is their position on the theological value of these cross-fertilizations? Will
Latina/o theologians condemn Latinas/os who include non-Catholic elements in their everyday Catholic practices and worldviews or will they
go against the official teachings of the church? Can the Latina/o Catholic
epistemology constructed by Latina/o theologians remain true to both
Latinas/os and the official church? Second, Latina/o theologians must
broaden their sources to better understand the religious worldviews of
their communities and how they shape Latina/o Catholicism. In the area
of Afro-Cuban religion, perhaps no theologian has offered a greater contribution on this theme than Orlando O. Espín.[25] Espín's scholarship on
Afro-Latin religions is a vital contribution to this conversation. In his own
research he has taken seriously how Afro-Cuban religions in particular
are fundamental for understanding the Latina/o Caribbean Catholic
ethos. A third methodological challenge is the product of the first two,
namely, in approaching these non-Catholic religious traditions, will Lat-
ina/o theologians dare say Latina/o Catholicism can benefit from the

knowledge gleaned from these other religious worldviews? Linked to this is the question of how the truth claims of non-Christian religions will affect Latina/o theology as a whole. What criteria will be used to assess these non-Christian beliefs and practices? Many Latina/o Catholics clearly feel, for example, that the close connection one can have with the dead through communication and an active relationship with their departed loved ones is vital to their spirituality. Similarly, the sense of active participation with the sacred that one finds in Santería rituals and through ritual faith healing is vital for many Latinas/os. Many of the non-Christian religious practices I outlined above are shaped by a Christian epistemological ethos yet also introduce other elements into Latina/o epistemology. Finally these traditions challenge Latina/o theologians to expand their focus to incorporate Latin American and Caribbean Catholicism. Not only is it here that we find the roots of Latina/o Catholicism, but also with our contemporary globalized world and the fluidity of immigration, we cannot limit ourselves to the U.S. context.

Whether it is described as popular religion, lived religion, folk religion, or vernacular religion, the everyday religious practices of Latina/o Catholics stretch beyond the confines of official doctrinal Catholicism. Latina/o Catholics are a product of the hybridity of cultures, races, and religions that constitute them as a people. It would be naive to think that this will not have an impact on their spirituality. Interestingly, some of the practices outlined in this essay are not new to Christianity; for example, belief in the evil eye was part of the Mediterranean world in which Christianity first flourished.[26] We must therefore learn from our history as we address contemporary theological questions. In a sense the Latina/o theologian is trapped at a crossroads between the intellectual tradition that informs the academic discipline of theology and the Latina/o popular Catholicism that has evolved independently of that academic discourse. The frustration of the Latina/o theologian is to attempt to use the discourse and tradition of the academy while remaining true to the beliefs and practices of Latinas/os. Latina/o theologians, I suspect, will never be able to fully respond to this challenge, yet must always keep it at the forefront of their work. The difficulty that I pose to Latina/o Catholic theologians is how they will concretely learn from and respond to the "faith of the people" when that faith is in contradiction with "the faith of the official Church and the academy."

❧ "Racism is not intellectual": Interracial Friendship, Multicultural Literature, and Decolonizing Epistemologies

PAULA M. L. MOYA

Racism is not intellectual.
I cannot reason these scars away.
—LORNA DEE CERVANTES

In a searingly powerful poem that serves as the fulcrum of her award-winning first book of poetry, *Emplumada*,[1] the Chicana poet Lorna Dee Cervantes responds to a young, white male acquaintance who has charged her with being altogether too concerned with the existence of racial discord.[2] Over the course of "Poem for the Young White Man Who Asked Me How I, an Intelligent, Well-Read Person Could Believe in the War Between Races," Cervantes attempts to explain to her interlocutor why she has been unable to transcend the emotional predispositions and structures of feeling that have mediated her race-conscious perspective on their shared social world. Hers is a perspective, she contends, that has its roots in the emotionally toxic fallout of her everyday experiences of racism: the schoolyard experiences that have left her with an " 'excuse me' tongue, and [the] / nagging preoccupation with the feeling of not being good enough"; the "slaps on the face" that her daily experiences of racism bring to her; the powerful enmity she feels from the "real enemy" outside her door who "hates [her]."[3] In response to the young man's implied argument that any perspective that participates in the logic of race-consciousness is the result of error-prone beliefs that can and should be eradicated through education, Cervantes insists that the accusation he has leveled at her cannot be adequately answered within the terms he has set forth: "Racism," she tells him, "is not intellectual. / I can not reason these scars away."[4]

Cervantes' assertion that racism is both imbued with emotion and resistant to pure reason has found resonance in the work of several philosophers. For example, in a paper he gave at a 2001 conference titled "Passions of the Color Line," Michael Stocker argues against the philosophical view that emotions only involve or arise from beliefs. Such an account, he explains, "undergirds the hopeful view that racism or at least the emotions of racism could be eliminated by changing the beliefs giving rise to those emotions."[5] Stocker makes his argument by drawing on the work of Sartre to trace out the intractability of feelings of loathing and contempt among anti-Semites who are confronted with evidence that logically contradicts the rationalizations they construct to justify their feelings. He then demonstrates the futility of trying to change beliefs without attending to the emotions they are inextricably bound up with.

It would not be enough that anti-Semites come to see that a particular act by a particular Jew is an everyday, ordinary act, or is even a fine act. That thought must be integrated into, and seen to conflict with, their anti-Semitism. And further, *this conflict must matter to them.* It cannot be seen just as a puzzling anomaly, of the sort that besets many, if not most, theories and generalizations. Nor can it be defended against in ways that stop it from mattering to them or moving them. They must be—and this means that almost certainly they must make themselves be—emotionally available and open to that thought and (what I see as) its obvious implications.[6]

Stocker's point bears repeating: If the anti-Semite is not, at a profound level, emotionally moved or bothered by the contradiction between what she observes and what she "knows," she need not make adjustments to her way of thinking. Even if she acknowledges that the act she has observed is a "fine act," she can interpret it as an anomaly—as the proverbial exception to the general rule. As such, she can incorporate the act into her consciousness without having her anti-Semitic beliefs challenged in the least. Her emotional involvement is thus a prerequisite to overcoming her logically unfounded views about Jews.

The philosophers Eduardo Mendieta and William Wilkerson similarly reject the rigid distinction between thought and emotion. In his contribution to the "Passions of the Color Line" conference, Mendieta prefaces his analysis of exoticization as a technology of the racist self, with an argument against the view that sees a bifurcation between mind and body. He observes that "the parceling between emotions and ideas, or between emotive responses and cognition, is but a manifestation of a [by now discredited] technology of the self, which dictates that we have to attribute to our biological natures an element of unpredictability and animalistic connotation, and to our cognitive and mental capacities a calculative, predictive nature."[7] Such a technology of the self, Mendieta reminds us, has arisen as a result of a historically contingent (specifically Cartesian) regime of subjection that fails to account for the way in which emotions are both cognitive and evaluative. Contra this view, Mendieta sees emotions as epistemically valuable. Emotions, he explains, "place us in particular relationships to the world, which is made up of things as well as other selves." Insofar as emotions help us to make sense of others and ourselves they serve as crucial hermeneutic devices—they "interpret the world for us."

Similarly, in a compelling essay about the experience of "coming out" as gay or lesbian, William Wilkerson presents some phenomenological considerations about experience that suggest thought and emotion are necessarily bound up with one another.[8] Drawing on the work of philosophers in both the analytic and continental traditions, Wilkerson argues that emotions are more than simply decorations or distractions to our thoughts.

[O]ur moods and emotional states are not merely an extra feeling laid over our ordinary thoughts and behaviors; they are part of a horizon that actually changes and molds our thoughts and behaviors, even as our behaviors and experience reinforce our emotions. If I am angry, my anger is not just a reaction to frustrating happenings or disappointed expectations. Rather, my anger has both a reactive and an anticipatory element. . . . When I am writing while angry and my pencil breaks, I may lash out in frustration, even though in a different mood I may simply get up and sharpen it and begin again. The experience is altered by the antecedent context of being angry, and being angry is not just an inner feeling but also a whole style of being in the world.[9]

Although Wilkerson chooses anger as the illustrative emotion in his example, his argument holds for all sorts of emotional states. Indeed, Wilkerson suggests that emotional states—as much as "taken-for-granted cultural meanings" and sedimented "habits of action and thought"— inevitably guide the initial direction that any interpretation may take by directing the interpreter's attention to some elements of the hermeneutic situation while obscuring others.[10]

One of Wilkerson's aims in the essay is to defend the realist contention (put forward by Satya Mohanty and myself, among others) that attending to one's own and others' emotions is a crucial part of those knowledge-generating projects that strive for a more objective and humane understanding of the social world.[11] Elsewhere, I have argued that although emotions are always experienced subjectively, the meanings they embody transcend the individuals who are doing the experiencing.[12] Insofar as people learn from others around them what are considered to be appropriate emotional reactions to specific social situations, emotions are at least partially conditioned by the particular social and historical contexts in which they emerge. In other words, emotions are mediated by the shared ideologies through which individuals construct their social identities. As such, emotions necessarily refer outward—beyond individuals—to historically and culturally specific sorts of social relations and economic arrangements.

Under the view I am articulating here, emotions are not merely subjective; they are not circumscribed within one body, nor do they have their origin in an individual psyche. Rather, they literally "embody" larger social meanings and entrenched social arrangements. Recent work in the field of social psychology now provides empirical evidence for this view. The social psychologist Jeannie Tsai and her colleagues have run a number of studies over the past decade showing the cultural causes and behavioral consequences of what is considered to be an "ideal affect," and the importance of cultural and situational factors for understanding the links between self and emotion.[13] Thus, through attending to the meanings and origins of our often inchoate feelings we can begin to discern the outlines of the social arrangements that sometimes constrain, and sometimes enable, our relational lives. It is in this way that emotions have crucial epistemic value.

I have spent the past few pages arguing for the inextricable link between thought, emotion, and motivation primarily because claims about race and racism that are made by people of color are often dismissed by others as based in emotion—and as therefore irrational and epistemically unjustified. In presenting a case for the necessary interconnectedness between what goes on in our hearts and in our minds, I hope to forestall an easy dismissal of the idea that interracial friendships and multicultural literature can contribute to the project of decolonizing epistemologies. Rather than suggesting that the race-conscious perspectives and claims of people of color are not based in emotion, I acknowledge that they often are—even as I insist that such perspectives and claims can be both rational and epistemically justified. Moreover, rather than "clouding the issue" or "derailing the conversation," emotions surrounding race and racism must be seen as precisely that which we seek to understand. Insofar as emotions are key to the replication of racism, a sustained examination of how emotions about race figure into human motivation must be fundamental to any attempt to move beyond the socioeconomic arrangements that sustain racial inequality and ideologies of racism.

As I use it in this essay, *racism* describes a complex of ideas, emotions, and practices having to do with the denigration, hatred, dispossession, and/or exploitation of people who are visually, and often culturally, different from oneself in a way that is understood to be innate, indelible, and unchangeable.[14] It expresses itself through multiple registers, including folk beliefs, laws, court decisions, institutional structures, and everyday habits of interaction. In the subjective realm, those who are subjected to the racism of others experience it as emotional pain, anger, and self-doubt. In the economic realm, victims of racism experience it as a lack of opportunity or the physical dispossession of personal or communal property. In either case, the harms caused by racism are long lasting and can be handed down over many generations. Children who grow up in racist environments imbibe social attitudes about race along with their mothers' milk, whereas children whose parents have been emotionally scarred by experiences of social denigration may inherit lifelong preoccupations with the "feeling of not being good enough."[15] On a psychosocial level, it can be difficult for the racist and her victim alike to transcend the psychological habits of racism learned in childhood. In addition, the significant economic advantages gained by the ancestors of many white Americans at a time when the forebears of most racial minorities could be (and often were) legally dispossessed of their lands and labor have not dissipated. Although some people of color have succeeded in substantially improving their economic status, the majority of them confront a systemic economic disadvantage relative to white Americans—a situation that has been, and continues to be, perpetuated across generations both through differential access to educational and employment opportunities and the ongoing effects of institutional and interpersonal racism.[16] Moreover, racial minorities have had to cope with this disadvantage in a society that (1) measures people's worth largely in terms of what kind of home they live in, what kind of car they drive, and what sort of school they attend, and that (2) assumes that what people have is what they—in some sort of moral sense—deserve. Given all this, it should not be surprising that the statements about race and racism made by people who have been victimized by racism are often thoroughly imbued with expressions of strong emotion—pain, regret, outrage, resentment. On the other hand, because many people who participate in racist practices do so unwittingly and unintentionally simply as a result of being part of a society that is organized according to race,[17] it should not be surprising that their reactions to the emotionally charged claims of their accusers frequently cover the spectrum from denial and defensiveness, through shame, to a self-righteous claiming of racial privilege. A necessary part of any antiracist project will thus be a consideration of the strong and varied emotions that are the warp and the woof of the fabric of racial relations in this country.

So if we cannot fight racism with facts, then how can we fight it? How might we go about the process of changing people's emotional horizons—which is clearly a part of what needs to happen if the problem of racism is to be ameliorated? Without suggesting that these are the only avenues to take, I propose two possible ways through which we might engage in a decolonial project with respect to race: (1) interracial friendships and (2) the teaching of multicultural literature.[18] In addition to thinking proactively about how to best fight racism, I hope to highlight the significant benefits of interracial friendships by showing that they can be particularly rich contexts for learning about the structural inequalities that accompany our racial formations. Moreover, I want to emphasize the value of multicultural literature by showing that literature written by and about people outside the cultural and economic mainstream of a given society can play a crucial role in shifting and expanding a reader's epistemic and emotional horizons.

INTERRACIAL FRIENDSHIP

In her book *What Are Friends For?*, feminist philosopher Marilyn Friedman makes a cogent and compelling argument for understanding the institution of friendship as providing important opportunities for moral growth. Building on the work of Carol Gilligan, as well as on the work of Gilligan's critics, Friedman explores the sort of profound moral growth that can result from a deep and sustained attention to the best interests of a person other than oneself. She takes as her paradigmatic case the relation of friendship and identifies several features of friendship that make it conducive to fostering moral growth.[19]

Although my own interests are directed less toward the potential that friendships hold for moral growth than toward the potential that interracial friendships hold for expanding and decolonizing people's epistemic and emotional horizons, I find Friedman's account useful for her insightful explication of the dynamics of a certain type of friendship. Rather than including in my discussion every sort of relationship across cultures to which some people may give the name of "friendship," I focus on the sorts of relationships that are predicated on a strong degree of voluntarism, mutuality, sharing, and trust—that is, the type of friendship described and identified by Aristotle in his *Nicomachean Ethics* as a "character friendship." In what follows, I both build on and depart from Friedman's account to examine the way that interracial friendships can contribute in significant ways to the changing of people's attitudes about race. I start by enumerating several features that are common to character friendships before returning to a consideration of specifically interracial friendships. I propose that the sharing of experiences about race and racism within interracial friendships that are predicated on a strong degree of voluntarism, mutuality, sharing, and trust can lead not only to emotional growth regarding the illogic and evils of racism but also to an increase in the two friends' shared understanding about the way race functions in our society to maintain current relations of power. Key to my argument is the contention that both the epistemic and emotional dimensions of interracial friendships are central to forging an effective decolonial antiracist project.

There are several features of character friendship that makes it particularly conducive to epistemic and emotional transformation. The first and perhaps most important characteristic is that it is a voluntary association. When we say that we are friends with someone, we usually mean at least these two things: (1) that we have *chosen* our friend because we feel affection for her and (2) that our friendship with her exists independently of biological or attributed kinship ties. This is not to say that one cannot be friends with a member of one's family—friendships among family members are both possible and frequent. Nevertheless, when one develops a friendship with a biological child or a sister-in-law, describing that relation as "friend" implies that there is a crucial sense in which the relationship transcends the kinship tie. Moreover, the voluntary nature of character friendship ensures that it is inherently self-regulating in the way that other sorts of relationships often are not. In general, economic, familial, and social considerations weigh much more heavily on marital, sibling, and parental relations than they do on friendship.[20] Indeed, because friendships exist with comparatively less institutional support than marriages and other familial structures, the relationship will survive only as long as both friends attend to it—at least intermittently. Once one person ceases absolutely to participate in the complex negotiations required to keep each attentive to the other, or begins to demand more from the relationship than the other is willing to provide, the friendship will founder or cease to exist. Indeed, the always-present threat of the friendship's dissolution discourages both coercion and taking one's friend for granted.

A natural consequence of the egalitarian nature of friendships is that friends who wish to maintain their relationship will be disposed to take an interest in and show respect for each other's perspectives—even when those perspectives differ from one's own. Accordingly, friends often come to understand each other as *particular others* who are related to, but not coincident with, the self. In other words, persons engaged in a character friendship are more likely than those engaged in other sorts of relationships (i.e., marital or parent-child relationships) to see each other with what the feminist philosopher Marilyn Frye calls a "Loving Eye."

According to Frye, seeing with a Loving Eye is a way of looking at an other that requires a certain kind of self-knowledge—that is, the "knowledge of the scope and boundary of the self." In particular, Frye explains, "it is a matter of being able to tell one's own interests from those of others and of knowing where one's self leaves off and another begins."[21] Because the loving eye does not confuse the other with the self, it "is one that pays a certain sort of attention." It is "the eye of one who knows that to know the seen, one must consult something other than one's own will and interests and fears and imagination. One must look at the thing. One must look and listen and check and question."[22] The "Loving Eye" thus exists on one end of a continuum at the other end of which is the "Arrogant Eye." In contrast to the "Loving Eye," Frye explains, the "Arrogant Eye" organizes everything—including the interests, desires, and needs of the other—with reference to himself and his own interests.[23]

The kind of emotional openness encapsulated by Frye in her concept of the Loving Eye is a necessary prerequisite to a third important aspect of friendship—the sharing of experiences and stories. Close friends frequently share stories about things that have happened to them and that bear for them some moral or epistemic significance. This activity of sharing stories is important not only because it provides an occasion for amusement and social bonding, but also because it provides an opportunity for friends to learn from each other. As one friend recounts an experience to the other, she necessarily interprets the meaning of the event she is relating. In the process, she draws on the cultural myths, social meanings, and bodies of knowledge that she has access to. She thus gives her friend access to an experience and an interpretive framework that may be unfamiliar (or even objectionable) to the friend. Friedman explains, "In friendship, our commitments to our friends, as such, afford us access to whole ranges of experience beyond our own. . . . Friendship enables us to come to know the experiences and perspectives of our friends *from their own points of view.*"[24] Moreover, because we care about the people with whom we form friendships, we are inclined "to *take our friends seriously* and to take seriously what our friends care about."[25] Taking a friend seriously may mean that we reconsider our own experiences, values, and interpretations in the light of the experiences, values, and interpretations of that friend. Alternatively, it may mean that we feel compelled to engage our friend in conversation—or even argue with or rebuke her—when she touches on a subject, such as race, about which we have strong feelings. In both cases, our response will be conditioned by the intensity and nature of our emotional investment—in the friend *and* in the issue under consideration.

This brings me to one of the most crucial aspects of a voluntary friendship—the fact that friends are likely to trust each other. As Friedman notes, friends are likely to have confidence that their friend will bear "reliable 'moral witness.' "[26] Indeed, it is when friends trust each other's epistemic capacity (and moral goodness) that the sharing of stories can help both parties expand their epistemic and emotional horizons. This is because a person who trusts her friend's judgment is less likely to dismiss outright an interpretation of a story provided by that friend that radically differs from one she herself might have come up with. The listener may be doubtful, and may initially treat the story or the interpretation with suspicion. However, because she risks losing an important relationship if she persists in being dismissive or contemptuous, she will be compelled to consider seriously, even for the purpose of arguing against, the interpretation that her friend has advanced. Just as "friends don't let friends drive drunk," the person who cares deeply about her friend's character and well-being is unlikely to simply ignore those viewpoints her friend holds that she finds deeply problematic.

The interactive process that occurs when friends share stories is enhanced when one friend, in the act of helping, is called upon to participate in the process of interpreting the meaning of the other's experience. It is a common practice for a person who is having some sort of trouble—in her marriage, at her job, with her children, with the law—to seek advice from a friend she trusts. Sometimes she needs material help, but often she needs help with comprehending and analyzing the dilemma she is facing. In such a situation, she shares with her friend the details of her quandary, advances a tentative interpretation, and then seeks amendments to her reading of the situation. When the circumstances are especially troubling—as in those cases where the worldviews or abstract moral values of either friend are challenged—the process of analysis will be protracted, interactive, and even conflictive. This interactive (and occasionally conflictive) process can amount to a "testing" of the viewpoints and abstract moral guidelines both hold. It should be noted that the emotional component of this process is absolutely key to its success.

Unless both friends feel an emotional stake in the outcome of the discussion, one or both might well retreat into a position of epistemic or moral relativism. The problem with a relativist position is that it discourages genuine involvement in the dispute and prevents the person who holds it from evaluating the different interpretations as better and worse, as more and less truthful. Only when both friends care about and respect each other enough to take the other seriously, and have sufficient confidence in the other's affection to risk pushing the other past her comfort zone, does this interactive process contribute to their collective epistemic and emotional growth.

I turn now to a consideration of the significance of specifically interracial friendships. In her account of the opportunities presented by friendships for promoting moral growth, Friedman acknowledges that the kind of deep-level moral growth she esteems is a potential that is not always realized. She notes that "the more alike friends are, the less likely they are to afford each other radically divergent moral perspectives in which to participate vicariously."[27] Friedman does not elaborate on this insight, nor does she extend her investigation into the realm of antiracist activism. However, to the extent that we are interested in understanding racism for the purpose of epistemic and emotional decolonization, it makes sense to do so.

To begin with, we should acknowledge that we rarely become close friends with people who are radically different in every way (in terms of race, class, gender, sexuality, age, political commitments, religious affiliation, etc.) from ourselves. This is partly because we make friends with people with whom we come into sustained contact; we find our friends at work, at play, in school, at church, or in our neighborhoods. Consequently, when we make friends with people who have been racialized differently from ourselves, usually they are like us in at least a few other salient ways. For example, when two people who work together become friends, it is generally because they are comparably situated in the hierarchy of their organization. They are likely to be comparably compensated and to have a similar standard of living. The two friends may share a commitment to their profession or company and value similar kinds of activities and material goods. The most salient difference between them, in such a case, might well be how they are situated in the U.S. racial hierarchy.

Because race matters considerably for people's life experiences and opportunities in American society, friends who are differentially situated in the U.S. racial hierarchy are more likely to have had different experiences in (and to possess different perspectives on) their shared world than those who are substantially similarly situated within the racial hierarchy.[28] In the case of two friends with different racial associations, the strong potential exists that one friend will eventually share with the other her interpretation of an event that her friend might either perceive quite differently or never have had the opportunity to experience personally. Depending on how they are each identified in terms of gender, class, and sexuality, their differing views regarding what is at stake or what is to be done in response to the event might be widely divergent. It is in the process of talking through their contrary perspectives, and in discovering what it is about their own *particular* lives that might have caused them to think and feel so differently, that they can begin to imagine another way to be in the world. Thus, it is often against this backdrop of sameness of other parts of their lives that two friends of different races have the opportunity to compare the difficulties and opportunities that come their way. Through such a process of comparison, they are in a good position to learn about the differential effects of race on people who are differentially situated within the racial order.

The opportunities for the production of knowledge about how race functions in our society are, I contend, especially rich in the case of two nonwhite friends who are of different racial or cultural backgrounds. As people who have been victimized by racism—as people who have been forced to respond in some way to numerous unfair and inaccurate assumptions about their mental and moral capacities—people of color are more likely than white people to be attuned to the multifarious dynamics of race. Not only have they had to grapple with the prejudice they encounter in their own lives, but—by virtue of their close proximity to family members, friends, and neighbors who share their racial group associations—they are likely to have been witness to a wide range of racist experiences particular to their own group. Furthermore, they are familiar with the incredible variety of strategies (humor, denial, self-segregation, racism directed toward members of other racial groups, armed resistance, self-affirmation, reverse racism, etc.) that people in their communities employ to counteract racism's painful and debilitating effects. As a result of their socially located experiences, nonwhite people have access to a virtual storehouse of emotionally charged pieces of information about race and racism—even if they never figure out how best to organize, interpret, synthesize, or process that information.

Furthermore, many people of color have developed what W. E. B. Du Bois termed a "double-consciousness"; they understand that there is more than one way of interpreting a racially charged situation. Insofar as people of color are accustomed to the disjuncture between their own interpretations of racial incidents and hegemonic or "commonsense" interpretations of those same events (think here of the initial media coverage of the 1992 L.A. uprising versus the subsequent interpretations provided by the people who were directly affected by it), they may in fact be more open than most white people are to the possibility that there are alternative valid perspectives about the issue of race. People of color are thus likely to make better interlocutors for each other when the subject is race and racism. And finally, because two nonwhite friends from different racial groups are differentially situated within the system of white supremacy, their mutual exposure to each other's situations can help them better understand *together* the overall dynamics of what is an incredibly complex system. To be sure, while blacks, Latinas/os, Asians, American Indians, and Arabs are all disadvantaged within the system of white supremacy, the system itself is sufficiently variegated that it affects each of these groups (and significant subgroups within them) differently.[29] For all these reasons, when a person of color shares her observations and feelings about race with a nonwhite friend associated with a different racial group, both friends are admirably positioned to begin the difficult process of analyzing together the complexity and perniciousness of racial formations in the United States.[30] Moreover, under some circumstances, the bond of friendship between two nonwhite friends can serve as a kind of microcosm for the sort of multigroup resistance that is necessary to address and confront the large-scale, institutionalized, and quite powerful ideologies of racism in this country.

Friendship between two people who are differently situated within the racial order thus enables a healthy and informing kind of particularizing of consciousness. When a friend you love and trust has a radically different reaction to a particular issue or event than you do, you are presented with the opportunity to realize that the view you hold on that issue is not the only—and perhaps not even the best—view to have. Indeed, friends who take each other's differences seriously are less inclined than those people whose values have never been profoundly challenged *by people they care about* to understand their way of thinking or being in the world as the "normal" or "right" way be. A healthy particularizing of consciousness—which I contend is a significant effect of interracial friendships that endure over time—is a key step in moving away from a positivist, and therefore false, conception of objectivity. As such, it is the first step toward a fallible and nondogmatic conception of how we can (collectively) better understand the world we live in. In the case of interracial friendships, a friend who understands that her way of interpreting a racial situation is only *one* way (and maybe not the best way) is well on her way toward achieving a more objective understanding of the complicated and ever-changing meanings attendant on the racial formation in the United States. Thus, a friendship between two people associated with different racial groups in a society like our own that is organized by race always holds at least the potential for expanding each friend's epistemic and emotional horizons.

THE DIALOGIC POTENTIAL OF MULTICULTURAL LITERATURE

In this section, I elaborate my claim that literature written by racial and cultural minorities can also play a crucial role in the expansion of people's epistemic and emotional horizons. Indeed, engagement with a literary work written by a racial other replicates some of the processes of an interracial friendship, but it has the advantage of being more flexible in space and time. My point is not to suggest that reading multicultural literature is necessarily more effective or important than fostering an interracial friendship. Rather, I want to suggest that reading and teaching novels by socially subordinated people can also play a significant role in the decolonization of hearts and minds.

My interest in this issue was sparked, in part, by an anecdote that Marilyn Friedman includes in her book. At a 1987 American Philosophical Association conference where she presented a version of her argument, David Solomon asked Friedman whether works of literature could inspire the same sort of moral transformation that she attributed to friendship. Her response was not to deny the possibility but to downplay it.[31] She explains: "The literary work may be more articulate than my friend, but I can talk to my friend and she can answer me in her own terms, directly responsive to what I say and what I ask her. By contrast, I may have to extract 'responses' from the fixed number of sentences in a literary work and I am limited to interpreting those responses in my own, possibly uncomprehending, terms."[32] Curiously, Friedman's account in this quote of how communication between friends works simplifies her own very interesting and complex account of the potential that friendship holds for moral growth. On one hand it implies an unconstrained and unending responsiveness on the part of the friend who is being questioned, and on the other it ignores the possibility that the questioner will be unable to hear her friend's responses (should they be forthcoming) in her friend's "own terms." Thus, Friedman inadvertently paints a picture of intersubjective communication that is too transparent, too immediate. In fact, communication between friends—particularly among those who are talking about something about which they hold differing views—can be very oblique or be conducted in fits and starts. If the matter at hand is an especially difficult one, if it seriously challenges one or the other of the pair, then it is quite likely that the listener will initially, and perhaps even repeatedly, hear her friend's responses in *her* own (as opposed to her *friend's* own) terms. Moreover, the listening friend's ability to "get it" may come years later, after the fact, in a moment of private contemplation and reinterpretation of what her friend was telling her so many years before.

I am not sure why Friedman feels the need to downplay literature as a source for moral transformation. Perhaps she felt unprepared to deal adequately with Solomon's question, or perhaps she interpreted it (unnecessarily, I believe) as a challenge to her argument. Whatever her rationale, Friedman's defensive response causes her to paint a static and ultimately inadequate picture of the experience of writing and reading fiction. She writes:

> Moreover, my friend's life continues to unfold in new directions that may surprise even her; while she lives, her life is still an open book whose chapters she does not wholly author as a mere self-confirmation of her own preexisting moral commitments. Thus, the lived experiences of friends have the potential for a kind of authenticity and spontaneity not available in novels, leaving only biography and autobiography as relevant analogues.[33]

With this explanation, Friedman inadvertently disparages the literariness of autobiographies and biographies, such as the way they are "plotted" by an author who selects and arranges certain biographical facts (but not others) of the life under consideration. More crucially for the present discussion, however, Friedman underestimates the complexity and semantic open-endedness of literary texts. Most importantly, she misunderstands how readers engage with works of literature that move them in profound ways. The scene of reading literature is rich in the potential for epistemic and emotional decolonization for at least the following three reasons: (1) Reading is a practice involving a person's intellectual and emotional engagement with a text; (2) reading expands a reader's horizon of possibility for experiential encounters; and (3) works of literature are heteroglossic textual mediations of complex social relations.

To begin with, a reader of a long, narrative work such as a novel will engage with it both intellectually and emotionally. In the process of reading, a reader is called upon to participate in an act of interpretation, to actively make sense of the narrative and of the characters that inhabit it. This interactive process is far more dialogic and open-ended than Friedman's description of the reader who must "extract 'responses' from the fixed number of sentences in a literary work" would imply. After all, if a reader is not sufficiently engaged by a novel, she will put it down and stop reading; she will decline the offer of friendship (or profit or amusement) that the narrative proposes to her and go her separate way.[34] If, however, she finds herself drawn into the novelistic world presented to her, her involvement will be both cognitive and emotive. The two processes necessarily go together—it is virtually impossible to follow a story line or remember the details of a novelistic setting without caring in some sort of positive or negative way about the characters whose adventures and dilemmas power the story line and provide fodder for the reader's ruminations about her own life.

Second, reading a novel can expand a reader's horizon of possibility for experiential encounters even further than the realm of friendship can. When a person reads a complex literary work of substantial length, the potential exists for her to engage in a kind of " 'world'-traveling" whereby she enters into another and (depending on who she is and what the book is about) possibly quite alien, world.[35] A reader who takes up a book about a world that is far from her own will be exposed to situations, feelings, attitudes, and characters (implied people) that she does not encounter in her everyday life. Moreover, because of their transportability through space and time, literary works allow a reader who lives in a racially segregated and economically stratified society like our own to be exposed to a variety of alternative perspectives that she might not otherwise be exposed to. Although some people do have friends from a wide variety of racial, cultural, and economic backgrounds, many more people associate only with those who are very similar to themselves. As Friedman admits, "Our choices of friends are indeed constrained, both by the limited range of our acquaintances and by the responses of others to us as we extend gestures of friendship toward them. Thus, friendship is voluntary only within the limits imposed by certain external constraints."[36] So, in the case of literature written by racial and cultural others, the effect can be that the reader is pulled in and given a kind of access to a way of conceptualizing the world that she might otherwise never be exposed to, even if she lives and works side-by-side with people of other races.

Moreover, in the case of a long, complex narrative such as a novel, the engagement a reader has with a text can be profound. It is true that a reader's engagement with a novel can be an encounter of the type that leaves her untouched and unmoved—but it need not be. The sort of engagement I am interested in here is the sort that causes a reader to question profoundly her basic understandings and attitudes. As with friendship, the potential for epistemic and emotional growth within the scene of reading will not always be realized—much depends on the quality of the reader's intellectual and emotional engagement with the novel and the "fit" between a particular reader and a particular text. A reader's engagement with a literary text can thus replicate the situation of voluntarism that one finds in friendships. This is because a reader has the power to control her exposure to materials that challenge her. She can take up books that are a good "fit" for her capacity for engagement and refuse those that are either too challenging or that fail to offer enough pleasure to keep her reading.

Central to an understanding of how and why literature holds out the potential for epistemic and emotional expansion is a proper appreciation for the semantic open-endedness of long, complex works of literature. Here I turn to the literary critic M. M. Bakhtin, who famously theorized the constitutive *heteroglossia* of the novel form.[37] According to Bakhtin, the "novel can be defined as a diversity of social speech types (sometimes even diversity of languages) and a diversity of individual voices, artistically organized."[38] It is the multivoicedness he describes in this definition of a novel—a multivoicedness that is accomplished artistically in any given novel through characters' dialogue, the authorial voice(s), and the incorporation of other genres such as letters, news articles, poems, and so on—all of which bring with them their own worldview—that Bakhtin refers to with the concept of heteroglossia. The constitutive heteroglossia of the novel's form is what ensures that any given novel will open out differently into the consciousnesses of its various readers. It is, moreover, what accounts for the fact that the same novel will open out differently within the consciousness of the same reader over time.

By insisting on its fundamental heterogeneity and multivoicedness, Bakhtin in no way suggests that the novel form lacks unity or artistry. He explains, "The novel orchestrates all its themes, the totality of the world of objects and ideas depicted and expressed in it, by means of the social diversity of speech types and by the differing individual voices that flourish under such conditions."[39] Through his use of the term "orchestrates," Bakhtin implicitly and helpfully imagines the novel as a kind of linguistic symphony in which a variety of speech types, discourses, literary styles, and incorporated genres are arranged into a stylistic unity. Insofar as we compare the novel to a symphony, we can imagine the various voices, discourses, and genres that together make up a given novel as so many different melodies, rhythms, and instruments that sound in concert to make up an orchestrated whole. And just as the different melodies, rhythms, and instruments resonate differently for the various listeners of a symphony—some of whom will focus on the melodic line; others of whom will listen hard for the bass undertones; and others who will feel a thrill of pleasure upon detecting the strains of an incorporated folk song with which they are familiar—so will the different elements of the novel resonate variously for diverse readers.

The concept of heteroglossia is thus helpful for understanding how and why a truly complex, multilanguaged, multiperspectival novel will change for a reader over time and will, in a nontrivial sense, be a different novel for different readers. This is not to suggest that any particular novel lacks its own intentionality or that its author does not have a meaning or message that she wants to convey and that we would do well as responsible readers to try to discern. Rather, the concept of heteroglossia shows why the meaning of a novel is not exhausted either by the author's intentional or by the logic of the novel's plotline. Insofar as meaning only ever comes into existence through the interpretive process, it can never be absolutely fixed. So, although on one level heteroglossia must be there *in* the text, on another level the disparate elements of that heteroglossia must be recognized and *actively interpreted* for meaning to come into being in the consciousness of the individual reader. A reader's experience of a novel will depend to a significant extent on her past experiences, her formal training, her cultural exposure, and the circumstances in which she reads the novel—all of which together form her interpretive horizon and condition her readerly practices and expectations.[40] And because people change—because they have additional experiences, sometimes receive more formal training, and occasionally expand or narrow their cultural horizons, their experience of a given novel will also change with subsequent rereadings. I have modified my interpretation of Toni Morrison's novel *Sula* several times as my attitudes about the dynamics of female friendship, the implications of marital infidelity, and the desire for security vis-à-vis self-exploration have altered over the years. I still love the novel; I still think it is a great work of art; but my experience of the novel and my judgment about its "meaning" have changed over the course of many rereadings and in the light of several significant changes in the circumstances of my life.[41] Sometimes (as with my experience of *Sula*), a novel will seem to get "better," as a reader discovers ever-new subtleties and meanings. Other times, however, a novel will seem to get "worse," as a reader becomes bored with the thinness of the narrative or is newly offended by the themes and attitudes the novel conveys. The literary critic Wayne Booth describes something of this sort in his excellent argument for a serious reconsideration of the way literary critics think about ethical criticism. He writes, "The 'very same' *Count of Monte Cristo* that at sixteen I thought the greatest novel ever written is now for me almost unreadable."[42]

The richness of any particular novel is due to a great deal more, of course, than the novel form's constitutive heteroglossia. Much depends on the theme of the novel and the treatment its author has given to that theme. It is important to note here that the process of writing a novel involves a lot more than plotting out a narrative that merely confirms the author's preexisting ethical or political commitments. Certainly, there may be some authors who compose novels that way—authors who have political or ethical agendas and who will force the details of a plot to conform to their preexisting vision. But others, such as Toni Morrison, approach writing as a process of exploration. Indeed, Morrison writes as a way of delving into a question or situation that she finds intriguing or troubling. In a 1985 interview conducted by Bessie Jones, Morrison formulated the question that motivated the novel *Sula*: "If you say you are somebody's friend as in *Sula*, now what does that mean? What are the lines that you do not step across?"[43] Elsewhere in that same interview, Morrison explains that she views writing as a way of testing out the moral fiber of her characters in order to see how they respond to difficult situations. She writes, "Well, I think my goal is to see really and truly of what these people are made, and I put them in situations of great duress and pain, you know, I 'call their hand.' And, then when I see them in life-threatening circumstances or see their hands called, then I know who they are."[44] Moreover, because Morrison regards writing as a process of moral and epistemic investigation, she does not write about ordinary, everyday people or events. Instead, she plumbs the hard cases— the situations where "something really terrible happens." She explains: "That's the way I find out what is heroic. That's the way I know why such people survive, who went under, who didn't, what the civilization was, because quiet as its kept much of our business, our existence here, has been grotesque."[45] The process of writing a novel can thus be a process of exploration in which the "answer" surprises even the author.

The semantic open-endedness of all good novels, including those that treat racial and cultural difference in interesting and complex ways, might seem to pose a difficulty for my larger argument that multicultural literature can contribute to a better understanding of the functioning of the racial order in a given society and thus be useful in a decolonial project. But that would be the case only if I were arguing that reading a work of multicultural literature *always* or *directly* has the effect of making its reader less racist and more knowledgeable about her implication in structures of racial inequality. My claim is far more limited. Instead, I am arguing that the novel form's constitutive heteroglossia enables a reader to engage dialogically at a deep emotional and epistemic level with the difficult questions around race, culture, and inequality raised by good multicultural novels. Such a dialogic interaction can, I suggest, prompt a reader to question and then revise some of her assumptions about structures of racial and economic inequality and how they are sustained.[46] And while questioning does not lead ipso facto to epistemic and emotional growth, the former is at least a precondition for the latter.

The Cervantes poem with which I began this essay demonstrates the failure of understanding that occurs when the elements of friendship I have been extolling as necessary for decolonizing epistemologies are missing from a dialogue about race. The question that is implied by the title—"You are an intelligent, well-read person. All such persons understand that racism is silly and illogical. As an intelligent, well-read person myself, *I* do not believe in racial discord. How, then, can *you?*"— introduces the less than ideal terms under which the exchange between the poet and the. young white man is taking place. Because the young man's question implies a challenge to rather than a sincere interest in the poet's perspective—because he sees her with an "Arrogant Eye"—he begins the exchange by denying her interpretive capacity. He fails to extend to her the friendly presumption that she will bear "reliable moral witness" and so cannot consider the possibility that she may know something that he does not know about the way race works in their shared world. His "arrogant" stance toward the poet is what allows him to make an appeal to their sameness at the expense of the racial difference that she insists must be acknowledged if her experiences are to make any sense. Thus the poem is an answer to the young man's question and a passionate defense of the poet's race-conscious perspective on their shared social world. Finally, it is an anguished appeal for understanding that simultaneously acknowledges the far greater possibility of misunderstanding: "(I know you don't believe this. / You think this is nothing / but faddish exaggeration. But they / are not shooting at you)."[47] With this last line, the poet further demonstrates her recognition that the young man's social location inhibits his ability to recognize the. existence of a racial order that affects them each very differently; she perceives that as a white man in a social order that overvalues both whiteness and maleness, he has never been targeted by the "bullets" of racism that are "discrete and designed to kill slowly."[48] So, although she makes several appeals of her own that acknowledge her potential sameness to him,[49] the poet finally refuses to uphold the young man's arrogant perception of their shared social world—to do so would be to gloss over the racial difference that shapes her very experience of it. She tells him that despite her best efforts to shut out the "sounds of blasting and muffled outrage" that disrupt her poetic reverie, she finally cannot ignore the daily "slaps on the face" that racism, unbidden, brings to her.

In a heteroglossic statement near the end of the poem that is at once subtly ironic and heart-wrenchingly sincere, the poet assures her young white male interlocutor, "I am a poet / who yearns to dance on rooftops, / to whisper delicate lines about joy / and the blessings of human understanding."[50] The sincerity of the statement stems from the fact that she envisions a world in which "the barbed wire politics of oppression / have been torn down long ago" and in which "the only reminder / of past battles, lost or won, is a slight / rutting in the fertile fields."[51] The irony stems from the fact that this is finally a poem about racial *misunderstanding*. Unless the young white man starts to care about the poet enough to risk "trying on" her interpretive claim and its implications for his own epistemic and emotional growth, and until he enters into a dialogue that acknowledges her as a worthy interlocutor who might have something to teach him about the world he lives in, "the blessings of human understanding" will remain frustratingly out of reach for them both.

~ Mapping Latina/o Futures

❧ Epistemology, Ethics, and the Time/Space of Decolonization: Perspectives from the Caribbean and the Latina/o Americas

NELSON MALDONADO-TORRES

The Caribbean is a geopolitical zone characterized by colonialism, human slavery, misrecognition, and the search for liberation, among other features. It became the first site for the expression of the project of genocide, slavery, and conquest of a Christian Europe that began to change its identity precisely through such acts of violence and by notions of "discovery" that began to sever its dependence on a Christian framework that relied on ancient notions of geography. Enrique Dussel refers to it as the site where modern Western philosophy emerged, and we likely find there the first radical expressions of *espanto* (not simply fear or anxiety) and desires for liberation in the face of modern forms of colonization.[1]

One important feature of the Caribbean is that it is a zone formed by islands and continental territories connected by a sea. Different European empires divided these places, and they heavily, if not in some cases totally, eliminated native populations in the region. Also, Black Africans who were brought through the Middle Passage have made a strong mark in most of the Caribbean territories. Laborers from China, India, and other places in Asia also came to the region, sometimes with promises of a better life, but ending up in situations similar to slavery, if not in slavery itself. Jews and Muslims have also been present in the region for centuries, many of them escaping religious intolerance, or as slaves, as in the case of Black Muslims from West Africa.

As a result of this violent history of colonialism, genocide, diaspora, and multiple migrations of different kinds, time, memory, and space are heavily fractured in the region, rendering a shadow of illusion into projects and discourses that promise unity or fixed anchors in the past or in single cultural traditions. The de-investment in typically continental visions of cultural essence, substantiality, history, and origins is increased by the overarching presence of the sea, which connotes openness, as well as the possibility of change and exchange, escape and salvation, interrelation, as well as the infinite possibility of expanding horizons.[2]

Edouard Glissant has called attention to some of these features. According to John E. Drabinski, Glissant "affirms the specifically Caribbean *geography* of thinking, rather than rooting thought in tradition, History, or any notion that presupposes a coherent relation to the past."[3] This Caribbean geography of thinking could be arguably distinguished from dominant themes in continental philosophies of history and related discourses, including discourses about continental unity in Europe, Latin America, and the United States. But this does not mean that prevalent themes in the Caribbean do not appear elsewhere, or that themes of continental unity do not also find a place in regions like the Caribbean. It is a question of emphasis that cannot simply be explained by geography itself, but by ways of living in those geographies and by their histories. It is in that sense that it is possible to consider mapping decolonial spatialities, and of identifying decolonial elements in multiple spatial configurations and different spatial references in multiple forms of decolonial thinking.

This essay is an attempt to contribute to these efforts, which I consider part of what I have called postcontinental philosophy.[4] First, I briefly spell out linkages between Frantz Fanon's view of subjectivity and his Caribbean and migrant imaginary. I connect this with Gloria Anzaldúa's use of the concept of *borderlands* and discuss how this spatial reference informs her views on subjectivity and knowledge. This is part of an effort to connect Caribbean and Latina/o, and in this case specifically Chicana, philosophical views, in particular, conceptions of space, knowledge, and self that can inform other forms of reflection. In the second part of the essay, I focus on one space or intellectual site where the decolonial views of Fanon and Anzaldúa come together, or can come together, and become rich areas of investigation and reflection. This space is known as ethnic studies, with multiple fields, including African American and Africana studies, Asian American and Asian Diaspora studies, Latina/o studies, and Native American studies, among others. These areas engage questions that emerge from the exposure to colonialism, genocide, and multiple forms of segregation, and they owe their origin to decolonial thinking and activism. Each one of them offers concepts of space, time, subjectivity, methods, and objects of study that contrast with dominant views in nineteenth- and twentieth-century European sciences. I consider ethnic studies as a heretical, emancipatory, and postcontinental episte-mological and institutional space where decolonial philosophy and theol-ogy can join with other fields in the mapping of spatialities, views of the self, and epistemologies that contribute to the decolonization of the world.

ON SELF AND SPACE: FANON'S TRAVELS
AND ANZALDÚA'S BORDERLANDS

Frantz Fanon was a black Martinican, who was educated in Martinique and France, and lived the final years of his life in Algeria. His work is marked, both by the lived experience of being a black subject in the Caribbean, and by traveling to and living in different territories with distinct racial dynamics and struggles. As a black Martinican, he could not easily assume the comfort of adopting a continental identity, be that European, Latin American, or African. His philosophy expresses the sense of dislocation that no idea of naturalized continental unity could undo. His calls for Algerian nationhood and African unity themselves, which are possibly the closest parallels in his work to ideas of homogeniz-ing unity in continental discourses, are followed by a demand for decen-tralization, adequate representation and participation of minorities, and an international politics of solidarity with the *wretched of the earth*.[5] In a sense, he Caribbeanized the continent, instead of continentalizing the Caribbean.

Fanon's views of territoriality arguably find an expression or are con-nected to his views on the self. He believed that the self is constituted by metaphysical desires, or desires for entering in relation with others, and that the openness of the self and the offering to the Other are a prerequi-site for the formation of the "I."[6] This does not mean that identity is impossible or necessarily problematic, but that it is always already pre-ceded by an ethical dislocation that can potentially inspire a decolonial politics that opposes anything that betrays the ethical constitution of the self. Ethics and the politics of decolonization are in this way the corrective to, or orienting ideal of, the politics of identity, just as they also are the antidotes to the ontology of colonization and of continentality. The poetics of relation articulated by Fanon's fellow Martinican Edouard Glissant are in this way given a thoroughly ethical and political character. Texts such as Fanon's *Black Skin, White Masks* and Glissant's *Poetics of Relation* refuse the idea of continentality and bring up relationality as key, not only with regard to the Caribbean, but in relation to human existence in general.

Fanon resisted the appeal of adherence to ideas of continental unity (by virtue of culture or civilization) and rather sought for the human in the spaces *between* human beings themselves. His call for building "the world of the *You*" can be understood as a critique of liberation projects that are anchored in identity discourses that, by posing themselves against hegemonic continental and imperial forms of identity, turn themselves precisely into subaltern continental forms or discourses.[7] Similar conceptions of spatiality and ethico-political relationality appear in philosophical, literary, artistic, and religious conceptions of "sub-alter" identities and political projects. A prominent one in the United States is the Chicana/o or Xicana/o identity/political project. This ethnic name/political designator denotes a particular history, lived experience, and epistemological and political project. The epistemological and political projects among Chicana/os are not exactly the same, but, to use Jorge Gracia's words, they could be conceived as a family of projects grounded, not solely on history, as Gracia indicates, but also on sharing a geopolitical and social space, on being categorized similarly and thus on having related lived experiences and meanings, and on sharing a vision of social transformation.[8] However, when looking at ethnic groups, family resemblances themselves don't necessarily involve historical baptisms or marriages.[9] This conception of the formation of communities can lead to ignoring the force of the modern/colonial Manichean divide of colonizer and colonized, which overdetermines the relation between groups and introduces new conditions of existence.

Gloria Anzaldúa's *Borderlands/La frontera* illustrates the multiplicity of elements at play in the formation of Chicana identity. The book begins by locating the subject in time, and thus history is important. But this is far from the "official history." History here is presented more as a critical

form of remembering that portrays what could be assumed to be historical "marriages" as murder, rape, and other forms of violence. Anzaldúa
examines history, not only to find the "source of the self" in time, but
also to determine the unethical excesses that best illuminate her social
reality, and her lived experience, including her multiple composition as a
subject with ties to both the oppressor and the oppressed (e.g., Mexican
and indigenous) in particular places. In *Borderlands/La frontera* history is
part of a decolonial form of traveling through time or a temporal decolonial "pilgrimage," to use María Lugones' conception. The "border/
frontera" and the "pilgrimage/peregrinaje" stand as complementary images of spatial location and movement through space and time.[10]

After looking at history, Anzaldúa focuses on culture. And here again
the purpose is not solely to understand the cultural sources of her self,
but also the way in which such cultural sources sometimes betray the
peoples and subjects that hold them. That is, these cultures, like probably
a good number of cultures, can provide a source of self-affirmation and
pride, as well as legitimations of machismo and imperialism, and can
even lead to self-hate. Thus, traditions or cultures by themselves cannot
or should not determine the identity of human groups. Identities are
shaped in part by critique and praxis. Similar to Fanon, Anzaldúa opposes
whatever betrays the condition of the human as a bordered subject (sujeto fronterizo) who is open to others in relations of hospitality and generosity, and who can commit ethically and politically to and for a sub-
Other. This opposition serves as a constant source of possible critique for
any given culture or identity. And the reason is that, for Anzaldúa, ethnic
identity cannot be obtained at the expense of the proper affirmation of
fundamental features of humanity. This insight is similar to Fanon's critique of Négritude, and it indicates the need to articulate a philosophical
anthropology as a propadeutic to any philosophy of identity. Both Fanon
and Anzaldúa provide a metaphilosophical account of ethnic identity in
the form of a philosophical anthropology based on a phenomenology of
the lived experience and metaphysical desires (ethical, communicative,
and erotic) of the Black Caribbean subject and the Chicana, as well as on
postcontinental and decolonial views of space and time.

In the light of Anzaldúa's and Fanon's work, the search for ethnic
identity should not be primarily motivated by the search for ground or
foundation, but by the *care for the sub-other* and the determination of the

tasks of responsibility. This points to the existence of a decolonial ethics and politics at the heart of Fanon's and Anzaldúa's work, which undergird any project to build identity or any effort to produce identity politics of any kind, strategically or not.[11] Metaphorically speaking, one could say that the self is not a continent or a separate island, but, rather, a border, a point of encounter, an intersection, or even an archipelago, understood as a point of relation with other selves. In this way, Caribbean and Chicana spatial imaginaries serve to help understand the self, beyond accusations of extreme forms of existential humanism in Fanon or alleged essentialism in Anzaldúa's work. At the same time, it should be clear that the main point here does not imply a rejection of the importance of identity or identity politics but rather an indication of a decolonial ethico-political grounding that serves to orient and sometimes to criticize identity projects, to the point of rendering them secondary sometimes or calling for their own suspension.

But suspension is not evisceration or complete rejection. Decolonial ethics and politics themselves require a view into identity and the self, both because one's social position can demand justice, and because one should know who one is in order to become accountable for the way in which one has benefited from or been complicit with the oppressor. The self is also relevant in the process of getting to know those sub-others to whom one owes the most or to whom one's people should aim to respond. This is possible because every subject has the capacity to see parts of himself or herself as oppressed but also as oppressor, an insight that helps overcome what Marilyn Frye calls "arrogant perception."[12] Thus, any project of self-affirmation has to deal with debts of responsibility, which also indicate the need to formulate ideas of the human that can inform conceptions of identity that help break off complicities with domination.

The Fanonian and Anzalduan conception of the self as oriented ethically informs various philosophical positions such as that of the Chicana Chela Sandoval and her concept of decolonial love, and the Latino of Argentinean origin Walter Mignolo and his critique of continental ontologies, and appraisal of noncontinentalist spatial conceptions/projects in the Americas.[13] Their reference to praxis resonates with the work of María Lugones. The insistence of these writers on the epistemological value of lived experience finds echoes in the work of Linda Martín Alcoff,

Jacqueline Martínez, and Paula Moya.[14] Emma Pérez's work is indebted to Fanon through a line of Chicana and Chicano writers as well as through Homi Bhabha, all of whom were influenced by Fanon. Pérez's view of the Chicana subject is also highly informed by Anzaldúa.[15] Despite the important differences between all these authors, I suggest that they can be viewed as part of a family of postcontinental theorizing that proposes new conceptions of time, space, subjectivity, interrelationality, ethics, and politics. They are arguably part of a decolonial turn in philosophy, theory, and critique, which includes Fanon, Anzaldúa, and a number of other figures who present innovative views of time, space, self, and knowledge to facilitate decolonization.[16]

I see my work and my reflections here within the same family of postcontinental and decolonial theorizing.[17] Within the postcontinental philosophy "family," I see a difference in emphasis and method from (1) the work of those with poststructuralist leanings and the work of others who are more critical or skeptical of poststructuralism, (2) work that focuses on practices and that of others who take a systemic point of view, and (3) the work of those who focus on either identity, liberation, or consciousness. There are other lines of demarcation as well, such as the general approach to European theoretical sources—either sympathetic with European theory or not. I concentrate on decolonial ethics (or ethico-politics), philosophical anthropology, and epistemology.[18] Here, I focus on the subjective and ethical preconditions for the emergence of decolonial postcontinental philosophy. Decolonial postcontinental philosophy is critical of the homogenizing conceptions in continental ontologies and political projects, as it also challenges the affiliation between sub-alter identities, such as Latina/o, with continental imaginaries, such as "America" or Latin America. Different from Jorge Gracia's proposal about Latina/o identity, a postcontinental view of Latinas/os establishes a family relationship, not by looking at historical events, but by identifying similar spatial imaginaries. In this case, as Mignolo puts it in his postcontinental manifesto *The Idea of Latin America*, Latina/o identity (at least in its more progressive and postcontinental expressions) is closer in kind to indigenous, Caribbean, and Afro-descendant projects that question the integrity of Latin American identity—and, of continental identity in general—than to Latin America. Latinas/os in the United States and indigenous people in Latin America have more in common among them than Latinas/os have with Queen Isabel or the King of Portugal in the sixteenth century.[19] This observation has large implications for the self-conception of these groups, as well as for the scholarly study of these communities.

Postcontinental philosophy is a decolonial philosophy. And decolonization is a project grounded on the histories, lived experiences, and ethico-political imperatives of colonized peoples, as well as on their desires for open human interrelationality at the intimate, erotic, and public levels. This project has produced or inspired some institutions, yet, it largely remains a project in the making.

Decolonization is about knowledge as much as it is about praxis, and in fact, many who do decolonial philosophy challenge the absolute divide between the two (Anzaldúa, Fanon, Lugones, to name only a few of the most obvious). One crucial question in this context is that of the institution or institutional space where this knowledge can grow, ideally in relation to praxis. This space won't likely be the traditional Western secular academic university, grounded on the primacy of nations, and more recently, corporations. And it is not necessarily the theological seminary either. In fact, decolonization and postcontinental philosophy typically appear as *heresy* to both dominant secular and religious institutions.

An example of a place where decolonial thinking takes place as part of an institution is the Escuela Popular Norteña, where María Lugones and other intellectuals have worked for years offering education about overcoming cultural, sexual, racial, and class oppression. Another project in the making is the Latina/o Academy of Arts and Sciences, which seeks to create a common front by Latina/o intellectuals and their allies in the United States to challenge the notion of Latina/o assimilation into Western academia and promote the defense and rigorous exposition of methods of study that validate the intellectual work of Latinas/os and others interested in further exploring the links among knowledge, praxis, and social justice. In Latin America, one finds the doctorate in Latin American Cultural Studies designed and led by Catherine Walsh, among other places, some of which are led by indigenous and peasant communities across the continent.

A more traditional setting in the United States is the research university. There, decolonial thinking has for the most part flourished in various forms of ethnic, gender, and women's studies programs, departments, and research centers. Ethnic studies itself was born as an institutional space in the academy in 1969 in the context of student-led protests on a number of college campuses across the United States. It is important to note in the context of this essay, that ethnic studies first emerged in the attempt to establish Third World colleges, which brings geopolitics and spatiality to the forefront and seeks to expose the modern research university as a partial project largely complicit with a First World vision of the world. The Third World College was meant to be a space where Third World subjects and allies in the Third World and elsewhere would be able to cultivate their critical views of society and empower themselves to change it. The Third World College was conceived as the principal home for decolonial thinking and praxis within the academy, as well as a continued motor of change that sought the transformation of society and the academy itself. That is how ethnic studies was born: as a denunciation of the established geography of reason and as the desire for an opening that would allow the serious exploration of a larger cognitive map and a deeper knowledge of self and society. It is the place where the dislocations of the sea and the ruptures of the borderlands, among other spatial images, can be seriously investigated beyond the limits imposed by the "time" of the nation or the "space" of the continent.

When understood well, ethnic studies is often perceived as heresy for the academy and society at large, but it is a form of heresy that represents a privileged space for decolonial thinking in the academy. One could see ethnic studies as a heretical discourse that challenges the limits of both, the Western secular sciences as well as most theologies, including at least some theologies of liberation and identity. Since ethnic studies is a privileged space where one can think through the tropes of the sea and the borderlands intrepidly and without apologies, it can also be referred to as a postcontinental and decolonial heretical space. I now turn to offer an interpretation of this space that will make these and other claims clearer.

THIRD WORLD/ETHNIC STUDIES AS HERESY: THINKING BEYOND THE CONTINENT AND NATION IN THE TIME/SPACE OF DECOLONIZATION

Following the work of Sylvia Wynter, I offer a view of ethnic studies as part of a larger humanist revolution with decolonial intent that is particularly characterized by acts of invention and heresy. The goal of these acts is to subvert the multiple structures and interlocked chains of oppression while uncovering new ways of thinking about our collective humanity and about projects that seek to affirm what is best in it. Understood in this way, ethnic studies and related fields are not simply areas that aim to mirror social diversity at the university, but rather spaces that foment the systematic exploration of decolonial spatial and temporal imaginaries, as well as philosophical anthropologies, art, ethics, epistemology, and politics that further the unfinished project of decolonization in the United States, the Caribbean, and elsewhere.

Ethnic studies is the result of social struggles, and it bears the mark of its origins. But it is housed in the Western university, an institution of at least seven to eight hundred years of existence that for the most part of its history has been not only complicit with but an actual participant in the colonization of knowledges and peoples that has been a central part in the history of European expansion. Ethnic studies is often looked at as an illegitimate member of the Western university: more like the result of an undesired concession with political motives than as a legitimate advance in the sophistication of the knowledge produced in the university. Thus it is often believed that any serious academic work on topics that have been introduced by ethnic studies or in which ethnic studies focuses (for example, ethnicity itself) are best produced in the traditional departments and out of ethnic studies. From this perspective the real contribution of ethnic studies to the university is helping to maintain its diversity profile by predominantly offering jobs and courses to professors and students of color, and even sometimes that is questioned.

I propose that instead of looking at ethnic studies as the result of a particular historical moment that interrupted the life of the university in ways that led it to adopt new, apparently "bastard" fields (such as Black, ethnic, and women's studies), we must see it the other way around: The formation of these fields represents perhaps the first time or one of the few times in the history of the Western university (from the European Middle Ages to today) when such an institution has been directly challenged from below to systematically transform itself in relation to its approach to themes or areas that it has systematically excluded. The 1960s in general and the emergence of black, ethnic, and women studies in particular perhaps find only two antecedents in the history of the Western university. These previous arguably comparable moments were moments of deep transformation that have come to define how we understand the university, its structure, and its function until today.

I am taking my cue for this interpretation from the work of one of the foremost but less-known theoreticians of color today, the Afro-Caribbean writer and theorist Sylvia Wynter.[20] Wynter argues that there is a parallel between the heresy of Renaissance humanists in the face of medieval Christian theological absolutism and the different form of heresy enunciated by people and intellectuals of color in the 1960s in the face of secular and religious colonialism, racialism, and patriarchalism. The Renaissance humanists were those who defended the value and relative autonomy of "Man" and his creations against a view that reduced human beings to the status of sinful creatures. This heresy is the foundation of the *studia humanitas*, or the humanities, which gradually became a fundamental part of the Renaissance university. The Renaissance university opened a space for man as the foundation for knowledge about human beings, gradually displacing the role of God and theology in the Western university.

Whereas Renaissance humanists questioned God and gradually opened up a space for autonomous Man as a ground for secular knowledge and understanding, people of color throughout the last five centuries, and particularly in the twentieth century, revealed other problems with these two foundations. They pointed out that God and Man were not simply general concepts, but that both were infused with heterosexual, patriarchal, and racist connotations. God and Man were White Male Homophobic God and White Male Heterosexual and Homophobic Man. And just as the humanists and the nonnoble laity were systematically excluded from circles of power in the Middle Ages, just so in similar fashion and even more brutally and profoundly women, people of color, and homosexuals have been systematically excluded from power in different but related forms throughout all of modernity. To be sure, the exclusion of women and homosexuals in the Christian West precedes the invention of the color line and the problem of the proletariat, which means that the Renaissance revolution and later on the revolution of the Enlightenment (which, I would argue, following Wynter, is the second antecedent to the revolution of the '60s) did not respond to all the systematic exclusions of the dominant epistemes in their day, but that they actually contributed with more. From here also those interested in forging a different form of heresy and *studia* beyond those of the colonial racist patriarchal heterosexual and capitalist God and man and their equally colonial racist patriarchal heterosexual and capitalist forms of knowledge production find a historical challenge today.

If the previous considerations have a ring of truth, it will be difficult to understand ethnic studies solely as a national phenomenon specific to the United States or concerned only with studying discrete ethnoracial communities or minoritized subjects. Ethnic studies can rather be seen not only as an instrument for the betterment of certain specific populations in the United States, but more generally as a center for the production of heresy in regard to the foundational constructs of the modern Western episteme. In order to uncover the sophisticated ways in which such constructs work, heresy needs to take an interdisciplinary and comparative approach that combines theory with the concrete empirical and archival work. That is, the heretical function of ethnic studies scholars demands that they relate knowledges, histories, and struggles and that they conceive of identities as nodes in networks of power rather than as fixed essences. The wealth of people of color is not in capital, as those who supported European humanists in the past; their wealth is perhaps more than anywhere else in the multiple forms of strategies of survival, resistance, and transformation that they have mobilized historically against the supremacy of racist and patriarchal God and Man. Attention to and focus on specific groups is absolutely important and should be continuously cultivated, but it acquires further significance when done in relation to the larger structures that affect all and in connection to the experiences and histories of resistance that are found in multiple communities and practices locally, nationally, and transnationally.

These practices of ethnic studies scholarship could be conceived as acts of heresy in the form of epistemic decolonization. By decolonization here I do not mean specific acts or forms of thinking against colonial administrations, or actions that were specific to the twentieth-century movements of decolonization. Decolonization is rather an activity that seeks to overcome the modern logic of colonization of natural resources, of the body, and of the mind of everyone, but particularly of people of color—that is, of the colonized and enslaved and their descendants. Decolonization is also a name for the project of heresy against racial, heteronormative, homophobic, and patriarchal God and Man. In this sense, if the concept of the Renaissance were used to refer to the project of returning to the classics in order to forge a new appreciation of Man, and the Enlightenment came to be likened to the idea of maturity as rational progress, I propose that we use decolonization to refer to the age of heresy that Wynter identifies and celebrates. Conceived in this way, decolonization is the project of systematic critique and overcoming of the limits and contradictions in modernity, including those of the Renaissance and the Enlightenment. It is important to insist that decolonization refers then not to peculiar nineteenth- and twentieth-century processes, but to a more general epistemic revolution that seeks to dramatically change the foundational concepts and priorities of the modern Western episteme and its main institutions, such as the state and the university. It is true that today we are in the epoch of colonizing readjustments, as well as in the time of the corporatization of the social world and of public institutions, but it continues to be an age of decolonization, which remains as an unfinished project.

Understood in this way, ethnic studies is a theoretical and intellectual arm in the project and the age of decolonization. It shares this attribute with multiple institutions that have been created in the last four decades to contribute to the project of decolonization, including indigenous universities and centers of study in some places in the Third World. Those, and not the traditional Western university, are its closer allies. Indeed, ethnic studies as a new form of *studia* resists incorporation into the existing academy, its arts and its sciences—which often appear to it as white arts and sciences. That is one reason why ethnic studies is often perceived with skepticism from the standard academic point of view. Many theologians in the Renaissance were not too happy and didn't have the best opinions of humanists either. Scientists and humanists in Western universities occupy the same structural position today that dogmatic theologians occupied several centuries ago. Indeed, one could go as far as regarding them as their heirs. It is thus natural that people of color and other populations who continue to be systematically excluded tend to appear as incoherent bastards or unsophisticated scholars. In many cases they are instead forging a new basis to understand and produce knowledge about human beings and the world as a whole, which is why ethnic studies scholars appear to some as threatening despite the fact that their numbers are not high and they don't have much power. Their threatening appearance largely lies in that they seek to advance views from another time/space that disrupts the temporal and spatial coordinates that give sense to the modern/colonial world and its institutions, including the secular university and the religious seminary.

206 | NELSON MALDONADO-TORRES

The roots of ethnic studies in the proposal for Third World Colleges at San Francisco State University and the University of California, Berkeley make clear that ethnic studies is anchored in an spatial imaginary and in an internationalist vision deeply connected with decolonization movements worldwide. The reading of ethnic studies as heresy in the context of the long durée of the university locates it within a genealogy of Western revolutions. But heresy also denotes the questioning of the uncontestable primacy of that genealogy and the opening to exploring multiple spaces and temporal narratives beyond national and continental ontologies. It is here that the sea, migration, travel, the borderlands, pilgrimages, and decolonial love find a space in the academy and where, in conjunction with participation in multiple other spaces, philosophies and theologies of hope, community, and liberation, they can exploit their postcontinental and decolonial potential.

❧ Thinking Bodies: The Spirit of a Latina Incarnational Imagination

MAYRA RIVERA RIVERA

Habla con dejo de sus mares bárbaros,
con no sé qué algas y no sé qué arenas;
reza oración a dios sin bulto y peso.
—GABRIELA MISTRAL, *la extranjera*

She speaks in the tones of her barbaric seas
With who knows what algae and what sands;
She prays to god without baggage and weight.
—GABRIELA MISTRAL, *the foreigner*

Como un oleaje perpetuo, fragante,
ella hace sonidos del mar.
Inclinada se extiende y así
suspira como si fuera una resaca delgadísima,
como si fuera una palabra de ausencia.
Entonces en el lienzo del silencio
y en la misma orilla del tiempo,
ella se inclina toda desnuda y desnuda
se mira con el rostro
del agua en sus palabras.
—MARJORIE AGOSÍN, *idiomas*

Like a perpetual, sweet-smelling surf,
she makes sounds of the sea.

Bent over, she stretches out,
sighs as if she where a reed-thin tide,
as if she were a word of absence.
Then, on the canvas of silence
and on the very shore of time,
she bends over, naked, and naked
regards herself with the face
of water in her words.
—MARJORIE AGOSÍN, *languages*

Speaking a language shaped by the sea, with the face of the water in their words, both Gabriela Mistral and Marjorie Agosín evoke in their poems geographies of a country they have left behind. Their words have traces of algae and sand, of a naked body embraced by the sea. The poets' fragrant verses have seduced me—though I tried to resist the spell of words about body and sea, alert to the dangers of bringing "body" too close to "nature." Will her body be washed away by the sea's unruly powers and be lost in its uncontrollable depth? Will she be seen as "merely" flesh, her carefully crafted words drowned in incomprehensibility, again dismissed as inadequate for theory or ineffective for politics? Her god too intimate with the turbulence of matter to be the subject of philosophy?

Fearing being caught in the fate that awaits nature/native/body, afraid that perception of irrationality may flood the wisdom of bodies, I tried to resist the poets' enchantment. But thinking of bodies, I too conjure images of the sea.

Questions of bodies, foreign words, and fragrant seas may appear as strange openings for a discussion of epistemology, concerned as it is with discerning the proper, reliable foundations for knowledge. In Western epistemological traditions sensuality and bodies have often been considered distractions to be overcome in order to attain true knowledge. Decolonizing epistemology implies questioning the privilege of those traditions. Indeed, taking epistemology as a central concern, decolonial theorists not only explore the implications of the power structures in the production of knowledge but also seek to articulate alternative understandings and visions. Focusing on Latina body-words, this essay seeks resources to think not only beyond the legacy of colonial/imperial knowledge but also beyond its disembodied definitions of "knowledge."

In the variegated intellectual traditions that constitute Latina studies, explorations of the legacies of colonialism in the Americas commonly imply theorizations of embodiment. There are very concrete reasons for this: Colonial-sexual violence against the African and indigenous women of the Americas indelibly marked the bodies of many of their descendants. Greed, violence, and enslavement *literally* became incarnate. They have left "memories in the flesh"—to adapt Luce Irigaray's phrase[1]—and memories of the flesh seek theoretical articulation. Despite the evident dangers of being perceived yet again as one uttering barbaric words carrying who knows what algae or sand, or perhaps precisely because of the oceanic force of such speech, Latina efforts to decolonize epistemologies cannot abandon body-words.

The corporeal effects of colonial histories cannot be neatly separated into physical and cognitive elements, for the genealogical traces of colonial-sexual violence are experienced in conjunction with the materialization of social and familial arrangements also introduced by colonial power. These new structures served as tools for "the organization of relations of production, of property rights, of cosmologies and ways of knowing," all of which would have lasting effects in local and global understandings and experiences of embodiment.[2]

In response to the codification of bodies and the organization of humanity based on biological traits, Latina decolonial theories uncover the constructed character of body-talk in ways that would be familiar to feminists attuned to Simone de Beauvoir's celebrated statement: "One is not born a woman, but becomes one."[3] In Latina theory, these becomings are distinctively historicized, not only in relation to patriarchy or sexual politics but also in relation to broader networks of power. Latina theory entails multidimensional deconstructions at the boundaries of identity that revolve around gender, sexuality, race, nationality, and coloniality of power.[4] One might assert that Latina theories attend to the ambivalence of the identities that emerge from colonial encounters— identities that are openly and intensely sexualized, gendered, and racialized. But one would need to add that the aim is not simply to *describe* the configurations of power that have affected Latina bodies, but more significantly to *reconfigure* them by offering alternative theorizations of embodiment.

The Latina works discussed here are marked by absence and longing, troubled by past memories and present uncertainties, moved by the elusive and fleeting touch of sensuality. They even thematize their silencing, the derision of their words along with the materiality they embrace. Attempting to speak the unspeakable is for these discourses not only revealing, but also a part of becoming.[5] As they are understood in these works, bodies are not simply objects of study; body-words are not merely representational, but also performative and creative. Mythology is often creatively reinterpreted, including perceptive, creative musings into the spiritual dimensions of corporeal becomings. In their creative, ecstatic moves such body-words both intersect with and unsettle Christian metaphors, inciting the present reinterpretation of spirit and flesh.

I must add a word of clarification here. The works of Chicana writers such as Cherríe Moraga and Gloria Anzaldúa are paradigmatic of the distinctive reconfigurations of the corporeal imaginary that we have come to associate more generally with Latina epistemologies.[6] My discussion of Latina body-words is profoundly influenced by the works of these and other Chicana writers and especially by the works of theorists who have espoused their contributions beyond the fields of literary and ethnic studies. Yet I approach those contributions with a deep awareness of the violence implied in the slippage between "Chicana" and "Latina," and of the particularities of Caribbean experiences veiled by both labels.[7] The voices of Caribbean and other Latina theorists I included here therefore add important dissonance. However, I trust that the different collectivities that embrace a "Latina" stance may also embrace each other's contributions to the task of theorizing embodiment, while carefully avoiding illusions of wholeness—in definitions of our fields as much as in models of embodiment.

This essay engages a diverse group of Latina theorists to consider what they contribute to an exploration of flesh and spirit. I am suggesting that Latina theorizations of embodied becomings, what Moraga famously called a "theory-in-the-flesh," offer important resources for reimagining spirit. I hope these reflections will illustrate how Latina body-talk inflects spirit-talk, and how those challenges and visions may unfold in new perspectives on spirit-flesh. To discern these possibilities, I consider body-words as they have already appeared in Latina theology and in Latina theory, and with this in mind I meditate toward the end of the essay on the incarnational spirit of those body-words.

THEOLOGICAL BODIES

The Argentinean theologian Marcella Althaus-Reid stands out for her consistent—and insistently transgressive—attempts to place bodies at the center of theology. She grounds her theology of the body in a basic tenet of liberation theology, namely that "Latin American liberation theology is based on the search for the materiality of transcendence." That search leads liberation theologies to people's stories, to everyday experiences, "because they reveal the falsity of the border limits between the material and divine dimensions of our lives."[8]

In U.S. Latina/o theology, this interest in the deconstruction of the rigid boundaries between materiality and divinity is evidenced in the privilege it has given to popular religiosity. As Roberto Goizueta describes it, Latina/o popular Catholicism recovers a medieval appreciation for a creation infused with divine presence. This was a faith "firmly anchored in the body: the body of the cosmos, the body of persons, the Body of Christ."[9] That worldview was almost lost both in the Reformation attacks against images and saints and in Catholic responses to such attacks, but its traces are still visible in "the faith of Hispanic people" which is "primarily embodied and expressed in and through symbol and ritual."[10] Through their interpretations of these religious practices, Latina/o theologians have emphasized the sacred elements in materiality and physicality, especially in the context of ritual practices.

More direct explorations of the body appear in Latina/o theologians' discussions of mestizaje/mulatez, which Ada María Isasi-Díaz identifies as "the locus theologicus" of her work.[11] In colonial contexts, mestizaje/mulatez were pejorative terms for those of "mixed blood," but they have now been reclaimed and redefined by Latina/o thinkers as a way of bringing together cultural, historical, and corporeal aspects of identity. Mestizaje/mulatez is, in Isasi-Díaz's words, "the Hispanic/Latino incarnation of hybridity and diversity."[12] Benjamín Valentín observes that Latina/o theologians have used the concepts of mestizaje/mulatez to elucidate "the abstruse evocations of rejection, pain, and spiritual searching" as well as the redemptive potential that they hold for self and society.[13] These discussions about mestizaje/mulatez are part of Latina theology's body-talk, and their broader implications for constructive theology continue to be debated and developed.

Latina/o theologians' attention to popular religiosity and embodied identities is consistent with liberation theology's commitment to foreground the concrete experiences and material struggles of marginalized people: of the poor and the disappeared, of those in pain and hungry, of those persecuted and tortured. What Althaus-Reid calls a "theology of the spiritually concrete and the materially spiritual"[14] is an attempt to reclaim and extend that liberationist pledge, for the bodies in Latin American liberation theology ended up being too neatly organized, too readily sorted according to accepted political and theological categories, Althaus-Reid contends.[15] In that neat and "decent" organization, liberation theology neglected rebellious, unruly, queer bodies. Furthermore, in the interest of concrete representations, these theologies lost a certain ghostliness that is also part of embodied life: the unseen, the ungraspable, and the no-longer-living in and among us.[16]

Althaus-Reid's work seeks to move beyond these tendencies of orderliness by attending to common objects—not only in devotional contexts—and to rejected, disruptive bodies. She does not shy away from disorder. Althaus-Reid's texts are populated with unruly bodies and body parts: Dirty feet are carefully observed in "Feetishism," and numerous sexual organs are (perhaps fetishistically?) presented throughout *Indecent Theology*.[17] These intensely carnal images coexist in her writings with other ghostly presences: rebellious corpses that refuse to disappear and poor, displaced people who haunt the living cities only in the shadows of the night—as fleeting presences.[18] Their appearances disturb the boundaries of corporeality.

The challenge to the myth of the stable, whole body performed through the irruption of multiple and incomplete bodies into theological discourses should be read, I think, alongside other attempts by Latina theorists to subvert "the founding myth of original wholeness, with its inescapable apocalypse of final return to a deathly oneness"—as Chela Sandoval describes it.[19] This is an unavoidable step toward disrupting the myth of the unchangeable wholeness of truth. To seek what María Pilar Aquino calls "an *evolving*-becoming truth"[20] entails the interrogation of the image of a self-present God, whose simple oneness depends on remaining unaffected by multiple, changing bodies. Given the power of the impassible, unchanging God in Christian imaginaries, incomplete and incoherent bodies may seem strange places to search for the materiality of transcendence—or for transcendence in materiality. But this strangeness points to a key aspect of this project: a rethinking of divine transcendence that does not presuppose completeness or absolute separation, one that is more amenable to the flux and disruptions of the flesh.

Whereas Althaus-Reid's body images hardly add up to an organized, whole, unified body—or to a coherent theory of embodiment—they do produce aesthetic effects that are theologically significant. These effects may be similar to what Patricia Cox Miller describes, in her reading of hagiographic texts, as "visceral seeing."[21] Miller explores "narrative pictorial strategies" that draw readers "into the images by virtue of their very bodies."[22] Displaying "ambiguous corporealities"—bodies that are both ephemeral and tangible, both fragmented and whole—such texts "induced a stance for the beholder to occupy, a stance in which the senses had cognitive status and in which the intellect was materially engaged."[23] Miller argues that such sensory realism is aimed at teaching "the reader how to see that the everyday life is saturated with the palpable" presence of the holy.[24] Similarly, by displaying starkly carnal images and ambiguous corporealities, Althaus-Reid's texts seem to aim at inciting visceral reactions in their readers and challenging the assumed boundaries between the sociopolitical, corporeal, and spiritual.

However, Althaus-Reid's shocking rhetorical strategies often threaten to reinscribe the all-too-familiar stereotypes of the hypersexual Latina—a problem that needs more careful attention. If coloniality of power produces not one but two or maybe more different gender systems for colonizing and colonized subjects, as María Lugones has persuasively argued, Latina critiques need to address the differences in constructions of gender and sexuality across the colonial divide.[25] That is, they need not only challenge Victorian gender images by, for instance, reclaiming the spiritual dimensions of eroticism, as Althaus-Reid does. They must also address the intense sexualization of women on the other side of the colonial divide: what Lugones calls the "dark side" of the gender system, that is, the gender structures imposed on the colonized.

Given this tendency of theological discourses either to ignore real bodies altogether or to idealize their beauty and their capacity for pleasure,

Althaus-Reid's work is a welcome provocation.[26] Turning that provocation into a theoretical critique that attends to the resistance of bodies to rigid ordering systems and recognizes even the "untouchable" bodies of society[27] entails first a closer look at the paradoxes of embodiment. For that analysis I now turn to works in Latina studies (outside of theological fields), and in so doing I return to the sea.

DISRUPTIVE BODIES

The Puertorrican poet Luz María Umpierre links her critique of the dominant ordering of bodies to a well-known symbol of the island: the walls of the city of San Juan.[28] Built to protect the city against foreign invasion during the Spanish colonial period, the old walls are today proudly displayed in souvenirs and tourism advertisements. That a fortified city may signify Puertorrican identity provokes Umpierre, who sees in it an appropriate symbol of the traps of the closed ideals of national identity and its compulsory heteronormativity. The walls of the city lock bodies in restrictive scripts; the walls of the city isolate the island from the sea. To allow for the needed contact between island and sea, Umpierre calls for words: "for the sea to come / to touch that island's land / one needs / your words."[29] These words are needed not to impose order on the unruly sea, but to liberate the sea from the wall. These are not the seemingly disembodied words commonly associated with creation myths; this is not a version of logocentrism. These are body-words that emerge from the islanders' bodies, from their mouths, stomachs, esophaguses, and so forth. Body-words contain for the poet the force that can erode the oppressive walls of nationalism and heteronormativity and expose identities to the touch of the sea—the watery medium of connection between shores and an agent of continual change.[30]

The effects of colonial history and nationalism on the bodies of the island and its subjects, to which Umpierre alludes, are not unrelated to the effects of racial ideologies in Latina bodies. For even when focusing mainly on the corporeal experiences that take place in the continental United States, Latina discourses generally stay in touch with the movements between shores and across borderlands that mark and shape people's bodies.[31] Standing between shores, in literal or figurative "exile," such bodies are often also in "sexile." As in Umpierre's poem, Latina body-words seek to erode the confining structures of U.S. national, racial, and sexual ideologies.

The structures that constrain and regulate identities function in part through appeals to the body that naturalize social constructions. Yet the boundaries between discursive claims and bodily experience are hardly impermeable. Bodies are formed and deformed as they are read in their social contexts, as they are touched by others. Those who are stigmatized often experience being caught in the dominant gaze, which affects the developments of their "bodily schema," as Fanon would put it.[32] The wounds produced by the seemingly disembodied gaze are felt viscerally, but their meanings might remain inscrutable. Such experiences are often characterized by a deep sense of uncertainty: Those who are subject to an objectifying gaze are unable to fully decipher just what the observed body signifies to the observer. Against the expectations of certainty produced by the naturalization of corporeal markers of identity, Latina/o body-talk often foregrounds—even dramatizes—puzzlement. The meaning of his own skin color is Richard Rodriguez's recurrent question in *Brown*.[33] Rodriguez ponders how the import of his brown skin shifts as he moves between worlds: the world of white Americans, where he "felt least certain about the meaning of [his] brown skin"; the racially diverse world of the early civil rights movement, where he felt "as safe as [he] ever felt"; the later world of clearly demarcated identities, where he no longer felt at home in the gatherings of ethnic groups other than his own. Brownness, he concludes, is not only an unstable sign; it is also an elusive one that simultaneously invites and resists being deciphered.[34]

The uncertainties of corporeal identity affect not only public interactions like the ones just described, but also intimate familiar relations. Pained by the awareness that her own light skin has given her privileges that are denied to her own mother, Moraga calls attention to the unreliable grounds of social identification.

See this face?
    Wearing it like an accident
Of birth
        It was a scar sealing up
A woman . . . [35]

Thus Moraga describes her experience of having her body read in the United States: a complex heritage reduced to the visible: a face, a sign, a scar. As Martín Alcoff observes, although "structural power relations . . . [determine] the meanings of our identities . . . the focal point of power most often operates precisely through the very personal sphere of our visible social identities."[36] The fissures of a racially divided social body fracture families along the differences in visible traits of their members. Even when those differences are the random outcome of genetic chance, they acquire added weight as signs of "the real" and thus as perceived evidence for social classification.

Visible corporeal traits become social data; social classifications become bodily wounds. Thus, the critical power of body-words stems from their ability, on the one hand, to resist the reduction of the body to biological inheritance and, on the other hand, to avoid the illusion of freedom to choose social affiliations unencumbered by the body and its history. Indeed, by highlighting the effects on her most intimate relationships of her corporeal entanglements with oppressive value systems, Moraga avoids such illusions of absolute freedom. Skin for Moraga is not only a mark of her ancestry, but also and simultaneously its mask. It is an accident and a scar that separates her from her mother—and unites her with her oppressor. Although a lighter skin can easily lead to participation in a system of clearly demarcated fields of power, it is often also a source of estrangement. This estrangement can be felt viscerally, for as she says, "The object of oppression is not only someone *outside* my skin, but the someone *inside* my skin."[37] The tension is inescapable. "Both strains [the conquistador and the native] contributed to their bodies, to their waking spirits," Rodriguez writes, as he draws the crucial implication: "Righteousness should not come easily to any of us."[38]

Locating the subject in relation to the native/conquistador dyad, however, obliterates the African influence that is essential for the Caribbean body imaginary, a problem that Isasi-Díaz has tried to address by insisting that we link mestizaje to the term mulatez. The simple dyadic structure native/conquistador may also, and more problematically, lead to construing identity as biological inheritance made up of the mixture of discrete substances. A theorization of embodiment needs to challenge such reductive understandings of inheritance. Yet, as an *epistemological* critique, allusions to the native/African/conquistador elements exemplify the multiplicity of relationships that constitute a body—incorporating the familiar and the unknown, the visible and the invisible, the nurturing and the oppressive. Attending to that multiplicity contributes to the disruption of myths of homogeneous subjectivity and unambiguous identification.

It is not only the complexity and irreducible multiplicity of biological inheritance that we must assert; we also need to scrutinize the analytical categories used for such work. Such a critique is implicit in Gloria Anzaldúa's question: "Just what did she inherit from her ancestors? . . . [W]hich is the baggage from the Indian mother, which is the baggage from the Spanish father?"[39] Highlighting the implications of differentiating between race, ethnicity, and social ideology, Anzaldúa adds, "Pero es difícil differentiating between lo heredado, lo adquirido, lo impuesto."[40] The uncertainties of heritage are clearly irreducible.[41] In contrast to the apparent clarity and stability of the theoretical categories that are used to describe it, self-identity is conflictive and puzzling, and its articulations should resist the illusions of epistemological certainty. Highlighting the perplexity of their own attempts at self-representation, Latina bodywords may call into question the compartmentalization of identity produced by the naturalization of categories of analysis, not by ignoring the body, but by bringing theory closer to the flesh.

The apparent celebration of the racial impurity associated with Latina theories is best understood in conjunction with its critique of, and invitation to move beyond, the illusion of purity in U.S. culture. At the heart of U.S. culture's privilege of purity, Rodriguez observes, is a repression of a male erotic fantasy and an enforced silence around the history of race in the United States. "When mulatto was the issue of white male desire, mulatto was unspoken, invisible, impossible."[42] And brown bodies may be seen as icons of terrifying, unnamed desires of the American symbolic. Rodriguez's goal is to turn that anxiety into a provocation that may lead to a deeper questioning of the very foundations of U.S. racial ideology. He turns brown into a category of analysis. "Brown made Americans mindful of tunnels within their bodies, about which they did not speak; about their ties to one another, about which they did not speak. This undermining brown motif, the erotic tunnel, was the private history and making of America."[43] The return of such suppressed knowledge, appearing in a story or body, produces violent anxiety.[44]

The challenge to acknowledge, perhaps even embrace, impurity entails for Rodriguez an epistemological shift to recognize "the ability of language to *express* two or several things at once, the ability of bodies to *experience* two or several things at once."[45] And this affirmation of multiplicity is a sexual challenge too. We observed that in Moraga's work a woman's skin appears as the site of memories of the touch of the maternal connection as well as of painful and guilt-ridden separation from her brown mother. However, despite her light skin, heterosexual ideologies "darken" her; because she desires women, Moraga considers her sex "brown."[46] A body acquires contrasting meanings in relation to different axes of power: Visible traits clash with familiar and biological bonds; sexual desires disturb ethnic affiliations, and so on. The disparate social meanings projected onto a body unavoidably mark it with incongruent desires and irreducible tensions, though never completely or unilaterally. The contradictory effects that different ideologies have on a body do not entail a simple internalization of social differences. Espousing subjectivities where "the individual is herself seen as 'fragmented' and 'contradictory,'" does not entail "displacing attention from the distinctions that exist *between*" bodies, Paula Moya asserts.[47] Instead, the goal here is to trace how the rifts that divide collectivities from one another, fragmenting the social body, materialize in unique but complex forms of embodiment—and in their transfigurations.

Corporeal pain, difficulty, and failure are undeniable effects of patterns of social discrimination, but their articulation cannot be reduced to expressions of victimhood or fatalism. If bodies have the ability to experience several things at once, they can also hold together pain and joy, failure and hope—and creatively transform those experiences. Whereas Yvonne Yarbro-Bejerano characterizes Moraga's depictions of identity as "non-redemptive,"[48] I read in such refusals to resolve the tensions of sociocorporeal existence glimpses of an open-ended view of salvation. In this model, redemption is never accomplished once and for all: It takes place in the transient, finite events of our lives and in the midst of the ambiguities and potentialities of our social relations. Exposing social structures and practices that inhibit corporeal flourishing reveals possibilities for unsettling them, thus opening spaces where new relationships may emerge. Yet the envisioned end is not the elimination of the tensions of corporeality in order to produce a coherent, whole body. Such an ideal would reinscribe what we referred to before as "the founding myth of original wholeness, with its inescapable apocalypse of final return to a deathly oneness,"[49] that in effect covers up multiplicity under ideologies of purity or homogeneity. Instead, we are seeking visions of redemption in which bodies become capable of embracing their multiplicity without having to become one.

A creative articulation of such longing for the transfiguration of bodily experience is represented in the song titled *"Raza Pura"* (Pure Race). The context is not the U.S. "mainland," but Puerto Rico. Based on the first verses of the song—"I am of a pure race / pure and rebellious"—the song may seem to espouse a problematic celebration of racial purity. But as the song proceeds to describe the conflict and violence that marks the subject's history, it demonstrates the impossibility of any simplistic acceptance of that ideal of purity. Indeed, the song displaces the logic of purity through parodic repetition. The claims to a "pure race" are immediately followed by a first-person description of its wounded body: "I am of a pure race which has had nails in its hands / and scars on its knees." The implicit links between Jesus' crucifixion and slavery lead to a redefinition of the claimed "purity": "I am Borincano / black and gypsy / I am taíno." Clearly and defiantly, the song affirms the irreducible multiplicity of the narrator's genealogy. But it simultaneously constitutes its complex corporeal history as the basis for a strange purity defined not by assumed biological homogeneity, but in relation to struggle, survival, and transformation. "I am tears and also pain / for all that I've lived / for all that I've suffered / I am of a pure race / pure and rebellious." While foregrounding experiences of violence and pain, the subject is not depicted as an object defined by victimization, but rather an active agent who makes "song with the chains," "escaping from the whip / and stealing magic from death." The body appears as the site of historical conflict and oppression as well as the source of mysterious, creative powers for resisting, challenging, and transgressing the logic, the "knowledge," that supports her subordination. The memory of an incarnate past and the articulation of improbable hopes combine—even in song—to effect the materialization of a new self.

In these transformative visions, bodies do not leave behind their memories of pain and loss; nor do they dream of attaining absolute freedom .

from social constraints in such a way that bodies could re-create themselves independently of others. At its most fundamental level, bodies are
constituted, understood, and experienced in relation to others—not only
to those others under whose gaze we feel the power of social controls
but also those familiar bodies among which we first learned to see ourselves as individuals. Physically and cognitively, bodies are shaped by
other bodies and through them they are marked by their meanings in
society. Those processes are fraught with uncertainty, yet they are also
dynamic and open to transformation through performative interventions: the ritual practices of popular religiosity, artistic creations, social
activism, critical writing. Those performative interventions are inherently relational: emerging from and limited by social and familiar bonds,
lured and empowered by the movements of the spirit in the flesh.

SPIRIT-FLESH

The ceremony always begins for me in the same way . . . always
the hungry woman. Always the place of disquiet moves the writing
to become a kind of excavation, an earth-dig of the *spirit found
through the body*. The impulse to write may begin in the dream, the
déjà-vu, a few words, which once uttered through my own mouth
or through the mouth of another, refuse to leave the body of the
heart.

Cherríe Moraga

The body-words presented in the previous sections emerge from
places of disquiet. Uneasiness, tremors, and desire give impulse to hungry
searches and distinctive modes of writing. Latina body-words attempt to
articulate not only the historical and social determinations of corporeality
but also that which exceeds representation and yet gives impulse to
speaking and writing: the body's unruly materiality, its mysterious spirituality. Such modes of writing invite an explicitly theological reading.
The aim of this reading is not to Christianize Latina theoretical contributions by subsuming them under doctrinal language. Instead I seek to
allow Christian discourses to be affected, to be disturbed yet again, by
accounts of the movements of the spirit found through the bodies of
those it has often ignored.[50]

A discussion of "the spirit found through the body," of spirit *in* the flesh, can hardly avoid engaging the ancient insights of the "incarnation": that central teaching of God *in carne*. The earliest authorities of the Christian tradition declared it a heresy to undermine the startling affirmation of divinity in the flesh. But theology all too often moves in the opposite direction—turning away from the realm of unruly earthy bodies. In its dogmatic formulations, the incarnation tends to be safely contained within Jesus' skin or reconceived in highly abstract, metaphysical terms that in effect distance the incarnation from our ordinary bodies: from the everyday experiences of working and dancing, praying and protesting, making bread and making love.

To take Latina theory as a starting point for an incarnational imagination, as I am suggesting here, is already to resist the tendency to circumscribe the incarnation to one body or to a one-time event that proves the rule of an otherwise disembodied deity. It is to affirm with Ivone Gebara that "the incarnation, the presence of the greatest of mysteries in our flesh, is more than Jesus of Nazareth."[51] Rather than setting the incarnation in opposition to our carnality, this reading seeks to embrace the incarnation's unfettered bond to our flesh. Attending to the spirit in the flesh of rejected, disorderly bodies is hardly to dismiss Jesus' body. Instead we read his body—a material, finite, stigmatized, vulnerable body—as revealing the scandal of divinity in the flesh, or more accurately, of the divine *becoming* flesh. We take ever more seriously the transformative power of a singular person, a unique history, the significance of the wounds that mark even a glorified body.

An interpretation of the incarnation as "the greatest of mysteries in our flesh" implies, methodologically, openness to learn from real, finite bodies, to seek the wisdom of body-words and their transformative power. This in turn entails a challenge to entrenched assumptions about the orientation of spiritual pursuits. The mind/body, spirit/matter dualisms pervasive in Western epistemologies lead to depictions of human development (and knowledge) as movements away from bodily "instincts" toward "rational thought," away from flesh/nature/mother toward culture conceived as the realm of the "free spirit." This reign of culture, it is well known, has been consistently associated with the agency of men/fathers, specifically of those who, by occluding their own dependence on the physical labor of women and disenfranchised men, may entertain the fantasy of life unencumbered by materiality or relationships. Reason and culture are thus imagined as rising above bodies and matter. Standard depictions of spiritual development assume the same path. Christian theologians and mystics commonly describe spiritual growth as ascension toward the airy heavens. In contrast, I am intentionally adopting Moraga's depiction of the spiritual pursuit as a movement of excavation or an earth-dig—a movement that takes us deeper into our fleshliness.

Through my reading of the Latina theorizations of corporeality, I have sought to foreground the dynamic and relational nature of such fleshliness. The challenges to the myths of original wholeness, homogeneous subjectivity, unambiguous identification, the illusions of purity and visual certainties, for instance, attempt to open up spaces for a complexly political model of carnality. In that view, bodies are always becoming through processes of identification and differentiation, objectification and transgression, fragmentation and transmutation. A theology-in-the-flesh also complicates and implicates the divine in these corporeal processes—the materialization of social relations, the enfleshment of the past in genes and memories, the transfiguration of corporeal wounds and social relations.

The intricate constitution of bodies that are simultaneously social, material, and spiritual would be undermined by conceptions of the spirit as a simple being or as a force that aims at permanent completion and wholeness—views that betray an epistemological privilege of oneness over plurality. The spirit that I am invoking here is not imagined as an alien element added to earthy objects. It is not an external container, a teleological goal, or an archetypal form that would gather the complexity of flesh into a unified whole. The spirit is that intrinsic part of the flesh. To emphasize the continuity between material and spiritual dimensions of embodiment I use the term "spirit-flesh." Just as "body-words" names discourses grounded on the continuity between corporeality and language, "spirit-flesh" emphasizes the inseparability of these concepts. In "spirit-flesh," the hyphen marks a boundary of distinction that does not tend to separation. Spirit and flesh flow into one another, each transfigures the other. The boundary between them remains as elusive as it is vital.[52]

Spirit-flesh is the substance of corporeality—its matter and energy—which is shaped by, but may also unsettle, layers of social and historical inscription and may disrupt old patterns of materialization. Yet, the living energy of the spirit-flesh does not eliminate the ambiguities of bodies that are ephemeral and tangible, fragmented and manifold, neither whole nor deficient. Thus the spirit is not to be associated with triumphalism or ideologies of absolute purity or perfection. Pain, difficulty, and failure are not antithetical to the movements of the spirit-flesh, for it is not independent of sociocorporeal life. In the transient events of finite, vulnerable existence, the spirit-flesh makes possible the transfiguration of our wounds and the incarnation of improbable hopes. This is the spirit, not of simple belongings, but of hybrid becomings.

The common depictions of spirit as primordially immaterial are challenged by these affirmations of spirit-flesh as constitutive of our bodies, while recognizing the spirit also in the nonhuman elements on which life depends. The biblical images of spirit as fire, water, and wind capture the material qualities of its life-sustaining energies, as well as its fluid and transforming power. We can recover the dynamic materiality of these images of the spirit as part of the work of countering received traditions that dismiss the epistemic import of materiality. These elemental images—like those of sea, algae, and sand identified in this essay's opening poems—may also help us reclaim the importance of the nonhuman elements in shaping of our corporeality. Regarding ourselves "with the face of water in [our] words" is to begin to erode the anthropocentrism of modern cosmologies and their ideologies of dominance.

The spirit-flesh is never simply our own; it can never be fully contained within the boundaries of the self. In contrast to atomistic views of embodiment, this reading asserts that our bodies are irreducibly linked to the nonhuman elements that sustain life; the marks of savage seas are sometimes legible in our body-words. Our bodies are shaped by some others whom we see and touch, as well as by those we perceive only as ghostly presences.[53] Earlier I referred to Althaus-Reid's allusions to the ghostly as a way to bring to our attention the traces of the no-longer-living in our selves, to the unseen presences of the excluded ones, as well as to the indeterminate aspects of bodily identity. Forgotten histories, suppressed knowledge, and ignored relationships do return, but they do not always appear with the weight of certainty that accompanies "reasonable" facts that can be observed from a safe distance. Instead they are experienced as fleeting insights or disquieting tremors *in* our bodies. We cannot be certain about just what we inherited from our ancestors— "which is the baggage from the Indian mother, which is the baggage from the Spanish father," which is the baggage from the African parents? We cannot clearly differentiate "between lo heredado, lo adquirido, lo impuesto."[54] Yet we know that the past is not simply superseded by the present, the ancestors are not merely outside our skin. Certain elements of the past and some aspects of the bodies of others are inherent in our own; as ghostly presences they remind us of our elusive, intimate connections with them.

Ghostly presences remind us that the spirit-flesh is never ahistorical, even if it lures us beyond what has been. The longings and courage to articulate hidden memories of the flesh are also associated with the movements of the spirit. Indeed, encounters with the past are sometimes represented as the presence of the spirits. Although modern Christianity has not been generally hospitable to talk of spirits from the past and has attempted to clearly differentiate the Holy Ghost from all other ghosts, we do find an image of the spirit as facilitator of memory in the Gospel of John. In that gospel's narrative, the spirit that was in Jesus infuses his followers and witnesses after his death. Tellingly, the spirit comes to them from the stigmatized body of a man who had been executed, a spectral body now able to walk through walls and yet still visibly wounded, still bearing the marks of violence on his flesh. How can this image not remind us of the ghostly appearances that populate the pages of the narratives of oppressed communities? The spirit that Jesus breathes into his followers is aptly called the spirit of truth, for it will remind the emerging community what they learned and experienced; it will also help them understand the baffling events of their past. The Johannine spirit is thus divine presence in remembrance—indeed, the very possibility of relating to the past. Latina theory's commitment to remember may resonate with the image of a spirit of remembrance as a spirit of truth. It may imagine the spirit enlivening memories in our flesh, inspiring attunement to their concreteness and their fluidity, while acknowledging in humility the irreducible uncertainties of remembrance.

The spectral elements, disconcerting as they may be, are not opposed to the body: They represent the fluent, fluid, dispersive aspects of flesh, of subjects that defy objectification. Ancestral memories haunt our present experiences, yet these do not exhaust the spectral elements of embodiment. A kind of ghostliness haunts even the most concrete characterizations, pointing beyond the represented to that which eludes representation, that for which we don't have concepts or words, that which unsettles established rationality and resists closure.

"I perceived a language of the ephemeral, the unseen, and the half-present that expressed the spiritual as a reference either to the divine or to that which is socially ghostly—certain bodies, desires, cultures, even locations. In this sense, the artwork itself was altar-like."[55] Thus Laura Pérez describes her analysis of Chicana art.[56] By depicting the unrepresented and unrepresentable elements in the spiritual and social realms, such artistic works invite us to explore corporeal mystery in nonreductive ways. "Spirit works," as Pérez aptly calls them, do not simply uncover suppressed knowledge, they "teach us to perceive and imagine differently."[57] Corporeal mystery is thus not dismissed as just a regrettable effect of ignorance or mystification. For in our dark or light skins, in our visible and invisible traits, in our unruly desires and sensitive wounds, the mysterious powers of spirit-flesh enable the materialization of unforeseeable possibilities.

This vision of spirit-flesh strives to maintain the balance between an awareness of vulnerability and a defiant trust in life. Refusing to leave behind the body of the heart or the memories of our flesh, we trust the energies of spirit-flesh. Such a trust differs from the sense of security found behind a fortified wall. Instead it is the kind of trust found by those who expose themselves to the connecting, transforming touch of the sea. Turning what we have been toward what we may yet become, a Latina image of spirit-flesh reclaims the wisdom of bodies to re-envision "salvations" that do not abandon corporeality, finitude, or its wounds. By uttering words impregnated with traces of sand and sea, Latina thought may keep drawing epistemology and body closer, as it brings forth incarnate words.

❧ Decolonizing Religion: Pragmatism and Latina/o Religious Experience

CHRISTOPHER TIRRES

Perhaps in the near future, as a new generation of scholars and philosophers begins to develop, mature, and conceive of a greater America that includes all of its subcontinents, we will begin to think of a larger geo-political and world-historical school of American philosophy from this hemisphere. This younger generation will read Emerson along with Rubén Darío, Peirce with Ingenieros, Dewey with Vasconcelos, Zea with Wilson, Rorty with Dussel, as they become so many canonical figures in one larger continental tradition.
—EDUARDO MENDIETA, *Latin American Philosophy: Currents, Issues, Debates*

The colonization of indigenous peoples in the Americas relied not only on harsh forms of physical subjugation—such as rape, torture, and death—but also on various forms of ideological control. U.S. Latino theologian Virgilio Elizondo describes this ideological control in terms of a violent attempt "to destroy the conquered's inner worldvision, which gives cohesion and meaning to existence."[1] Central to this world vision, Elizondo notes, are religious sensibilities and symbols. When these are destroyed, one moves from significant order into meaningless chaos, or from "nomos" to "anomie," as the sociologist Peter Berger would say. Indeed, the colonial encounter in the Americas could well be described as a situation in which "reality and identity [were] malignantly transformed into meaningless figures of horror."[2]

Various attempts to colonize indigenous worldviews were no doubt aided by the introduction of Western, dualistic epistemologies. These epistemologies often separated body and mind, flesh and spirit, life and death, and the sacred and the secular. In doing so, they ruptured indigenous cosmologies that integrated these pairings in a seamless way.

Indigenous modes of knowing had their own dualities: Indigenous gods such as Ometeotl, for example, were both female and male, and single poetic ideas were often expressed by the conjunction of two words (*difrasismos*). However, these indigenous "dualities" were not "dualisms" in the Western sense. They did not constitute separate or autonomous "parts" of reality. Rather, indigenous dualities were porous and fluid realities that interpenetrated each other. Sylvia Marcos, a scholar of religion and gender, has shown, for instance, that Nahua epistemologies concerning the body evade the modern, master narrative of spirit over flesh through their stress on concepts such as equilibrium and fluidity. As Marcos explains, maintaining equilibrium meant constantly combining and recombining opposites. In the Nahua realm of thought, "opposites are integrated: cold and hot, night and day, sun and moon, sacred and profane, feminine and masculine."[3] Western dualisms, in contrast, tend to maintain oppositions, thereby reinforcing a hierarchical logic that often pits one end of the polarity against the other. Most disastrously, perhaps, this is seen in the hierarchies of masculine over feminine and the sacred over the profane.

In myriad ways, U.S. Latina/o theologians and scholars of religion have contributed to efforts that attempt to overcome dominant Western epistemological dualisms. This work has been aided by a number of methodologies, including feminist critical theory, postcolonial theory, and deconstructionism. Indeed, the range of methodological orientations in this very volume is a testament to the many ways in which scholars may undertake the task of decolonizing epistemology.

In what follows, I explore how a native American philosophy, U.S. pragmatism, may further help in this task. As I suggest, pragmatism may be a useful ally in helping us theorize the religious dimension of human experience in a way that avoids problematic dualisms. In this essay, I focus on how pragmatism helps us integrate the aesthetic and ethical dimensions of religious faith, which—in the modern, colonial mythos—are often considered to be two different "types" of religious experience. As I demonstrate, pragmatism avoids a sharp separation between these two dimensions in two ways. First, it espouses a metaphysics in which these two dimensions are *qualities* of experience rather than as sui gene-ris *types* of experience. Experience, for the pragmatist, is not so much made up of discrete units of experience as it is an emerging process that is teeming with qualities that are always changing. Second, prag-matism ties this metaphysical outlook to a nonreductionistic epistemol-ogy that helps account for *how* religious faith changes and grows. As such, pragmatism has something to say not only about the integral and emerging "structure" of experience—of which aesthetic and ethical qualities play a central part—but also it helps us see how these qualities interrelate dynamically in experience. These insights, I suggest, may significantly aid current decolonial efforts to overcome problematic epistemological dualisms. The first two parts of this essay will deal with these contributions.

If pragmatism helps us overcome certain epistemological dualisms that were introduced by the colonial religious imaginary, what does postcolo-nial religious experience have to offer to pragmatism? In particular, what does Latina/o religious experience have to say to a pragmatic philosophy of religion? In the final part of this essay I look at some of the ways in which Latina/o faith experience adds significantly to traditional prag-matic accounts of religious faith. As I show, U.S. Latina/o approaches to religion help critique and rectify what have traditionally been some of the weakest parts of William James's and John Dewey's philosophies of religion, namely, their underappreciation of the social dimensions of reli-gion and their general neglect of pastoral approaches to faith.[4]

UNDERSTANDING PRAGMATISM

The philosophy of U.S. pragmatism is often misunderstood, owing in large part to how we use the word "pragmatic" in ordinary speech. Denotative definitions of "pragmatic," for example, often suggest that the word refers to practical matters of fact as opposed to intellectual, artistic, or idealistic matters. Today, the term often comes up in reference to business or politics. A pragmatic individual is someone who can make tough decisions and who can "get the job done." In the best light, this means that such a person weighs all possible evidence and renders clear-cut decisions. In the worst light, this person becomes a kind of crass utilitarian who does what is most expedient or efficient, regardless of the consequences.

The truth of the matter, however, is that "pragmatism" and "pragmatic" carry quite different meanings within the context of U.S. pragmatism, a distinctive philosophical tradition that emerged in the United States around the turn of the twentieth century, largely through the work of Charles Sanders Peirce, William James, John Dewey, and George Herbert Mead. Contrary to what many denotative definitions suggest, U.S. pragmatism is, in fact, quite open to artistic matters and idealistic concerns. In fact, as I will suggest in a moment, such considerations are key building blocks for a pragmatic theory of religious faith.

Much can be said about the history and meaning of pragmatism, but for the sake of brevity, let me simply say that pragmatism may be understood in four complementary ways. First, pragmatism refers to a philosophical method that takes seriously the indissoluble link between theory and practice. It seeks to address practice by relentlessly interrogating the theory that informs it. More precisely, pragmatism is a method that looks at ideas and beliefs in terms of their practical and social effects rather than in terms of timeless or inherent truths. To understand the meaning of an idea, for example, one should look to what this idea *does*, which is to say how it *orients* us in a particular way in the world. To this extent, pragmatism is indeed interested in the "practical" bearings of thought.

Second, pragmatism is also a nonreductive discourse about experience. It is a form of empiricism that seeks to give a credible account of experience in all its richness, particularity, and complexity. Like today's contextual theologies, pragmatism places a premium on "actual" and "everyday" forms of experience without reducing experience to that which is quantifiable and measurable. After all, "actual" and "practical" experience contains within it ideal and aesthetic aspects that may be better assessed qualitatively than quantitatively. As a robust empiricism, pragmatism does not shy away from matters of quality since they too exist in "actual" experience.

Third, pragmatism is, at its best, a critical theory, or a tool for social criticism. Pragmatists are quite aware that all social institutions have their moorings in habits of thought. Pragmatists probe these underlying habitual ways of thinking not only to clarify their meaning, but more importantly to change them. As scholars such as Cornel West and Rebecca Chopp have noted, pragmatism offers a set of interpretations that not only attempt "to explain America to itself at a particular moment" but also to "change what is into a better what can be."[5]

Last, pragmatism may be understood as an evolving and contested tradition. It is, in many ways, on ongoing debate about the meaning of pragmatism. Such debates add to the vitality of the tradition. As we see today, pragmatism is being put to use in an impressive variety of ways. Scholars of color and feminists, for example, have begun to draw on pragmatism in ways that are congenial to decolonial and liberating approaches to religion. One notes, for example, the pioneering work of Cornel West in philosophy and religious studies; Charlene Haddock Seigfried and Eduardo Mendieta in philosophy; Donald Gelpi, Rebecca Chopp, and Sheila Greeve Davaney in theology; and Eddie Glaude Jr. in religious studies and African American studies. One could also add to this list the thought-provoking philosophical work of Gregory Fernando Pappas, who has argued that—contrary to what many would expect— pragmatism "reflects values that are cherished by Latin, not North American, culture."[6] Such interpretations of pragmatism can go a long way to correct prominent misunderstandings of it, such as those coming from Latin America. Although Latin American philosophy and pragmatism share a host of family resemblances and emancipatory aims, Latin American philosophy has unfortunately often equated pragmatism with a kind of shallow utilitarianism or expedient technologism. As recent scholarship suggests, a new conversation between these two traditions is sorely needed.[7]

As a Mexican American who identifies with and values subaltern epistemologies, I consider my own work to be very much a part of this larger attempt to reinterpret pragmatism "from the margins." I take to heart Roberto Unger's recent call for a "radicalized pragmatism," which treats concepts less as reflections of the natural order of things and more as tools, or valuable weapons, for social change. My pragmatic approach to religious faith is also deeply indebted to the "prophetic pragmatism" of Cornel West, for whom the option for the poor and oppressed is central. This being said, my work brings to light some key aspects of a pragmatic theory of religious faith that go largely unexplored by Unger and West. Although both scholars rightly highlight the political implications of pragmatic instrumentalism—particularly John Dewey's version of it— they do not, on my reading, fully reckon with the ways in which Dewey's philosophy of religion intimately connects a metaphysical outlook with an instrumentalist epistemology.[8] This connection, I argue, provides a crucial key for more fully understanding Dewey's philosophy of religion and, by extension, for better grasping its import for decolonial thought.[9]

PRAGMATISM AND RELIGION

Just as pragmatism is commonly misidentified as a philosophy of technological efficiency, so too is it often assumed to have little or nothing to say about religion. Pragmatism is unfortunately identified as a form of secular humanism or atheism. Such assessments, however, miss the mark of what the classic pragmatists actually said about religious faith. A number of scholars, including myself, are helping to set the record straight: The classical pragmatists indeed "took the religious life seriously and made vital contributions to understanding what it means."[10]

Of all of the classical pragmatists, John Dewey—educator, philosopher, and social critic—was most interested in socially engaged forms of faith. He saw faith not as a matter of assent to doctrine, but rather, as a matter of lived praxis. Dewey explored the ways in which the religious aspect of human experience could be used as a vital force to promote more just and democratic forms of living. As one of his foremost biographers notes, Dewey's philosophy of religion evolved into what many today would call a form of liberation theology.[11]

Given this affinity between Dewey's philosophy of religion and liberationist thought, I explore how Dewey's philosophy of religion helps subvert the modern dichotomization between the aesthetic and the ethical dimensions of faith. As I show, Dewey's starting point is an important one: These dimensions of human experience are not sui generis or self-generating types of experience, but rather continually changing qualities of experience.

This shift in thinking from discrete types of experience to shared qualities of experience opens up a promising avenue for decolonial thought, since it does not dissect experience into different "parts." To see the full significance of this shift from type of experience to quality of experience, consider, for a moment, how moderns have tended to view "religious experience" as a particular type of experience. Owing largely to the influence of Kant, moderns have been obsessed with the question: In what fundamental capacity of human nature does religion fit—thoughts, actions, or feelings? Kant himself pursued the question in his three *Critiques*, ultimately opting for ethical action as the proper basis for religion. Yet, the debate hardly ended there. As Walter Capps has pointed out, various options emerged in the wake of the "Kantian paradigm," including (1) the further development of Kant's ethical position (as seen, for example, in the work of Ritschl), (2) alternative answers within Kant's tripartite schema (such as Schleiermacher's turn to the aesthetic *feeling* of "absolute dependence"), and (3) the proposal of new paradigms altogether (such as Rudolf Otto's concept of "the Holy," which is an attempt to surpass rationalistic, ethical, and aesthetic accounts of religious experience).[12]

If we take the "Kantian paradigm" as our starting point, it would be fair to say that pragmatists have opted for choice number 3, the development of a new paradigm. To be sure, however, the pragmatic alternative differs greatly from Otto's proposal. Rather than searching for "the religious" as a discrete type of experience, which is still reflected in Otto's search for a religious a priori, pragmatists tend to focus on the religious as a qualitative and active dimension of life. As William James says, "Religion, whatever it is, is man's total reaction upon life."[13] The question for the pragmatist, then, is not so much "In what human capacity is religion located?" but rather, "*How* do we react upon life, and in what ways may this reaction qualify as 'religious'?" Although he doesn't write explicitly as a pragmatist, the scholar of religion Wilfred Cantwell Smith captures the pragmatic position well when he observes that the religious aspect of human experience is best understood not as a noun, an entity, or a thing—as in "*a* religion"—but rather as an adjective and adverb—that is, how we live in a *religious way*.

The pragmatic shift from "type" of experience to "quality" of experience proves significant because it points to a fundamentally revised metaphysics and epistemology, which, in pragmatism, are intimately related. To begin with, it is important to keep in mind that pragmatism espouses a nonreductive form of empiricism. Its object of study is experience as it is "actually lived." Put negatively, this means that pragmatism turns away from idealistic, transcendental, or universalizing presuppositions that have no basis in the ebb-and-flow of "actual experience." Put positively, however, this turn to experience alternatively signals a deep appreciation for the richness, plurality, and depth of experience. Thus, without succumbing to a transcendental metaphysics, pragmatism acknowledges that experience is always more than what meets the eye. It eschews reductive empiricisms (such as certain forms of British empiricism) that value only that which is quantifiable, measurable, or readily apparent to the senses.

Pragmatism may be said, then, to straddle a middle ground between positivistic and transcendental accounts of experience. With the positivists, pragmatists indeed narrow the object of study to actual experience, yet with the transcendentalists, they acknowledge that actual experience is much more subtle, complex, and even "ineffable" than we have been taught to think.[14] Pragmatic empiricists take quite seriously, in other words, what James refers to as the "rich thicket of reality."[15]

As regards knowledge, pragmatists believe that we engage experience both reflectively and prereflectively. Knowledge, strictly speaking, is a *reflective* account of past events. It is a memorandum, using sequences and relations, of things that happen to us "immediately." At the same time, however, we also experience reality in countless *prereflective*, aesthetic, or "immediate," ways. "Immediate experience" describes our engagement with reality prior to our fully making sense of it. It is experience that "hits us" viscerally and emotionally, and it is qualitatively "had" rather than quantitatively "known."[16] The immediate things of aesthetic experience may thus be said to serve as the raw fodder for knowledge.

The experience of being scared by a sudden sound would be an example of immediate experience. This event has a distinctive quality all its own, and it is only after we attempt to make sense of this noise ("From where is it coming? What is its source? Am I really in danger?") that the distinctive quality of this experience changes. At the point of being scared, the quality of the experience may be primarily visceral, emotional, and indeterminate. On reflection, however, the quality of the experience may change to one that is intellectual, rationalistic, and determinate.

The significance of such an account is twofold. First, it underscores the need for empirical analysis to account not only for intellectual and reflective modes of experience but also for visceral and prereflective modes. A robust empiricism demands that we take account of determinate situations as much as indeterminate ones, since both are part-and-parcel of experience as it is "actually" experienced. Second, such an account highlights the fact that the qualitative experience *changes* as knowledge takes hold of it. For the pragmatist, experience is nothing other than the interaction of an organism with its environment. Taking their cue from Darwin, pragmatists acknowledge that this interaction grows, recedes, and emerges once again.

These general insights into experience and knowledge have specific corollaries within pragmatic accounts of religious faith. Like experience in general, the religious aspect of human experience may surface in both prereflective and reflective ways. Dewey refers to the prereflective experience of the religious as "natural piety," and he calls its reflective manifestations "moral faith."

"Natural piety" is a form of immediate experience that involves what we may call aesthetic "undergoing."[17] It is a visceral sense of consummation that is freely given in nature (of which humans are a part), and it incites in us a sense of wonder and awe. We may undergo natural piety, for example, when we are wowed by the sight of the Grand Canyon, entranced by the flicker of a flame, comforted by the occasional moments of silence around us, or engulfed in meaningful conversation with others. Dewey honors these kinds of immediate experience. He insists, however, that such experiences need not be explicitly connected to a particular religious institution, nor need they be automatically attributed to a supernatural power. But because natural piety contains a sense of "internal integration" and "fulfillment," this experience may be described, at least provisionally, as an end-in-itself, given that it is marked by a certain self-sustaining quality of its own.

Whereas natural piety may be understood in terms of aesthetic "undergoing," moral faith is akin to ethical "doing." Moral faith refers to an active and engaged sense of faith. It involves the construction of meaningful ideals and the active pursuit of these ideals through the use of intelligence and human action. To return, momentarily, to our earlier discussion of modernity's "Kantian paradigm," if natural piety may seem to imply a Schleiermachian emphasis on the aesthetic feeling of "undergoing" experience (or being "beholden" to it), moral faith suggests a more classical Kantian emphasis on actively transforming experience to fulfill a moral good.

Given what I have said thus far, one might be inclined to conclude that "natural piety" refers to the aesthetic dimension of faith whereas "moral faith" captures its ethical dimension. This is a fair assessment, but only insofar as it does not treat these dimensions of faith as discrete and autonomous types of experience. In other words, one should not so quickly accept the terms of the "Kantian paradigm" whereby the aesthetic and ethical "dimensions" of faith are thought to be like different "rooms." In such an interpretation, these rooms are clearly set apart. Their relationship is, at best, structural and formal.

A pragmatic theory of religious faith avoids this kind of spatial conceptualization, which tends to reinforce certain epistemological hierarchies. For the pragmatist, the aesthetic and ethical "dimensions" of faith are not so much discrete "spaces" or "rooms" within human experience, but rather, qualities that may inhabit any and all forms of human experience. These two dimensions are more like the colors of a room rather than the rooms themselves. Indeed, these colors may be applied to any and all rooms. Among other things, the pragmatic contribution is to show that the qualities that "color" experience are as real as physical and material things. Experience, for the pragmatist, is both actual and ideal.

Moreover, a pragmatic theory of religious faith acknowledges that these qualities change as knowledge takes hold of them. To return to our earlier example, we saw how an indeterminate experience of being scared became a determinate one through the process of inquiry. The "immediate experience" of fright changes as one begins to ask questions about it. Inquiry thus helps expand the meaning of a given situation, and, in so doing, it guides us toward new paths of action.[18] Rather than being caught in a perpetual state of fright, for example, inquiry helps us "settle" problematic or indeterminate situations so that we can move forward with new courses of action.

Pragmatism builds on this insight by adding a further observation: The transformation of indeterminate experience into determinate experience is not a linear process, but rather a spiraling one. If this process were linear, the goal of inquiry would be to surpass all indeterminate and "imperfect" forms of knowledge—which aesthetic and religious rationalities are often assumed to be—in order to reach a determinate and verifiable form of knowledge. Fortunately, pragmatism does not espouse such a "straight-line," or positivistic, view of knowledge.[19] Instead, pragmatists recognize that experience becomes truly meaningful when it draws on both reflective and prereflective modes of knowing. Dewey is explicit on this point. Knowledge, he says, "becomes something more than knowledge because it is merged with non-intellectual elements to form an experience worth while as an experience."[20] In other words, nonintellectual elements are needed, even in science, to help "round off" experience in meaningful ways. In short, aesthetic quality "cannot be sharply marked off from intellectual experience since the latter must bear an esthetic stamp to be itself complete."[21]

These insights prove significant for efforts to decolonize religion because they help us see that moral faith—which relies on the "method of intelligence"—cannot be sharply marked off from natural piety—which bears its own "aesthetic stamp." Although analytically distinct, moral faith and natural piety are functionally related. This observation is especially crucial because skeptics are likely to assume that pragmatism is interested in only moral, and intelligent, forms of faith at the expense of expressions of natural piety. Quite the contrary. As Dewey says, the essentially unreligious attitude is that which denies natural piety, "that which attributes human achievement and purpose to man in isolation from the world of physical nature and his fellows."[22] To drive home this point further, Dewey speaks sympathetically of mystical experience as one form of natural piety. In a passage that may surprise many, Dewey, echoing Santayana, writes, "There is no reason for denying the existence of experiences that are called mystical. On the contrary, there is every reason to suppose that, in some degree of intensity, they occur so frequently that they may be regarded as normal manifestations that take place at certain rhythmic points in the movement of experience."[23] In this statement, we find an amazing openness to the glory of natural experience.

To be sure, Dewey does indeed turn to moral faith and the method of intelligence as a means to appreciate better natural piety as a natural—and not supernatural—phenomenon. But it is important to note that his recourse to moral faith is not meant to be a definitive antidote to natural piety, wherein moral faith's "intelligent action" serves to correct, once and for all, the admittedly "transitory and unstable" elements of natural piety.[24] If this were the case, Dewey's view of knowledge would indeed amount to a "straight-line" instrumentalism. Instead, Dewey lauds moral faith because he believes that it can lead us on to newer, and qualitatively richer, forms of "immediate experience." Just as natural piety—as a form of aesthetic experience—demands the reflective processes of moral faith, so too can moral faith, in turn, give rise to new forms of aesthetic experience. At their best, moral faith and natural piety functionally complement each other in an emerging and spiraling fashion. A marriage between the two helps both to grow.

The great payoff of this whole process is the development of an enduring pragmatic attitude. Indeed, the idea of cultivating an "enduring attitude" is a key motif for pragmatic philosophy in general and for a pragmatic theory of faith in particular. This idea greatly expands the often-held assumption that pragmatism is nothing more than a philosophy of "getting things done," or, as we will see momentarily, a philosophy of "adaptation." Peirce articulated early on, however, that how we get things done—that is, how we "adapt" ourselves to the world, or how we shape and reshape our habits—has tremendous implication for the long run, for habitual action determines, in large part, the kind of people and society we truly are. Thus, while intelligence, as a means for solving particular problematic situations, is certainly a key feature of pragmatism, the more significant payoff is the *total way of life* that is gained through its repeated and habitual use.

In terms of religion, this total way of life may be described as a type of spirituality that is not necessarily dependent on institutional religion or its usual recourse to supernaturalism. This pragmatic spirituality grows through the functional interplay between intelligence and moral action, on the one hand, and appreciation for the aesthetics of the natural world and everyday human life, on the other. James hints at this type of spirituality when he writes of "man's total reaction upon life," and Dewey describes it as a deep-seated "adjustment" in life.

Religious "adjustment" is different from other forms of human response like "accommodation" and "adaptation." "Accommodation" implies a largely passive, or submissive, reaction to external circumstances. We accommodate ourselves, for example, to changes in the weather or to uncontrollable changes in income. In comparison, "adaptation" implies a more active and engaged response to one's environment. Books are carefully "adapted" into movies; houses are remodeled to meet the needs of growing families; cell phones are redesigned to meet new consumer demands. In short, whereas in accommodation we accommodate ourselves to conditions, in adaptation we modify conditions so that they will conform to our purposes and desires.

"Adjustment" suggests a more significant type of response. It involves a process of self-transformation and self-realization that is "much more inclusive and deep seated" than the other two forms of response. Unlike accommodation and adaptation, adjustment is not a specific response to specific circumstances, but rather, an attitude that is forged over time and that is shaped, in part, by countless "accommodations" and "adaptations." Adjustment does not depend, then, on any particular resolve or volition, for it "lasts through any amount of vicissitude of circumstances, internal and external." Rather, it is a fundamental "change *of* will"— when "will" reflects the organic wholeness of the self—rather than "any special change *in* will."[25]

Adjustment, in short, proves to be Dewey's highest form of religiosity, after "natural piety" and "moral faith." Adjustment is the "general attitude" that is gained when, over multiple occasions (or, indeed, over the course of a lifetime), moral faith and natural piety interact and grow, thereby leading to a "unification of the self." As a naturally occurring form of spirituality, adjustment is the enduring way of life that is gained when one intelligently mobilizes natural piety and moral faith in a manner that sustains and enriches both.

So what does this all tell us? Why is this pragmatic theory of faith significant for efforts to decolonize religion? First, on the most general level, pragmatism offers a theory of religious faith that is not beholden to institutional forms of religion. This is particularly significant given the colonizing histories of most major world religions. Indeed, the very concept "religion" is a modern invention that has been fueled by a variety of colonial encounters. Colonizers have often constructed differences in "religion" in order to further increase their distance from the indigenous "other."[26] Because pragmatism does not root its theory of faith in particular religious doctrines or dogmas, it is more apt to avoid certain hierarchical logics that often characterize the colonial religious imaginary. As I will develop further in the next section, however, just because pragmatism is not beholden to institutional forms of religion does not mean that it cannot be harmonized with them. In other words, I see no necessary antinomy between a pragmatic theory of faith and institutional forms of religion. There are, after all, important subversive counter-traditions within institutional religions that critique colonizing and imperialistic tendencies. One sees this, for example, in certain articulations of liberation theology, beginning with Bartolomé de Las Casas's heroic defense of the Amerindians in the sixteenth century, and in religious movements of nonviolence, such as those led by Mahatma Gandhi, Martin Luther King Jr., and César Chávez.

Second, and more substantively, like indigenous cosmologies, pragmatism approaches experience in an integral, holistic, and nonreductionistic way. It calls into question dominant Western dualisms by putting forth a view of experience that is at once fluid, porous, and complex. As with indigenous cosmologies, pragmatism acknowledges that while certain pairings may be analytically distinct, they are nevertheless fluid, changing, and emerging realities. Pragmatism, I have tried to show, unpacks this insight in two ways. First, it espouses a metaphysics in which experience is best approached as a compendium of interrelated *qualities* rather than discrete *types* of experience. Second, it offers an instrumentalist epistemology that accounts for *how* these qualities interrelate with one another.

Decolonial and liberationist efforts share pragmatism's interest in offering an alternative metaphysics that subverts modern, colonial dichotomies. Oftentimes, these efforts are aided by turning to premodern cosmologies or to postmodern theory. Indeed, scholars such as Sylvia Marcos and María Lugones creatively and simultaneously weave in aspects of both. The introduction of alternative cosmologies is no doubt a crucial move, yet, a subsequent question must also be broached: Within these alternative metaphysics, *how*, exactly, do fluid dualities interrelate? How can we retain an analytic distinction between complementary dualities—like the aesthetic and ethical dimensions of religion—and still adequately account for their integral and holistic relation? Pragmatic instrumentalism, I have suggested, offers a useful pathway forward, for it makes the function of knowledge central to this inquiry. Pragmatism helps show how prereflective forms of knowledge (such as natural piety) interact with reflective forms of knowledge (such as moral faith) so as to give rise to an enduring attitude (or deep-seated form of spirituality). In doing so, a pragmatic hermeneutic offers decolonial thought insight into

the *process* of a naturally occurring form of faith formation that is beholden neither to traditional religions nor to the dichotomizing epistemologies that often accompany them.

STRENGTHENING PRAGMATISM: SOME CONTRIBUTIONS
OF U.S. LATINA/O FAITH EXPERIENCE

If a pragmatic theory of faith can contribute to contemporary efforts to
decolonize religion, what does U.S. Latina/o liberation thought offer to
the discussion? In what follows, I highlight three possibilities.

First, Latina/o religious experience helps pragmatists better appreciate
the social and communal nature of faith practice. For all the attention
that the classical pragmatists give to a critical community of inquirers
(Peirce) and to the social ramifications of pragmatism (Dewey), early
pragmatists are often lacking when it comes to the social dimensions of
faith. This is especially the case with William James and John Dewey. In
the *Varieties of Religious Experience* (1902), for example, James interprets
the social dimension of faith largely in terms of the institutional church,
for which he has little patience. James warns that in churches the "spirit
of politics and the lust of dogmatic rule are . . . apt to enter and to
contaminate the originally innocent thing." The "originally innocent
thing" is, for James, "first-hand religious experience" that resides "within
the private breast."²⁷ Both for good and for ill, James believes that the
churches capture "but a fractional element" of faith when compared to
the power of individual religiosity.

Dewey's *A Common Faith* (1934) unfortunately employs the same basic
distinction. What James describes as the calcifying tendencies of institutional churches Dewey labels "religion," and what James refers to as the
individual spontaneous spirit Dewey commonly refers to as "the religious." Repeatedly, Dewey pits these two concepts against each other,
as seen in the title of his introductory chapter: "Religion vs. The Religious." It is both ironic and unfortunate that Dewey—one of the preemi-
nent social philosophers of his time—adds little to the question of the
social dimensions of religion in *A Common Faith*.

In contrast, Latin American and Hispanic liberation thinkers have
worked hard to highlight the social dimensions of faith. Because liberation thinkers take seriously the biblical mandate to serve "the least of

these," faith becomes less a strictly private affair and more an interpersonal expression of solidarity and love. Though faith always has an irreducible individual dimension, liberation thinkers understand that faith often proves most significant and meaningful when the option for the poor and oppressed is central to its expression.

Latin American and Latina/o liberation thinkers have illuminated both the *intrinsic* and *extrinsic* social dimensions of faith. As regards the intrinsic social nature of faith, many liberation thinkers begin with a basic Durkheimian insight: Community is the birthplace of the self. Just as one's cultural identity emerges out of a community, so too does individual faith depend, in large part, on the communities that sustain it. Among others, Virgilio Elizondo has described the intrinsic, relational anthropologies that inform Latin American and Latina/o faith practice. "For our native forefathers," Elizondo writes, "it was not the individuals who by coming together made up the community, but rather it was the community . . . which actually brought the individual person into existence." Babies were born "faceless," which, within the context of indigenous Mesoamerica, meant without personality and individual identity. To rectify this situation, the community "called forth the individuality of the person." Individual existence was thus based on one's "indivisible unity with the group."[28] In a substantive way, the community *made* the individual person.

Liberation thinkers have developed further the theoretical significance of this kind of intrinsic, relational anthropology. One group that has been especially important in this regard are mujerista and Latina feminist theologians. Owing much to the groundbreaking work of Ada María Isasi-Díaz and María Pilar Aquino, these scholars have argued that feminist ways of "thinking relationally" represent valid alternatives to patriarchal approaches to human subjectivity, which rely on stratified gender hierarchies and a false sense of individuality. In so doing, Latin American and U.S. Hispanic theologians—along with their Euro-American and womanist counterparts—have articulated a variety of egalitarian, relational, communal, and embodied anthropologies. Collectively, these constructive proposals strive toward "an egalitarian vision of humanity as created in the image of God," and they offer new models of God as a form of "relational transcendence."[29]

For their part, philosophers of liberation have productively explored the intrinsic, "intersubjective" character of ethical discourse and religious faith. The Latin American philosopher Enrique Dussel has been especially important in this regard, and Dussel's work has influenced a host of Latina/o philosophers, such as Eduardo Mendieta, Nelson Maldonado-Torres, and Linda Martín Alcoff, as well as Latina/o theologians such as Roberto Goizueta and René Sanchez. Dussel's engagement with "discourse ethics," in particular, is reflected especially in the work of Mendieta and Goizueta, who, in their own ways, explore how ethics is grounded in the very structure and context of human communication. Significantly, this insight into the ethical significance of human communication has roots in the pragmatic tradition. One can trace this influence back to Dussel's substantial engagement with continental thinkers like Jürgen Habermas and Karl-Otto Apel, who, in turn, have drawn inspiration from classical pragmatists like Charles Sanders Peirce and George Herbert Mead.[30]

A third group of liberation thinkers has explored the intrinsic nature of social faith by returning more directly to the early pragmatism of C. S. Peirce and Josiah Royce. Among these theologians are Alejandro García Rivera, Robert Lassalle-Klein, and Nancy Pineda-Madrid. These scholars, who have ties to the Graduate Theological Union in Berkeley, California, have used Peirce's and Royce's theories of interpretation to elucidate the communal character of Latina/o culture and religion. Each has made a case that the semiotics of Peirce and/or Royce gives philosophical clarity to significant themes in U.S. Latina/o theology, including theological aesthetics, Guadalupe and mestizaje, and popular ritual. Specifically, García-Rivera shows that Peirce's and Royce's semiotics lend philosophical credibility to Hans Urs von Balthasar's idea of "seeing the form" of divine Beauty. Lassalle-Klein uses Peirce, among other things, to deepen Virgilio Elizondo's social-cultural interpretation of la Virgen de Guadalupe as a powerful symbol that mediates the liberating message of Jesus, on the one hand, and the historical violence of mestizaje, on the other. Lassalle-Klein does this by showing how Peirce's triadic semiotics helps us see with greater clarity how the Guadalupe symbol serves as a powerful "interpretant," which Peirce understands as a highly developed sign that makes "ultimate" claims on human beings insofar as it produces new habits of action. Nancy Pineda-Madrid, with the help of Royce and

Catherine Bell, has shown that ritual practices can legitimately be understood as sign interpretation. When such a hermeneutic is employed, one can better see how rituals sustain community and facilitate the transmission of faith.[31]

Aside from showing that faith is intrinsically social, Latin American and Latina/o liberation thinkers have also helped to expand our idea of social faith as it is *extrinsically* manifested in religious institutions and practice. Whereas James and Dewey tend to look on churches and other religious institutions with disdain, liberation thinkers, especially theologians, have wisely called for reinterpretations of "church" that move well beyond top-down, hierarchical models. Leonardo Boff's work in ecclesiology has been exemplary in this regard. Boff, a native of Brazil, has argued persuasively that "the hierarchical function is essential in the church—but it does not subsist in and for itself." Rather, the hierarchical function must be understood "as subsisting within the faith community and in its service."[32] Boff therefore proposes a model of the church that emerges from the poor and is based in the radically egalitarian experience of Pentecost. In such a model, the church gains power not by "accumulation and absorption, but in integration and coordination." The church's "charism," in other words, is "not outside the community, but within it; not over the community, but for the good of the community."[33]

U.S. Latina/o theologians have learned much from these insights, and they have expanded further the meaning of church as the "community of the faithful" by looking at the extraecclesial practices of popular religion. The theologian Orlando Espín—who, not inconsequentially, studied with Leonardo Boff in Brazil—has offered some of the most significant studies of Latina/o popular Catholicism. Espín recounts how his own approach to popular religion changed significantly from the mid-1970s to the mid-1990s. As a pastoral agent on the Haitian-Dominican border in the mid-'70s, Espín recounts that the poor people with whom he worked were Catholic, "but not in the way [he] had been used to or trained to appreciate." At this time in his life, Espín viewed their religious practices as "incorrect, insufficient, or superstitious," and he saw their "bastardized form of Christianity" as a "very serious impediment to their understanding the social and economic forces that were oppressing them, and a real obstacle for a liberating praxis."[34]

With the passing of two decades, however, Espín, like so many other U.S Latina/o theologians, came to understand the faith of the people in a more sympathetic way. He became aware of his own "theologically colonizing" disposition toward popular religion. Over time, he grew to see popular Catholicism as "the real faith of the real Church."[35] In saying this, Espín acknowledges that written texts make up an important part of tradition, but equally, if not more, important, he adds, is "the living witness and faith of the Christian people."[36] For Espín and other Latina/o theologians, popular Catholicism embodies this living witness. It is a source of revelation insofar as it embodies the *sensus fidelium*, or "sense of the faithful."

In addition to attending to the intrinsic and extrinsic social dimensions of faith, Latina/o liberation thinkers have also underscored the importance of a pastoral approach to faith. Through their pastoral interventions, liberation thinkers often help bridge the "practice" of faith at the popular level with the "theory" of faith-reflection at the professional level.[37] Many are academic professionals as well as active leaders and participants in churches and other faith-based initiatives. As pastoral agents, they help people connect their own personal experiences to larger gospel narratives and themes.

Such a pastoral approach has much to add to contemporary pragmatic interpretations of religious faith. As I see it, the pragmatic tradition has bequeathed two related, yet distinct—and, at times, somewhat competing—approaches to faith. The first, which owes much to Charles Sanders Peirce's work in logic, can be described as a "conceptual and logical" approach to faith that is concerned with the conceptual clarity of religious ideas. The second, which is more akin to John Dewey's theory of education, may be labeled a "developmentalist" approach that understands faith in terms of the ongoing process of transforming experience. The two approaches are closely connected. After all, our experience is always informed and shaped by the conceptual categories we use to describe it. Concepts not only help us to make sense *of* experience, but in their own way, they, too, *make* experience. To this extent, the two approaches are intimately related.

Yet, they are also distinct. Pragmatic thinkers have put varying degrees of emphasis on these two approaches. Dewey himself weighs their difference in his classic book on education, *Democracy and Education* (1916). On the one hand, Dewey speaks positively on behalf of scientific method, which rests on logical clarity. Science signifies "the *logical* implications of any knowledge."[38] It is "rational assurance" and "logical warranty."[39] By way of example, Dewey explains that a competent zoologist can reconstruct an animal just by looking at a few bones. Similarly, the specialist in mathematics or physics can often form an idea of a larger system of truths just by looking at a single formula. The logical inference of science allows for such possibilities.

On the other hand, however, Dewey also acknowledges that "to the non-expert" such a logical approach may often prove to be a "stumbling block." From the standpoint of the learner, Dewey notes, "scientific form is an ideal to be achieved, not a starting point from which to set out. . . . To the layman the bones are a mere curiosity. Until he had mastered the principles of zoölogy, his efforts to make anything out of them would be random and blind."[40]

Accordingly, Dewey tempers his enthusiasm for the logical method of the expert or specialist. Education also requires a "chronological" or "psychological" method, which educators today would refer to as a "developmentalist" approach to learning.[41] Such an approach begins with the experience of the learner. It organizes subject matter so as to coordinate it with the interests and abilities of the student. Once these conditions are met, the teacher may indeed choose to move on to more logic-based methods. The crucial point, however, is that the new learner is first engaged with the subject matter in a developmentally appropriate way. Such an approach helps guarantee that "what the pupil learns he at least understands."[42] This is no doubt one of Dewey's most pivotal educational insights. Unfortunately, however, he fails to apply it the realm of religion and the ongoing "educational" process of faith formation.

Owing much to the pedagogical work of Paulo Freire, many liberation thinkers today approach religion in developmentalist terms, thereby making this link explicit. They understand that religious faith is an ongoing process that requires continual reflection and cultivation. Since religious individuals experience faith in a variety of ways and in countless different contexts, it follows that the role of the religious educator should have less to do with putting forward ironclad logical propositions and more to do with offering metaphors, symbols, rituals, and stories that can speak to adherents in a number of different ways.⁴³ When deployed effectively, these metaphors, symbols, rituals, and stories may help adherents make new connections between their "life of faith" and their "life-at-large." The religious educator thus "educates" by meeting people where they are and by inviting them to take their present experience and to transform it on a continual and ongoing basis.⁴⁴

As I have shown, liberation thinkers offer some important lessons for a pragmatic theory of faith, especially in those areas where it is weakest. Liberationists make clear that the intrinsic social dimensions of faith are often more subtle and complex than many pragmatists would admit. Liberationists also show that there is no *necessary* antinomy between a sense of personal religiosity and institutional religion, and they make a strong case for pastoral—versus strictly logical—approaches to religious faith. Although one can certainly find these liberationists and pastoral impulses in pragmatic writings, these themes are often muted or disparate. Liberationist thought thus serves as a useful conversation partner to help foreground their importance.

But just as liberationists have much to offer pragmatism, so too does pragmatism have much to offer liberation and decolonial thought. I began this essay by showing how pragmatism provides a strong philosophical method for making more explicit the integral relationship between the aesthetic and ethical dimensions of faith. Rather than treat these pairings as discrete types of religious experience—which continues to be the norm in modern epistemologies—pragmatism underscores their functional relation in experience. Pragmatism's nonreductive empiricism and its generative and spiraling instrumentalism allow for an integration of these qualities as changing and fluid functions of experience. Such insights serve as valuable building blocks for further decolonizing religious faith.

✧ The Ethics of (Not) Knowing: Take Care of Ethics and Knowledge Will Come of Its Own Accord

EDUARDO MENDIETA

THE EPISTEMIC MACHINE: AN ATTEMPT AT DISMANTLING IT

Over the gates that open to our modern age there hangs a sign, cast in iron but radiant like so many neon signs in Manhattan's Times Square: "Knowledge shall make you free." This is the shibboleth that since Francis Bacon, Isaac Newton, Galileo Galilei, and René Descartes has set apart our period from those coming before it. From Bacon, we get the catchphrase "knowledge is power." From Newton and Galileo, we inherited the idea that to decipher the language of the book of nature requires that we crack its mathematical syntax: God's thoughts are written in the language of mathematics. From Descartes, we receive the carte blanche of radical doubt that would leave standing only that which cannot be doubted—the certainty of the thinking "I." The Cartesian project of laying an unshakable ground of epistemic certitude led to the ethical and moral evisceration of the subject.

Although our age is called the "modern age," the age of reason, and the age of science, where each one of these designators is the Janus face of the other, it can also be called the age of knowledge. We have pursued reason, against faith, to obtain knowledge that could be functionalized into technology. In fact, our science and technology have been one since Bacon launched the age of science. The metastasizing of science and technology into technoscience has been epitomized by Leonard da Vinci as no one else has epitomized it. We have become modern as we chased after an elusive "modernity" by pursuing knowledge. Knowledge, so goes the mythology of the West, has made us modern. Knowledge is thus always juxtaposed against tradition. Tradition is what we received from our predecessors. Knowledge is what we wrest from the body of nature. Tradition makes us old, that is, traditional. Knowledge makes us new, that is, utterly modern. Knowledge thus is about being dehistoricized by being catapulted into the not yet, the future. Knowledge appears atemporal, although what makes us distinct is in fact temporal or, rather more precisely, historical. Knowledge raises us above history, whereas tradition grounds us in history.

This is one seductive story, but it is hardly the whole story, or for that matter the real story of how our time, our own historicality, has been constituted by a more intricate and dissimulated project. Even if there is a kernel of truth in this self-congratulating and self-aggrandizing story about the "rise of the West," the story has to be localized and placed within a larger narrative about how the pursuit of knowledge is accompanied by the constitution or construction of certain types of knowing subjects. Before there is knowledge, there is a knower. The project of the pursuit of knowledge, additionally, commands the mapping, or gerrymandering, of regions of knowledge. A knower knows something, some things about some things. The project of knowing thus requires the construction of a reservoir of entities to be known. This mapping, bounding, and circumscribing exclude by including. The modern epistemological project, the project of becoming modern by becoming atemporal, presupposed the construction of a particular type of subject that would be, to use Donna Haraway's apropos expression, the "authorized ventriloquist"[1] of that object world in which it had been traced, encircled, duly registered. This subject, the modern subject, is the knower par excellence, that is, as a knower he (and we know that the proper, legitimate, reliable, and trustworthy knower is gendered without gender, that is, as male) would be transparent, reflective, impassioned, passive, a perfect surface on which the object of knowledge would be faithfully reflected. Again, in Haraway's language, this "credible" and "authorized" knowing subject would be one in which "subjectivity would be objectivity."[2] The story of the rise of the West thus is a story about the invention of this epistemic machine that empties out his subjectivity so as to become a receptacle for objectivity. This epistemic machine, however, is a device, what Michel Foucault would have called a *dispositif*, that is, an artificial ensemble that performs certain functions while not performing other ones. At the same time, this epistemic machine, this *dispositif* of the West, attends to a particular ontological region, over which it toils and guards diligently: the realm of nature, the realm of the eternal, the unchanging. The knowing subject is thus also a deculturing device. To eviscerate the subjectivity of the knowing subject demands that this subject become dehistoricized, without a tradition, even a natural language. The ideal epistemic machine speaks in the language of math, equations, statements about objective states of affair. It is the ventriloquist of nature. For this reason, Haraway points out that this "modest witness" (the term she appropriates from Steve Shaping and Simon Schaffer) is one that inhabits the "culture of no culture."[3]

In the following I want to challenge the great fable about how the West became modern by launching the age of reason, science, and knowledge by arguing that such a story presupposes that knowledge can be transparent, pristine, disinterested, and dehistoricized, in a word, timeless and reliable. I will argue that there is a fundamental and insurmountable asymmetry between knowing and unknowing that renders all knowledge precarious, revocable, and perishable. Knowledge is wrested from ignorance, but it also projects its own shadow: unknowing, and disavowed knowledge. I also argue that behind the mask of impassioned obdurate determination downed by the epistemic machine that the epistemological project of the West presupposes is a particular type of ethical subject. The "modest" witness, the credible, authorized, reliable epistemic subject is in fact a moral subject. Knowing is always itself an ethical act. Epistemology presupposes ethics, just as knowledge presupposes a certain type of virtue. More precisely, I argue that knowing is an ethical trope: a turning-in-from-toward—a knowing subject, a knowing agent, is always in a world—in which it localizes itself, by which it is localized, and from which it aims to know by turning toward a certain thing in that world. There is no knowledge that is not situated, historical, and thus woven into a whole culture of what can be known, how it can be known, and by whom it can be known. The challenge therefore is less to demystify a particular fable and more to dismantle the Western epistemological dispositif that evacuates the moral and historical elements that make us into distinct human beings.

Yet, the aim of this project of dismantling the "epistemic machine" presupposed and constructed by the fable of the West is to contribute to the project that Walter Mignolo, Nelson Maldonado-Torres, Lewis Gordon, Anibal Quijano, and Ramon Grosfoguel have called "decolonizing epistemology," or the "decolonial" turn. My argument is that this project gets tangled in a double bind: In order to challenge the way in which epistemology has been used to legitimate and advance the hegemony of the West, over the "rest," it calls for its cleansing, its purification, its sanitation, its reformation, and eventual redemption. The project of decolonizing epistemology, in short, enters the territory of contestation on the terms already determined by the priority of epistemology that is an essential part of the myth of the superiority of the West, the home of modernity. The question to be asked is what comes after we have "decolonized" epistemology? Will a more "objective" epistemology have emerged? Will a better epistemology result, one that is not impaired, distorted, manipulated, instrumentalized, weaponized by some imperial, male chauvinist, racist, homophobic ideology? Is not the pursuit of an epistemology without blinkers, without gendered, raced, classed glasses, precisely how we fell prey to the epistemological project of the West? At the end of the path of decolonizing epistemology is the end of the priority of epistemology, not a better, improved, and reformed epistemology.

THE EPISTEMOLOGY OF IGNORANCE

The guiding metaphor that orients all thinking about knowledge in Western philosophy is that of light: Light is to reason as darkness is to ignorance.[4] In the staging of this metaphor the mind is a lighthouse whose beacon guides us through the hazards of the ocean of opinion, ignorance, and faith onto the continent of knowledge. This is how Kant put it in the *Critique of Pure Reason.* The metaphor has also been staged as an escape in Plato's famous allegory of the cave.[5] In book 7 of the *Republic*, Plato manages to give us an encompassing theory that links epistemology, ontology, ethics, and the vocation of the philosopher in terms of the allegory of the ascent from the prisons of the ephemeral and the shadows of ignorance. For Plato, knowledge is the ascent from the depth of darkness to the heights of luminosity. Plato, however, acknowledges that this ascent can be blinding. The light of the true, the eternal, that which is and thus endures, blinds. The eye of the mind must turn from the blinding light, as it must also turn away from the shadows in the walls of the cave, to the true source of light, which is outside the cave. Knowledge is thus a turning of the mind away from shadows to light, but also from light to the shade. This is important to note because this turning is the moment of not knowing. The shadows, copies of the true objects of knowledge, are caught in this play of light and shadow, knowledge and ignorance. If light is to reason as darkness is to ignorance, and the mind is like a lighthouse, knowledge stands on top of the very darkness of its blinding light—it is darkest at the foot of the lighthouse.

Perhaps Plato and Kant were trying to pay tribute to Socrates' most famous formulation, namely that "he only knows that he does not know" (*Apology*, 21d). We could venture the affirmation that Western philosophy is born with the Socratic recognition of "the fecundity of ignorance." Knowledge is always shadowed by its other: doxa, opinion, ignorance. So, when we speak about the production of knowledge, we must also talk about the production of unknowledge, ignorance, what Socrates called "mere opinion." The production of knowledge is also the production of unknowledge. This is what the scholars Robert Proctor and Londa Schiebinger have called *agnotology*.[6] For Schiebinger the history of the production of knowledges has also been the relentless and vigorous production of ignorance. In her outstanding book *Plants and Empire*, Schiebinger studies the ways in which European botanists appropriated local indigenous botanical knowledge and traditions of botanical pharmacology.[7] The appropriation, however, was accompanied by a process of erasure of the sources of that knowledge. Additionally, Schiebinger notes that the process of the colonial appropriation of local knowledges was caught in an inter-imperial epistemological struggle, in which Spanish and Portuguese jealously guarded their stolen knowledge from British and French colonial botanists. The rush for the Amerindian lands was also a rush for the riches of their indigenous knowledges.

Proctor and Schiebinger's term "agnotology," the logos of nonknowledge, is provocative and evocative because it directs our attention to what I referred to above as the shadowing of knowledge by ignorance. The term, a neologism, suggests that ignorance is not a mere absence of knowledge, in the way in which darkness is a mere absence of light. Rather, the term indicates that ignorance has a logos, that unknowing is a product, a result. The science of ignorance, if we translate agnotology literally, turns out to be about the production of what has been called in hermeneutics occultation, concealment. This has to be underscored: Ignorance is not the absence of knowledge. Ignorance is not the negative supplement of knowledge. Ignorance, unknowledge, has its own ontological status. Ignorance is not privative but affirmative.

Since this text is addressed partly to theologians, agnotology should be analogized with theodicy. Such a comparison would be useful and illuminating, as theodicy is precisely about the way in which evil and injustice exist not because of an absence of God's goodness, or an absence of goodness in general, but because there has been a willful, deliberate turning away from God. In Augustine's work, we can find at least three different answers to the question of theodicy. First, evil exists because of the freedom of our will; second, we let our will be turned away from God's law by our cupidity or concupiscence; and finally, evil exists because as mortal creatures we cannot know God's plan. So, evil is not just about the will, but also about knowledge. For Augustine, particularly in *On the Free Choice of the Will*, it is not enough not to will something. One must positively will its opposite. In other words, evil results not just when we will something immoral and unjust but also when we do not deliberately and avowedly will the good. Evil as ignorance, or rather theodicy as the epistemology of ignorance, tells us that we must guard against what we do not know and seek what can and should be known. Even in Augustine knowledge is haunted by ignorance, and this is what we can find in his theodicy, as it is presented in both *On the Free Choice of the Will* and the *Civitas Dei*.

The point of this comparison between agnotology and theodicy is to arrive at the clarification that knowledge is produced with its other and, most important, that ignorance and unknowledge are indispensable to knowing knowledge, or what we could most properly be called reflexive knowledge. The comparison allows us to argue for what Du Bois called a double vision: to look in order to know, but to look while knowing that we are also producing unknowing. Thus, to know is to see while seeing what is not seen because it is looked at with a certain gaze, with certain eyes. But, mutatis mutandis, to know is not to see what is not seen because it was looked at with a certain gaze. I think this is what Shannon Sullivan and Nancy Tuana called the epistemology of ignorance.

Sullivan and Tuana, in an extremely important anthology, gathered a group of philosophers to unpack and unfurl the layered folds of knowing ignorance and ignorant knowing produced by racism.[8] In their anthology, we can read the original and pioneering essays by Charles Mills and Linda Alcoff, but for the moment, let me flag Mills's essay "White Ignorance," because in it Mills links ignorance to culpability, or rather Mills links unknowing to an economy of absolution or, more precisely, a moral economy of disavowal. Toni Morrison called this moral economy of disavowed ignorance "the crime of innocence."[9] Later on I will return to the crime of innocence, but linked to the crime of gendered ignorance.

I want to descend, not all the way down to the darkest corner of the Platonic cave, but to the shadowy world of the mundane. I do so by quoting someone infamous, and thus I apologize in advance if I offend anyone. As we all now know, or ignorantly know, as the U.S. occupation in Iraq was unraveling into chaos, civil war, and a bloody anti-imperialistic heroic resistance, then Secretary of Defense Rumsfeld shielded his inactivity and incompetence behind an "epistemology of ignorance," which he articulated in this way: There is what we know we know; then there is what we know we do not know; and then there are the unknown unknowns. Now, Slavoj Žižek, in a wonderful little essay in *In These Times*, argued that Rumsfeld's unknown unknowns are the American unconscious, that is to say, that which we repress in order for Americans to retain a modicum of justification for the performance of their benevolent violence. We don't have to appeal to Lacan or Freud or Žižek to understand that the unknown unknowns that Rumsfeld was talking about are produced by certain dynamics of power. In Sullivan and Tuana's language, we could say that unknown unknowns result from judicious epistemologies of ignorance that are sustained by political economies of power and violence.

I could summarize my conclusions thus far by saying that agnotology and epistemologies of ignorance point us in the direction of the political economies of the production of knowing and unknowing, knowledge and ignorance. The linkage between political economy and epistemology, however, puts on the table for our consideration the ensemble of relations in which epistemic subjects are disclosed to be relay mechanisms. Epistemic subjects are caught in ensembles of knowledge/ignorance production, and in this sense they have neither priority nor primacy. Let me explain what I mean by this.

In his 1979 book, *Philosophy and the Mirror of Nature*, Richard Rorty set out to dismantle what he thought was a distorting and no longer tenable metaphor of the mind and knowledge.[10] The metaphor is named in the title of the book: The mind is a mirror of nature. Another metaphor was that of a tabula rasa. Essentially, however, both metaphors implied the same thing: a passive, atomized, desocialized, and unencumbered observer, who impartially and impassively lets the world affect his mind, or lets his mind reflect what nature projects on to it. Rorty called this model of the mind and knowledge the Cartesian-Kantian epistemological paradigm. He proceeded in this book to show that this naive and distorting view of the mind had been rendered obsolete, at best, and pernicious, at worst, by the shift from analyzing mental states to analyzing statements. In short, Rorty announced the end of epistemology and the turn toward the philosophy of language.

Indeed, there is no way to make epistemic claims without making them in some sort of language, which can never be but a natural language. Rorty had already claimed in several essays from the seventies, prior to *Philosophy and the Mirror of Nature*, what he put tersely in the introduction to that book, namely that the most important philosophers of the twentieth century were Dewey, Wittgenstein, and Heidegger. They were the most important philosophers, he believed, because each in his own way in their youthful works tried to provide unassailable foundations for philosophy but in their late works gave up on such projects. Instead, all three embraced in their mature work what Rorty called the "therapeutic" model of philosophy, a model that says that philosophy is at its best when it is curing our culture of most of its misguided and misleading metaphors and sacred idols.

Perhaps the most entrenched myth that these three philosophers tried to save us from was that of the lonely knower. If we use the language that these three philosophers coined, we could say that knowledge is a practice that is embedded in particular lifeworlds and that knowledge is but an abstraction or hypostatization of hermeneutical horizons. Knowledge, in other words, is the name for something that is extracted from primordial practices of understanding. Understanding, however, is a doing that is enabled within a lifeworld. To that lifeworld correspond certain practices, or what Wittgenstein called language games. Knowledge is thus a language game that is caught in deep practices that are enabled within specific life-forms or lifeworlds.

It was, however, Michel Foucault who best articulated this critique of the Cartesian and Kantian epistemic paradigm when he provided us with an "archeology of knowledge." Very briefly, Foucault showed how knowledge is produced within certain authorized institutions, which sanction certain disciplinary approaches, in discourse and theory, about specific truths or truth domains. Knowing subjects, or rather knowing agents, are products of the interaction among these different levels: institutions, disciplines, object domains. More pointedly, knowing subjects are authorized as such. Thus, knowledge claims are enabled by sanctioned or authorized knowledge agents. Knowledge here is an aftereffect of legitimate authority. And knowledge can be dispensed from a certain locale, or site. In Walter Mignolo's language, knowledge is about the loci of enunciation, and about who can ascend to specific pedestals from which only certain types of knowledge claims can be enunciated.

We are now in the position to summarize, and thus establish the ground on which I want to begin to build an analysis of the gendered economy of epistemologies of ignorance. Knowledge is always entangled with its other, ignorance or unknowing. Knowledge is not found; nor is it the by-product of a certain form of inactivity or passivity. The mind is not an empty receptacle; nor is it a nondistorting mirror. Knowledge is always produced. The production of knowledge is embedded within political economies of ignorance and moral exculpation. Most important, perhaps, epistemic subjects are not Leibnizian monads, Cartesian cogitos, or Kantian transcendental "I's." A knower is a social, embedded, corporeal agent. Knowledge and unknowing are forms of agency. Knowledge is the name for a practice, a language game, which is always part of a certain lifeworld. We do not receive knowledge without producing it, and we produce it, reproduce it, and circulate it as a commodity within institutional spaces, using specific authorized disciplines that are legitimated to excavate only certain object or truth domains. All knowing, however, is also the production of accompanying forms of ignorance, a culpable ignorance. To the crime of innocence there corresponds the responsibility for ignorance. Knowing ignorance and ignorant knowing are always morally suspect.

THE PRIORITY OF TRUTHFULNESS OVER TRUTH

In order to elucidate the entwinement of knowledge and ignorance I referred to Plato's allegory of the cave. Now, I refer to another aspect of

Plato's work that is often neglected, namely, that it is one prolonged, sustained, and at times vitriolic polemic against the sophists. The *Republic*, in fact, is the culmination of Plato's debate with and against the sophists. We can speak of a Platonic tetralogy of antisophist texts that is made up of the *Sophist*, *Protagoras*, the *Gorgias*, and the *Republic*. At the heart of these texts is the polemic against the sophist dictum that the sophist can teach anything without the sophists' having any first person knowledge of what they teach, that they can persuade anyone of the truth of what they argue even if it is not true, and that virtue can be taught by a teacher who lacks virtue. The sophist provides opinion, mere belief, the semblance of the true, what Plato calls cookery and rhetoric in the *Gorgias*, whereas the philosopher leads one to the true and just. For these reasons Plato juxtaposes the philodoxer to the true philosopher in the *Republic*. At the center of Plato's polemic against the sophists, I want to argue, is the distinction between truthfulness and truth. The sophists do not think there is truth. They are proto-relativists and in many cases even radical skeptics. But they do believe in the power of speech, or rhetoric, to lead people to believe what they want them to believe. For them, public speech is at the service of power; it is self-serving rhetoric. It is from this use of rhetoric that we get the term "demagogue"—the one who leads the people by the power of rhetoric. The demagogue uses sophistry. Tyrants are sophists and demagogues. It is against the disastrous consequences of sophistry that Plato draws the exalted picture of Socrates, who uses speech and rhetoric, not for his own self-aggrandizement and benefit, but for the health of the polis.

Yet, Socrates is also the one who confesses that he is the wisest because he knows that he does not know. Is he a relativist like Gorgias, Protagoras, or even Thrasymachus? Plato will partly answer this question in the *Republic*, precisely through the allegory of the cave and his onto-epistemology that postulated the realm of ideas, of the eternal forms. But, what is Socrates' position on this question? For Socrates there may be a truth, but not for him, not in his lifetime at least. Philosophy may be the quest for truth, for knowledge, for wisdom, but for Socrates, the goal is less important than the path toward it. It is for this reason that there are at least two shibboleths we immediately link with Socrates: "Know thy self," and "the unexamined life is not worth living." Both crystallize into one basic orientation: truthfulness. Be truthful to yourself, to your compatriots, to your polis, to your god, even if it means dying, unjustly. In the absence of truth, all we have is the orientation toward it. If philosophy is the royal path toward knowledge, truthfulness is the royal path toward our own "examined" life.

Socrates was a historical person who lived, taught, and inspired Plato, but he is also a metonym, which is why I have undertaken this brief exegesis. Socrates is the metonym for the priority of truthfulness over truth. Socrates is the name for the one who aims to speak truthfully, courageously acknowledging ignorance, one who unmasks epistemic hubris. Only a truthful person may obtain truth and communicate it. This is one of the messages we get from Plato's polemic against the sophists. But what is truthfulness, at least in the way Socrates embodies it and Plato illustrates it? From the earliest dialogues to the last, we know one thing about Socrates, and that is that he refuses to accept received opinion, or doxa. He refuses knowledge that is paid for. He refuses to lead or to abuse his "professional" authority, even when his students try to seduce him. He is blunt, frank, and impassioned. For this reason, sometimes he strikes readers as arrogant and dismissive. His irony is misperceived as derogation, when it is a rhetorical device to unmask unacknowledged assumptions. His not knowing is not feigned, but truthful, which is why most of the dialogues in which Socrates is the protagonist and speaks in his own voice, rather than as a ventriloquist for Plato, are inconclusive. At least we arrive at this point: That which we assumed we knew, is not true, or it is too muddled. As Bernard Williams put it, devotion to "truthfulness" and suspicion of truth are intricately linked.[11] Truthfulness is an orientation to oneself by way of relating to others. It is an ethos and a way of life. For Socrates, his philosophical vocation was a divine calling. To philosophize, for him, was to lead a certain type of life. We could say, appropriating a phrase from Foucault, that truthfulness is an *ethopoetic* device: It is a way of forming ethos, forms of living, ways of relating to the world and others, and by way of them to oneself.[12] How does truthfulness operate ethopoetically? Truthfulness is related to sincerity, honesty, accuracy, courage, fearlessness, respect, and fidelity. To be truthful is to speak one's mind, as this is available to us; to speak without subterfuge or connivance; to speak what is; to be faithful to the object of knowledge as much as it is in our power to do so; not to distort or dissimulate; to speak the truth without fear of the benefits or adverse consequences of doing so; and to speak out of loyalty and respect for our interlocutors and ourselves. Truthfulness turns around the kind of ethical subject we seek to be.

An important passage in Friedrich Nietzsche's *The Gay Science* aims precisely at the ethical ground on which knowledge and truth are built. Paragraph 344, poignant and incisive, reads:

> We see that science, too, rests on a faith; there is simply no "presup-positionless" science. The question whether *truth* is necessary must get an answer in advance, the answer "yes," and moreover this answer must be so firm that it takes the form of the statement, the belief, the conviction: "*Nothing* is *more* necessary than truth; and in relation to it, everything else has only secondary value." This unconditional will to truth—what is it? Is it the will not to let oneself be deceived? Is it the will *not to deceive*? For the will to truth could be interpreted in this second way, too—if "I do not want to deceive *myself*" is included as a special case under the generalization "I do not want to deceive." But why not deceive? But why not allow oneself to be deceived? . . . Consequently, "will to truth" does *not* mean "I do not want to let myself be deceived" but—there is no alternative—"I do not want to deceive, not even myself"; *and with that we stand on moral ground.*[13]

Let me bracket the references to science, as important as they are, and simply focus on the last phrase: "*and with that we stand on moral ground.*" The will to truth, the will to knowledge, the will to know how things stand in the world is itself a subspecies of a more encompassing will, the will not to deceive, and above all, not to deceive even oneself. Why does the "will not to deceive" find its source in the will not to deceive even oneself? What is this "even"? For Nietzsche, as all of us who have stood on either side of deception know so well, to deceive others is more difficult than to deceive oneself. There is another way to get to Nietzsche's point, and it is by paraphrasing a question that Socrates asks in the *Gorgias:* "Is it better to be done wrong to than to do wrong?" (469a and following). For Socrates, the answer is unequivocal and transparent: It is better to be done wrong to than to do wrong (473a). Would you rather be deceived than be the deceiver? Is it better to be deceived than to deceive? Is it better to deceive others than yourself? Is it better to deceive oneself than others? Here, the questions of truth and knowledge lead us to the question of why we must will the truth, why we must will knowledge, and why this makes us stand on "moral ground." This moral ground, as Nietzsche aptly notes, nourishes the faith in science but also the faith in others and even in ourselves. Truthfulness has priority over truth because only a certain ethos can lead to truth. Truth is an accomplishment, or at the every least, something that is produced by social agents in specific conditions of the production of knowledge, as Otto Maduro notes in his contribution to this volume.

If knowledge is intricately entwined with ignorance, as I argued above, is it not also possible that truthfulness is intricately entwined with dishonesty, or if not outright lying, then with a willful disregard for "truth"? Dishonesty may be deliberate, but what about "ignorance"? Am I culpable for my ignorance? Is ignorance related to innocence, if by innocent we mean someone who is not culpable or liable? There is an important passage in Toni Morrison's novel *Tar Baby* that I think can help me elaborate the point I am trying to make.

He thought about innocence there in his greenhouse and knew that he was guilty of it because he had lived with a woman who had made something kneel down in him the first time he saw her, but about whom he had known nothing; had watched his son grow and talk but about whom he had known nothing. And there was something so foul in that, something in the crime of innocence so revolting it paralyzed him. He had not known because he had not taken the trouble to know. He was satisfied with what he did know. Knowing more was inconvenient and frightening. All he could say was that he did not know. He was guilty therefore of innocence. Was there anything so loathsome as a willfully innocent man? Hardly. An innocent man is a sin before God. Inhuman and therefore unworthy.[14]

It has been argued that this is the key organizing trope of Morrison's literature, namely the crime of innocence, that we sin when we proclaim our innocence, or aim to shield our culpability behind the excuse of our not knowing.[15] But, not knowing is a form of action, by way of inaction.

Not knowing is a result of a decision. It is an abandonment or lassitude. Innocence is a form of moral turpitude, and in this sense we are responsible for it. For this reason, Morrison thinks that innocence is a form of criminality, something for which we are accountable.

Whether feigned or produced, deliberate or inadvertent, ignorance has political, economic, and moral consequences, and no one has elaborated the political economy of ignorance, and feigned innocence, like Charles Mills has. For Mills, the modern polity is a racialized/racial polity.[16] It is structured around white racial privilege, but this structure and structuring are maintained by what he calls an epistemology of ignorance. Evidently, a racialized polity that builds up a racial hierarchy that exploits some for the benefit of others presupposes the deliberate occlusion of the effects of its generative inequity. This racial polity can be sustained only through enforced ignorances and the deliberate granting of epistemic privilege to certain types of agent. The social costs of racial supremacy and the sustained ethical and epistemic derogation of its *Untermenschen* can endure only at the expense of a remorseless act of forgetfulness and purging of the social archive. Social amnesia is a form of racialized epistemic ignorance. The social contract, which Mills demythologizes as a racial contract, is constructed and sustained by an epistemological contract that licenses and necessitates certain forms of unknowing, ignorance, feigned innocence.[17] In fact, the epistemological contract that underwrites the racial contract really entails an analysis of what Mills called recently "moral ignorance."[18]

Moral ignorance, I would argue, is an instance of what, with a different connotation, has been called by feminists "epistemic privilege."[19] What Mills calls moral ignorance—which is not just not knowing what the ethical thing to do is but also that what we do not know itself has moral effects—is what Toni Morrison called "the crime of innocence." But, for both, such "innocence" is a luxury of a power position. Only a certain type of subject, in a certain location can afford not to know, or can derive substantive benefits from not knowing, or from being in the orchestrated position of being able to claim "plausible deniability"—i.e., "I did not know, could not have known, would not have known." Thus, in contrast to the feminist positive inflection of "epistemic privilege" I want to argue that the epistemology of ignorance that Mills and Morrison are describing is also a form of "epistemic privilege"—racial, gendered, class, and civilizational privilege. Not to know is a luxury afforded by a social situation in which epistemic assets, powers, and standpoints are unequally and prejudicially distributed.

If there is "epistemic privilege" in the sense that I have just described, then there is what Miranda Fricker has called "epistemic oppression," which in turn is a species of the genus "hermeneutical injustice."[20] By this Fricker means that there are social experiences and epistemic resources that are excluded, disauthorized, derogated, and marginalized from informing and guiding our world-forming interpretative practices. If by "hermeneutics" we mean the art of making sense of those practices through which we have constructed our social world, then hermeneutic injustice means that there are some practices that are attached to social experiences and locations that are not counted, or considered worth counting. The social world is socially made, but under conditions of hermeneutic injustice, this world is claimed to be mapped and oriented by privileged hermeneutical standpoints. But why should we will to count, to include every experience that can contribute to our interpretative acts? Why include? Why not exclude? Why be solicitous toward those hermeneutical agents we deride, discriminate against, or simply neglect? Why interpret the world in the most capacious and encompassing way that is possible? Why should we engage in what Fricker calls "hermeneutical affirmative action"?[21] Why not deceive? Why be hermeneutically humble and generous? Here, we have to say with Nietzsche, *we stand on moral ground.*

WHAT COMES AFTER DECOLONIZATION? NOT YET A CONCLUSION

The "decolonial turn" or the project of "decolonizing the social sciences," and within it epistemology, is a theoretical paradigm that emerged from the productive convergence and synthesis of at least five different theoretical/philosophical strands: Dusselian liberation philosophy, grounded in a Levinasian-Schellingian phenomenology that is married to a post-Eurocentric, post-Hellenophilic, post–pax Americana hermeneutics with planetary reach; Wallerstenian world systems theory refracted through the lens of the Atlantic slave trade; the Quijanoian post-Eurocentric, post-occidentalist critique of the "coloniality of power"; and the Fanonian phenomenological critique of the racial geography and corporeality of occidental reason, as has been elaborated eloquently by Lewis Gordon and Nelson Maldonado-Torres; and last but not least, Mignolian border gnosis or Nepantlism.[22] Each of these currents is nourished by a formidable and extensive bibliography—veritable libraries. Even the most cursory of overviews of the massive amount of scholarship that has been produced by this group of Latina/o, Latin American/Caribbean scholars would reveal an important contribution to rethinking the major characteristics and contours of the West and the Americas.

This group of scholars accomplished two major conceptual breakthroughs from which neither the social sciences nor the humanities can retreat.[23] First, the "modern" world, what we were miseducated to take as a synecdoche for the West, namely "modernity," was materially, conceptually, and symbolically made possible by the so-called discovery of the New World. The boundaries of reason were literally redrawn because the map of the world itself had been redrawn with the "invention" of "America." The "West" invented/discovered itself by inventing/discovering the "New World." Second, this so-called modernity, this ever new West, had coloniality as its other side. There is no modernity without coloniality, because all modalities of modern power, whether epistemic, gender, racial, religious, and so on, are suffused with coloniality. In this very precise sense, of the *coloniality of all power*, we have to recognize that we can never get beyond either modernity or coloniality.

For this reason, the postmodern and postcolonial projects are but other means to echo the sycophancy of the West. The decolonial project has shown us the way out of this echo chamber. Europe has been provincialized. The West has been unmasked as a fable. The decolonial turn, understood in the expansive sense I propose here as the convergence of these five currents, profiles itself as one of the most thorough critiques of the "West" and its symbolic order with its "Orients," "Africas," "Macondo Latin Americas." At the very least, collectively this group of scholars has made it impossible for us to be "innocent" about how we were "imagined" to have become "modern," the exemplary children of modernity.

Now, all this has been accomplished because what the "decolonial" project was doing was precisely a critique of the production of knowledge. In fact, a more proper name for what this group of scholars has been doing is a "critique of the global production of knowledge." The decolonial turn is really a "political economy of the global production of knowledge." It is part and parcel of this critique qua political economy to defetishize, decommodify, demystify "epistemology." In fact, one of the accomplishments of the decolonial turn is to have shown that epistemic universality, universality as such, is an elusive, nay impossible standpoint. What the Colombian philosopher Santiago Castro-Gómez called the "hubris of the zero point" was the dispositif that allowed the "West" to put epistemology on an unassailable pedestal above hermeneutics.[24] It was for this reason that Dussel and Mignolo called for a "pluriversal" or "diversal" reason that would always remain under construction and unaccomplished.[25] What Grosfoguel has called "the epistemic decolonial turn" suggests we take one step forward and two back. When Grosfoguel writes "that a truly universal decolonial perspective cannot be based on an abstract universal (one particular that raises itself as universal global design),"[26] he is giving back to the Baconian/Cartesian/Kantian "unencumbered" subject the power, enchantment, and unassailability that the decolonial turn has deconstructed and shown to be a founding mythology. The way to move forward with decolonization is to dismantle, rather than to merely jam or rewire, the epistemic machine.

I have argued so far that knowledge is not found, but produced. The production of knowledge is accompanied by the production of its other: ignorance, or unknowing. Knowledge is produced not by individuals, but by social agents within specific political economies. These political economies of knowledge authorize or deauthorize certain loci from which agents may or may not be able to make certain knowledge claims. Knowledge production thus has to do with social geographies of race, gender, and class. All knowledge production is thus raced, gendered, and classed. In this essay I have focused on the ways in which ignorance is not a privation, an absence, but a productive positivity. Ignorance is not innocent, but culpable, incurred, and, more important, ethically condoned or tolerated.

Specifically, I have wanted to begin to sketch the loci from which Latina/os subjects can or cannot produce knowledge. Our locus of enunciation is certainly distinct: We are postcolonial, postimperial, post–pax Americana, post-occidental subjects avant la lettre. Such a locus is not triangulated by a temporal sequence that reenacts the theodicies of Western teleological histories, but rather it is determined by the questioning of the spatializations of a quasi-divine history (the histories of progress toward modernity as secular versions of *Heilsgeschichte*). Latina/os must continuously negotiate their locus of enunciation from which knowledge may be claimed, produced, as it lifts the veil from the face of ignorance. But, it is the social locus that coordinates an ethical standpoint, an ethical standpoint that turns toward a critique of the imperial knowledge maps that force us to be plagued by Cartesian epistemic anxiety. My analysis suggests that given the last half a century of changes and emergence of a framework of a set of conditions of epistemic agency, Latina/o agencies/subjectivities are being constrained within vicious cycles of economic, cultural, political, and educational marginalizations and disenfranchisements. These marginalizations and disenfranchisements can result only in the denuding, atrophy, and eventual evisceration of emergent Latina/o gendered economies of knowledge.[27] But, as the many essays that shoulder and support this one, Latina/o gendered economies of knowledge are also unsuspectingly generative, productive, challenging, disconcertingly fresh but also full of memory, remembrance, and insurrected yearning.

NOTES

DECOLONIZING WESTERN EPISTEMOLOGY / BUILDING DECOLONIAL EPISTEMOLOGIES | WALTER MIGNOLO

1. Humberto Maturana and Bernhard Poerksen, *From Being to Doing: The Origins of the Biology of Cognition* (Heidelberg: Auer International, 2004), 63.
2. "Da qualche tempo nessuno dei grandi eventi che scuotono il mondo è più interpretabile fuori della categoria di biopolitica." http://www.ici-berlin.org/de/docu/esposito/.
3. More details on decolonial strategies in Walter Mignolo and Madina Tlostanova, *Learning to Unlearn: Decolonial Meditations from Eurasia and América* (Athens: Ohio University Press, 2012).
4. Fausto Reinaga, *La revolución India* (La Paz: Partido Indio de Bolivia, 1970), 382.
5. See *La teoría política en la encrucijada descolonial*, compiled and introduced by Alejandro J. De Oto; preface by Walter Mignolo, and contributions by Sylvia Wynter and Lewis Gordon (Buenos Aires: Ediciones del Signo / CGSH; Durham, N.C.: Duke University, 2009).
6. Anibal Quijano, "Coloniality and Modernity/Rationality" (1992), in *Globalization and the De-colonial Option*, ed. Walter Mignolo and Arturo Escobar (London: Routledge, 2010), 22–32.
7. The original Spanish is: "El Manifiesto del Partido Indio de Bolivia (PIB), no tiene por qué sujetarse a un modelo, regla de lógica formal e intelectual de los partidos politicos del cholaje blanco-mestizo de Bolivia e Indoamérica. No es un Manifiesto de una clase social. Es un Manifiesto de una raza, de un pueblo, de una Nación; de una cultura oprimida y silenciada. No se puede establecer parangón con el Manifiesto Comunista de Marx. Porque el genial 'moro' no se enfrentó con el Occidente. Enfrentó la clase proletaria

con la clase burguesa; y propuso como solución de la lucha de clases, dentro de la 'civilización occidental' la Revolución comunista." Walter Mignolo, "La opción de-colonial: desprendimiento y apertura. Un manifiesto y un caso." *Tabula Rasa: Revista de Humanidades*, Universidad de Cundinamarca, 2008, 8, available online at http://www.revistatabularasa.org/numero8 .html; http://dialnet.unirioja.es/servlet/articulo?codigo=2346538; in http:// dialnet.unirioja.es / servlet / revista?tipo_busqueda = CODIGO&clave_revista = 1906; http://dialnet.unirioja.es/servlet/listaarticulos?tipo_busqueda = EJEM PLAR&evista_busqueda = 1906&clave_busqueda = 163010 (issue dedicated to Etnicidad en América Latina: Relatos de colonialismo, identidad, resistencia y agencia), 43–72. For the decolonial turn see Nelson Maldonado-Torres, "Césaire's Gift and the De-colonial Turn," *Radical Philosophy Review* 9, no. 2 (2006): 11–138.

8. See "The Decolonial Virgin in a Colonial Site: It's Not about the Gender in My Nation, It's about the Nation in My Gender," in *Our Lady of Controversy: Alma López's "Irreverent Apparition,"* ed. Alicia Gaspar de Alba and Alma López (Austin: University of Texas Press, 2011), 180–202; Emma Pérez, "De-colonial Queer Theory," presented at the workshop titled Decolonizing Epistemology: New Knowing in Latina/o Philosophy and Theology, Drew University, 8th Interdisciplinary Colloquium, November 2008.

9. On decolonizing gender epistemology see María Lugones, "Methodological Notes toward a Decolonial Feminism," in this volume.

10. See Marcelle Maese-Cohen, "Introduction: Toward Planetary De-colonial Feminisms," *Qui Parle: Critical Humanities and Social Sciences* 18, no. 2 (2010): 3–27.

11. On this topic, see also Emma Pérez, "De-colonial Border Queers: Case Studies of Chicana/Mexicana/of Lesbians, Gay Men, and Transgendered in El Paso/Juarez," in *Performing the US Latin@ Borderlands*, ed. Arturo J. Aldama, Peter J. Garcia, and Chela Sandoval (Bloomington: Indiana University Press, 2012).

12. I am referring to Quijano's concept of coloniality and Dussel's "geopolitics and philosophy" and the crucial concept of "analectical moment" introduced in his *Philosophy of Liberation* (1977), translated from Spanish by Aquilina Martinez and Christine Morkovsky. (Eugene: Wipf and Stock, 1982), paragraphs 1.2 and 5.3 respectively.

13. "The Rhetoric of Modernity, the Logic of Coloniality, and the Grammar of De-Coloniality," first presented at a conference titled "Coloniality, Transmodernity, and Border Thinking," Berkeley 2005, it was published in *Cultural Studies* 21, no. 2–3 (2007), and reprinted in *Globalization and the De-colonial Option*, ed Walter Mignolo and Arturo Escobar (London: Routledge, 2010), 303–68.

14. Carl Schmitt, "Postscript: On the Current Situation of the Problem: The Legitimacy of Modernity," In *Political Theology II. The Myth of the Closure of Any Political Theology*, translated and introduced by Michael Hoelzl and Graham Ward (Malden, Mass.: Polity Press, 2008), 117.

15. Partha Chatterjee, "Talking about Our Modernity in Two Languages," in *A Possible India: Essays in Political Criticism* (Calcutta: Oxford University Press, 1998), 263–85.

16. I am alluding here to Madina Tlostanova's argument in the conclusion of her book *Gender Epistemologies and Eurasian Borderlands* (New York: Palgrave Macmillan, 2010). The title of the chapter is "Why Cut the Feet in Order to Fit Western Shoes?"

17. Walter D. Mignolo, "The Darker Side of the Enlightenment: A De-colonial Reading of Kant's Geography," in *Reading Kant's Geography*, ed. Stuart Elden and Eduardo Mendieta (Albany: State University of New York Press, 2011), 319–44.

18. Chatterjee, "Talking about Our Modernity," 273–74.

19. Mignolo, "Darker Side," 275.

20. Walter D. Mignolo, "Epistemic Disobedience and the Decolonial Option: A Manifesto," in *Critical Stew: Philosophy/Theory/Conjecture*, February 2, 2008, http://criticalstew.org/?p=193.

21. Linda Tuhiwai Smith, *Decolonizing Methodologies: Research and Indigenous Peoples* (London: Zed Books, 1999), 25.

22. Fazlur Rahman, *Islam and Modernity: Transformation of an Intellectual Tradition* (Chicago: University of Chicago Press, 1982).

23. Ibid., 46–47.

24. Kishore Mahbubani, *Can Asians Think?* (Singapore: Marshall Cavendish International, 2004).

25. Maxime Rodinson, *Islam and Capitalism*, translated from the French by Brian Pearce (1966; London: Sagi Essentials, 1974); Aidit Ghazali, *Development: An Islamic Perspective* (Petaling Jaya: Pelanduk Publications, 1990); Sri Mulyati et al., *Islam and Development: A Politico-Religious Response* (Montreal: Permika and Lembaga and Penerjemah and Penulis Muslim Indonesia, 1997).

26. Malik Bennabi, *The Question of Ideas in the Muslim World*, translated with a foreword by Mohamed El-Tahir El-Mesawi (Kuala Lumpur: Islamic Trust, 2003), 104. On Bennabi's basic ideas see Alwi Alatas, "Malik Bennabi on Civilization," http://alwialatas.multiply.com/journal/item/74; see also Mohamed El-Tahir El-Mesawi, "Religion, Society, and Culture in Malik Bennabi's Thought," in *The Blackwell Companion to Contemporary Islamic Thought*, online, ed. Ibrahim M. Abu-Rabi' (London: Blackwell, 2007), 213–56.

27. Walter Mignolo, "Coloniality of Power and De-colonial Thinking," in *Globalization and the De-colonial Option*, ed. Walter Mignolo and Arturo Escobar (London: Routledge, 2010), 1–21.

28. Gloria Anzaldúa, *Borderlands / La Frontera: The New Mestiza* (San Francisco: Aunt Lute Books, 1987), 193.

MUJERISTA DISCOURSE: A PLATFORM FOR LATINAS' SUBJUGATED KNOWLEDGE | ADA MARÍA ISASI-DÍAZ

1. For a fuller description of mujerista theology and ethics see Ada María Isasi-Díaz, *En La Lucha—In the Struggle: Elaborating a Mujerista Theology*, 2nd ed. (Minneapolis: Fortress Press, 2004).

2. I am greatly influenced by Gloria Anzaldúa, *Borderlands/La Frontera: The New Mestiza* (San Francisco: Spinsters/Aunt Lute, 1987). Also see Walter D. Mignolo, *Local Histories/Global Designs—Coloniality, Subaltern Knowledges, and Border Thinking* (Princeton: Princeton University Press, 2000), particularly chapter 1 and afterword.

3. Paulo Freire, *Pedagogy of the Oppressed* (New York: Continuum Press, 1973), 24.

4. Ibid., 47.

5. Ibid., 52–53.

6. See the essay by Walter Mignolo in this volume.

7. This is based on, but does not replicate exactly, the schema elaborated in Iris Marion Young, *Justice and the Politics of Difference* (Princeton: Princeton University Press, 1990), 39–65. In this essay I do not have the space to explain each of these modes of oppression from the perspective of Latinas. For such an explanation, see Ada María Isasi-Díaz, *Mujerista Theology—A Theology for the Twenty-first Century* (Maryknoll, N.Y.: Orbis Books, 1996), 105–27.

8. I use "impoverished" instead of "the poor" to indicate that poverty is not an inherent condition but rather is the result of how certain sectors of society are exploited. I thank Dr. Peter Kanyandago from Uganda for this insight in his presentation "Everyday Life: Site of Interchange or of New Colonization between the North and the South," at the Program of Dialogue North-South, San Leopoldo, Porto Alegre, Brazil, May 2010. See also Pedro Casaldáliga, *Cartas a mis amigos* (Madrid: Editorial Nueva Utopía, 1992), 112: "We in Latin America want to avoid the poor being thought of as spontaneously poor, isolated, outside the structures that exploit and marginalize them; that is why we speak about the 'impoverished.'"

9. In valuing the experience of the oppressed, I want to highlight their epistemological contribution. I make a difference between "raw data," what happens, which I am quick to admit we never know except through the lens that we use to see it, and experience, which has two elements: what happens and how we explain it. For a theoretical framework to understand the point I am making, see Paula M. L. Moya, *Learning from Experience: Minority Identities, Multicultural Struggles* (Berkeley: University of California Press, 2002), 38–39.

10. For a fuller explanation of "conscientization" see Freire, *Pedagogy of the Oppressed.*

11. I believe that those who seek an individualistic way out or who simply want to get ahead within oppressive structures exclude themselves from those who struggle for liberation, for at the heart of all liberative praxis lies the conviction that no one will be fully liberated unless everyone is liberated, and that the struggle for liberation is about radical structural change.

12. Martin Buber, *Between Man and Man* (New York: Macmillan, 1965), 14.

13. Clifford Geertz, *Local Knowledge* (New York: Basic Books, 1983), 74–76.

14. Daniel H. Levine, *Popular Voices in Latin America Catholicism* (Princeton: Princeton University Press, 1992), 317.

15. I am not following the postmodern trend of denouncing universals. I do believe that universals are possible, as long as they start from the specific, the historical, and proceed to point out shared understandings and practices. For a thorough discussion of this see Martha C. Nussbaum, *Women and Human Development: The Capabilities Approach* (Cambridge: Cambridge University Press, 2000), particularly chap. 1.

16. See the essay in this book by Linda Martín Alcoff for the meaning of and reason for the term "ethnoracism."

17. Geertz, *Local Knowledge,* 85–86. This description of *lo cotidiano* uses elements of Geertz's analysis of "common sense."

18. Michel de Certeau, *The Practice of Everyday Life,* trans. Stevan Rendall (Berkeley: University of California Press, 1984), 254–55.

19. Raúl Fornet-Betancourt, Introduction to *Everyday Life: Space for Interchange or a Space for New Colonization between North and South, Dokumentation des XIV Internationalen Seminars des Dialogprogramms Nord-Süd,* ed. Raúl Fornet-Betancourt (Mainz: Wissenschaftsverlag, 2010), 29.

20. Ibid., 45.

21. It is important to notice how the negative view of the Palestinians, the Iraq war, and the war in Afghanistan are understood and talked about as "defending the American way of life."

22. For a much more elaborated explanation of this point see Virginia Ascuy, "Pobreza y hermenéuticas. Senderos para una resurrección de las relaciones sociales," in *Suena la "Campana de Palo,"* ed. Virginia Ascuy and Octavio Groppa (Buenos Aires: Centro de Estudios Salesianos de Buenos Aires, 2003), 11–32.

23. Douglas Brinkley, *Rosa Parks: A Life* (New York: Penguin Books, 2000).

24. Frederick John Dalton, *The Moral Vision of Cesar Chavez* (Maryknoll, N.Y.: Orbis Books, 2003).

25. Robert F. Worth, "How a Single Match Can Ignite a Revolution," New York Times, January 21, 2011, at http://www.nytimes.com/2011/01/23/weekinreview/23worth.html?src=twrhp; accessed March 1, 2011.

26. The interconnection between the one who knows and the one who is known, the relations between the epistemologies of both, is an important argument for insisting that academics need to be in touch with the cotidiano of the oppressed and impoverished. See Irene Vasilachis de Gialdino, "Del sujeto cognoscente al sujeto conocido: una propuesta epistemológica para el estudio de los pobres y de la pobreza," in *Pobres, pobreza y exclusión social* (Buenos Aires: Ceil-Conicet, 2000), 21–45.

27. Eleonore Stump, *Wandering in Darkness: Narrative and the Problem of Suffering* (Oxford: Oxford University Press, 2010), 56.

28. For a rich discussion on these two types of knowledge, see, particularly part 1 of Stump, *Wandering in Darkness*.

29. There is an expression that is difficult to translate into English that is for me the best way of describing an individual: *"dueño y señor de sí mismo,"* owner and lord of himself. It is an expression used often in everyday Spanish to refer to someone who does not take anyone else into consideration.

30. See Sheena Iyengar, "On the Art of Choosing," at http://www.ted.com/talks/sheena_iyengar_on_the_art_of_choosing.html; accessed August 7, 2010.

31. Raúl Fornet-Betancourt, "Para una crítica filosófica de la globalización," in *Resistencia y solidaridad—globalización capitalista y liberación,* ed. Raúl Fornet-Betancourt (Madrid: Editorial Trotta, S.A., 2003), 56. All translations from the Spanish are my own.

32. Ibid., 57.

33. Stephen J. Pope, "Proper and Improper Impartiality and the Preferential Option for the Poor," *Theological Studies* 54, no. 2 (1993): 246.

34. Ibid.

35. Juan Luis Segundo, *The Liberation of Theology* (Maryknoll, N.Y.: Orbis Books, 1979), 231ff.

36. I follow here the arguments presented by Pope, "Proper and Improper Impartiality," 264–67.

37. William O'Neill, "No Amnesty for Sorrow: The Privilege of the Poor in Christian Social Ethics," *Theological Studies* 55, no. 4 (1994): 648.

38. This understanding of fairness and impartiality has some faint resemblance to the liberal understandings of John Rawls and others. However, it radically disagrees with the priority given by liberalism to individual negative liberty (liberty from absence of interference) over social positive goods, and to negative rights or immunities over social and economic rights. In this discussion I follow the arguments of O'Neill, "No Amnesty for Sorrow," 642–46.

39. Ibid., 647.

40. Pope, "Proper and Improper Impartiality," 265.

41. Margaret Urban Walker, "Partial Consideration," *Ethics* 101 (July 1991): 773.

42. Ibid.

43. Roger Shinn, *Forced Options: Social Decisions for the Twenty-First Century*, 3rd ed. (Cleveland: Pilgrim Press, 1991), 3.

44. Ibid., 4.

45. Segundo, *Liberation of Theology*, 116–20.

46. For a concise theological explanation of grace see Karl Rahner and Herbert Vorgrimler, *Dictionary of Theology*, new rev. ed. (New York: Crossroad, 1990), 196–200. Though this explanation is from a Catholic perspective, much of what it says is acceptable to other Christian denominations.

47. Diana Viñoles, "Opción Fundamental y Opción Preferencial por los Pobres—Diálogo entre Ambos Paradigmas," in *Suena la "Campana de Palo,"* 109.

48. Casaldáliga, *Cartas a mis amigos*, 70–71.

49. For the differences in meaning between kingdom of God and kin-dom of God see Ada María Isasi-Díaz, "Kin-dom of God: A *Mujerista* Proposal," in *In Our Own Voices: Latino/a Renditions of Theology*, ed. Benjamín Valentín (Maryknoll, N.Y.: Orbis Books, 2010).

METHODOLOGICAL NOTES TOWARD A DECOLONIAL FEMINISM | MARÍA LUGONES

The sources of the epigraphs are Alfred Arteaga, *Chicano Poetics: Heterotexts and Hybridities* (Cambridge: Cambridge University Press, 1997), 5; Emma Perez, *The Decolonial Imaginary: Writing Chicanas into History* (Bloomington: Indiana University Press, 1999), 78; Walter Mignolo, *Local Histories/Global Designs* (Princeton: Princeton University Press, 2000), x.

1. As I am following the logic of the formation of Women of Color feminisms in the United States and seeking a larger decolonial feminism, I begin by committing the colonial/racist reduction of all Latinas, Native American, Asian, Afro-American "women" to a separate understanding of them. The term Women of Color, the colonial litany with a coalitional, multiplicitous, differential creative opposition.

2. Women of Color feminists do not rely on postmodern critiques of essentialism in criticizing the separability of race and gender. Rather, we rely on understanding the history of the race/gender inscriptions and their relation to the processes of creating meaning. See Kimberlé Crenshaw as one the first theorists to work with the concept of intersectionality; she gave the concept this name, but her work has already been addressed by other theorists.

3. This is Johannes Fabian's analytical concept of a lack of contemporaneity.

4. Since the eighteenth century, the dominant Western view "has been that there are two stable, incommensurable, opposite sexes and that the political, economic, and cultural lives of men and women, their gender roles, are somehow based on these 'facts'" (Thomas Laqueur, *Making Sex: Body and Gender from the Greeks to Freud* [Cambridge, Mass.: Harvard University Press, 1990], 6). In this same text, Laqueur tells us that historically differentiations of gender preceded differentiations of sex (62). What he terms the "one-sex model" he traces through Greek antiquity to the end of the seventeenth century (and beyond): a world where at least two genders correspond to but one sex, where the boundaries between male and female are of degree and not of kind (25). Laqueur tells us that the longevity of the one-sex model is due to its link to power. "In a world that was overwhelmingly male, the one-sex model displayed what was already massively evident in culture: man is the measure of all things, and woman does not exist as an ontologically distinct category." The question of perfection is summed up by Laqueur as he tells that for Aristotle and for "the long tradition founded on his thought, the generative substances are interconvertible elements in the economy of a single sex body whose higher form is male" (42).

5. I agree with Oyeronke Oyewumi, who makes a similar claim for the colonization of the Yoruba in *The Invention of Women: Making an African Sense of Western Gender Discourses* (Minneapolis: University of Minnesota Press, 1997). But I complicate the claim, because I understand both gender and sex as colonial impositions. That is, the organization of the social in terms of gender is hierarchical and dichotomic, and the organization of the social

in terms of sex is dimorphic and related the male to the man even to mark a lack. The same is true of the female. Thus, Mesoamericans who did not understand sex in dimorphic, separable terms, but in terms of fluid dualisms, became either male or female. Linda Alcoff (*Visible Identities: Race, Gender and the Self* (New York: Oxford University Press, 2005) sees the contribution of sperm and egg in the reproductive act as in some way entailing the sexual division and the gender division. But the contribution of sperm and egg is quite compatible with intersexuality. From "contributes the ovum" or "contributes sperm" to a particular act of conception, it does not follow that the sperm contributor is either male or a man, and it does not follow that the egg contributor is female or a woman, unless, of course, one declares it tautological. But nothing about the meaning of "male" or "man" would unequivocally point to a sperm contributor who is markedly intersexed as a male man, except again as a matter of normed logic. If the Western modern gender dichotomy is conceptually tied to the dimorphic sexual distinction and if production of sperm is the necessary and sufficient condition of maleness, then of course, the egg donor is male and a man. Hormonal and gonadal characteristics are notoriously insufficient in determining gender. Think of the dangerous misfit of male to female transsexuals being housed in male prisons to get a feel for this perception embedded in language and popular consciousness.

6. Nelson Maldonado-Torres, "The Coloniality of Being," *Cultural Studies* 21, no. 23 (2007): 240–70.

7. Anibal Quijano understands the coloniality of power as the specific forms that domination and exploitation take in the constitution of the capitalist world system of power. It refers to the classification of the world's populations in term of races, the racialization of the relations between colonizers and colonized; the configuration of a new system of exploitation that articulates in one structure all forms of control of labor around the hegemony of capital, where labor is racialized (waged labor as well as reciprocity, slavery, servitude, small commodity production became all racialized forms of production, all new forms as they were constituted at the service of capitalism); eurocentrism as the new mode of production and control of subjectivity; a new system of control of collective authority around the hegemony of the nation-state that excludes populations racialized as inferior from control of collective authority. See Quijano, "La Colonialidad del actual patron de poder," CAOI, *Estados Plurinacionales Comunitarios*.

8. In the chapter "Street Walker Theorizing," in my book *Pilgrimages/Peregrinajes* (Lanham, Md.: Rowman and Littlefield, 2003), I introduce the concept of

active subjectivity to capture the minimal sense of agency of the resister to multiple oppressions whose multiple subjectivity is reduced by hegemonic understandings/colonial understandings/racist-gendered understandings to no agency at all. It is her belonging to impure communities that gives life to her agency.

9. Walter Mignolo, "Delinking: The Rhetoric of Modernity, the Logic of Coloniality, and the Grammar of De-coloniality," *Cultural Studies* 21, no 23 (2007): 339–514.

10. A further note on the relation of intersectionality and categorical purity: intersectionality has become pivotal in U.S. women of color feminisms. As said above, one cannot see, locate, and address women of color (U.S. Latinas, Asian, Chicanas, African Americans, Native American women) in the U.S. legal system and in much of institutionalized U.S. life. As one considers the dominant categories, among them "woman," "black," "poor," they do not articulate in a way that includes people who are women, black, and poor. The intersection of "woman" and "black" reveals the absence of black women rather their presence. That is because the modern categorical logic constructs categories as homogenous, atomic, separable, and constituted in dichotomous terms. That construction proceeds from the pervasive presence of hierarchical dichotomies in the logic of modernity and modern institutions. The relation between categorical purity and hierarchical dichotomies works as follows. Each homogenous, separable, atomic category is characterized in terms of the superior member of the dichotomy. Thus "women" stands for white women. "Black" stands for black men. When one is trying to understand women at the intersection of race, class, gender, nonwhite, black, mestiza, indigenous, Asian women are impossible beings. They are impossible because they are neither European bourgeois women nor indigenous males. Intersectionality is important when showing the failures of institutions to include discrimination or oppression against women of color. But here I want to be able to think of their presence as being both oppressed and resisting. So I have shifted to the *coloniality of gender* at and from the *colonial difference* to be able to perceive and understand the fractured locus of colonized women/fluent in native cultures as agents.

11. Anibal Quijano, "La Colonialidad," in *Festschrift for Immanuel Wallerstein, Part I. Journal of World-System Research* 11, no. 2, special issue (2000): 378.

12. María Lugones, "Heterosexualism and the Modern Colonial Gender System," *Hypatia* 22, no. 1 (2007): 186–209.

13. Irine Silverblatt, *Moon, Sun, and Witches* (Princeton: Princeton University Press, 1987).

14. Carolyn Dean, "Andean Androgyny and the Making of Men," in *Gender in Pre-Hispanic America*, ed. Cecilia Klein (Washington, D.C.: Dumbarton Oaks, 2001).

15. Maria Esther Pozo and Jhonny Ledezma, "Género: *trabajo* agrícola y tierra en Raqaypampa," in *Las Displicencias de Género en los Cruces del Siglo Pasado al Nuevo Milenio en los Andes*, ed. Maria Esther Pozo and Nina Laurie (Cochabamba, Bolivia: CESU, San Simón University Press, 2006).

16. Pamela Calla and Nina Laurie, "Desarrollo, poscolonianismo y teoría," in *Las Displicencias de Género en los Cruces del Siglo Pasado al Nuevo Milenio en los Andes*, ed. Maria Esther Pozo and Nina Laurie (Cochabamba, Bolivia: CESU, San Simón University Press, 2006).

17. Silvia Marcos, *Taken from the Lips: Gender and Eros in Mesoamerican Religions* (Leiden: Brill, 2006).

18. Paula Gunn Allen, *The Sacred Hoop: Recovering the Feminine in American Indian Traditions* (Boston: Beacon Press, 1986).

19. Filipe Guaman Poma de Ayala, *Nueva Coronica y Buen Gobierno* (Mexico: Siglo Veintuno, 1615).

20. Filomena Miranda Casas, *Metaforas de la oposicion de genero chacha-warmi "hombre-mujer" en el aymara de La Paz y Oruro* (La Paz : Instituto de Estudios Bolivianos—IEB; Facultad de Humanidades y Ciencias de la Educacion; Universidad Mayor de San Andres—UMSA, 2009), 288.

21. Paula Gunn Allen tells us of *koskalaka* that they "have a singular power" that "can (potentially, at least) override that of men, even very powerful medicine men such as the one in my story" (*The Sacred Hoop: Recovering the feminine in American Indian traditions* (Boston: Beacon Press, 1986) 260.

22. *Chachawarmi* is a particular set, of opposites, not in the sense of being negations of each other but in the sense of a tension that provokes movement and generation, but not in the restricted sense of procreation. *Chachawarmi* are also in a relation of complement with respect to their community.

23. Oyenronke Oyewumi tells us that *obinrin* is not equivalent to the English "female" because "*rin* suggests a common humanity" and "the basic terms *okunrin* and *obinrin* are best translated as referring to the anatomic male and anatomic female." Oyewumi, *Invention of Women*, 33.

24. This passage should be understood as offering an understanding of *qamaña* and *utjaña*.

25. *Chhixi* cannot simply be understood as "mixed." Silvia Rivera Cusiqanqi shows the complexity of the term when she identifies herself as *chhixi*. She says: "Personalmente, no me considero *q'ara* (culturalmente desnuda,

usurpadora de lo ajeno) porque he reconicido plenamente mi origin doble, aymara y europeo, y porque vivo de mi propio esfuerzo. Por eso me considero *chhixi*, y considero a ésta la traduccion más adecuada de la mezcla abigarrada que somos las y los mestizos." ("Personally, I do not consider my self *q'ara* [culturally naked, usurper of that which belongs to someone else] because I have fully recognized my double origin, Aymara and European, and because I live by my own effort. That is why I consider myself *chhixi* and consider this to be the most accurate translation of the dense mixture of those of us who are mestizo [both *chacha* and *warmi*]," author's trans.) Silvia Rivera Cusiqanqi, *Rivera Cusicanqui, "Chhixinaka utxiwa*: Una reflexion sobre practices y discursos descolonizadores," in *Modernidad y Pensamiento Descolonizador*, ed. Mario Yapu (La Paz: University PIEB and Ifea, 2006), 11.

26. Mignolo, *Local Histories*, ix.

27. Ibid., ix.

28. Ibid.

29. Ibid.

30. Ibid., x.

31. Ibid.

32. Ibid.

33. Ibid.

34. Ibid., 37.

35. Ibid.

36. Ibid., 45.

37. Ibid., 267.

38. Brinda Mehta does this work beautifully, carefully, and imaginatively in her *Diasporic Dis(locations): Indo-Caribbean Women Negotiate the "Kala Pani"* (Kingston, Jamaica: University of the West Indies Press, 2004).

39. Audre Lorde, *Sister Outsider: Essays and Speeches* (Berkeley, Calif.: Crossing Press, 2007).

40. Chela Sandoval, *Methodology of the Oppressed* (Minneapolis: University of Minnesota Press. 2000).

41. Lorde, *Sister Outsider*.

42. Gloria Anzaldúa, *Borderlands/La Frontera: The New Mestiza* (San Francisco: Aunt Lute Books, 1986).

43. I mean to include here not just the coalitional feminisms of Lorde, Anzaldúa, and Sandoval, among others, but I also think of transnational feminisms, third world feminisms, and intersectional feminisms.

AN(OTHER) INVITATION TO EPISTEMOLOGICAL HUMILITY: NOTES TOWARD A SELF-CRITICAL APPROACH TO COUNTER-KNOWLEDGES | OTTO MADURO

1. The works of Karl Marx and Friedrich Engels, particularly those collected in *The Marx-Engels Reader*, edited by Robert C. Tucker, 2nd ed. (New York: W. W. Norton, 1978), constitute the point of departure of most (including my) approaches to knowledge as a social construction both shaped by, and fulfilling significant functions in, asymmetric power dynamics.

Karl Mannheim's *Ideology and Utopia: An Introduction to the Sociology of Knowledge,* translated by Edward Shils, preface by Louis Wirth (San Diego: Harvest Book/Harcourt, 1985), and Peter L. Berger's and Thomas Luckmann's *The Social Construction of Reality: A Treatise in the Sociology of Knowledge* (reprint, Garden City, N.J.: Anchor Books/Doubleday, 1990) went deeper into the analysis of human knowledge as a social product and its relations to conflictual power arrangements.

Maligned or misunderstood when not simply forgotten, especially among English-speaking social theorists right and left, Max Weber's *The Methodology of the Social Sciences,* translated and edited by Edward A. Shils and Henry A. Finch; foreword by E. A. Shils (New York: Free Press, 1949), is a key point of reference for an examination of human knowledge as both a social outcome and a social instrument.

For anybody who is familiar with the work of Pierre Bourdieu, its influence will be more than evident throughout the lines of this essay. A sociologist/anthropologist/philosopher anchored—among others—in the Marxist, the Weberian, and the Durkheimian traditions, using each to complement and criticize the other two, Bourdieu's could be called a critical sociological epistemology: he was convinced of the essential role of lopsided power dynamics in shaping human knowledge, "individual" as well as collective, no less than of the decisive weight of acquired, shared, "legitimate" knowledges in the understanding of, participation in, and limitations for changing social inequalities. Among Pierre Bourdieu's most important writings for this endeavor at hand are *The Craft of Sociology: Epistemological Preliminaries,* with Jean-Claude Chamboredon and Jean-Claude Passeron, edited by Beate Krais, translated by Richard Nice (Berlin: Walter de Gruyter, 1991); *An Invitation to Reflexive Sociology,* with Loïc J. D. Wacquant (Chicago: University of Chicago Press, 1992); *Distinction: A Social Critique of the Judgement of Taste,* trans. Richard Nice (Cambridge, Mass.: Harvard

University Press, 1984); *Outline of a Theory of Practice*, 2nd ed. (Cambridge, UK: Cambridge University Press. 1977); "The Social Space and the Genesis of Groups," *Theory and Society* 14, no. 6 (1985): 723–44; Pierre Bourdieu, "Forms of Capital," in *Handbook of Theory and Research for the Sociology of Education*, edited by John G. Richardson (New York: Greenwood Press, 1986), 241–58; *Language and Symbolic Power* (Cambridge, Mass.: Harvard University Press, 1991); "Legitimation and Structured Interests in Weber's Sociology of Religion," in *Rationality and Modernity*, edited by Scott Lash and Sam Whirmster (London: Allen and Unwin, 1987), 119–36; and "Genesis and Structure of the Religious Field," *Comparative Social Research*. no. 13 (1991): 1–44), among many other works.

Other significant contributions to a more complex understanding of human knowledge as a bio-psycho-social product are to be found, on the one hand, in the works of Jean Piaget, particularly his *Biology and Knowledge: An Essay on the Relations between Organic Regulations and Cognitive Processes*, translated by Beatrix Walsh (Chicago: University of Chicago Press, 1971), and, on the other, in the "antipsychiatry" movement, especially in some of the works of Ronald D. Laing, where human perception is intriguingly scrutinized in its linkages to family systems, emotional development, etc.: *The Politics of Experience, and, The Bird of Paradise* (Harmondsworth, UK: Penguin, 1967); *The Politics of the Family and Other Essays* (New York: Pantheon Books, 1971); *The Divided Self: An Existential Study in Sanity and Madness* (London: Routledge, 1999); *Sanity, Madness, and the Family: Families of Schizophrenics* (London: Routledge, 1999); *Self and Others* (London: Routledge, 1999); *Do You Love Me?: An Entertainment in Conversation and Verse* (New York: Pantheon Books, 1976); and *Knots* (London: Routledge, 1999).

Two key anthropological works on the social-cultural construction of the self have also marked my epistemological views. They are Marcel Mauss's "A Category of the Human Mind: The Notion of Person," translated by W. D. Halls, in *The Category of the Person: Anthropology, Philosophy, History*, edited by Michael Carrithers, Steven Collins, and Steven Lukes (Cambridge, Eng.: Cambridge University Press, 1985), 1–25, and his disciple Maurice Leenhardt's *Do Kamo: Person and Myth in the Melanesian World*, translated by Basia Miller Gulati, preface by Vincent Crapanzano (Chicago: University of Chicago Press, 1979).

The philosophy and history of science have yielded important works enriching and broadening the reflection on human knowledge as both an artifact and a factor of social, historical, and cultural power dynamics. Noteworthy here are Paul Feyerabend's *Against Method*, 3rd ed. (London: Verso/

New Left Books, 1993) and Thomas S. Kuhn's *The Structure of Scientific Revolutions*, 3rd ed. (Chicago: University of Chicago Press, 1996). I think worthwhile reading in this area includes the works of Fritjof Capra, especially *Uncommon Wisdom: Conversations with Remarkable People* (Toronto: Bantam Books, 1989) and *The Tao of Physics: An Exploration of the Parallels between Modern Physics and Eastern Mysticism*, 4th ed. (Boston: Shambhala, 2000), and the works of Karl Popper, maybe starting with his *Unended Quest: An Intellectual Biography* (Glasgow: Fontana/Collins, 1976).

Likewise, the epistemological concerns of the British philosophy of history have been deeply influential on my own social-constructivist understanding of knowledge. Prominent here are Edward Hallett Carr, *What Is History?* (London: Macmillan, 1961); R. G. Collingwood, *The Idea of History: With Lectures 1926–1928*, edited and introduction by Jan van der Dussen (Oxford: Oxford University Press, 1994), as well as his *An Autobiography*, reprint, introduction by Stephen Toulmin (Oxford: Oxford University Press, 1978). Three German philosophers are also significant for my reflections on knowledge, language, and power: Ernst Cassirer, *The Philosophy of Symbolic Forms*, vol. 1: *Language*, translated by Ralph Manheim, preface and introduction by Charles W. Hendel (New Haven, Conn.: Yale University Press, 1953); Max Horkheimer, *Critique of Instrumental Reason: Lectures and Essays since the End of World War II*, 2nd ed., translated by Matthew J. O'Connell et al. (New York : Continuum, 1985); and Jürgen Habermas, *Knowledge and Human Interests*, 2nd ed., translated by Jeremy J. Shapiro (London: Heinemann Educational, 1978).

The feminist tradition introduced a crucial set of approaches and questions to the whole discussion of knowledge, culture, and power. Classic among the pioneering works in this area is Carol Gilligan's *In a Different Voice: Psychological Theory and Women's Development*, 2nd ed. (Cambridge, Mass.: Harvard University Press, 1993); Mary Field Belenky, Blythe McVicker Cinchy, Nancy Rule Goldberger, and Jill Mattuck Tarule, *Women's Ways of Knowing: The Development of Self, Voice, and Mind*, 2nd ed. (New York: BasicBooks, 1997), as well Sandra Harding and Merrill B. Hintikka, eds., *Discovering Reality: Feminist Perspectives on Epistemology, Metaphysics, Methodology, and Philosophy of Science*. 2nd ed. (Dordrecht: Kluwer Academic, 2003) are important, early anthologies in this respect. Patricia Hill Collins, *Black Feminist Thought: Knowledge, Consciousness, and the Politics of Empowerment*, rev. 10th anniv. ed. (London: Routledge, 2000), introduced the decisive angle of racial constructions, power dynamics, and conflicts, and their epistemological consequences. Also important from a sociological perspective are the works of Dorothy E. Smith: *The Everyday World as Problematic: A Feminist Sociology* (Milton Keynes, Eng.: Open University Press, 1988); *The Conceptual Practices of Power: A Feminist Sociology of Knowledge* (Boston, Mass.: Northeastern University Press, 1990); *Texts, Facts, and Femininity: Exploring the Relations of Ruling* (London: Routledge, 1990); *Writing the Social: Critique, Theory, and Investigations* (Toronto: University of Toronto Press, 1999); and *Institutional Ethnography: A Sociology for People* (Walnut Creek, Calif.: AltaMira Press, 2005). More recently, I have been deeply impressed by the approach of Elizabeth Kamarck Minnich in her *Transforming Knowledge*, 2nd ed. (Philadelphia: Temple University Press, 2005).

Among the major Latina feminist/mujerista contributions to this conversation are Gloria E. Anzaldúa, *Borderlands/La Frontera. The New Mestiza*, 2nd ed. (San Francisco: Aunt Lute Books, 1999); Cherríe L. Moraga and Gloria E. Anzaldúa, eds., *This Bridge Called My Back: Writings by Radical Women of Color*, 2nd ed. (Latham, N.Y.: Kitchen Table: Women of Color Press, 1984); and Ada María Isasi-Díaz, *En La Lucha/In the Struggle: Elaborating a Mujerista Theology*, 2nd ed. (Minneapolis: Augsburg Fortress Press, 2004).

Several Latin American and Hispanic philosophers, theologians, and other thinkers have also helped me make the connections of many of the diverse threads underlying these reflections, both among themselves and with the history, circumstances, and critical thinking emerging since the late 1960s in Latin America and among U.S. Hispanics. Among these thinkers are Rubem Alves with his *Filosofia Da Ciencia: Introdução ao jogo e suas regras*, 3rd ed. (São Paulo: Editora Brasiliense S. A., 1982), *Estórias de quem gosta de ensinar*, 2nd ed. (São Paulo: Cortez Editora-Autores Asociados, 1982), and *Conversas com quem gosta de ensinar*, 8th ed. (São Paulo: Cortez Editora-Autores Asociados, 1988); Renato Rosaldo: *Culture and Truth: The Remaking of Social Analysis*, 2nd ed. (Boston: Beacon Press, 1993); Linda Martín Alcoff and Eduardo Mendieta, eds., *Thinking from the Underside of History: Enrique Dussel's Philosophy of Liberation* (Lanham, Md.: Rowman and Littlefield, 2000); Ivone Gebara, *Longing for Running Water: Ecofeminism and Liberation*, translated by David Moulineaux (Minneapolis: Augsburg Fortress Press, 1999); Dolores Delgado Bernal, C. Alejandra Elenes, Francisca E. Godínez, and Sofia Villenas, eds., *Chicana/Latina Education in Everyday Life: Feminista Perspectives on Pedagogy and Epistemology* (Albany: State University of New York Press, 2006); Orlando Espín, *The Faith of the People: Theological Reflections on Popular Catholicism* (Maryknoll, N.Y.: Orbis Books, 1997); Orlando Espín and Miguel H. Diaz, eds., *From the Heart of Our People:*

Latino/a Explorations in Catholic Systematic Theology (Maryknoll, N.Y.: Orbis Books, 1999); Walter D. Mignolo, *Local Histories/Global Designs: Coloniality, Subaltern Knowledges, and Border Thinking* (Princeton, N.J.: Princeton University Press, 2000); David T. Abalos, *Latinos in the United States: The Sacred and the Political*, 2nd ed. (Notre Dame, Ind.: University of Notre Dame Press, 2007); and Claudio Canaparo, *Geo-epistemology: Latin America and the Location of Knowledge* (Oxford: Peter Lang, 2009).

Michel Foucault's *Power/Knowledge: Selected Interviews and Other Writings, 1972–1977*, edited and translated by Colin Gordon (New York: Pantheon Books, 1980), is another key work for these discussions. And, in my very personal case, two disparate, out-of-the-ordinary books helped me frame with a smile these issues that are all too often entangled with very real, massive human pain: Robert M. Pirsig's *Zen and the Art of Motorcycle Maintenance: An Inquiry into Values*, 25th anniv. ed. (New York: Quill, 1999), and Bernard McGrane's *The Un-TV and the 10 mph Car: Experiments in Personal Freedom and Everyday Life* (Fort Bragg, Calif.: Small Press, 1994).

Finally, two previous writings of mine have summarized earlier elucidations of my views in these matters: "Avertissements épistémologico-politiques pour une sociologie latino-américaine des religions," *Social Compass* 26, no. 2–3 (1979): 179–94, and *Mapas para la fiesta*, 2nd ed. (Atlanta: Asociación para la Educación Teológica Hispana, 1999).

ANTI-LATINO RACISM | LINDA MARTÍN ALCOFF

1. This essay is a significantly revised version of "Latinos beyond the Binary," *Southern Journal of Philosophy* 47, supplement (2009): 112–28.
2. Justin Pritchard, "Mexican Worker Death Rates Rise Sharply Even as Overall Job Safety Improves," Associated Press, March 20, 2004.
3. The demographer and sociologist Richard Alba contests the claim that Latino immigration will continue to increase, and yet the perception of a possibly unending increase remains a motivating factor for the current hysteria. See Richard Alba, *Blurring the Color Line: The New Chance for a More Integrated America* (Cambridge: Harvard University Press, 2009).
4. See Adrian Piper, "Xenophobia and Kantian Rationalism," *Philosophical Forum* 24, no. 1–3 (1992–93): 188–232; J. L. A. Garcia, "The Heart of Racism," *Journal of Social Philosophy* 27, no. 1 (1996): 5–45.
5. Lewis Gordon, *Bad Faith and Antiblack Racism* (Atlantic Highlands, N.J.: Humanities Press, 1995), 102.
6. The arguments of this section were initially developed in my "Latinas/os, Asian-Americans and the Black/White Paradigm" *Journal of Ethics* 7, no. 1 (2003): 5–27.

7. See, for example, David Theo Goldberg, *Racist Culture: Philosophy and the Politics of Meaning* (Oxford: Blackwell, 1993).

8. Nell Irvin Painter, *The History of White People* (New York: W. W. Norton, 2010).

9. Stuart Ewen and Elizabeth Ewen, *Typecasting: On the Arts and Sciences of Human Inequality* (New York: Seven Stories Press, 2006).

10. For an explanation of the concept of cultural racism, see Ramón Grosfoguel, "'Cultural Racism' and Colonial Caribbean Migrants in Core Zones of the Capitalist World-Economy," *Review: Fernand Braudel Center* 22, no. 4 (1999): 409–34.

11. Religions, such as Islam, can become stand-ins for cultures in this way.

12. On this view, the problem with Latinos is not just that they are seen as foreign but that their cultural background makes them ineluctably foreign, both incapable of and unmotivated toward assimilation to the superior, mainstream, white Anglo culture. Debates over bilingualism thus invoke the specter of a concerted resistance to assimilation rather than language rights, and the public celebration of nationally specific holidays, such as "Puerto Rican Day" or Mexican Independence Day, and even the presence of ethnic-specific cuisines can come to signify a threat to the imagined community of Anglo nationalism. Despite the fact that Mexican Americans have been living within the current U.S. borders for longer than most Anglo-Americans, they are all too often seen as squatters on U.S. soil, interlopers who "belong" elsewhere.

13. Samuel Huntington says in fact that Latinos must assimilate to Anglo-Protestant values and begin "dreaming in English" or the coherence of the United States is in danger; see *Who Are We?: The Challenges to America's National Identity* (New York: Simon and Schuster, 2004), esp. chaps. 4 and 9.

14. For a more extended discussion of the relationship between Latinos and the category of race, see my *Visible Identities: Race, Gender, and the Self* (New York: Oxford University Press, 2006), chap. 10.

15. Goldberg, *Racist Culture*, 75.

16. Max Weber, "Ethnic Groups," in *Theories of Ethnicity: A Reader*, ed. Werner Sollors (New York: New York University Press, 1996), 55–57.

17. Ibid., 56.

18. Angelo Corlett's odd formulation of ethnic identity as determined by genealogy bridges this divide but in ways he does not acknowledge, since he characterizes his account as only about ethnicity, and not about race. See his *Race, Racism, and Reparations* (Ithaca, N.Y.: Cornell University Press, 2003), 130–31.

19. See, e.g., Jean Bethke Elshtain, *Democracy on Trial* (New York: Harper Collins, 1995).

20. Anthony Appiah, *In My Father's House: Africa in the Philosophy of Culture* (New York: Oxford University Press, 1992); Nancy Fraser, *Justice Interruptus: Critical Reflections on the "Postsocialist" Condition* (New York: Routledge, 1997); and Paul Gilroy, *Against Race: Imagining Political Culture beyond the Color Line* (Cambridge, Mass.: Belknap Press, 1992).

21. Weber, "Ethnic Groups," 55.

22. Nathan Glazer and Daniel Patrick Moynihan, *Beyond the Melting Pot: The Negroes, Puerto Ricans, Jews, Italian, and Irish of New York City*, 2nd ed. (Cambridge, Mass.: MIT Press, 1970).

23. See, e.g., Jorge Gracia, *Surviving Race, Ethnicity, and Nationality: A Challenge for the 21st Century* (Lanham, Md.: Rowman and Littlefield, 2005).

24. "'Ethnic, ethnical, ethnicity, *ethnie, ethnique*': Entries from *Oxford English Dictionary* (1961) and *Supplement* (1972), and *Grand Robert* (1985)," in *Theories of Ethnicity: A Classical Reader*, ed. Werner Sollors (New York: New York University Press, 1996), 2–12.

25. Ibid.

26. Michael Omi and Howard Winant, *Racial Formations in the United States: From the 1960s to the 1980s* (New York: Routledge, 1986).

27. See, e.g., José Cruz, *Identity and Power: Puerto Rican Politics and the Challenge of Ethnicity* (Philadelphia: Temple University Press, 1998).

28. See, e.g., Cristina Beltran, *The Trouble with Unity* (New York: Oxford University Press, 2010).

29. See, e.g., Mario Barrera, *Race and Class in the Southwest: A Theory of Racial Inequality* (South Bend, Ind.: University of Notre Dame Press, 1979).

30. Linda Martín Alcoff, "Comparative Race, Comparative Racisms," in *Black Ethnicity/Latino Race?* ed. Jorge Gracia (Ithaca, N.Y.: Cornell University Press, 2007).

31. See, e.g., Arthur H. Goldsmith, Darrick Hamilton, and William Darity Jr., "Shades of Discrimination: Skin Tone and Wages," *American Economic Review* 96, no. 2 (2006): 242–45.

32. See, e.g., the definitive, longitudinal study by Edward E. Telles and Vilma Ortiz, *Generations of Exclusion: Mexican Americans, Assimilation and Exclusion* (New York: Russell Sage, 2008). Telles and Ortiz found it necessary to conceptualize Mexican Americans as a "racialized ethnic group," and show that assimilation to a white norm remains a fiction for most.

33. Eduardo Bonilla-Silva, *Racism without Racists: Color Blind Racism and the Persistence of Inequality in America* (Lanham, Md.: Rowman and Littlefield, 2009).

34. Of course, this will not be news to social scientists, but it has not yet seeped into the general discussions of even critical race theory as evidenced by the often weak analyses of recent electoral phenomena.

THE ACT OF REMEMBERING: THE RECONSTRUCTION OF U.S. LATINA/O IDENTITIES BY U.S. LATINA/O MUSLIMS | HJAMIL A. MARTÍNEZ-VÁZQUEZ

1. I am using the concept of imaginary to name the overarching set of ideological, philosophical, and theoretical paradigms that guide the social, economic, political, and academic structures of society. Imaginary should not be seen or interpreted as something that lacks factual reality. The imaginary is responsible for discourses, theories, ideologies, and philosophies that dictate the way we live in the world.

2. Although I focus my attention on the importance of Muslim traditions in the construction of U.S. Latina/o identities, it is important to acknowledge that the restoring of the medieval history of Spain as a source of historical consciousness also applies to U.S. Latina/o Jews, especially (but not limited to) those who have their roots in the tradition of Crypto-Jews in the Southwest. See Gloria Golden, *Remnants of Crypto-Jews among Hispanic Americans* (Mountain View, Calif.: Floricanto Press, 2004).

3. Juan Flores, "Broken English Memories: Languages of the Trans-Colony," in *Postcolonial Theory and the United States: Race, Ethnicity, and Literature*, ed. Amritjit Singh and Peter Schmidt (Jackson: University Press of Mississippi, 200), 338.

4. Arif Dirlik, *Postmodernity's Histories: The Past as Legacy and Project* (Lanham, Md.: Rowman and Littlefield, 2000), 48.

5. Ibid., 48–49. U.S. Latina/o Muslims draw on "distant forgotten memories" in their process of identity construction.

6. Ibid., 48.

7. Flores, "Broken English Memories," 338.

8. See Arcadio Díaz-Quiñones, *La Memoria Rota: Ensayos Sobre Cultura y Política* (Río Piedras, P.R.: Ediciones Huracán, 1993).

9. Flores, "Broken English Memories," 340.

10. Ibid., 342.

11. Ibid., 347.

12. Jeanette Rodríguez and Ted Fortier, *Cultural Memory: Resistance, Faith, and Identity* (Austin: University of Texas Press, 2007), 11.

13. Ibid.

14. Mieke Bal, Introduction to *Acts of Memory: Cultural Recall in the Present*, ed. Mieke Bal, Jonathan Crewe, and Leo Spitzer (Hanover, N.H.: University Press of New England, 1999), vii.

15. Jan Assmann, *Religion and Cultural Memory: Ten Studies*, trans. Rodney Livingstone (Stanford, Calif.: Stanford University Press, 2006), 11.

16. Ibid., 27.

17. Anzaldúa refers to the concept of *la facultad*, as "an acute awareness mediated by the part of the psyche that does not speak, that communicates in images and symbols which are the faces of feelings, that is, behind which feelings reside/hide" (Gloria Anzaldúa, *Borderlands/La Frontera: The New Mestiza* [San Francisco: Aunt Lute, 1987], 38.) U.S. Latinas/os have this *facultad* because their condition as outcast, marginalized, and persecuted people awakens and increases this psychic awareness. They can discover the past through new lenses, and in doing so their identity construction becomes a subversive practice, debunking the traditional and normative understanding of the past as fixed and finished.

18. Rodríguez and Fortier, *Cultural Memory*, 10.

19. Ibid., 11.

20. Gilbert R. Cadena, "Religious Ethnic Identity: A Socio-Religious Portrait of Latinos and Latinas in the Catholic Church," in *Old Masks, New Faces: Religion and Latino Identities*, ed. Anthony M. Stevens-Arroyo and Gilbert R. Cadena (New York: Bildner Center for Western Hemisphere Studies, 1995), 33.

21. Virgilio Elizondo, "Popular Religion as the Core of Cultural Identity Based on the Mexican American Experience in the United States," in *An Enduring Flame: Studies on Latino Popular Religiosity*, ed. Anthony M. Stevens-Arroyo and Ana María Díaz-Stevens (New York: Bildner Center for Western Hemisphere Studies, 1994), 114.

22. This primary role of religious experience in the construction of cultural identities is not specific to U.S. Latinas/os, as it also applies to other racial/ethnic groups in the United States (e.g., U.S. African Americans and U.S. Irish Americans).

23. This is particularly important to acknowledge since the histories of colonization of the Americas prove the fact that religion can be used as an assimilation tool. For example, the history of the "Americanization" of Puerto Rico after 1898 cannot be understood without the Protestant missionary activity that served as a catalyst of new identities, while also intended to do away with the existing Catholic cultural identity of the country.

24. Rodríguez and Fortier, *Cultural Memory*, 3.

25. Ibid.
26. Ibid.
27. Elizondo, "Popular Religion," 117.
28. Richard R. Flores, "Para El Niño Dios: Sociability and Commemorative Sentiment in Popular Religious Practice," in *An Enduring Flame: Studies on Latino Popular Religiosity*, ed. Anthony M. Stevens-Arroyo and Ana María Díaz-Stevens (New York: Bildner Center for Western Hemisphere Studies, 1994), 184.
29. Rebecca Sachs Norris, "Converting to What? Embodied Culture and the Adoption of New Beliefs," in *The Anthropology of Religious Conversion*, ed. Andrew Buckser and Stephen D. Glazier (Lanham, Md.: Rowman and Littlefield, 2003), 171.
30. U.S. Latina/o Muslims do not convert because they want to be subversive and challenge the traditional understandings of their cultural identities, but they engage in these activities after conversion in order to reconstruct their identities so they can fit their newfound religious experience. In this sense, conversion to Islam for U.S. Latinas/os turns into a subversive activity, a radical act of remembering, even if the intention of converting is not subversive.
31. Alberto Hernández, "Hispanic Cultural Identity and the Recovery of Lost Memory: Response to Raúl Gómez-Ruiz's *Mozarabs, Hispanics, and the Cross*," *Perspectivas* 12 (Fall 2008): 41.
32. Ibid.
33. Ibid., 44.
34. Ibid.
35. Yahya 'Abu Ayah' López, "What's in a Word," *Latino Muslim Voice*, July–September 2002, http://www.latinodawah.org/newsletter/july-sept2k2.html#12.
36. Edmund A. Arroyo, "A Perspective from Chicago of the Latino Muslim Experience," *Latino Muslim Voice*, October–December 2002, http://www.latinodawah.org/newsletter/oct-dec2k2.html#4.
37. Interview with María in New York City (July 23, 2006). I use a pseudonym to ensure privacy.
38. Juan Galván, "Who Are Latino Muslims?," *Islamic Horizons* (July/August 2008), 28.
39. Raheel Rojas, "In Between Religions (Regresa a tu Senior y tu Cultura Latino)," *Latino Muslim Voice*, April–June 2006, http://www.latinodawah.org/newsletter/oct-dec2k2.html.

40. Kenny Yusuf Rodríguez, "Latino Muslims: Islamic Roots of Spanish Culture," *Islamic Horizons* (July/August 2002), 40–41.

41. Hisham Aidi, "Olé to Allah: New York's Latino Muslims," Beliefnet, http://www.beliefnet.com/story/9/story_996.html?rnd=543.

42. Américo Castro argues that Spanish attitudes toward indigenous populations and enslaved Africans came as a direct result of their attitudes toward Muslims and Jews in Spain who were used as servants. At the same time, Castro also recognizes the Islamic style in the construction of churches (columns), which underscore the connection to Islamic culture. Américo Castro, *Iberoamérica: Su Historia y su Cultura* (New York: Holt, Rinehart and Winston, 1954), 9–12.

43. Mary Elizabeth Perry, *The Handless Maiden: Moriscos and the Politics of Religion in Early Modern Spain* (Princeton: Princeton University Press, 2005), 37.

44. Ibid.

45. The interest in dis-covering this history is demonstrated in the large number of essays on the topic in U.S. Latina/o Muslim newsletters. For example see Samantha Sánchez, "Islamic Resurgence in Spain and Beyond," *Latino Muslim Voice*, July–September 2002, http://www.latinodawah.org/newsletter/oct-dec2k2.html, and Mariam Santos García, "Musulmanes en la Peninsula Ibérica," *Latino Muslim Voice*, July–September 2003, http://www.latinodawah.org/newsletter/july-sept2k3.html, among others.

46. Yvonne Yazbeck Haddad, "The Quest for Peace in Submission: Reflections on the Journey of American Women Converts to Islam," in *Women Embracing Islam: Gender and Conversion in the West*, ed. Karin van Nieuwkerk (Austin: University of Texas Press, 2006), 21.

47. Guillermo Araya Goubet, "The Evolution of Castro's Theories," in *Américo Castro and the Meaning of Spanish Civilization*, ed. José Rubia Barcia and Selma Margaretten (Berkeley: University of California Press, 1976), 47.

48. Michelle González, *Afro-Cuban Theology: Religion, Race, Culture, and Identity* (Gainesville: University Press of Florida, 2006), 9.

49. Ibid. While I agree with González's assessment, I find that it is not simply their emphasis on culture, but the understanding of culture as something fixed. This is different from my argument that culture should be a guiding point to the construction of identities because I see culture as fluid and ever-changing, not fixed in some particular past or tradition.

50. Miguel A. De La Torre, "Religion and Power in the Study of Hispanic Religions," in *Rethinking Latino(a) Religion and Identity*, ed. Miguel A De La Torre and Gastón Espinosa (Cleveland: Pilgrim Press, 2006), 288.

51. González, *Afro-Cuban Theology*, 22.

52. Ibid., 24.

53. Manuel A. Vásquez, "Rethinking *Mestizaje*," in *Rethinking Latino(a) Religion and Identity*, ed. Miguel A De La Torre and Gastón Espinosa (Cleveland: Pilgrim Press, 2006), 139.

54. Ibid.

55. Ibid., 140.

56. Ada María Isasi-Díaz, "A New Mestizaje/Mulatez: Reconceptualizing Difference," in *A Dream Unfinished: Theological Reflections on America from the Margins*, ed. Eleazar S. Fernández and Fernando F. Segovia (Maryknoll, N.Y.: Orbis, 2001), 204.

57. Ibid., 207.

58. Ibid., 208.

59. Ibid.

60. I am arguing for the reconceptualization of the term "mestizaje," but in order to strip it from the almost "absolute" characterization that this hybrid condition exists only as a result of the colonization of the Americas, overlooking the diversity of cultural and religious experiences within the Latina/o historical consciousness. In other words, we have to readdress the issue of mestizaje, so that our conceptions of *latinidades* are redefined with new epistemological character. For example, this concept has to be deconstructed in order to analyze if it follows the tradition of "racial purity" established in Europe, and commercialized by Spain, and turns out to be just another classification that serves more to limit than to include. For a further discussion on the issue of racial purity, see Santiago Castro-Gómez, "(Post)Coloniality for Dummies: Latin American Perspectives on Modernity, Coloniality, and the Geopolitics of Knowledge," in *Coloniality at Large: Latin America and the Postcolonial Debate*, ed. Mabel Moraña, Enrique Dussel, and Carlos A. Jáuregui (Durham, N.C.: Duke University Press, 2008), 259–85.

61. Vásquez, "Rethinking *Mestizaje*," 142.

62. Raúl Gómez-Ruiz, "Ritual and the Construction of Cultural Identity: An Example from Hispanic Liturgy," *Perspectivas* 12 (Fall 2008): 9. Also see Raúl Gómez-Ruiz, *Mozarabs, Hispanics, and the Cross* (Maryknoll, N.Y.: Orbis, 2007).

63. Hernández, "Hispanic Cultural Identity," 48.

64. Ibid., 36.

65. Ibid.

66. Coloniality, here, refers to the way that the domination of a colonial discourse is exercised, leaving other discourses and knowledges (subversive

and subaltern) outside of the imaginary through silence or erasure. For further discussion on coloniality, see Walter Mignolo, *Local Histories/Global Designs: Coloniality, Subaltern Knowledges, and Border Thinking* (Princeton: Princeton University Press, 2000).

67. González, *Afro-Cuban Theology*, 32.
68. Ibid.
69. Hernández, "Hispanic Cultural Identity," 52.

IF IT IS NOT CATHOLIC, IS IT POPULAR CATHOLICISM? EVIL EYE, ESPIRITISMO, AND SANTERÍA: LATINA/O RELIGION WITHIN LATINA/O THEOLOGY | MICHELLE A. GONZÁLEZ

1. Laura de Mello e Souza, *The Devil and the Land of the Holy Cross: Witchcraft, Slavery, and Popular Religion in Colonial Brazil*, trans. Diane Grosklaus Whitty (1986; Austin: University of Texas Press, 2006), 46.
2. Ibid., 48.
3. Anthony M. Stevens-Arroyo, "The Contribution of Catholic Orthodoxy to Caribbean Syncretism: The Case of La Virgen de La Caridad del Cobre in Cuba," *Des Sciences Sociales des Religion* 117 (January–March 2002): 42.
4. William A. Christian, *Local Religion in Sixteenth-Century Spain* (Princeton, N.J.: Princeton University Press, 1981), 3.
5. The emphasis on hot and cold has been traced to the Greek classical medicine that was brought to Latin America, called humoral pathology. Linda-Anne Rebhun, "Contemporary Evil Eye in Northeast Brazil," in *Folklore Interpreted: Essays in Honor of Alan Dundes,* ed. Regina Bendix and Rosemary Lévy Zumwalt (New York: Garland, 1995), 218.
6. In his classic study, "Wet and Dry, The Evil Eye," Alan Dundes proposes four elements of evil eye belief: the dependence on liquid for life; the idea that goodness is limited; a balanced view of the universe where one's fortune can affect another's misfortune; and symbolic equivalence between eyes and sexual organs.
7. Sheila Cosminsky, "Guatemala: The Evil Eye in a Quiché Community," in *The Evil Eye,* ed. Clarence Maloney (New York: Columbia University Press, 1976), 163–74.
8. While *ladino* has been historically used in Guatemala, today a trend toward using *mestizo* is also apparent to describe individuals of racially mixed descent.
9. Mario A. Núñez Molina, "Community Healing among Puerto Ricans: *Espiritismo*," in *Healing Cultures: Art and Religion as Curative Practices in the*

Caribbean and Its Diaspora," ed. Margarite Fernández Olmos and Lizbeth Paravisini-Gebert (New York: Palgrave, 2001), 119.

10. Hippolyte Léon Denizard Rivail (1804–1869), popularly known as Allan Kardec, was a well-known scholar of pedagogy when he began to study spirit mediumship. These studies cemented his beliefs in reincarnation, the astral body, and communication with spirits through mediums. Belief in reincarnation is a fundamental marker that distinguishes Spiritism from Anglo-Saxon Spiritualism. Our reincarnation is linked to Kardec's notion of the moral progression of the soul through the many lives we live. Kardec believed that the soul became more morally elevated or evolved as it became incarnated in its different lives. He understood his doctrine as a scientific account of the spirit world that was grounded in Christian morality.

11. Núñez Molina, "Community Healing among Puerto Ricans," 117–18.

12. "In Cuba people from all the Yoruba subdivisions were mixed together with people from all over West and Central Africa. They were classified into groups called *naciones* (nations), and each bore a distinctive name. Descendents of the Yorubas and some of their neighbors became the Lucumi nation. . . . Lucumi is a secondary phenomenon in Cuba, a result of the inclusion of heterogeneous Yoruba subgroups within an exploitative system of urban and rural slavery alongside Africans from other areas." George Brandon, *Santería from Africa to the New World: The Dead Sell Memories* (Bloomington: Indiana University Press, 1993), 55.

13. Anthony B. Pinn, *Varieties of African American Religion* (Minneapolis: Fortress Press, 1998), 58.

14. Citing the work of E. Bolaji Idowu, Ramos describes the term *orisha* as a corruption of the word *orishe*. *Ori* means head or source, and *she* means to begin. "The name *orisha* would then be an ellipsis of *ibiti ori ti she*—the origin or source of *ori*: Olodumare himself." Miguel "Willie" Ramos, "Afro-Cuban *Orisha* Worship," in *Santería Aesthetics in Contemporary Latin American Art*, ed. Arturo Lindsay (Washington, D.C.: Smithsonian Institution Press, 1996), 56.

15. The January 6 festival of Epiphany, *El Día de Reyes*, was perhaps the most significant feast day for Afro-Cubans. As described by renowned ethnographer Fernando Ortiz, "That day, black Africa, its people, its costumes, its music, its tongues, its song and dance, its ceremonies, its religion and political institutions, were brought across the Atlantic to Cuba, especially Habana." Fernando Ortiz, *Los cabildos y la fiesta afrocubanos del Día de los Reyes* (Havana, Cuba: Editorial de Ciencias Sociales, 1992), 1.

16. Jospeh M. Murphy, "YéYé Cachita: Ochún in a Cuban Mirror," in *"Òsun across the Waters: A Yoruba Goddess in Africa and the Americas*, ed. Joseph M.

Murphy and Mei-Mei Sanford (Bloomington: Indiana University Press, 2001), 87.

17. Miguel Barnet, *Afro-Cuban Religions* (Princeton, N.J.: Markus Wiener, 1995), 7–8.

18. Mary Ann Clark, "Godparenthood in the Afro-Cuban Religious Tradition of Santería," *Religious Studies and Theology* 22, no. 1 (2003): 45–62.

19. Ramos, "Afro-Cuban *Orisha* Worship," 59.

20. Ibid.

21. Luis León, " 'Soy Una Curandera y Soy Católica': The Poetics of a Mexican Healing Tradition," in *Horizons of the Sacred: Mexican Traditions in U.S. Catholicism*, ed. Timothy Matovina and Gary Riebe-Estrella (Ithaca, N.Y.: Cornell University Press, 2002), 95–118.

22. Prayers for the dead are ultimately prayers for the second coming of Christ and should not be reduced to merely individualistic petitions. Also, prayer for the dead does not mean participation in séances and directly communicating with the dead. "Attempts to make direct contact with the dead would be absolutely unchristian and uneschatological, and would amount to spiritualism." Elmar Klinger, "Purgatory," in *Sacramentum Mundi: An Encyclopedia of Theology*, ed. Karl Rahner et al., vol. 5 (London: Burns and Oates, 1970), 168.

23. Lara Medina and Gilbert R. Cadena, "Día de Los Muertos: Public Ritual, Community Renewal, and Popular Religion in Los Angeles," in *Horizons of the Sacred: Mexican Traditions in U.S. Catholicism*, ed. Timothy Matovina and Gary Riebe-Estrella (Ithaca, N.Y.: Cornell University Press, 2002), 69–84.

24. The importance of difference for Latinas and Latinos is made obvious by the insistence in Hispanic/Latino theology, including mujerista theology, on recognizing the importance of mestizaje/mulatez, a concept which originally referred to the mingling of Amerindian and African blood with European blood, but which now also includes the present-day mixtures of people from Latin America and the Caribbean both among ourselves and with people of other ethnic/racial and cultural backgrounds here in the United States. Ada María Isasi-Díaz, "A New *Mestizaje/Mulatez*: Reconceptualizing Difference," in *A Dream Unfinished: Theological Reflections on America from the Margins*, ed. Eleazer S. Fernandez and Fernando F. Segovia (Maryknoll, N.Y.: Orbis Books, 2001), 203. Her sentiments are echoed in the writings of Roberto S. Goizueta, who sees the coming together of Latin America and the United States as a second *mestizaje* and the convergence of Latina/o cultures in the United States as a third *mestizaje*. Roberto S. Goizueta, *Caminemos con Jesús: Toward a Hispanic/Latino Theology of Accompaniment* (Maryknoll, N.Y.: Orbis Books, 1995), 8.

25. See Orlando O. Espín, *Grace and Humanness: Theological Reflections because of Culture* (Maryknoll, N.Y.: Orbis Books, 2207).

26. See, for example, John H. Elliot, "Paul, Galatians, and the Evil Eye," in *The Social World of the New Testament*, ed. Jerome H. Neyrey and Eric C. Stewart (Peabody, Mass.: Hendrickson, 2008), 223–34.

"RACISM IS NOT INTELLECTUAL": INTERRACIAL FRIENDSHIP, MULTICULTURAL LITERATURE, AND DECOLONIZING EPISTEMOLOGIES | PAULA M. L. MOYA

1. *Emplumada* was the winner of the 1982 American Book Award. The poem under consideration is situated right in the middle of the second (and middle) section of the book.

2. For their insightful comments and helpful criticisms, I am indebted to David Kim, Michael Hames-García, Ernesto Martínez, and Alex Woloch.

3. Lorna Dee Cervantes, "Poem for the Young White Man Who Asked Me How I, an Intelligent, Well-Read Person Could Believe in the War between Races," in *Emplumada* (Pittsburgh: University of Pittsburgh Press, 1981), 36. Hereafter Cervantes, *Emplumada*.

4. Ibid.

5. This quote and the block quote below are taken from a paper prepared by Michael Stocker for the proceedings of the "Passions of the Color Line" conference: "Some Issues About Emotions and Racisms" (unpublished manuscript, 2001), 1–29 The planned publication has not appeared in print. Some of the material around the quote cited in this paper can be found in the book Stocker wrote with Elizabeth Hegeman titled *Valuing Emotions* (New York: Cambridge University Press, 1996).

6. See Stocker, "Some Issues About Emotions and Racisms," 1–29 (my italics). See also Stocker with Hegeman, *Valuing Emotions*.

7. This and the following quotation are taken from a paper prepared by Eduardo Mendieta for the same, never published, conference proceedings: "Technologies of the Racist Self" (unpublished manuscript, 2001), 1–15.

8. William S. Wilkerson, "Is There Something You Need to Tell Me? Coming Out and the Ambiguity of Experience," in *Reclaiming Identity: Realist Theory and the Predicament of Postmodernism*, ed. Paula M. L. Moya and Michael R. Hames-García (Berkeley: University of California Press, 2000), 256–67.

9. Ibid., 259–60.

10. Ibid., 260.

11. When I speak of objectivity, I am not appealing to a God's-eye "view from nowhere" but rather to a postpositivist conception that acknowledges the

unavoidability, and indeed, epistemic necessity of interpretive bias. By itself, the "subjectivity" of emotion does not disqualify it from contributing to projects that strive for objectivity.

12. See Paula M. L. Moya, "A Symphony of Anger," *Phoebe: An Interdisciplinary Journal of Feminist Scholarship, Theory and Aesthetics* 8, no. 1/2 (1996): 1–13; Paula Moya, "Postmodernism, 'Realism,' and the Politics of Identity," in *Reclaiming Identity: Realist Theory and the Predicament of Postmodernism*, ed. Paula M. L. Moya and Michael R. Hames-Garcia (Berkeley: University of Califonia Press, 2000), esp. 91–99. See also Susan Babbitt, "Feminism and Objective Interests," in *Feminist Epistemologies*, ed. Linda Alcoff and Elizabeth Potter (New York: Routledge, 1993); Satya P. Mohanty, "The Epistemic Status of Identity: On 'Beloved' and the Postcolonial Condition," *Cultural Critique*, no. 24 (1993): esp. 45–55.

13. See Yulia E. Chentsova-Dutton and Jeanne L. Tsai, "Self-Focused Attention and Emotional Reactivity: The Role of Culture," *Journal of Personality and Social Psychology* 98, no. 3 (2010): 507–19; Jeanne L. Tsai, "Ideal Affect: Cultural Causes and Behavioral Consequences," *Perspectives on Psychological Science* 2, no. 3 (2007): 242–59; Ying Wong and Jeanne Tsai, "Cultural Models of Shame and Guilt," in *Handbook of Self-Conscious Emotions*, ed. R. Robins Tracy and J. Tangney (New York: Guilford Press, 2007), 210–23 .

14. I follow historian George Fredrickson's understanding of racism as "not merely an attitude or set of beliefs" but rather something that "expresses itself in the practices, institutions, and structures" in a way that "either directly sustains or proposes to establish a *racial order*, a permanent group hierarchy that is believed to reflect the laws of nature or the decrees of God." George M. Fredrickson, *Racism: A Short History*, (Princeton, N.J.: Princeton University Press, 2002), 6. See also Michael Omi and Howard Winant, *Racial Formation in the United States: From the 1960s to the 1990s* (New York: Routledge, 1994), esp. 69–76.

15. Cervantes, *Emplumada*, 36.

16. See Hazel Rose Markus and Paula M. L. Moya, eds. *Doing Race: 21 Essays for the 21st Century* (New York: W. W. Norton, 2010); Matthew Desmond and Mustafa Emirbayer, *Racial Domination, Racial Progress: The Sociology of Race in America* (New York: McGraw Hill, 2010); Omi and Winant, *Racial Formation in the United States*.

17. Markus and Moya, *Doing Race*.

18. I use the term "multicultural" here as a kind of shorthand to refer to those works of literature that treat in interesting and complicated ways the social fact of race, the dynamics of cross-cultural encounters, and the destructive

294 | NOTES TO PAGES 174-81

capacity of racism. Generally, though not always, such works are written by persons who have been racialized as "subaltern" or "minority" subjects in a society (such as our own) that is largely economically and socially stratified along lines of class, gender, ability, and race.

19. By friendship, Friedman means "a relationship that is based on approximate equality (in at least some respects) and a mutuality of affection, interest, and benevolence. Friendship, in this sense, can occur between or among lovers or familial relations as well as between or among people not otherwise affiliated with one another." Marilyn Friedman, *What Are Friends For? Feminist Perspectives on Personal Relationships and Moral Theory* (Ithaca, N.Y.: Cornell University Press, 1993).

20. Frye notes that it "is one mark of a voluntary association that the one person can survive displeasing the other, defying the other, dissociating from the other." Marilyn Frye, *The Politics of Reality: Essays in Feminist Theory* (Trumansburg, N.Y.: Crossing Press, 1983), 73.

21. Ibid., 75.

22. Ibid.

23. Ibid., 66-67.

24. Friedman, *What Are Friends For?*, 197-98 (my italics). She continues: "Through seeing what my friend counts as a harm done to her, for example, and seeing how she suffers from it and what she does in response, I can try on, as it were, her interpretive claim and its implications for moral practice. I can attend to what happens as a result of her acquiescence and accommodation or as a result of her resistance and rebellion" (198).

25. Ibid., 192-93.

26. Ibid., 189.

27. Ibid., 202-3.

28. When and if race no longer "matters," this statement will no longer hold true.

29. For a discussion of this point, see Linda Martín Alcoff, "Anti-Latino Racism," in this volume.

30. I am speaking, of course, from experience. Over the past twenty-one years, I have had many friends of various backgrounds who have taught me a great deal about the way race is implicated with other social hierarchies such as class, gender, and sexuality to produce the U.S. racial formation. Perhaps the two friends from whom I initially learned the most about race in this country are two African American women with whom I worked closely (at different times in my life) over the course of several years—one an academic, the other a former schoolteacher and civil servant. These two

women are very different from each other (and from me) in a number of salient ways (sexuality, religious affiliation, age, life trajectory, work experiences, geographic location), but what they have in common (besides the fact that they are both middle-class, college-educated African American women) is that they are incredibly intelligent women who can articulate insightfully what race has meant for the way they and others around them have been gendered, sexualized, and situated within a global economic order. Additionally, they have in common the fact that I care deeply about them. In each case, we have seen and helped each other through some of life's most difficult transitions (death, divorce, job loss, breakups, affairs, moves across the country, parental disappointments, intimate betrayals, murder, and suicide) and celebrated together some of life's most affirming events (marriage, graduations, school acceptances, new romances, new home purchases, parental achievements, job offers, and job promotions). They have each, at different times and in different ways, through their words and through their experiences, helped me discern the subtle racial dynamics that infuse our daily lives and permeate our most intimate interactions. We have learned together through humor and with laughter, in anger, though sorrow, and by way of profound emotional pain. We have pushed each other way past our comfort zones on several notable occasions, and I am the wiser for it.

31. Friedman writes: "I certainly do not preclude the possibility that all of these sources and more, not solely friendship, may contribute to moral transformation." Friedman, *What Are Friends For?*, 202.

32. Ibid., 201.

33. Ibid., 201–2.

34. For an excellent book that uses the metaphor of friendship to discuss how readers interact with books they read, see Wayne C. Booth, *The Company We Keep: An Ethics of Fiction* (Berkeley: University of California Press, 1988), esp. 169–79.

35. I am taking up María Lugones's suggestive phrase "'world'-traveling" to indicate the different subjective worlds we humans occupy. See Lugones, "Playfulness, 'World'-Traveling, and Loving Perception," in *Pilgrimages/Peregrinajes: Theorizing Coalition against Multiple Oppressions* (Lanham, Md.: Rowman and Littlefield, 2003), 77–100.

36. Friedman, *What Are Friends For?*, 209.

37. Bakhtin focused his theorizing on the novel. However, his insights can be usefully extended to other genres, many of which have been, as Bakhtin notes, "novelized." See M. M. Bakhtin, *The Dialogic Imagination: Four Essays*,

trans. Caryl Emerson and Michael Holquist (Austin: University of Texas Press, 1981). The heteroglossic advantage of the novel (after it fundamentally changed the landscape of literature so that all genres had been "novelized") is that it is longer (more voices can enter the text simply by virtue of the fact that there is more space for them to exist in) and that its form is looser (thus allowing for a wider variety of types of voices to be incorporated into the same work).

38. Ibid., 262.

39. Ibid., 263.

40. I do not have the space to develop this idea in this essay, but I want to briefly note that seeing a long, complex work as a heteroglossic orchestrated unity that sounds differently to different people can help us to think more complexly about the question of literary value. Those of us who work in the academy are duly educated into some works of literature—but not others. It is quite possible, then, that some canonical works of literature may not so much have trans- or cross-cultural value as that their new readers are taught to become "good" readers of them—that is, the new readers (as part of their entry fee to the academy) take on as their own the culture or worldview of the canonized texts.

41. Toni Morrison sees this sort of contextual dialogism as a desirable aspect of the novel-reader relation. She explains: "The open-ended quality that is sometimes problematic in the novel form reminds me of the uses to which stories are put in the black community. The stories are constantly being retold, constantly being imagined within a framework." Nellie McKay, "An Interview with Toni Morrison," *Contemporary Literature* 24, no. 4 (1983): 413–29. Hereafter McKay, *Contemporary Literature*.

42. Booth, *Company We Keep*, 34–35.

43. Bessie Jones, "An Interview with Toni Morrison," in *The World of Toni Morrison: Explorations in Literary Criticism*, ed. Bessie Jones and Audrey Winson (Dubuque, Iowa: Kendall/Hunt, 1985), 138.

44. Ibid., 141. Morrison reiterates this interest in an interview with Nellie McKay. She says, "It's the complexity of how people behave under duress that is of interest to me—the qualities they show at the end of an event when their backs are up against the wall." McKay, *Contemporary Literature*, 420.

45. Jones, "Interview with Toni Morrison," 141.

46. If I am to believe my many students who tell me so (and I have no reason not to), good multicultural literature really does have the capacity to powerfully implicate its readers and make them examine their own relation to

the economic and social structures that reinforce racial and cultural hierarchies.

47. Cervantes, *Emplumada*, 35.

48. Ibid., 36.

49. For instance, Cervantes begins the poem with a reference to her own imaginative universe, a land in which there are "no distinctions . . . no boundaries . . . no hunger, no / complicated famine or greed." Later she asserts, "I am not a revolutionary. / I don't even like political poems."

50. Ibid., 36.

51. Ibid., 35.

EPISTEMOLOGY, ETHICS, AND THE TIME/SPACE OF DECOLONIZATION: PERSPECTIVES FROM THE CARIBBEAN AND THE LATINA/O AMERICAS | NELSON MALDONADO-TORRES

I thank Ada María Isasi-Díaz for requesting this contribution and organizing the conference where it was first shared, and Eduardo Mendieta for his insightful comments to an earlier version of the essay.

1. Enrique Dussel, "Origen de la filosofía política moderna: Las Casas, Vitoria y Suarez (1514–1617)," *Caribbean Studies* 33, no. 2 (2005): 35–80. For an elaboration of the concept of "espanto" see Nelson Maldonado-Torres, "La descolonización y el giro des-colonial," *Tabula Rasa* (Colombia) 9 (July–December 2008): 66.

2. Esiaba Irobi, "The Philosophy of the Sea: History, Economics, and Reason in the Caribbean," *Worlds and Knowledges Otherwise* 1, no. 3 (2006): http://www.jhfc.duke.edu/wko/dossiers/1.3/EIrobi.pdf (February 14, 2010).

3. This passage is taken from a summary of John E. Drabinski's book manuscript entitled *Abyssal Beginnings: Glissant, Philosophy, and the Middle Passage* posted by the author in http://www.jdrabinski.com/Abyssal_Beginnings .html. See also J. Michael Dash, "Writing the Body: Edouard Glissant's Poetics of Re-membering," *World Literature Today* 63, no. 4 (1989): 609–12.

4. See Nelson Maldonado-Torres, "Post-Continental Philosophy: Its Definition, Contours, and Fundamental Source," *Worlds and Knowledges Otherwise* (Fall 2006). http://www.jhfc.duke.edu/wko/dossiers/1.3/1.3contentarchive .php (February 14, 2010); see also Nelson Maldonado-Torres, "Toward a Critique of Continental Reason: Africana Studies and the Decolonization of Imperial Cartographies in the Americas," in *Not Only the Master's Tools: Theoretical Explorations in African-American Studies*, ed. Lewis Gordon and Jane Anna Gordon (Boulder, Colo.: Paradigm Press, 2006), 51–84.

5. See, for instance, Frantz Fanon, *Wretched of the Earth*, trans. Constance Farrington (New York: Grove Press, 1965), 197–98.

6. See Emmanuel Lévinas, *Totality and Infinity: An Essay on Exteriority*, trans. A. Lingis (Pittsburgh: Duquesne University Press, 1991), 33–48. For more on this Levinasian reading of Fanon, and a Fanonian critique and expansion of Lévinas, see Nelson Maldonado-Torres, *Against War: Views from the Underside of Modernity* (Durham, N.C.: Duke University Press, 2008), 93–162.

7. See Frantz Fanon, *Black Skin, White Masks*, trans. Charles Markmann (New York: Grove Press, 1967), 232.

8. Jorge J. E. Gracia, *Hispanics/Latinos in the United States: Ethnicity, Race, and Rights* (New York: Routledge, 2000); Jorge J. E. Gracia, *Latinos in America: Philosophy and Social Identity* (Malden, Mass.: Wiley-Blackwell, 2008). For a critical analysis of Jorge Gracia's position, see Paula M. L. Moya, "Why I Am Not Hispanic: An Argument with Jorge Gracia," *American Philosophical Association Newsletter* 00, no. 2 (2001): 100–105; Nelson Maldonado-Torres, Review of *Latinos in America: Philosophy and Social Identity*, by Jorge Gracia, *Latino Studies* 7, no. 2 (2009): 284–86.

9. For a related critique see Moya, "Why I Am Not Hispanic."

10. See María Lugones, *Pilgrimages/Peregrinajes: Theorizing Coalition against Multiple Oppressions* (Lanham, Md.: Rowman and Littlefield, 2003).

11. For a development of decolonial ethics see Maldonado-Torres, *Against War*.

12. Marilyn Frye, *The Politics of Reality: Essays in Feminist Theory* (Berkeley: Crossing Press, 1983), 66–72. This is also a crucial point in Lugones, *Pilgrimages,/Peregrinajes*, which is in dialogue with Frye's concept of "arrogant perception."

13. Chela Sandoval, *Methodology of the Oppressed* (Minneapolis: University of Minnesota Press, 2000); Walter Mignolo, *The Idea of Latin America* (Malden, Mass.: Blackwell, 2005).

14. Lugones, *Pilgrimages/Peregrinajes*; Linda Martín Alcoff, "Phenomenology, Post-structuralism, and Feminist Theory on the Concept of Experience," in *Feminist Phenomenology*, ed. Linda Fisher (Dordrecht, The Netherlands: Kluwer Academic, 2000), 39–56; Linda Martín Alcoff, "Toward a Phenomenology of Racial Embodiment," in *Race*, ed. Robert Bernasconi (Malden, Mass.: Blackwell, 2001), 267–83; Linda Martín Alcoff, *Visible Identities: Race, Gender, and the Self* (Oxford: Oxford University Press, 2006); Jacqueline M. Martinez, *Phenomenology of Chicana Experience and Identity: Communication and Transformation in Praxis* (Lanham, Md.: Rowman and Littlefield, 2000); Paula M. L. Moya, *Learning from Experience: Minority Identities, Multicultural Struggles* (Berkeley: University of California Press, 2002).

15. Emma Pérez, *The Decolonial Imaginary: Writing Chicanas into History* (Bloomington: Indiana University Press, 1999).

16. "Mapping the Decolonial Turn: Philosophical Contributions to Philosophy, Theory, and Critique" was the title of a conference at UC–Berkeley on April 21–23, 2005, that brought together Latin American, Latina/o, and Caribbean philosophers. It is also the title of a forthcoming special issue in the journal *Transmodernity* (2011).

17. See also the web dossier on postcontinental philosophy in the web journal *Worlds and Knowledges Otherwise,* http://www.jhfc.duke.edu/wko/dossiers/1.3/1.3contentarchive.php.

18. See, for instance, Maldonado-Torres, *Against War.*

19. I am combining insights from Paula Moya's critique of Gracia and Mignolo's account of Latina/o identity in response to Jorge Gracia's account of historical families in regards to Latinos.

20. See, for instance, Sylvia Wynter, "The Ceremony Must Be Found: After Humanism," *Boundary 2* 12, no. 3 (1984): 19–65.

THINKING BODIES: THE SPIRIT OF A LATINA INCARNATIONAL IMAGINATION | MAYRA RIVERA RIVERA

The first epigraph is from Margot Arce de Vazquez, *Gabriela Mistral: The Poet and Her Work,* trans. Helene Masslo Anderson (New York: New York University Press, 1964); trans. modified. The second epigraph is from Marjorie Agosín, *Sargasso,* bilingual edition (Spanish/English), trans. Cola Franzen (Fredonia, N.Y.: White Pine Press, 1993), 28 (Spanish), 29 (English, trans. modified).

1. Luce Irigaray, *An Ethics of Sexual Difference,* translated by Carolyn Burke and Gillian C. Gill (1984; Ithaca, N.Y.: Cornell University Press, 1993), 191.

2. María Lugones, "Heterosexualism and the Colonial/Moderm Gender System," *Hypatia* 22, no. 1 (2007): 186.

3. Simone De Beauvoir, *The Second Sex,* trans. H. M. Parshley (New York: Alfred A. Knopf, 1953), 281.

4. "Coloniality of power" is a term used by Lugones, Anibal Quijano, and others to denote the system that "introduces the basic and universal social classification of the population of the planet in terms of the idea of race." Lugones, "Heterosexualism and the Colonial/Modern Gender System," 190.

5. Nancy Raquel Mirabal argues that these discourses acknowledge that "expressing the inexpressible and speaking the unspeakable are often part of

the becoming, of the revealing, inherent in knowledge production" (Introduction to *Technofuturos: Critical Interventions in Latina/o Studies*, ed. Nancy
Raquel Mirabal and Agustín Laó-Montes (Lanham, Md.: Lexington Books,
2007), 19.

6. Lázaro Lima, *The Latino Body: Crisis Identities in American Literary and Cultural Memory* (New York: New York University Press, 2007), 129. Lázaro
Lima argues that Anzaldúa and Moraga reconfigure "citizenship as a gendered, racialized, and desiring mobile imaginary written on the body" (129).

7. On the problematics of the homogenization of the representations of "Lat-
ina/o" experience in theology, specifically the creation of "a *mexicanized*
construction of Latino/a identity" (12), see Michelle Gonzalez, *Afro-Cuban
Theology: Religion, Race, Culture, and Identity* (Gainesville: University Press
of Florida, 2006), especially 15–33.

8. Marcella Althaus-Reid, *Indecent Theology: Theological Perversions in Sex, Gender, and Politics* (New York: Routledge, 2000), 148.

9. Roberto Goizueta, "The Symbolic Realism of U.S. Latino/s Popular Catholicism," *Theological Studies* 65, no. 2 (2004): 263.

10. Ibid., 262.

11. Ada María Isasi-Díaz, *Mujerista Theology: A Theology for the Twenty-First Century* (Maryknoll, N.Y.: Orbis Books, 1996), 64.

12. Ada María Isasi-Díaz, *La Lucha Continues: Mujerista Theology* (Maryknoll,
N.Y.: Orbis Books, 2004), 159.

13. Benjamin Valentin, *Mapping Public Theology: Beyond Culture, Identity, and
Difference* (New York: Trinity Press, 2002), 53. For an overview of Latino/a
theologians' contributions and debates on the subject of mestizaje/mulatez
see also Gonzalez, *Afro-Cuban Theology*, 21–29.

14. Marcella Althaus-Reid, "Feetishism: The Scent of a Latin American Body
Theology," in *Toward a Theology of Eros: Transfiguring Passion at the Limit of
Discipline*, ed. Virginia Burrus and Catherine Keller (New York: Fordham
University Press, 2006), 137.

15. Ibid., 144–45.

16. Ibid.

17. Ibid., and Althaus-Reid, *Indecent Theology*.

18. Marcella Althaus-Reid, "El Tocado (Le Toucher): Sexual Irregularities in
the Translation of God (the Word) in Jesus," in *Derrida and Religion: Other
Testaments*, ed. Yvonne Sherwood and Kevin Hart (New York: Routledge,
2004), 393–406. As discussed later in this essay, Laura Pérez finds in Chicana
art a similar emphasis on the ghostly in the midst of the concrete, as that
which expresses both the spiritual and the socially ephemeral elements of

life (Laura E. Pérez, *Chicana Art: The Politics of Spiritual and Aesthetic Altarities* [Durham, N.C.: Duke University Press, 2007]).

19. Donna Haraway, cited in Chela Sandoval, *Methodology of the Oppressed* (Minneapolis: University of Minnesota Press, 2000), 171.

20. María Pilar Aquino, "Latina Feminist Theology: Central Features," in *A Reader in Latina Feminist Theology: Religion and Justice*, ed. María Pilar Aquino, Daisy L. Machado, and Jeanette Rodriguez (Austin: University of Texas Press, 2002), 150.

21. Hagiography is also Suzanne Bost's description of Chicanas' approach to history. She proposes that "hagiography" "is a more appropriate term for the ways in which these writers use the past, since it focuses on mystical bodies and the lessons learned from their lives. Hagiographies reflect on the sacred significance of individuals' everyday experiences, pain, and symbolic illness. . . . Rather than being faithful to one chronological account, hagiographies are outside of normative histories and more marvelous than they are true to material facts" (*Encarnación: Illness and Body Politics in Chicana Feminist Literature* [New York: Fordham University Press, 2010], 54).

22. Patricia Cox Miller, "Visceral Seeing: The Holy Body in Late Ancient Christianity," *Journal of Early Christian Studies* 12, no. 4 (2004): 392.

23. Ibid., 398.

24. Ibid., 399.

25. Lugones, "Heterosexualism and the Colonial/Modern Gender System."

26. Most discussions of the body in contemporary theology have focused on sexuality and in the recovery of eroticism. Although this is a crucial aspect of body theology—and has been central to Latina theory—the attention to bodies exclusively as sources of pleasure leads to romanticized views of embodiment.

27. Althaus-Reid, "El Tocado (Le Toucher)."

28. My discussion of Luz María Umpierre's work is based on Lázaro Lima's insightful reading of her poetry (*Latino Body*, 130–39).

29. Ibid., 138.

30. The sea as symbol of fluid, rhythmic connection is a recurrent image in Caribbean philosophy, richly developed in Antonio Benitez Rojo's *La isla que se repite: el Caribe y la perspectiva posmoderna* and Édouard Glissant's *Poetics of Relation*.

31. Many of these theorists, myself included, move between zones dominated by the nationalisms of their countries of origin and by the racial ideologies of the United States. Thus rather than using the idea of exile literally, I use it mainly to indicate the experience of living in a place where one's body is read as a foreign body—regardless of political status.

32. Frantz Fanon, *Black Skin, White Masks* (New York: Grove Press, 1967), 109–40.

33. Richard Rodriguez, *Brown: The New Discovery of America* (New York: Viking, 2002).

34. Ibid., 15.

35. Cherríe L. Moraga, "It Got Her Over," in Cherríe L. Moraga, *Loving in the War Years: Lo que Nunca Pasó por sus Labios* (Cambridge, Mass.: South End Press, 2000), 64.

36. Linda Martín Alcoff, *Visible Identities: Race, Gender, and the Self* (New York: Oxford University Press, 2006), viii.

37. Moraga, *Loving in the War Years*, 46. As Moya observes, "In her own articulation of a theory in the flesh, Moraga emphasizes the materiality of the body by conceptualizing 'flesh' as the site on or which the woman of color experiences the painful material effects of living in her particular social location" (Paula M. L. Moya, *Learning from Experience: Minority Identities, Multicultural Struggles* [Berkeley: University of California Press, 2002], 50).

38. Rodriguez, *Brown*, 228.

39. Gloria Anzaldúa, *Borderlands/La Frontera: The New Mestiza* (San Francisco: Aunt Lute Books, 1999), 104.

40. Ibid. "But it is difficult to differentiate between what is inherited, what is acquired, what is imposed."

41. Some Latina/o thinkers attempt to stabilize the meanings of visible identities by splitting race from ethnicity, assuming either that (1) race is inherited and ethnicity is acquired or (2) race is visible and unavoidable and ethnicity implies choice. Such distinctions are implicit in claims such as "I am a woman of color who is racially white." Although this helps foreground the differences between subjective agency and socially imposed limits, I wonder if such distinctions unwittingly reproduce the myths of race as nature. Do such distinctions in effect split body and culture, reducing corporeal inheritance to a limited set of recognizable features—most often skin color—thus occluding the cultural arbitrariness of racial categories? A similar problem has affected the distinction between sex and gender, a split that may lead to assume that sex is natural and gender is socially constructed.

42. Rodriguez, *Brown*, 133.

43. Ibid.

44. For a discussion of the parallel projections of "guilty imagination" onto black bodies see Dwight N. Hopkins, "The Construction of the Black Male Body," in *Loving the Body: Black Religious Studies and the Erotic*, ed. Anthony B. Pinn and Dwight N. Hopkins (New York: Palgrave Macmillan, 2004).

45. Rodriguez, *Brown*, xi.

46. "To be fully human necessitated my claiming the race of my mother. My brother's sex was white. Mine, brown" (Moraga, *Loving in the War Years*, 90).

47. Moya, *Learning from Experience*, 24.

48. Yvonne Yarbro-Bejarano, *The Wounded Heart: Writing on Cherríe Moraga* (Austin: University of Texas Press, 2001).

49. Haraway, cited in Sandoval, *Methodology of the Oppressed*, 171.

50. I am focusing here on the challenges of these theories for Christian conceptions of Spirit, rather than offering a survey of Latinas' allusions to spirit—which would require a more extensive exposition than this project allows for.

51. Ivone Gebara, *Longing for Running Waters: Ecofeminism and Liberation* (Minneapolis: Fortress Press, 1999), 184.

52. The continuity between matter and energy in postmodern science may be an apt metaphor for rethinking the relationship between spirit and flesh. Perhaps flesh is a particular material form of the spirit?

53. For a reading of spirit as a figure of memory see my "Ghostly Encounters: Spirits, Memory, and the Holy Ghost," in *Planetary Loves: Gayatri Spivak, Postcoloniality, and Theology*, ed. Stephen D. Moore and Mayra Rivera (New York: Fordham University Press, 2011). For a discussion of the relevance of ghostly images in sociology see, Avery F. Gordon, *Ghostly Matters: Haunting and the Sociological Imagination* (Minneapolis: University of Minnesota Press, 1997).

54. Anzaldúa, *Borderlands/La Frontera*, 104.

55. Pérez, *Chicana Art*, 6.

56. Ibid.

57. Ibid., 306.

DECOLONIZING RELIGION: PRAGMATISM AND LATINA/O RELIGIOUS EXPERIENCE | CHRISTOPHER TIRRES

1. Virgilio Elizondo, "Mestizaje as a Locus of Theological Reflection," in *Mestizo Christianity: Theology from the Latino Perspective*, ed. Arturo Bañuelas (Maryknoll, N.Y.: Orbis Books, 1995), 10.

2. Peter Berger, *The Sacred Canopy: Elements of a Sociological Theory of Religion* (New York: Anchor Books, 1990), 22.

3. Sylvia Marcos, "Embodied Religious Thought: Gender Categories in Mesoamerica," *Religion* 28, no. 4 (1998): 374. See also Kay Read, *Time and Sacrifice in the Aztec Cosmos* (Bloomington: Indiana University Press, 1998).

4. Latina/o philosophers and scholars of religion have much to teach pragmatism in other ways as well. Some of these lessons, which are outside of the scope of the present essay, include insights into the geopolitics of gender and the role of embodied agents, the effect of imperial histories in the constitution of citizenship, and the general instability of race. I am thankful to Linda Martín Alcoff and Eduardo Mendieta for my exchanges with them regarding these issues.

5. Cornel West, *The American Evasion of Philosophy: A Genealogy of Pragmatism* (Madison: University of Wisconsin Press, 1989), 240. Rebecca S. Chopp, "Feminist Queries and Metaphysical Musings," *Modern Theology* 11, no. 1 (1995): 47–62.

6. Gregory Fernando Pappas, "The Latino Character of American Pragmatism," *Transactions of the Charles S. Peirce Society* 34, no. 1 (1998): 93–112. See also Gregory Fernando Pappas, "Dewey and Latina Lesbians on the Quest for Purity," *Journal of Speculative Philosophy* 15, no. 2 (2001): 152–61, and José Medina, "Pragmatism and Ethnicity: Critique, Reconstruction, and the New Hispanic," *Metaphilosophy* 35, no. 1/2 (2004): 115–46.

7. For a good review of the Latin American reception of pragmatism, see Jaime Nubiola, "The Reception of Dewey in the Hispanic World," *Studies in Philosophy and Education* 24, no. 6 (2005): 437–53, and Gregory Fernando Pappas and Jim Garrison, "Pragmatism as a Philosophy of Education in the Hispanic World: A Response," *Studies in Philosophy and Education* 24, no. 6 (2005): 515–29.

8. I suspect that the influence of Richard Rorty has something to do with this oversight, given Rorty's Wittgensteinian belief that the core of pragmatism lies primarily within the realm of linguistic affairs. As Leonard Skof rightly points out, however, Rorty may tend unnecessarily to "clos[e] the door on rich nonlinguistic and prereflective 'facts' as endorsed by radical empiricism." Leonard Skof, "Thinking between Cultures: Pragmatism, Rorty, and Intercultural Philosophy," *Ideas y Valores: Revista Colombiana de Filosofía* 57, no. 138 (2008): 51.

9. Along these lines, I have been greatly aided by recent scholarship on Dewey, including the work of Thomas Alexander, Richard Bernstein, Raymond Boisvert, Jim Garrison, Giles Gunn, David Hildebrand, Hans Joas, Gregory Fernando Pappas, Steven C. Rockefeller, Melvin Rogers, and Richard Shusterman.

10. Richard J. Bernstein, "Pragmatism's Common Faith," in *Pragmatism and Religion: Classical Sources and Original Essays,* ed. Stuart Rosenbaum (Urbana: University of Illinois, 2003), 130. See also Giles Gunn, "Religion and

the Recent Revival of Pragmatism," in *The Revival of Pragmatism: New Essays on Social Thought, Law, and Culture*, ed. Morris Dickstein (Durham, N.C.: Duke University Press, 1998), and M. Gail Hamner, *American Pragmatism: A Religious Genealogy* (New York: Oxford University Press, 2003). I am currently working on a book manuscript that reconstructs Dewey's philosophy of religion in a way that responds to current issues in liberation theology.

11. Steven C. Rockefeller, *John Dewey: Religious Faith and Democratic Humanism* (New York: Columbia University Press, 1991), 129. See also William M. Shea, *The Naturalists and the Supernatural* (Macon, Ga.: Mercer, 1984), 127n27.

12. Walter H. Capps, *Religious Studies: The Making of a Discipline* (Minneapolis: Fortress Press, 1995), 7–52.

13. William James, *The Varieties of Religious Experience: A Study in Human Nature*, in *Writings, 1902–1910* (New York: Viking, 1987), 39.

14. "Immediacy of existence," an idea that I will address momentarily, "is ineffable," says Dewey. "But there is nothing mystical about such ineffability; it expresses the fact that of direct existence it is futile to say anything to one's self and impossible to say anything to another." LW1:74. This and all subsequent citations of John Dewey's works are taken from the thirty-seven-volume critical edition *The Collected Works of John Dewey, 1882–1953*, edited by Jo Ann Boydston (Carbondale: Southern Illinois University Press, 1967–90). Citations give the name of the text, series abbreviation (EW [Early Works], MW [Middle Works], LW [Later Works]), volume number. and page number.

15. William James, "What Pragmatism Means," in *Writings, 1902–1910* (New York: Viking, 1987), 517.

16. "Things in their immediacy," Dewey writes, "are unknown and unknowable, not because they are remote or behind some impenetrable veil of sensation of ideas, but because knowledge has no concern with them." Dewey, *Experience and Nature*, LW1:74. For the classic treatment of immediate experience, see Dewey, "The Postulate of Immediate Experience" (1905), MW 3:158–67.

17. The idea of natural piety is borrowed from George Santayana's notion of "cosmic piety," which he develops in *Reason and Religion*, the third volume of *The Life of Reason; or, The Phases of Human Progress* (New York: Charles Scribner's Sons, 1928–31).

18. Dewey describes his instrumentalism in the following way: "Knowledge is instrumental to the enrichment of immediate experience through the control over action that it exercises." LW 10:294.

19. Larry A. Hickman, *John Dewey's Pragmatic Technology* (Bloomington: Indiana University Press, 1990), 13.

20. John Dewey, *Art as Experience*, LW 10:294.

21. Ibid., 45. There are ongoing debates between Dewey scholars regarding the nature of the relationship between aesthetic imagination and reflective deliberation. Compare, for example, Steven Fesmire's *John Dewey and Moral Imagination: Pragmatism in Ethics* (Bloomington: Indiana University Press, 2003) and Jennifer Welchman's *Dewey's Ethical Thought* (Ithaca: Cornell University Press, 1995).

22. John Dewey, *Common Faith*, LW 9:18.

23. Ibid., 26.

24. John Dewey, *Quest for Certainty*, LW 4:241–42.

25. Dewey, *Common Faith*, LW 9:12–13.

26. Jonathan Z. Smith, "Religion, Religions, Religious," in *Critical Terms for Religious Studies*, ed. Mark C. Taylor (Chicago: University of Chicago Press, 1998), 269–85; Talal Asad, *Genealogies of Religion: Discipline and Reasons of Power in Christianity and Islam* (Baltimore: Johns Hopkins University Press, 1993).

27. James, *Varieties of Religious Experience*, 306.

28. Virgilio P. Elizondo, *La Morenita: Evangelizer of the Americas* (San Antonio: Mexican American Cultural Center, 1980), 8.

29. See Michelle A. Gonzalez, *Created in God's Image: An Introduction to Feminist Theological Anthropology* (Maryknoll, N.Y.: Orbis Books, 2007), 108, and Mayra Rivera, *The Touch of Transcendence: A Postcolonial Theology of God* (Louisville: Westminster John Knox Press, 2007).

30. See especially Enrique Dussel, *Ética de la Liberación en la Edad de la Globalización y la Exclusión* (Madrid: Trotta, 1998), and *The Underside of Modernity: Apel, Ricoeur, Rorty, Taylor, and the Philosophy of Liberation*, trans. and ed. Eduardo Mendieta (Atlantic Highlands, N.J.: Humanities Press, 1996); Roberto S. Goizueta, *Caminemos con Jesús: Toward a Hispanic/Latino Theology of Accompaniment* (Maryknoll, N.Y.: Orbis Books, 2005); and Eduardo Mendieta, *The Adventures of Transcendental Philosophy: Karl-Otto Apel's Semiotics and Discourse Ethics* (Lanham, Md.: Rowman and Littlefield, 2002).

31. Alejandro García-Rivera, *The Community of the Beautiful: A Theological Aesthetics* (Collegeville, Minn.: Liturgical Press, 1999); Robert Lassalle-Klein, "The Potential Contribution of C. S. Peirce to Interpretation Theory in U.S. Hispanic/Latino and Other Culturally Contextualized Theologies," *Journal of Hispanic/Latino Theology* 6, no. 3 (1999); Nancy Pineda-Madrid, "Traditioning: The Formation of Community, the Transmission of Faith,"

in *Futuring Our Past: Explorations in the Theology of Tradition*, ed. Orlando Espín (Maryknoll: Orbis Books, 2006), 204–26. See also Cecilia González-Andrieu, "Theological Aesthetics and the Recovery of Silenced Voices," *Journal of Hispanic/Latino Theology* (http://latinotheology.org), September 2, 2008, which draws inspiration from the work of Garcia-Rivera.

32. Leonardo Boff, *Ecclesiogenesis: The Base Communities Reinvent the Church*, trans. Robert R. Barr (Maryknoll, N.Y.: Orbis Books, 1986), 23.

33. Ibid., 28. See also *Church, Charism, and Power: Liberation Theology and the Institutional Church*, trans. John W. Diercksmeier (London: SCM Press, 1985).

34. Orlando O. Espín, *The Faith of the People: Theological Reflections on Popular Catholicism* (Maryknoll, N.Y.: Orbis Books, 1997), 1.

35. Ibid., 3.

36. Ibid., 65.

37. Clodovis and Leonardo Boff offer a helpful discussion of the three interrelated levels of liberation theology—professional, pastoral, and popular—in *Introducing Liberation Theology*, trans. Paul Burns (Maryknoll, N.Y.: Orbis Books, 1987), 11–21.

38. John Dewey, *Democracy and Education*, MW 9:227.

39. Ibid., 198.

40. Ibid., 227.

41. James W. Garrison, "John Dewey's Philosophy as Education," in *Reading Dewey: Interpretations for a Postmodern Generation*, ed. Larry A. Hickman (Bloomington: Indiana University Press, 1998), 69–70.

42. Dewey, *Democracy and Education*, MW 9:228.

43. Patrick W. Collins, *More than Meets the Eye: Ritual and Parish Liturgy* (New York: Paulist Press, 1983).

44. Daniel S. Schipani, *Religious Education Encounters Liberation Theology* (Birmingham, Ala.: Religious Education Press, 1988); Joseph Betz, "John Dewey and Paulo Freire," *Transactions of the Charles S. Peirce Society* 28, no. 1 (1992): 107–26.

THE ETHICS OF (NOT) KNOWING: TAKE CARE OF ETHICS AND KNOWLEDGE WILL COME OF ITS OWN ACCORD | EDUARDO MENDIETA

1. Donna Haraway, *Modest_Witness@Second_Millennium.FemaleMan@_Meets_OncoMouse™: Feminism and Technoscience* (New York: Routledge, 1997), 24.

2. Ibid.

3. Ibid., 25.

4. See Hans Blumenberg, "Light as a Metaphor of Truth: At the Preliminary Stage of Philosophical Concept Formation," in *Modernity and the Hegemony of Vision*, ed. David Michael Levin (Berkeley: University of California Press, 1993), 30–62.

5. See Hans Blumenberg, *Salidas de caverna* (Madrid: A. Machado Libros, 2004).

6. Robert Proctor and Londa Schiebinger, eds., *Agnotology: The Making and Unmaking of Ignorance* (Stanford, Calif.: Stanford University Press, 2008).

7. Londa L. Schiebinger, *Plants and Empire: Colonial Bioprospecting in the Atlantic World* (Cambridge, Mass.: Harvard University Press, 2004).

8. Shannon Sullivan and Nancy Tuana, eds., *Race and the Epistemologies of Ignorance* (Albany: State University of New York Press, 2007).

9. For a discussion of this theme in Toni Morrison's work see Barbara Christian, "The Crime of Innocence," in *The Good Citizen*, ed. David Batstone and Eduardo Mendieta (New York: Routledge, 1999), 51–64.

10. Richard Rorty, *Philosophy and the Mirror of Nature* (Princeton: Princeton University Press, 1979).

11. Bernard Williams, *Truth and Truthfulness: An Essay in Genealogy* (Princeton: Princeton University Press, 2002), 1.

12. Michel Foucault, *The Hermeneutics of the Subject: Lectures at the Collège de France 1981–1982*, trans. Graham Burchell (New York: Picador, 2004), 237.

13. Friedrich Nietzsche, *The Gay Science*, ed. Bernard Williams, trans. Josefine Nauckhoff (Cambridge: Cambridge University Press, 2001), 200–201.

14. Toni Morrison, *Tar Baby*, quoted in Christian, "Crime of Innocence," 57.

15. Terri Otten, *The Crime of Innocence in Toni Morrison's Fiction* (Columbia: University of Missouri Press, 1989).

16. See Charles Mills, "Racial Polity," in *Blackness Visible: Essays on Philosophy and Race* (Ithaca, N.Y.: Cornell University Press, 1998), 119–37.

17. Charles W. Mills, *The Racial Contract* (Ithaca, N.Y.: Cornell University Press, 1997), 96–97.

18. Charles W. Mills, "White Ignorance," in *Agnotology*, ed. Proctor and Schiebinger, 235.

19. For a positive definition of "epistemic privilege" see Linda Alcoff and Elizabeth Potter, eds., *Feminist Epistemologies* (New York: Routledge, 1993).

20. See Miranda Fricker, "Epistemic Oppression and Epistemic Privilege," in *Civilization and Oppression*, ed. Catherine Wilson (Calgary: University of Calgary Press, 1999), 191–210. See also Miranda Fricker, *Epistemic Injustice: Power and Ethics of Knowing* (Oxford: Oxford University Press, 2007).

21. Fricker, "Epistemic Oppression and Epistemic Privilege," 210.

22. For an excellent overview see Walter Mignolo's introduction to the special issue of *Cultural Studies* on the coloniality of power and decolonial thinking, *Cultural Studies*, 21, no. 2–3 (2007): 155–67. This special issue is a major resource about the proposal of the "decolonial turn." See also the indispensable volume edited by Mabel Moraña, Enrique Dussel, and Carlos A. Jáuregi, *Coloniality at Large: Latin America and the Postcolonial Debate* (Durham, N.C.: Duke University Press, 2008), as well as Ramón Grosfoguel, Nelson Maldonado-Torres, and José David Saldívar, eds., *Latin@s in the World System. Decolonization Struggles in the 21st Century U.S. Empire* (Boulder: Paradigm, 2005).

23. See Eduardo Mendieta, "Postcolonialism, Postorientalism, Postoccidentalism: The Past That Never Went Away and the Future That Never Arrived," in *Emerging Trends in Continental Philosophy*, vol. 8 of *History of Continental Philosophy*, ed. Todd May (Durham, N.C.: Acumen, 2011), 149–71.

24. Santiago Castro-Gómez, *La Hybris del Punto Cero: Ciencia, raza e ilustración en la Nueva Granada* (1750–1816) (Bogotá, Colombia: Pontificia Universidad Javeriana, 2005).

25. See my discussion in Eduardo Mendieta, "From Imperial to Dialogical Cosmopolitanism," in *Ethics and Global Politics*, 2, no. 3 (2009): 241–58.

26. Ramón Grosfoguel, "The Epistemic Decolonial Turn: Beyond Political-Economy Paradigm," in *Cultural Studies* 21, nos. 2–3 (2007): 211–23.

27. See my essay "Migrant, Migra, Mongrel: The Latin American Dishwasher, Busboy, and Colored/Ethnic/Diversity (Philosophy) Hire," in *Critical Perspectives on the Profession of Philosophy: Latin-American and African-American Voices*, ed. George Yancy (Albany: State University of New York Press, forthcoming).

CONTRIBUTORS

Linda Martín Alcoff is Professor of Philosophy at both Hunter College and the CUNY Graduate Center. Her latest book is a collection coedited with John Caputo titled *Feminism, Sexuality, and the Return of Religion* (Indiana University Press, 2011). She is also the author of *Visible Identities: Race, Gender, and the Self* (Oxford University Press, 2005). For more information go to www.alcoff.com.

Michelle A. González is Associate Professor of Religious Studies at the University of Miami. Her latest books are *Caribbean Religious History* (co-authored with Ennis B. Edmonds (New York University Press, 2010) and *Shopping: Christian Explorations of Daily Living* (Fortress, 2010).

Ada María Isasi-Díaz is Professor of Christian Social Ethics and Theology (Emerita) at Drew University Theological School. Her forthcoming book is titled *Justicia—A Reconciliatory Praxis of Care and Tenderness* (Fortress Press, 2012).

María Lugones teaches at the Philosophy, Interpretation, and Culture Program at Binghamton University–State University of New York. She is the author of *Peregrinajes: Theorizing Coalition against Multiple Oppressions* (Rowman and Littlefield, 2003), and is currently working on a book on decolonial feminism. Maria Lugones is a popular educator at the Escuela Popular Norteña.

Otto Maduro is Professor of World Christianity and Latin American Christianity at Drew University Theological School. His last book, *Mapas para la fiesta,* was published in Bolivia in 2008 and is awaiting publication in English. He was elected President of the American Academy of Religion for 2011–12 and has been National Director of the Hispanic Summer Program since 2006.

Nelson Maldonado-Torres is Associate Professor in the Department of Latino and Hispanic Caribbean Studies with a joint appointment in Comparative Literature at Rutgers University. Author of *Against War: Views from the Underside of Modernity* (Duke University Press, 2008), he is currently working on a book manuscript titled *Fanonian Meditations.*

Hjamil A. Martínez-Vázquez is the author of *Latina/o y Musulman: The Construction of Latina/o Identity among Latina/o Muslims in the United States* (Pickwick, 2010) and is working on *Religious History from a Latina/o Perspective: New Methodologies in the Search for Memory* (Baylor University Press).

Eduardo Mendieta is Professor of Philosophy at Stony Brook University. His most recent books are the coedited collections titled *The Power of Religion in the Public Sphere* (Columbia University Press, 2011) and *Habermas and Religion* (Polity, 2011).

Walter Mignolo is William H. Wannamaker Professor in the Program of Literature, Romance Studies and Cultural Anthropology at Duke University. His forthcoming book is *The Darker Side of Western Modernity: Global Future, Decolonial Options* (Duke University Press, 2012).

Paula M. L. Moya is Associate Professor of English at Stanford University. Her latest book is a collection coedited with Hazel Rose Markus titled *Doing Race: 21 Essays for the 21st Century* (Norton, 2010). She is the author of *Learning from Experience: Minority Identities, Multicultural Struggles* (University of California Press, 2002).

Mayra Rivera Rivera is Assistant Professor of Theology and Latina Studies at Harvard Divinity School. She is author of *The Touch of Transcendence* (Westminster/John Knox, 2007).

Christopher Tirres is Assistant Professor of Religious Studies at DePaul University. He is currently working on his first book, *The Shock of the Immediate: Liberation Theology and Pragmatism.*

INDEX

Abalos, David T., 281n1
Abduraheem Ocasio, Ramón Omar, 140
affirmative action, 61–62, 111
Afghanistan war. *See* war in Afghanistan
African Americans, 110–11, 120, 122–24;
  Muslims, 141
Afro-Latinos, 120, 134
agency, 9, 72, 76–77, 221, 255, 264, 274n8;
  collective, 11, 118, 121; moral, 52, 62,
  65
agnotology, 251–53
Agosín, Marjorie, 207–8
Alba, Richard, 281n3
Alcoff, Linda Martín, 3, 10–11, 16, 198,
  216, 242, 253, 273n5, 280n1; "Compara-
  tive Race, Comparative Racisms," 122
Algerian Front de Liberation, 19–20
Ali, Ben, 56
Althaus-Reid, Marcella, 211–14, 223; and
  "Feetishism," 212; *Indecent Theology*,
  212
Alves, Rubem, 280n1
amalgamation model, 122
American Philosophy Association
  (APA), 182
American philosophy, 226
Amerindian. *See* indigenous peoples
analectical moment, 266n12

analytic philosophy, 109, 171
anthropocentrism, 223
antipsychiatry movement, 278n1
Anzaldúa, Gloria, 13–14, 42, 72, 82, 132,
  194, 196–200, 210, 217, 276n43, 280n1,
  285n17, 300n6; *Borderlands / La frontera*,
  196–97
Apel, Karl-Otto, 242
Appiah, Kwame Anthony, 117
Aquinas, Thomas, 28
Aquino, María Pilar, 212, 240
Araya Goubet, Guillermo, 142
archeology of knowledge, 255
Aristotle, 24, 27, 175, 272n4; *Nicomachean
  Ethics*, 175
Arpaio, Joe, 107
"arrogant eye," 177, 189
Arroyo, Edmund A., 138
Arteaga, Alfred, 68
ashé, 162
assimilation, 113, 121, 134, 165, 200,
  282n12, 282n13, 283n32, 285n23
Ataturk, Mustafa Kemal, 37
Augustine, St., 252; *Civitas Dei*, 252; *On
  the Free Choice of the Will*, 252
authority, 37–38, 70, 86, 91, 93–96, 255,
  273n7; discursive, 99–100
Aztecs. *See* indigenous peoples

Bacon, Francis, 247
Baconian/Cartesian/Kantian unencumbered subject, 263
Bakhtin, M. M., 185–86, 295n37
Bartolomé de Las Casas, 34, 239
Bell, Catherine, 243
Bennabi, Malik, 22, 28
Berger, Peter, 226, 277n1
Bhabha, Homi, 199
bilingualism, 123, 282n12
biopolitics, 20, 29
"black," 68–69, 119, 274n10
blackness, 110, 120, 125–26
bodily schema, 215
body-words, 14–15, 208–11, 214–16, 220–23
Boff, Leonardo, 243
Bolivian Indian Party (PIB), 21
Bonilla-Silva, Eduardo, 124–25
Booth, Wayne, 187
border thinking, 26, 81–83
bordered subject, 13–14, 194, 197, 214
Bost, Suzanne, 301n21
Bouazizi, Mohamed, 56
Bourdieu, Pierre, 87, 93, 95, 277; *Outline of a Theory of Practice*, 87
"brown," 122, 215, 217–18, 303n46
brownness, 215
Buber, Martin, 47
Busby, James, 33

Cadena, Gilbert R., 165
Canaparo, Claudio, 281n1
Cantwell Smith, Wilfred, 232
capitalism, 21–23, 37–38, 74–75, 84; and Islam, 273n7
Capps, Walter, 232
Capra, Fritjof, 279n1
Cartesian, 171, 247, 250, 255, 264
Cartesian-Kantian epistemic paradigm, 249–50
Cassirer, Ernst, 279n1
Castro, Américo, 287n42
Castro-Gómez, Santiago, 263
Catholicism; folk, 155, 158–59; institutional, 155, 164, 168; national, 99; popular, 12, 151, 158, 167–68, 211, 243–44;

Spanish, 147, 151, 155, 156; syncretism, 151–53, 155–56, 158–59, 161–64, 167–68
Cervantes, Lorna Dee, 169–70, 189–90, 297n49; *Emplumada*, 169; "Poem for the Young White Man Who Asked Me How I, an Intelligent, Well-Read Person Could Believe in the War Between Races," 169, 189–90
Césare, Aimé, 34
character friendship, 175–76
Chatterjee, Partha, 8, 27, 30–32, 35, 38
Chávez, César, 56, 239
Chicana, 194, 196–97, 199, 210; art, 225, 300n18
Chopp, Rebecca, 229–30
Christian, William, 152
Christian theology, 14, 23, 27, 40, 44
Christianity, 12, 22, 27, 32, 36, 146; colonial mission, 73–74, 141; leftist, 22; liberationist, 145; syncretism, 151, 158, 167–68, 224, 243
civil disobedience, 36
civil rights, 115
civil rights movement, 56, 61, 215
class, 21–22, 46–47, 51, 73, 75, 121, 124, 152; ethno-class, 28; middle class, 42, 46–47, 51, 55, 158; relations, 34, 101; working class, 21–22, 42, 51, 203
Collingwood, R. G., 279n1
colonial matrix of power, 21, 24–27, 38–39
colonialism, defined
coloniality: defined, 20–21, 23–24, 288n66; of gender, 9, 72, 74–81, 83–86; of knowledge, 24, 29, 86; of power, 6, 75, 81–83, 86, 213, 261, 273n7, 299n4
colorism, 112, 114–15
Cominsky, Sheila, 155
communal futures, 8, 29
communism, 21, 22
comunidades de base, 5
Confucianism, 38, 82
Continental philosophy, 109, 171, 193–96, 198–99, 226, 242
Corinthians 1:26–31, 65
Corlett, Angelo, 282n18

cosmic piety, 309n17
Council of Trent reforms, 151–52
counter-discourses, 143
counter-knowledges, 87–89, 100–1
Crenshaw, Kimberlé, 272n2
critical race theory, 284n34
critical theory, 41–42, 227, 229
Crusades of the Reconquest, 141
Cugoano, Ottobah, 24, 32
cultural memory, 11, 129, 132–36, 138, 142, 148–49
curanderismo, 154, 158, 163

da Vinci, Leonardo, 247
Darío, Rubén, 226
Darity, Sandy, 123–24
Darwin, Charles, 234
Davaney, Sheila Greeve, 230
Day of the Dead, 164–65
de Beauvoir, Simone, 25, 209
de Certeau, Michel, 51
De La Torre, Miguel, 143
de Mello e Souza, Laura, 151–52
Dean, Carolyn, 78
decolonial feminism, 9, 72, 76–77, 85
decolonial option, 7, 22, 25, 34–36, 40
decolonial turn, 199, 250, 261–63, 309n22
decoloniality, defined, 7, 8, 20, 23–25, 37–38
deconstructionism, 227
Defoe, Daniel, 9
dehumanization, 7, 9, 71, 73, 75, 84
Delgado Bernal, Dolores, 280n1
Derrida, Jacques, 42
Descartes, René, 28, 247
Dewey, John, 15, 226, 228–31, 236–38, 240, 254, 304n9, 305n10, 305n14, 305n16, 309n18; A Common Faith, 240; Democracy and Education, 244; epistemology, 234, 243–45, 306n21
Diaspora Cultural Center, 159
Diaz, Miguel H., 280n1
Díaz-Quiñones, Arcadio, 131
diversal reason, 263
diversity, 3, 35, 50, 103, 166, 186, 202
double consciousness, 70, 79, 181

Drabinski, John E., 194
Drew University Transdisciplinary Theological Colloquium, 4–5, 7
Du Bois, W. E. B., 181, 252
Dumas, Alexandre, 187
Dundes, Alan, 289n6
Durkheimian, 241, 277n1
Dussel, Enrique, 26–27, 193, 226, 242, 263, 266n12; and liberation philosophy, 261

Einstein, Albert, 41
Ejército de Liberación Nacional, 19
Ejército Zapatista de Liberación Nacional, 19
el buen vivir, 4
Elenes, C. Alejandra, 280n1
Elizondo, Virgilio, 135, 144–46, 226, 241–42
embodiment, 79, 209–10, 213–14, 216, 218, 222–23, 225, 304n4; gendered, 15
Emerson, Ralph Waldo, 226
empiricism, 229, 232–34, 246, 304n8
Engels, Friedrich, 277n1
English-only policies, 122
Enlightenment, 14, 30–31, 137, 203–5
epistemic hegemony, 3, 29
epistemic privilege, 3, 35, 260–61
epistemology: of ignorance, 252–53, 260; political, geopolitical, 8, 29
Escuela Popular Norteña, 200
Espín, Orlando O., 167, 243, 244, 280n1
Espiritismo, 12, 151, 156–59, 162–64, 166–67
Esposito, Roberto, 20
essentialism, 35, 119, 198, 272n2
ethnic studies, 13–14, 194–95, 200–2, 204–6, 210
ethnicity, 11, 62, 115–23, 125–27, 217, 282n18, 302n41
ethnoclass, 24, 28
ethnorace, 10, 62, 115, 120–22, 125–26
ethnoracism, 3, 10, 12, 49, 61
Eurocentrism, 23, 39, 82, 273n7
evangelicals, 100
evil eye, 12, 151, 153–56, 162–63, 164, 167–68, 289n6

Ewen, Elizabeth, 113
Ewen, Stuart, 113
existential humanism, 198

Fabian, Johannes, 272n3
la facultad, 132, 285n17
fairness/impartiality, 60–63
Fanon, Frantz, 13–14, 34, 194–95, 197–200, 215; *Black Skin, White Masks*, 196
Feyerabend, Paul, 278n1
Field Belenky, Mary, 279n1
First Nation Peoples. *See* indigenous peoples
Flores, Juan, 130–31
Flores, Richard, 135
folk religion, 151–55, 158–59, 168
Fortier, Ted, 133
Foucault, Michel, 25, 30–31, 36, 248, 255, 257, 281n1
Fraser, Nancy, 117
Frederickson, George, 293n14
Freire, Paulo, 44, 99, 245
Freud, Sigmund, 253
Fricker, Miranda, 261
Friedman, Marilyn, 175, 178–79, 182–85, 294n24, 295n31; *What Are Friends For?*, 175
la frontera, 197
Frye, Marilyn, 176–77, 198

Galilei, Galileo, 247
Galván, Juan, 139, 142
Gandhi, Mahatma, 36, 239
Garcia, Jorge, 109
García Rivera, Alejandro, 242
Gebara, Ivone, 221, 280n1
Geertz, Clifford, 296n17
Gelpi, Donald, 230
Gilligan, Carol, 175, 279n1
Gilroy, Paul, 117
Glaude, Eddie Jr., 230
Glazer, Nathan, 118
Glissant, Edouard, 194, 196; *Poetics of Relation*, 196
globalization, 2, 50, 97, 102
God: displacement of, 28, 203, 204; grace of, 64–66; image of, 241; love for the poor, 64–67

Godínez, Francisca E., 280n1
Goizueta, Roberto, 211, 242, 291n24
Goldberg, David Theo, 115–16; *Racist Culture*, 115
Gómez-Ruiz, Raúl, 147
González, Michelle A., 11–12, 143–44, 146–48, 287n49
Gordon, Lewis, 110, 250, 262; *Bad Faith and Antiblack Racism*, 110
Gracia, Jorge, 196, 199, 299n19
Graduate Theological Union, 242
Grosfoguel, Ramón, 250, 263
Guaman Poma de Ayala, Filipe, 24, 32, 78
Gunn Allen, Paula, 78, 275n21

Habermas, Jürgen, 242, 279n1
hagiographic text, 213
hagiography, 301n21
Hallett Carr, Edward, 279n1
Haraway, Donna, 248–49
Harding, Sandra, 279n1
Heidegger, Martin, 254
Heisenberg, Werner, 41
Hemingway, Ernest, 51
hermeneutical humility, 9–10, 16
hermeneutics, 3, 5, 60, 172, 252, 254, 261, 263; post-Eurocentric, post-Hellenophilic, post–pax Americana, 261; pragmatic, 239
Hernández, Alberto, 137, 147
heteroglossia, 186–88
heteroglossic, 184, 190, 296n37, 296n40
heteronormativity, 43, 214
Hill Collins, Patricia, 279n1
Hintikka, Merrill B., 279n1
Hispanic, 11–12, 89, 94, 147–48, 211, 280n1
Hobbes, Thomas, 28
Horkheimer, Max, 25, 40–41, 279n1
Hountondji, Pauline J., 31
human rights, 115
Hume, David, 32
Huntington, Samuel, 114, 282n13

Iberian, 11, 72, 145
identity proliferation, 11, 125
Idowu, E. Bolaji, 290n14

imaginary, defined, 284n1
immigrants, 2–3, 91; anti-immigrant sentiment, 107–8, 110–11; Latina/o 89, 108; undocumented, 98, 108, 115, 126
impoverished, 8, 46–47, 57, 61, 63, 66–67
impurity. *See* purity
incarnational, 14, 211, 221
indigenous movement, 80
indigenous peoples, 69, 73, 82, 78, 114, 120, 226, 239, 291n24; Aymara, 34–35, 80, 83; Aztecs, 164; Bolivia, 9, 21; Maori, 8, 33–35; Maya, 155–56
infrapolitics, 9, 71, 76
Ingenieros, José, 226
Institute for Cultural Inquiry (ICI), 20
instrumentalism, 230, 237, 239, 246, 305n18
interracial friendship, 12–13, 173–76, 179–82
invisible hand, 98
Iraq, U.S. occupation of, 253, 266n12
Irigaray, Luce, 209
Isasi-Díaz, Ada María, 8, 15, 145–46, 166, 211, 216, 240, 280n1, 291n24
Islam, 11, 22, 28, 37–39, 99, 114, 128, 138–41, 146–47, 167; conversion, 129, 136, 286n30; leftist, 22; Shiite, 99

Jackson, Michael, 29
James, William, 15, 228–29, 232–33, 237, 240, 243; *Varieties of Religious Experience*, 240
Jesus of Nazareth, 14, 64–65, 144, 219, 221, 224, 242
Jewish, 11, 40, 118, 128, 137
Jones, Bessie, 188
Jose Crow laws, 124

Kamarck Minnich, Elizabeth, 280n1
Kant, Immanuel, 30–32, 231–32, 250–51; *Critique of Pure Reason*, 250; "What Is Enlightenment?" 30
Kantian: paradigm, 232, 234–35; philosophy, 38, 232; transcendental "I," 250
Kardec, Allan, 158–59, 290n10
Kardecan spiritism, 158

King, Martin Luther Jr., 22, 36, 239
Kuhn, Thomas, 279n1

La Caridad del Cobre. *See* Our Lady of Charity
La Via Campesina, 40
labor: immigrants, 115, 122–23; race, 122; unskilled, 108
Lacan, Jacques, 253
Ladino, 155, 289n9
Laing, Ronald D., 273n1
language games, 254–55
Laqueur, Thomas, 272n4
Lassalle-Klein, Robert, 242
Latin Muslim Voice, 140
Latina, 1–2, 8–9, 44, 210; embodiment, 14
Latina/o Academy of the Arts and Sciences, 200
latinidad, 11, 110, 120, 128–29, 144, 148–49, 288n60; conversion to Islam, 138–41
"Latino," 69, 124–26
Leenhardt, Maurice, 278n1
Leibnizian monads, 250
Lenin, Vladimir Ilyich, 20–22
León, Luis, 163
liberation theology, 25, 45, 134, 211–12, 231, 239, 305n10
Lima, Lázaro, 300n6
lo cotidiano, 8, 15, 46–48; defined, 48–51; disvaluing of, 52, 54–57; example of, 51–54; moral agency, 52, 62, 65
Locke, John, 28
locus historicus, 10
locus theologicus, 8, 64, 145, 211
logocentrism, 214
Lopez, Yahya 'Abu Ayah', 138
Lorde, Audre, 72, 85, 276n43
"loving eye," 176–77
Luckmann, Thomas, 277n1
Lucumí people. *See* Yoruba people
Lugones, María, 9, 25–26, 39, 197–98, 200, 213, 239, 295n35, 299n4
Luke 6:20, 64
Lumumba, Patrice, 21

Machiavelli, Nicolò, 24
machismo, 197

Maduro, Otto, 9–10, 259
Mahbubani, Kishore, 37; *Can Asians Think?*, 37
Maldonado-Torres, Nelson, 7, 13–14, 25, 40, 75, 242, 250, 262
Manichean divide, 196
Mannheim, Karl, 277*n*1
Marcos, Sylvia, 227, 239
Marrano, 11
Martínez, Jacqueline, 199
Martínez-Vázquez, Hjamil, 11–12
Martinican, 195–96
Marx, Karl, 20–22
Marxism, 22–24, 34, 40, 99, 277*n*1
Marxist-Leninist, 19–20
Matthew 25:31–46, 64
Mattuck Tarule, Jill, 279*n*1
Mauss, Marcel, 278*n*1
McGrane, Bernard, 281*n*1
McKay, Nellie, 296*n*44
McVicker Cinchy, Blythe, 279*n*1
Mead, George Herbert, 229, 242
Medina, Lara, 165
Mendieta, Eduardo, 16, 171, 226, 230, 242, 280*n*1; *Latin American Philosophy: Currents, Issues, Debates*, 226
mestizaje, 15, 120, 148, 166, 288*n*60, 289*n*8; theology, 144–46
mestizaje/mulatez, 145, 211, 216, 291*n*24, 300*n*13
metanarratives, 130–31
metaphilosophical, 197
Mexican, 3, 108–10, 114, 124
Mexican American, 56, 89, 144, 165, 230, 282*n*12
Mignolian border gnosis, 262
Mignolo, Walter, 7–8, 45, 81–83, 250, 255, 263, 281*n*1, 299*n*19; critique of ontology, 198–99; *The Idea of Latin America*, 199; *Local Histories, Global Designs*, 81–82
Miller, Patricia Cox, 213
Mills, Charles, 16, 253, 260; "White Ignorance," 253
Mirabal, Nancy Raquel, 299*n*5
Miranda, Filomena, 78, 80–81

Mistral, Gabriela, 207–8; *la extranjera / the foreigner*, 207
Modern philosophy, 231
modernity, 14, 20, 23–26, 36, 43, 247–48; critique of, 29, 36, 205; modernity/coloniality, 26–27; our/their modernity, 27, 29–32, 35, 38, 40; Western, 27, 35
Mohanty, Satya, 172
Montesquieu, Charles-Louis de Secondat, Baron de, 28
Moors, 11, 12, 138–40
Moraga, Cherríe, 210, 215–16, 218, 220, 222, 300*n*6, 302*n*37
Moriscos, 141
Morrison, Toni, 16, 187–88, 253, 259, 260, 296*n*41, 296*n*44; *Sula*, 187–88; *Tar Baby*, 259
Moya, Paula, 12–13, 199, 218, 299*n*19, 302*n*37
Moynihan, Daniel Patrick, 118
Mughal Sultanate, 27
mujerista, 8, 44–46; theology, 8, 64, 145, 241, 291*n*24
mulatez, 146, 166, 216
multicultural literature, 12–13, 173–75, 182, 188, 296*n*46
multiplicity, 70–71, 84–85, 217–19
Murphy, Joseph M., 160–61
Muslim. *See* Islam
Muslim Brotherhood, 37

Napoleon Bonaparte, 21, 30
national security, 108
national socialism, 99
Native American. *See* indigenous peoples
nativism, 108, 111–12, 114–15
Négritude, 197
New World, 33, 262
Newton, Isaac, 247
Nietzsche, Friedrich, 36, 258–59, 261; *The Gay Science*, 258
Nuñez Molina, Mario, A. 157

Obama, Barack, 111, 124–25
occidentalism, 21, 38–39
Omi, Michael, 119

ontology of colonization, 196
the oppressed, 46–50, 55–61, 63, 64–67, 76–77
oppressing → ← resisting process, 78
oppressing → ← resisting relation, 9, 76
Ortiz, Fernando, 290n15
the Other, 146, 176, 195, 114; Latina/o Muslims, 142–43; negation of, 109, 141; sub-Other, 19–98
Otto, Rudolf, 232
Our Lady of Charity, 144, 159–61
Our Lady of Guadalupe. *See* Virgin of Guadalupe
Oxford English Dictionary, 119
Oyewumi, Oyeronke, 78, 275n23

Painter, Nell, 113
Pappas, Gregory Fernando, 230
Parks, Rosa, 55
patriarchy, 26, 43, 209
Peirce, Charles Sanders, 226, 229, 240, 242, 244
Pentecostalism, 98, 99, 134, 243
Pérez, Emma, 25–26, 40, 199
Pérez, Laura, 225, 300n18
Perry, Mary Elizabeth, 141
Peter the Great, 41
phenomenology, 171, 197; Fanonian, 261; Levinasian-Schellingian, 261; phenomenological critique, 261–62; Sartrean, 110
philosophical anthropology, 197, 199, 202
Piaget, Jean, 278
PIB. *See* Bolivian Indian Party
"pilgrimage"/"peregrinaje," 197
Pineda-Madrid, Nancy, 242–43
Piper, Adrian, 109
Pirsig, Robert M., 281n1
Plato, 24, 27, 250–51, 255–57; allegory of the cave, 250–51, 253, 255–56; *Apology*, 251; *Gorgias*, 256, 258; *Protagoras*, 256; *The Republic*, 250, 255; *Sophist*, 256
Platonic forms, 256
Pletsch, Carl, 31

pluriversal reason. *See* diversal reason
poetics of relation, 196
political biography, 28–29
political egology, 28–29
political theology, 28–29
poor. *See* impoverished
Popper, Karl, 279n1
popular religion, 4–5, 133, 145, 165, 168, 243–44
positivistic, 233, 236
postcolonial subject, 6, 263
postcolonialism, 23, 45, 227, 262
postcontinental philosophy, 13, 194, 197, 199–201
post-imperial subject, 263
postmodern, 29–30, 35–36, 239, 262, 269n15, 272n2
post-occidental subject, 263
post–pax Americana subject, 263
postpositivist, 292n11
postracial erasure, 111
poststructuralism, 29, 199
Pozo, Maria Esther, 78
pragmatism, 13, 15, 227–28, 231–33, 237, 246, 304n4, 304n7; defined, 229–30; epistemology, 232–33, 236, 239; moral faith, 234–39; natural piety, 234–39; pragmatic instrumentalism, 230; prophetic pragmatism, 230; religion, 15, 232, 235, 238–40
preferential option for the poor/oppressed, 8, 57–58, 60–66
Proctor, Robert, 251
purity, 217–19, 222–23, 274n10, 288n60

Quechua, 83
Queen Isabel, 200
queer bodies, 212
queer theory, 42–43
queer thinking, 26, 40
Quijano, Anibal, 6, 23, 25, 27, 75, 77, 199n4, 250, 266n12, 273n7
Quijanoian critique, 261

race: biological view, 113, 116, 117, 119; defined, 116–20; Foucauldian account,

119; gender, 9, 69–70, 78, 272; pheno-
type, 1, 11, 112–14, 116, 119–20, 124, 216
racial eliminativism, 122
racialization, 3, 28, 72, 77; gender, 9,
69–71; Latinas/os, 121
racism, 3, 13, 21, 26, 37–38, 43, 70, 88, 109,
111–15, 169, 235; anti-black, 110, 112,
122–23, 126; anti-Latina/o, 10, 89, 108,
110, 112, 114–15, 121, 125–26; anti-Mexican, 126; defined, 112, 173; emotions,
170, 174
Rahman, Fazlur, 36–38
Ramos, Miguel "Willie," 159, 290n14
rationality, 23–28, 41, 45, 63, 113, 221, 262
Rawls, John, 271n38
Raza Pura (song), 219
reflective/prereflective knowing, 236
Regla de Ocha. See Santería
relationality, 13–14, 58–60, 196
relativist, 179, 256
Renaissance, 14, 23, 28, 30, 140, 203–5, 213
Revolución India, 23
Reynaga, Fausto, 21, 23, 26
Rice, Condoleezza, 22
right to free speech, 31, 35, 38
Ritschl, Albrecht, 232
ritual, 12, 162, 167, 211, 243
Rivail, Hippolyte. See Kardec, Allan
Rivera Cusiqanqi, Silvia, 275n25
Rivera Rivera, Mayra, 14–15
Rodríguez, Jeanette, 133
Rodríguez, Kenny Yusuf, 140
Rodriguez, Richard, 215–18
Rojas, Raheel, 140
Rorty, Richard, 15, 226, 304n8; Philosophy
and the Mirror of Nature, 254
Rosaldo, Renato, 280n1
Royce, Josiah, 242
Rule Goldberger, Nancy, 279n1
Rumsfeld, Donald, 243

Sachs Norris, Rebecca, 136
Sanchez, René, 242
Sandoval, Chela, 72, 198, 212, 276n43
Santayana, George, 236, 305n17
Santería, 12, 151, 159–62, 166

Sartre, Jean-Paul, 110, 170; Being and
Nothingness, 110
Schaffer, Simon, 249
Schiebinger, Londa, 251
Schleiermacher, Friedrich, 232
Schleiermachian, 234
Schlesinger, Arthur, 114
Schmitt, Carl, 28
secularism, 28, 113
Seigfried, Charlene Haddock, 230
Seminario Evangélico de Teología, 59
semiotics, 242
September 11, 2001, 97
Shaping, Steve, 249
Shari'ati, Ali, 22
Shepard, Matthew, 97
Silverblatt, Irene, 78
skeptics, 256
skin color, 1, 119, 123–24, 215–16, 218,
302n41
Skof, Leonard, 304n8
slavery, 120, 123, 141, 159–60, 193, 209,
219, 273n7, 290n12; enslaved Africans,
73, 128, 133, 287n42; slave trade, 261,
144
Smith, Adam, 28
Smith, Dorothy E., 280n1
Smith, Linda Tuhiwai, 33–35
Sollors, Werner, 116
Solomon, David, 182
sophists, 256–57
Sotomayor, Sonia, 117
Sovereignty of Food, 40
Spanish (language), 1, 94, 108
spirit-flesh, 210, 220, 222–25
stereotypes, 127, 129–30, 133–34, 141, 147,
159, 213
Stevens-Arroyo, Anthony, 152
Stocker, Michael, 170
subjectivity, 194, 217, 222, 248–49, 273n7,
274n8, 293n11; active, 76, 79, 83, 274n8;
embodied, 84, 110; Fanon's view, 13,
194; intersubjective, 9, 59, 70–71, 76,
78, 86, 110, 241
Sullivan, Shannon, 252–53
syncretism, 12, 102, 152

Takagi, Dana, 111
Tel Quel, 42
terrorists, 108, 115
text, 12, 26, 100–1; hagiographic, 213; religious, 167; semantic open-endedness, 184, 186–87
theodicy, 252
theology of liberation, 25, 40, 45, 134, 201
theory-in-the-flesh, 210
Third World, 8, 22–23, 29, 31, 33
Third World College, 201, 206
Tirres, Christopher, 15
transcendence proposal, 122
transcendental metaphysics, 233
Truth, Sojourner, 69, 75
Tsai, Jeannie, 172
Tuana, Nancy, 252–53
Tuhiwai Smith, Linda, 8

Umpierre, Luz María, 214
unemployment, 54, 97, 123
Unger, Roberto, 230
universality, 24, 27, 263
universals, 39, 49, 109, 263, 296n15
university, 14, 200–3, 205–6

Valentín, Benjamín, 211
Vasconcelos, José, 144, 146, 226
Vásquez, Manuel A., 145, 146
Villenas, Sofia, 280n1
Virgin de Guadalupe, 144, 242

visceral seeing, 213
von Balthasar, Hans Urs, 242

Wallerstenian world systems theory, 261
Walsh, Catherine, 200
war in Afghanistan, 269n21
Weber, Max, 28, 116–18, 120
Weberian tradition, 277n1
Webster's Unabridged, 119
West, Cornel, 15, 118, 229–30
Western epistemology, 221, 226–27
Wilkerson, William, 171–72
Williams, Bernard, 257
Wilson, Colin, 226
Winant, Howard, 119
Wiredu, Kwasi, 31
Wittgenstein, Ludwig, 254
Wittgensteinian belief, 304n8
"woman," 69, 71–73, 274n10
Women of Color, 9, 70–72; coalition, 68; feminism, 72, 76, 79, 85, 272n1, 272n2, 274n10
Wynter, Sylvia, 201, 203, 205

xenophobia, 89, 109, 113

Yarbro-Bejerano, Yvonne, 218
Yoruba people, 159–62, 272n5, 290n12

Zea, Leopoldo, 226
Zedong, Mao, 22
Zionism, 99
Žižek, Slavoj, 253